ELEMENTARY GRAMMAR
OF THE
SANSCRIT LANGUAGE

ELEMENTARY GRAMMAR
OF THE
SANSCRIT LANGUAGE

PARTLY IN THE ROMAN CHARACTER
ARRANGED ACCORDING TO A NEW THEORY,
IN REFERENCE ESPECIALLY TO THE CLASSICAL LANGUAGES

With Short Extracts in Casn Brose

TO WHICH IS ADDED,
A SELECTION FROM

THE INSTITUTES OF MANU,

WITH COPIOUS REFERENCES TO THE GRAMMAR, AND AN ENGLISH TRANSLATION.

by

MONIER WILLIAMS, M. A.

GYAN

Published by

Gyan Publishing House
5, Ansari Road
Daryaganj, New Delhi-110002
Phone: 011-47034999, 9811692060
E-mail: books@gyanbooks.com

Distribution Network
gyanbooks.com
India, USA, Canada, UK, Australia, France

ISBN : 978-81-212-6166-1 (PB)
First Published, 1846

2nd Impression 2021

Printed at: Gyan Press, Delhi.

Elementary Grammar of the Sanscrit Language
Author: Monier Williams

THE ELEMENTS OF THE DEVANĀGARI CHARACTER.

NUMERICAL FIGURES.

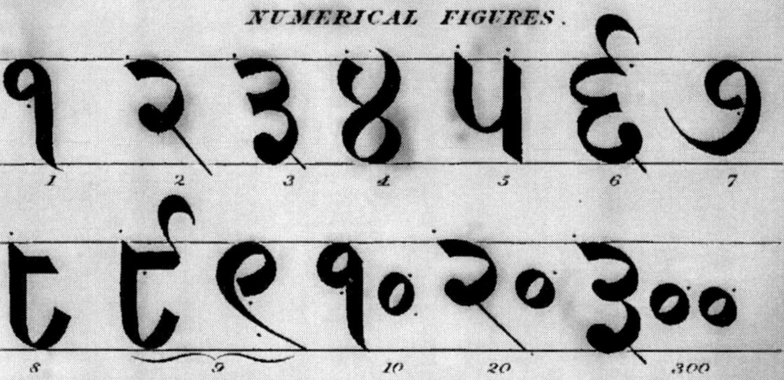

Sir C. Wilkins scrip^t

J. Barclay

W. H. Allen & Co London.

ELEMENTARY GRAMMAR

OF THE

SANSCRIT LANGUAGE,

PARTLY IN THE ROMAN CHARACTER

ARRANGED ACCORDING TO A NEW THEORY,

IN REFERENCE ESPECIALLY TO THE CLASSICAL LANGUAGES:

With short Extracts in easy Prose.

TO WHICH IS ADDED,

A SELECTION FROM

THE INSTITUTES OF MANU,

WITH COPIOUS REFERENCES TO THE GRAMMAR,

AND AN ENGLISH TRANSLATION.

BY MONIER WILLIAMS, M.A.

MEMBER OF THE ROYAL ASIATIC SOCIETY,

ONE OF THE PROFESSORS OF SANSCRIT IN THE EAST-INDIA COLLEGE,

LATE BODEN SANSCRIT SCHOLAR IN THE UNIVERSITY OF OXFORD.

PREFACE.

Sir William Jones has said of the Sūtras of Pāṇini that they are "dark as the darkest oracle;" and Colebrooke, in one of his Essays, has given a list of about one hundred and forty Indian grammarians and commentators who have followed in the footsteps of the great Patriarch of Sanscrit Grammar, and endeavoured to throw light upon the obscurity of his aphorisms. In this endeavour they have succeeded rather in shewing the depth of their own knowledge, than in making the subject more accessible to the generality of European students; and the explanations which they offer are sometimes more unintelligible than the original itself.

Happily, however, a writer has arisen in our own country competent to elucidate most thoroughly the difficulties of this subject. Professor Wilson, the greatest Sanscrit scholar of the present day, whose name the University of Oxford is proud to associate with its own, in the excellent Grammar which he has given to the public has added to his high reputation by his graceful adaptation of the English language to the exposition of the native system of grammatical teaching. It may be said of all this author's numerous works, that, as they abound in indications of surpassing genius, so they offer to the student of Oriental Literature the most valuable information on every topic of inquiry.

But notwithstanding the advantages thus afforded for the study of a language so interesting in its affinities, so rich in its literature, and so important in its bearing upon our interests in the East, it is remarkable that the greater part of the

English public are not merely indifferent to its acquisition, but ignorant of its character, and even of its very name. It must be confessed that this indifference on the part of the generality to a language which recommends itself to their attention by no considerations of immediate practical utility, ought not to excite surprise. It is even, perhaps, too much to expect that the study should flourish in the University of Oxford. Its neglect in this ancient seat of learning only points to a fact which has escaped the observation of those would-be reformers of the present system of education at Haileybury, who are not for wholly abolishing the study of so important a language, but would leave its cultivation to the will of the student: and this fact is, that to make any course of study voluntary in a place of public education is tantamount to its total abolition; and that no temptation of honour, or reward, or present or prospective benefit, and no amount of facilities or opportunities, and no degree of intrinsic excellence or interest in the subject itself, will ever attract any number of votaries to a study which is *not made compulsory upon all.*

But how does it come to pass, that in the East-India College, where this study is still, with true wisdom, made incumbent upon every one; where it is only reasonable to expect that the classical languages of the Hindus should be cultivated with as much ardour as the classical languages of Europe in the European Universities; and where to educate the minds of the future governors of India with any reference to the duties they are to fulfil, or at least to imbue them with any sympathy for the people they are to govern, is surely to give them some knowledge of the language which is the vehicle of that people's literature, the key to their opinions, the repository of all that they hold sacred, and the source of nearly all their spoken dialects;—how does it come to pass, that in this College the study of Sanscrit is not prosecuted with greater zest?

Many causes are assigned for this indifference. It might, indeed, be anticipated that ignorance and idleness would league themselves in a common crusade against any course of reading which entails a more than usual degree of mental effort and perseverance. But ignorance and idleness would not prevail, were it not in their power to make use of arguments that have a considerable shew of reason. To those who would excuse their indifference by alleging that a knowledge of this language is useless to the Civil servants of India, no reply need be given. Such an argument is unworthy of refutation, as proceeding from an utter ignorance of facts, and a stupid contempt for the authority of those eminent scholars, who have long since determined otherwise. To those who do not deny its utility, but affirm that many great men in India have succeeded very well without it, there is but one answer to return. No one disputes that such men have succeeded very well without a knowledge of this language, but no one can tell how much better they might have succeeded, or in how much less time they might have attained the same position, or how much more consideration they might have shewn for the feelings and prejudices of the natives in the course of their career, had the study of Sanscrit formed a part of their education. Our forefathers doubtless prospered very well without a knowledge of Latin and Greek; but now that so many beneficial effects are found to result from an acquaintance with these languages, and now that so many facilities exist for their acquisition, no one would think of making such an argument an excuse for the neglect of a branch of education which, as civilization and learning advance, becomes every day more essential.

But there are some who rest their objection to the study of Sanscrit on the ground of its difficulty. These adopt a very specious line of argument, and one which, it must be confessed, has every appearance of reason on its side. They maintain that the grammar alone is of itself too intricate to be mastered by men of ordinary abilities in their short course of two years at Haileybury; that too many other subjects are forced upon their attention to admit of their gaining any satisfactory insight into the literature of the language; that they pass their examinations by a mere forced effort of memory; and that the little they learn is as rapidly forgotten as it was rapidly acquired, and only serves to disgust, without leaving behind any solid or permanent advantage.

It is with the especial view of answering this latter class of objectors that the following short work has been composed. It was thought that any system of grammar, however excellent in itself, founded upon the esoteric method of teaching adopted by the Pandits of India, was certainly amenable to these objections. An elementary work has, therefore, been written, which rests its claim of adaptation to the wants of beginners on its opposition to the Indian scheme of grammatical tuition. For it should be borne in mind that in India we have presented to us the curious phenomenon of a literature elucidating grammar, rather than a grammar elucidating literature. The better to understand this, it may here be observed that the literature of the Hindus is referrible to three distinct phases, the natural, the philological, and the artificial. As the first and last of these are diametrically opposed to each other, so it may be shewn that the cause of this sudden transition from the one extreme to the other was the intervention of a rage for philological inquiry.

Nothing can exceed the simplicity and beauty of the writings which fall under the early period of Hindu literature. Witness some of the episodes of the two epic poems of the Rāmāyaṇa and Mahābhārata; witness some of the Purāṇas; witness the short specimens of the fables of the Hitopadesha and of the Laws of Manu, given at the end of this volume. The style in all of these is plain, unaffected, and in perfect good taste; and the amount of grammatical knowledge required for their perusal might have been compressed into much less space than the two hundred pages which follow these prefatory remarks.

But at some period or other not very far anterior to the Christian era, a passion for philological disquisition seems to have taken possession of the Hindu mind. The appearance of the Pāṇinīya Sūtras created an appetite for abstract speculation into the nature and capabilities of language, and caused a total revulsion in the character of literary composition. Numerous grammarians arose, whose laboured treatises were not intended to elucidate the national literature of the age, but rather had in view the formation of a distinct grammatical literature, existing solely for its own sake. Then succeeded the era of artificial composition, when poems were written, either with the avowed object of illustrating grammar, or with the ill-concealed motive of pompously exhibiting the depth of the author's philological research.

It cannot be wondered if, under these circumstances, when all the subtlety of Indian intellect wasted itself upon a subject such as this, the science of grammar should have been refined and elaborated to a degree wholly unknown in the other languages of the world.

The highly artificial literature, therefore, of later times, which resulted from such an elaboration, and was closely interwoven with it, cannot certainly be cultivated by the advanced scholar without the aid of a grammar, moulded in strict conformity with the native model. But, on the other hand, it may be suspected that a treatise of this character will always be unpalatable, and may even prove a stumbling-block rather than an aid, to the common class of students, who, with no extraordinary powers of mind, and with neither the time nor the inclination for mere abstract research into the capabilities of language, will certainly be content with such an amount of grammatical knowledge as may enable them to comprehend the earlier and purer specimens of Sanscrit composition. Indeed, it would almost appear as if the Pandits of the East had designed to shut out the knowledge of their language from the minds of the uninitiated vulgar. They require that the young student shall devote ten years to the grammar alone, and they have certainly contrived to provide him with ample occupation during this tedious period of his novitiate. The arrangement adopted in the best of their grammatical treatises would seem to have been made with the express purpose of exaggerating difficulties. Doubtless there are many real difficulties, but there are also many obvious parts of the subject the simplicity of which has been carefully concealed behind a tissue of mysticism. A complicated machinery of technical schemes and symbolical letters is constructed, which may be well calculated to aid the memory of the initiated natives themselves, or those who have become familiar with the native system by a long course of reading in the country, but only serves to bewilder the European tyro. The young English student has enough to do in conquering the difficulties of a strange character, and mastering the rules of combination, without puzzling himself in a labyrinth of servile, substituted, and rejected letters, and perplexing himself in his efforts to gain, by this indirect process, knowledge which is attainable more easily by the usual direct means.

It is enough to say of the present volume that it is the first really elementary Sanscrit Grammar ever published. Its defects will, therefore, it is hoped, not be too critically judged by those who propose to themselves a higher aim than the mere assistance of beginners. To administer to the wants of the *earliest* students has been the one object kept steadily in view; and subordinately an attempt has been made to exhibit the peculiarities which distinguish the study of this language from that of Latin and Greek. The plan adopted will sufficiently explain itself. It has been deemed desirable not to embarrass the student with too much at once. Types of two different sizes have therefore been employed; the larger attracts his eye to that which is of first importance: the smaller generally contains such matter as possesses no pressing claim to his immediate consideration. The Roman character has been applied to the expression of the Devanāgarī throughout the greater part of the Grammar, especially in treating of the rules which regulate the combination and permutation of vowels and consonants. There can be no doubt that the false opinion which prevails of the difficulty of Sanscrit may be traced to the labour imposed of thoroughly mastering these rules at the first entrance upon the study of the language. They form, as it were, a mountain of difficulty to be passed at the very commencement of the journey, and the learner cannot be convinced that, when once surmounted, the ground beyond may be more smooth than in other languages, the ingress to which is comparatively easy.

To simplify, as much as possible, this division of the subject has been the main object; and as an accurate acquaintance with the Devanāgarī letters is not here indispensable, they have not been introduced, except in cases where any doubt is likely to arise in the learner's mind. As he advances, he will find a more sparing use of the Roman character, and towards the end of the volume it has been entirely abandoned. For let it not be supposed that, by the mixed method of printing here adopted, any loose or inaccurate knowledge of the Sanscrit character is tacitly encouraged. Such inaccuracy is a too common obstacle to the sound acquisition of this language. The student satisfies himself at first with an imperfect knowledge of the Devanāgarī alphabet, and, having never conquered this difficulty at the outset, is ever after hampered by its perpetual recurrence.

The tabular views which have been given throughout this work, especially in the chapter on Verbs, will, it is hoped, conduce to the ready comprehension of the more complex parts of the subject. They contain some novelties, which might require an apology, had they not been suggested by a strong belief in the falsity of the native method of proposing, as the general scheme, a system of terminations which applies rather to the exceptions, and then, by a needless process of derivation and substitution, forcing it into universal application.

In the chapter on Syntax, the laws which determine the coalition of vowels have not been observed, as being out of place in a portion of the subject which aims only at the clear exhibition of inflectional changes.

The Selections which have been appended to the grammatical part of this book offer the greatest facilities to the early student in his first effort at translation. Those in prose are of the simplest character, and every word is explained either by notes or by references to the preceding pages of the grammar. Those in verse contain some few difficulties, but the style is plain, and an English translation has been subjoined, which may aid the text, as well as tend to shew that the matter contained in Sanscrit literature may not be so unprofitable as some have ignorantly assumed. The separation of each word from the next, and the use of a mark to indicate the division when the blending of vowels makes such separation impossible, will offend the eye of the advanced Oriental scholar; but the beginner can scarcely be expected to know which is the final or which the initial letter of a word which he never saw before. Why, therefore, refuse to give the only clue which is to guide him in his search for the word in the Dictionary; and why, by uniting those parts of the sentence which admit of separation, superadd this unnecessary source of perplexity to the necessary difficulty, unknown in other languages, resulting from the blending of vowels and the composition of words? The natives of the East ought, in this particular, to conform to a custom which the art of printing has made universally prevalent amongst civilized nations, if, at least, they desire their languages to be generally cultivated by the people of Europe. Nor does there seem any reason in the theory which would make such a conformity incompatible with the laws of euphony.

It only remains to add, that in a work, small and unpretending though it be, in which so many minute points and marks have been employed to represent the Sanscrit character by the Roman, the correction of the press has been a task of no small labour. In this labour Professor Johnson, an Oriental scholar of whose varied attainments the East-India College has reason to be proud, has cheerfully co-operated, and in other matters also has freely given the benefit of his valuable advice and great experience. But whilst to him much of the merit is due that may belong to this book on the score of accuracy, it must be distinctly understood that he is entirely free from the responsibility of its novel structure and arrangement. It is also fair to state that some of the detail of the following pages has been suggested by a careful perusal of Professor Bopp's Sanscrit Grammar, printed at Berlin.

EAST-INDIA COLLEGE,
July 1846.

CONTENTS.

CONTENTS.

SANSCRIT GRAMMAR.

VOWELS.

Initial	अ *a*	इ *i*	उ *u*	ऋ *ṛi*	ऌ *ḷri*	ए *e*	ओ *o*
	आ *ā*	ई *ī*	ऊ *ū*	ॠ *ṛī*	ॡ *ḷrī*	ऐ *ai*	औ *au*
Not initial		ि *i*	ु *u*	ृ *ṛi*	ॢ *ḷri*	े *e*	ो *o*
	ा *ā*	ी *ī*	ू *ū*	ॄ *ṛī*	ॣ *ḷrī*	ै *ai*	ौ *au*

SIMPLE CONSONANTS.

Gutturals,	क *k*	ख *kh*	ग *g*	घ *gh*	ङ *ṅ*		ह *h*
Palatals,	च *ch*	छ *chh*	ज *j*	झ *jh*	ञ *ñ*	श *sh*	य *y*
Cerebrals,	ट *ṭ*	ठ *ṭh*	ड *ḍ*	ढ *ḍh*	ण *ṇ*	ष *ṣh*	र *r*
Dentals,	त *t*	थ *th*	द *d*	ध *dh*	न *n*	स *s*	ल *l*
Labials,	प *p*	फ *ph*	ब *b*	भ *bh*	म *m*		व *v*

THE MOST COMMON OF THE COMPOUND CONSONANTS.

क्ष *ksh*, द्य *dy*, त्र *tr*, त्व *tw*, त्त *tt*, न्न *nn*, द्द *dd*, क्त *kt*, त्क *tk*, क्न *kn*, क्त्व *ktw*, ज्ञ *jn*, व्य *vy*, स्य *sy*, ष्य *ṣhy*, भ्य *bhy*, ध्य *dhy*, प्य *py*, त्र्य *try*, त्य *ty*, न्य *ny*, श्य *shy*, ख्य *khy*, च्य *chy*, ल्य *ly*, क्ष्य *kshy*, ग्ध *gdh*, ब्ध *bdh*, द्ध *ddh*, द्भ *dbh*, द्व *dw*, द्ग *dg*, द्ग्र *dgr*, प्त *pt*, प्म *pm*, प्र *pr*, श्र *shr*, श्च *shch*, श्व *shw*, श्न *shn*, ग्र *gr*, ग्न *gn*, क्र *kr*, द्र *dr*, छ्र *chhr*, र्क *rk*, र्म्म *rmm*, र्व्व *rvv*, र्य्य *ryy*, ङ्क *ṅk*, ङ्ख *ṅkh*, ङ्ग *ṅg*, द्ग *dg*, ञ्च *ñch*, ञ्छ *ñchh*, ञ्ज *ñj*, ण्ट *ṇṭ*, ण्ठ *ṇṭh*, ण्ड *ṇḍ*, न्त *nt*, त्न *tn*, ण्य *ṇy*, ण्ण *ṇṇ*, ष्ट *ṣhṭ*, ष्ठ *ṣhṭh*, ष्ट्र *ṣhṭr*, ष्ट्व *ṣhṭw*, ष्ट्य *ṣhṭy*, ष्ठ्य *ṣhṭhy*, ष्ण *ṣhṇ*, स्व *sw*, स्त *st*, स्त्र *str*, स्म *sm*, स्क *sk*, स्थ *sth*, स्न *sn*, न्त्व *ntw*, न्त्र *ntr*, न्त्य *nty*, न्त्र्य *ntry*, च्च *chch*, च्छ *chchh*, ज्ज *jj*, त्थ *tth*, त्त्व *ttw*, ह्य *hy*, ह्म *hm*, ह्ण *hṇ*, ह्न *hn*, ह्र *hr*, द्म *dm*, क्व *kw*, क्ल *kl*, ग्ल *gl*, क्क *kk*, ज्व *jw*, द्भ्य *dbhy*, द्ध्य *ddhy*, ग्र्य *gry*, ध्व *dhw*, ब्ज *bj*, ब्भ *bbh*, ध्न *dhn*, न्ध *ndh*, क्ष्ण *kshṇ*, क्ष्म *kshm*, क्त्र *ktr*, क्त्य *kty*, ङ्क्य *ṅky*, त्स्य *tsy*, त्म्य *tmy*, द्व्य *dwy*, द्र्य *dry*, ण्ड्य *ṇḍy*, छ्य *chhy*, ठ्य *ṭhy*, द्द्य *ddy*, ह्ल *hl*, स्ख *skh*.

SANSCRIT GRAMMAR.

CHAPTER I.

LETTERS.

THE Sanscrit language is written in the character called Devanāgarī. The following are the Devanāgarī letters, with their equivalents in the Roman character.

VOWELS, DIPHTHONGS, AND SEMI-VOWELS.

SHORT VOWELS.			LONG VOWELS.			IMPROPER DIPHTHONGS CALLED GUNA.			PROPER DIPHTHONGS CALLED VRIDDHI.			SEMI-VOWELS.	
Initial.	Not Initial.		Init.	Not Init.		Initial.	Not Initial.		Initial.	Not Initial.			
अ		*a*	आ	ा	*ā*								
इ	ि	*i*	ई	ी	*ī*	ए	े	*e*	ऐ	ै	*ai*	य	*y*
उ	ु	*u*	ऊ	ू	*ū*	ओ	ो	*o*	औ	ौ	*au*	व	*v* or *w*
ऋ	ृ	*ṛi*	ॠ	ॄ	*ṛī*	अर्		*ar*	आर्		*ār*	र	*r*
												ल	*l*

CONSONANTS.

	HARD CONSONANTS.		CORRESPONDING SOFT.		CORRESPONDING NASALS.	CORRESPONDING SIBILANTS.	ASPIRATE AND SEMI-VOWELS.		NASAL SYMBOL CALLED ANUSWĀRA.
							Initial or Medial.	Final called Visargah.	
Gutturals,	क *k*	ख *kh*	ग *g*	घ *gh*	ङ *n·*		ह *h*	ः *h*	ं *n* or *m*
Palatals,	च *ch*	छ *chh*	ज *j*	झ *jh*	ञ *ṅ*	श *sh*	य *y*		
Cerebrals,	ट *ṭ*	ठ *ṭh*	ड *ḍ*	ढ *ḍh*	ण *ṇ*	ष *ṣh*	र *r*		
Dentals,	त *t*	थ *th*	द *d*	ध *dh*	न *n*	स *s*	ल *l*		
Labials,	प *p*	फ *ph*	ब *b*	भ *bh*	म *m*		व *v* or *w*		

Observe that *ar* and *ār* are not distinct letters, but have been inserted amongst the diphthongs for reasons that will be afterwards apparent. That the semi-vowels have been placed in both Tables, as falling under the first, in their relation to *i, u, ṛi, ḷṛi;* under the second, in their relation to *j, ḍ, d, b.* That *h* at the end of a word stands for Visargah (:). That when *n* is found before the semi-vowels *y, v, r, l,* the sibilants *sh, ṣh, s,* and the aspirate *h* in the middle of a word, it represents the symbol Anuswāra; and that *m* at the end of a word always represents the same symbol. That the vowels ऋ and ॠ will be represented by *ṛi* and *ṛī,* as distinguished from रि *ri* and री *rī,* which represent the consonant *r* combined with the vowels *i* and *ī.* Lastly, that the palatal sibilant श will be represented by *sh,* as distinguished from *ṣh,* which represents the cerebral sibilant ष.

ON THE METHOD OF WRITING THE VOWELS.

The vowels assume two forms, according as they are initial or not initial. Thus, *ik* is written इक्, but *ki* is written कि; short *i,* when not initial, being always written *before* the consonant *after* which it is pronounced. Short *a* is never written, unless it begin a word, because it is supposed to be inherent in every consonant. Thus, *ak* is written अक्, but *ka* is written क; the mark ् under the final *k* being used to shew that it has no *a* inherent in it. The vowels *u, ū,* and *ṛi, ṛī,* not initial, are written under the consonants after which they are pronounced; as कु, कू, *ku, kū;* कृ, कॄ, *kṛi, kṛī.**

† The Sanscrit is said to possess another vowel, viz. ॡ *ḷṛi,* which has not been given, as it only occurs in one word in the language. The only use of introducing it in a Table like the above, is to shew the perfection of the Devanāgarī alphabet; for without it, we have no corresponding vowels or diphthongs to the semi-vowel ऌ *l;* but, with it, the last line of the Table may be filled up thus,

SHORT.	LONG.	GUNA.	VRIDDHI.	SEMI-VOWEL.
ऌ *ḷṛi*	ॡ *ḷṛī*	अल् *al*	आल् *āl*	ल *l*

* When, however, *u* follows र it is written thus, रु *ru;* and when *ū* follows र, thus, रू *rū.*

ON THE COMPOUND CONSONANTS.

Every consonant is supposed to have short *a* inherent in it, so that it is never necessary to write short *a* except at the beginning of a word. Hence, when any of the above simple consonants are seen standing alone in any word, short *a* must always be pronounced after them; but when they are written in conjunction with any other vowel, this vowel of course takes the place of short *a*. Thus, such a word as कलानतया would be pronounced *kalānatayā*. The question then arises, how are we to know when consonants have to be pronounced together, without the intervention of any vowel; as, for instance, *kl* and *nty* in the word *klāntyā?* This occasions the necessity for compound consonants: *kl* and *nty* must then be combined together thus, क्ल, न्त्य, and the word is written क्लान्त्या. And here we have illustrated the two methods of compounding consonants, viz. 1st, by writing them one above the other; 2dly, by placing them side by side, omitting in all, except the last, the perpendicular line which lies to the right.

Almost all compound letters are in this way resolvable into their component parts. There are two, however, which are not so, viz. क्ष *ksha* and ज्ञ *jna*. The last is commonly pronounced *gya*, and may therefore be represented by these letters. The following compound letters, being of very frequent occurrence, and not always obviously resolvable into their parts, are given with a view to attract the *first attention* of the student. He may afterwards study the list in Prof. Wilson's Grammar.

क्त *kta*, as in the word उक्तं *uktam;* र्म *rma*, as in the word कूर्म *kūrma*. And here remark, that when र *r* is the *first* letter of a compound consonant, it is written above in the form of a semicircle; when it is the *last* letter, it is written below in the form of a small stroke, as क्र *kra* in the word क्रमेण *kramena*. Again, श्च *shcha*, as in ततश्च *tatashcha*. Here remark, that श sometimes changes its form to श, when combined with another consonant. त्र *tra*, as in तत्र *tatra;* च्छ *chcha*, as in अन्यच्छ *anyachcha;* ष्ट *shṭa*, as in कृष्ट *kṛishṭa;* द्य *dya*, as in अद्य *adya;* द्ध *ddha*, as in बुद्धि *buddhi;* भ्य *bhya*, as in तेभ्यः *tebhyah;* त्त *tta*, as in सुहृत्तमाः *suhṛittamāh;* व्य *vya*, as in व्याध *vyādha;* द्व *dwa*, as in द्वार *dwāra;* स्य *sya*, as in तस्य *tasya;* स्त *sta;* म्य *mya;* द्भ *dbha;* ख्य *khya;* ङ्क *ṅka;* ङ्ग *ṅga;* ञ्च *ñcha;* ण्ड *ṇḍa;* न्त *nta*.

PRONUNCIATION OF THE VOWELS.

The following English words, written in the Sanscrit character, will furnish the best clue to the pronunciation of the vowels.

A as in रोमन्, "Roman"; *ā* as in लास्त्, "last"; *i* and *ī* as in the first and last syllables of इन् वलीद्, "invalid"; *u* as in पुष्, "push"; *ū* as in रूद्, "rude"; *ṛi* as in ऋल्, "rill"; *ṛī* as in शागॄन्, "chagrin"; *e* as in एर्, "ere"; *o* as in सो, "so"; *ai* as in ऐल्, "aisle"; *au* as *ou* in और्, "our"; *ar* and *ār* as in the words "inward," "regard."

Since short *a* is inherent in every consonant, the student should be careful to acquire the correct pronunciation of this letter. There are a few words in English which will afford examples of its sound, such as *Roman, temperance, husbandman, tolerable.* But in English this sound is often represented by *u,* as in *fun, sun;* or by *o,* as in *done, son;* or even by the other vowels; as by *e* in *her, vernal;* by *i* in *bird, sir.* The perfection of the Devanāgarī alphabet, as compared with the Roman, is at once apparent. Every vowel in Sanscrit has one invariable sound, and the beginner can never be in doubt what pronunciation to give it, as in English, or whether to pronounce it long or short, as in Latin.

PRONUNCIATION OF THE CONSONANTS.

The consonants are in general pronounced as in English. But *g* is always pronounced hard, as in *give*: *th* is not pronounced as in English, but is only *t* aspirated, and, when rapidly enunciated, hardly distinguishable from *t.* The same remark applies to the other aspirated letters. The true sound of *th* is exemplified by the word *anthill;* so also *ph,* by *uphill,* which might be written उफिल्. The cerebral class of consonants only differs from the dental in being pronounced with a duller and deeper sound. Each class of consonants has its own nasal; thus the sound *ink* would be written in Sanscrit इङ्क्; the sound *inch,* इञ्च्; the word *under* अण्डर्; the dental *n* would be written in the word *country,* pronounced as in Ireland; the sound *imp* would be written इम्प्. So, also, three of the classes have sibilants peculiar to them. Thus the final sibilant of the word ततस् *tatas,* when combined with the word च *cha,* must be written ततश्च *tatashcha;* when combined with

टीका *ṭīkā*, must be written ततष्टीका *tatashṭīkā*; when combined with तं *tam*, must be retained ततस्तं *tatastam*. So also each of the letters, *h, y, r, l, v*, is plainly referrible to its particular class. The ह *h* is pronounced from the throat, and therefore allied to the guttural class. The य *y* belongs to the palatal class, and in Bengali is always corrupted into *j*. The र is allied to the cerebral letters ड and ढ, and in Bengali these letters are often hardly distinguishable from *r* in sound. The ल *l* is evidently a dental. The व, although partly dental, belongs to the labial class; and is so allied to ब *b*, that, in Bengali, it is always pronounced like *b*, and, in Sanscrit, is often interchanged with it.*

† It may here be remarked, that although the column of nasals in the Table of Consonants (p. 1) has reference to the sibilants, aspirate, and semi-vowels, as well as to the other consonants; yet the mark Anuswāra (ं) is the proper nasal of these letters, and must always take the place of any other nasal that may be combined with them in the same word. Thus the preposition सम् and the participle स्मृत, when united in one word, are written संस्मृत; सम् and हार, संहार; सम and राग, संराग;† and so on. But in every one of these cases the Anuswāra takes the sound of the nasal of the class to which the following letter belongs. Thus संस्मृत is sounded as if written सन् स्मृत; संहार as if written सङ् हार; संलाप as if written सन् लाप. For the sake of brevity, however, the Anuswāra is, in many books, written as the representative of the nasal of any letter, and not merely of the aspirate, semi-vowels, and sibilants.

---

* In Sanscrit, however, the letter व is always pronounced either like *v* or *w*; like *v* when it stands by itself, or as the *first* member of a compound consonant, as in वा *vā*, व्याध *vyādha*; like *w*, when it forms the *last* member of a compound consonant, as in द्वार *dwāra*.

† सम्राट्, "an universal monarch," and सम्यक्, "properly," are the only words which violate this rule.

CHAPTER II.

SECT. I.—COMBINATION AND PERMUTATION OF LETTERS.

WE are accustomed in Greek and Latin to certain euphonic changes of letters. Thus *in*, combined with *rogo*, becomes *irrogo*; *rego* makes, in the perfect, not *regsi* but *reksi*, contracted into *rexi*; *veho* becomes *veksi* or *vexi*; *συν* with *γνώμη* becomes *συγγνώμη*; *ἐν* with *λάμπω*, *ἐλλάμπω*. These laws for the combination of letters are applied very extensively throughout the Sanscrit language; and that, too, not only in combining two parts of one word, but in combining all the words in the same sentence. Thus the sentence "*Rara avis in terris*" would require, by the laws of combination (called, in Sanscrit, Sandhi) to be written thus, *Rarāvir ins terrih*; and would, moreover, be written without separating the words, *Rarāvirinsterrih*. The learner must not be discouraged if he is not able thoroughly to understand *all* the numerous laws of combination at first. He is recommended, after reading them over with attention, to pass at once to the declension of nouns and conjugation of verbs: for to oblige him to learn by heart a number of rules, the use of which is not fully seen till he comes to read and construct *sentences*, must only lead to a waste of time and labour.

CHANGES OF VOWELS.

1. Nevertheless, there are some changes of letters which come into immediate application in the formation and declension of nouns, and the conjugation of verbs; and amongst these, the changes of vowels called Guna and Vriddhi should be impressed on the memory of the student, before he takes a single step in the study of the Grammar. When the vowels *i* and *ī* are changed to *e*, this is called the Guna change, or a change in *quality*; when *i* and *ī* are changed to *ai*, this is called the Vriddhi change, or an *increase*. Similarly, *u* and *ū* are often changed to their Guna *o*, and Vriddhi *au*; *ṛi* and *ṛī* to their Guna *ar*, and Vriddhi *ār*; and

a, though it have no corresponding Guna change, has a Vriddhi substitute in *ā*.

2. Let the Student, therefore, never forget the following rule, or he will be confused at every step. There is no Guna substitute for *a*, but *ā* is the Vriddhi substitute for *a*; *e* is the Guna, and *ai* the Vriddhi substitute for *i* and *ī*; *o* is the Guna, and *au* the Vriddhi substitute for *u* and *ū*; *ar* is the Guna, and *ār* the Vriddhi substitute for *ṛi* and *ṛī*.

Again, let him never forget that *y* is the semi-vowel of *i* and *ī*; *v* is the semi-vowel of *u* and *ū*; *r* is the semi-vowel of *ṛi* and *ṛī*.

3. Lastly let him bear in mind that the Guna dipthong *e* is supposed to be made up of *a* and *i*, and the Guna *o*, of *a* and *u*;* so that *a* and *i* may often coalesce into *e*, and *a* and *u* into *o*.

He will now understand the reason for the arrangement of vowels and semi-vowels given in the first Table. This Table is here repeated in the Roman character.

SHORT.	LONG.	GUNA.	VRIDDHI.	SEMI-VOWELS.
a	*ā*		*ā*	
i	*ī*	*e*	*ai*	*y*
u	*ū*	*o*	*au*	*v*
ṛi	*ṛī*	*ar*	*ār*	*r*

RULES FOR THE COMBINATION OF VOWELS.

4. If a word end with *a* or *ā*, when the next begins with *a* or *ā*, the two vowels are contracted into one long similar vowel. Thus *na asti* become *nāsti*.

A similar rule applies to the other vowels *i*, *u*, *ṛi*, short or long. Thus, *adhi ishwara*, *adhīshwara*; *kintu upāya*, *kintūpaya*; *pitṛi ṛiddhih* (पितृ ऋद्धिः), *pitṛīddhih* (पितॄद्धिः).

5. If a word end with *a* or *ā*, when the next begins with *i*, *u*, *ṛi*, short or long, then *a* and *i* coalesce into *e*; *a* and *u* into *o*;

* In the same way the Vriddhi diphthong *ai* is supposed to be made up of *a* or *ā* and *e*, and the Vriddhi *au* of *a* or *ā* and *o*.

a and *ṛi* into *ar*. Thus, *parama īshwara* become *parameshwara; hita upadesha, hitopadesha; gangā udakam, gangodakam; tava ṛiddhih* (तव ऋद्धिः), *tavarddhih* (तवर्द्धिः).

6. If a word end with *a* or *ā*, when the next begins with the Guna letters *e, o*, or the Vriddhi *ai, au*, then *a* or *ā* with *e* or *ai*, coalesce into the Vriddhi *ai; a* or *ā* with *o* or *au*, into *au*: as, *deva aishwaryam* become *devaishwaryam; vidyā eva* become *vidyaiva; alpa ojas, alpaujas; tathā aushadham, tathaushadham.*

7. If a word end with *i, u, ṛi*, short or long, when the next begins with any other dissimilar vowel, *i* and *ī* are changed to the corresponding semi-vowel *y; u* or *ū* to *v; ṛi* or *ṛī* to *r*: as, *prati uvācha* become *pratyuvācha; tu idānīm, twidānīm; mātṛi ānanda* (मातृ आनन्द) become *mātrānanda* (मात्रानन्द).

8. If a word end with the diphthongs *ai* or *au*, when the next begins with any vowel, *ai* is changed to *āy*, and *au* to *āv*. Thus, *tasmai uktah* becomes *tasmāyuktah; dadau annam, dadāvannam.*

9. If a word end in *e* or *o*, when the next begins with *a* short, then *e* and *o* remain unchanged, and the initial *a* is cut off. Thus, *te api* are written *te 'pi* (तेऽपि); *so api* are written *so 'pi* (सोऽपि).

10. If a word end in *e*, when the next begins with any other vowel except *a* short, then *e* is supposed to be first changed to *ay*; but the *y* is usually dropped, leaving the *a* uninfluenced by the following vowel. Thus, *te āgatāh* becomes *ta āgatāh*, (त आगताः).

† It so happens that *o*, as the final of a complete word, is never likely to come in coalition with any initial vowel but short *a*. But in the case of *e* or *o*, as the finals of roots or crude forms, when the termination to be annexed begins with any vowel, whether *a, ā, i*, or any other, then *e* is changed to *ay*, and *o* to *av*. Thus, *je ati* become *jayati, bho ati* become *bhavati.*

The following Table exhibits all the combinations of vowels at one view. Supposing a word to end in *ū*, and the next word to begin with *au*, the student must carry his eye down the first column (headed "final vowels") till he comes to *ū*, and then along the top horizontal line of "initial vowels," till he comes to *au*. At the junction of the perpendicular column under *au* and the horizontal line beginning *ū*, will be the required combination, viz. *v au.*

INITIAL VOWELS.	a	ā	i	ī	u	ū	ṛi	ṛī	e	ai	o	au
FINAL VOWELS.												
a	ā	ā	e	e	o	o	ar	ar	ai	ai	au	au
ā	ā	ā	e	e	o	o	ar	ar	ai	ai	au	au
i	y a	y ā	ī	ī	y u	y ū	y ṛi	y ṛī	y e	y ai	y o	y au
ī	y a	y ā	ī	ī	y u	y ū	y ṛi	y ṛī	y e	y ai	y o	y au
u	v a	v ā	v i	v ī	ū	ū	v ṛi	v ṛī	v e	v ai	v o	v au
ū	v a	v ā	v i	v ī	ū	ū	v ṛi	v ṛī	v e	v ai	v o	v au
ṛi	r a	r ā	r i	r ī	r u	r ū	ṛī	ṛī	r e	r ai	r o	r au
ṛī	r a	r ā	r i	r ī	r u	r ū	ṛī	ṛī	r e	r ai	r o	r au
e	e '	a ā	a i	a ī	a u	a ū	a ṛi	a ṛī	a e	a ai	a o	a au
ai	āy a	āy ā	āy i	āy ī	āy u	āy ū	āy ṛi	āy ṛī	āy e	āy ai	āy o	āy au
o	o '	av ā	av i	av ī	av u	av ū	av ṛi	av ṛī	av e	av ai	av o	av au
au	āv a	āv ā	āv i	āv ī	āv u	āv ū	āv ṛi	āv ṛī	āv e	āv ai	āv o	āv au

† Observe, that in this table the final letter, in its changed state, has been printed, for greater clearness, separate from the initial; except in those cases (in the second and third lines), where the blending of the two vowels made this impossible. But in a *sentence* they must be written without any separation, as already seen in the opposite page.

Sect. II.—COMBINATION OF CONSONANTS.

11. Before proceeding to the rules for the combination of consonants, let the alphabet be regarded attentively as divided into two grand classes, as exhibited in the following Table.

HARD OR SURD.		SOFT OR SONANT.			
k kh		*g gh*	*ṅ*	*h*	all the vowels.
ch chh	*sh*	*j jh*	*ñ*	*y*	
ṭ ṭh	*ṣh*	*ḍ ḍh*	*ṇ*	*r*	
t th	*s*	*d dh*	*n*	*l*	
p ph		*b bh*	*m*	*v*	

12. If any surd letter end a word when any sonant begins the next, the hard is changed to its own unaspirated soft; thus, *karmakṛit bhavati* becomes *karmakṛid bhavati; vāk asti, vāg asti; chitralikh asti, chitralig asti.*

† It may be proper here to remark, that in writing a Sanscrit sentence, when the words have undergone those changes which the laws of combination demand, they may either be written separately, as in the examples just given, or often more correctly without any separation; as, *karmakṛidbhavati* (कर्मकृद्भवति); *vāgasti* (वागस्ति). The student is therefore to observe, that although in the following examples, each word will, for greater clearness, be printed separately from the next, it would accord more with the practice of the natives of India to print them without any separation. There are two cases, however, in which there remains no option, but in which words must always be written together without separation. 1st, when a final and initial vowel blend together into one sound (see examples, r. 4—8); 2dly, when either crude forms or adverbs are joined with other words to form compounds (see Chap. IX. on Compound Words).

13. If any sonant letter end a word when any surd begins the next, the soft is changed to its own unaspirated hard.* Thus,

---

* If the final be an aspirated sonant letter, and belong to a root whose initial is *g*, *d*, or *b*, the aspirate, which is suppressed in the final, is transferred back to the initial letter of the root. Thus, *vedabudh asti* becomes *vedabhud asti.*

tad karoti becomes *tat karoti; vāg patih, vāk patih; kshudh pipāsā, kshut pipāsā.* But as very few words in Sanscrit end in any other consonants than *t* and *d*, the nasals, Visargah, the dental sibilant *s*, and *r*, it will be sufficient for all practical purposes that the attention be confined to the changes of these consonants. To begin, therefore, with *t* and *d*.

CHANGES OF FINAL *t* AND *d*.

General rule.

14. *T* becomes *d* before *g, gh, d, dh, b, bh, h, y, r, v*, and all vowels.* See example, rule 12.

D becomes *t* before *k, kh, t, th, p, ph, s*. See example, rule 13.

Before the nasals, palatals, and the letter *l*, final *t* and *d* undergo a change in *form* as well as quality, as in the following special rules.

Change of t or d to n, before n or m.

15. If *t* or *d* end a word when the next begins with a nasal, the *t* or *d* is usually changed to its own nasal. Thus, *tasmāt na* becomes *tasmān na; tasmāt mūrkha, tasmān mūrkha.*

† A final *k* is subject to a similar rule. Thus, *vāk mama* (वाक् मम) would become *vān-mama* (वाङ्मम).

Assimilation of t or d with ch, j, l.

16. If *t* or *d* end a word when the next begins with *ch, j*, or *l*, the *t* or *d* assimilates with these letters. Thus, *bhayāt lobhāt cha* becomes *bhayāl lobhāch cha; tad jīvanam, taj jīvanam.*

Combination of t or d with sh.

17. If *t* or *d* end a word when the next begins with श् *sh*, then

* Before the vowels of *terminations t* remains unchanged; thus, the accusative case of *Harit* is *Haritam*, not *Haridam*; and the third person singular of the verb *yat* is *yatate*, not *yadate*.

t or *d* are changed to *ch,* and the initial श् *sh* to छ् *chh.* Thus, *tat shrutvā* (तत् श्रुत्वा) becomes *tach chhrutvā* (तच्छ्रुत्वा).

Combination of t or d with h.

18. If a word end in *t* or *d* when the next begins with ह् *h,* the final *t* is changed to *d* (by rule 12), and the initial ह् to ध् *dh.* Thus, *tad harati* (तद् हरति) is written *tad dharati* (तद्धरति).

† By a similar rule, and on the same principle, are written words ending in *k* followed by initial ह्; as *vāk harati* (वाक् हरति), *vāg gharati* (वाग्घरति).

CHANGES OF THE NASALS.

Changes of final न् n before vowels and before t, ch, sh, l.

19. If the letter न् *n,* preceded by a *short* vowel, end a word when the next begins with any vowel, the *n* is doubled. Thus, *āsan atra* becomes *āsann atra; tasmin eva, tasminn eva.*

20. If *n* end a word when the next begins with *t, ch,* or their aspirates, a sibilant is inserted between the two words, according to the class of these last initial letters; and the न् *n* is then expressed by Anuswāra, according to rule (p. 5, †). Thus, *asmin tu* becomes *asminstu* (अस्मिंस्तु); *kasmin chit* becomes *kasminshchit* (कस्मिंश्चित्).

† If न् *n* end a word when the next begins with श् *sh*, they may either remain unchanged, or they may be combined in either one of the two following ways. 1st, the final न् may be changed to ञ् *ñ*; as, भवान् शूरः is written भवाञ्शूरः. 2dly, the श् may also be changed to छ्; as, भवाञ्छूरः.

If न् end a word when the next begins with *l*, the *n* assimilates with the *l*, and the mark ँ is placed over the preceding vowel. As, *pakshān lunāti* is written पक्षाँल्लुनाति.

If the crude form of a word end in *n*, this *n* is rejected in forming a compound word, or before any affix. Thus, *rājan purusha* is compounded into *rāja-purusha;* and स्वामिन् अर्थं into स्वाम्यर्थं; and *dhanin*, with the affix *twa*, becomes *dhanitwa.*

Change of न् n, not final, to ण् ṇ, after ṛi, r, ṣh, preceding in the same word.

21. The letters र् *r,* ष् *ṣh,* are *cerebrals,* and the vowel *ṛi* is allied to the cerebral *r.* Hence, if the letter *n* (*not final*) should follow

ṛi, ṛ, or *ṣh, in the same word,* the nasal must be written in the *cerebral* form ण् *ṇ*, even though *k, g, p, b* (or their aspirates), *h, y, v,* or *m,* should intervene. Thus, the English word *carbonic* would be written in the Sanscrit character thus, कार्बणिक्; and the accusative case of ब्रह्महन् is ब्रह्महणं; and the nominative plural of चर्मन् is चर्माणि; and the imperative mood of क्षिप, क्षिपाणि.* But the intervention of a dental, palatal, or cerebral, or of any letter whatever, if compounded with the nasal, prevents the operation of this rule, and requires the dental *n* to follow. Thus, the instrumental case of शृगाल is शृगालेन; the nominative plural of वर्त्मन्, वर्त्मानि; and in further illustration of the same law, may be taken the words सर्जनं, क्रीडनं, प्राप्नोति, राज्ञा.

Changes of final m.

22. If the letter म् *m* end a word when the next begins with *any* consonant, it may be represented by Anuswāra (ं); or it may, optionally, before those consonants which have a corresponding nasal, be changed to this corresponding nasal. Thus, *gṛiham gachchhati* is written either गृहं गच्छति or गृहङ्गच्छति.

23. When the next word begins with a vowel, the letter म् is always written. Thus, *gṛiham āpnoti*, गृहमाप्नोति.

CHANGES OF VISARGAH OR FINAL *h*.

Almost every nominative case, and nearly half the remaining cases of nouns in Sanscrit, besides many persons of the verb, end in Visargah (:), or the symbol used to denote the aspirate when final. And this final *ḥ* is liable to remain unchanged, to be changed to *s*, to *sh*, to *o*, to *r*, or to be dropped altogether, according to the nature of the initial letter following. At every step, therefore, these changes will meet the student's eye. *Therefore let him master the following five rules before he attempts to read a single sentence of Sanscrit, or he can never hope to make any real progress in the acquirement of this language.*

---

* The letter क्ष is, properly, a compound of क् *k* and ष् *ṣh*; although, in this Grammar, it is considered as a simple letter, and represented by *kṣh*.

RULE A.—WHEN IS VISARGAH OR FINAL *h* UNCHANGED?

24. *a.* Before *k*, *p* (and their aspirates), and before the sibilants स् *s*, श् *sh*.

b. Before a pause, *i.e.* at the end of a sentence, or when a word stands by itself.

RULE B.—WHEN IS VISARGAH CHANGED TO स् *s* AND श् *sh*?

25. *a.* Before *t* (and its aspirate) it is changed to the dental sibilant स् *s*; before *ch* (and its aspirate), to the palatal sibilant श् *sh*.*

b. Also in some books, before the sibilants स, श, Visargah is allowed to assimilate with these letters.

RULE C.—WHEN IS VISARGAH CHANGED TO *o*?

26. *a.* Final *ah* is changed to *o* before all sonant consonants.

b. Also before short *a* (this *a* being then cut off).

RULE D.—WHEN IS VISARGAH CHANGED TO *r*?

27. *a.* *Ih*, *īh*, *uh*, *ūh*, *eh*, *aih*, *oh*, *auh*, before *any sonant* (consonant or vowel), change the final *h* to *r*;

b. Unless *r* itself be the sonant following, in which case, to avoid the coalition of two *r's*, final *h* is dropped, and the vowel preceding it (if short) is lengthened.

RULE E.—WHEN IS VISARGAH DROPPED ALTOGETHER?

28. *a.* Final *ah*, before any other vowel except short *a*, drops the Visargah, and leaves the remaining *a* opening on the initial vowel of the next word without coalition.†

b. Final *āh*, before *any* sonant (consonant or vowel), drops the Visargah; and, if the initial letter of the next word be a vowel, the remaining *ā* is allowed to open upon it without coalition.

---

* So, also, before ट, ठ, Visargah is changed to the cerebral sibilant ष्; as, रविष् टीकते.

† By a special rule सः, "he," and एषः, "this," the nominative cases of the pronouns तद् and एतद्, drop their Visargah before *any consonant*.

In the following Table the nominative cases *Narah*, "a man," *Narāh*, "men," and *Harih*, "Vishṇu," joined with verbs, illustrate these rules at one view.

VISARGAH BEFORE SURD LETTERS.		VISARGAH BEFORE SONANT LETTERS.	
Before hard consonants.	Before sibilants.	Before soft consonants	Before vowels.
Narah karoti *Narāh kurvanti* *Harih karoti* } A. a.	*Narah sarati* *Narāh saranti* *Harih sarati* } A. a.	*Naro gachchhati* C. a. *Narā gachchhanti* E. b. *Harir gachchhati* D. a.	*Naro 'tti* C. b. *Narā adanti* E. b. *Harir atti* D. a.
Narah pachati *Narāh pachanti* *Harih pachati* } A. a.	*Narah shaknoti* *Narāh shaknuvanti* *Harih shaknoti* } A. a.	*Naro jayati* C. a. *Narā jayanti* E. b. *Harir jayati* D. a.	*Nara āpnoti* E. a. *Narā āpnuvanti* E. b. *Harir āpnoti* D. a.
Naras tarati *Narās taranti* *Haris tarati* } B. a.	or *Naras sarati* *Narās saranti* *Haris sarati* } B. b.	*Naro dadāti* C. a. *Narā dadati* E. b. *Harir dadāti* D. a.	*Nara īkshate* E. a. *Narā īkshante* E. b. *Harir īkshate* D. a.
Narash charati *Narāsh charanti* *Harish charati* } B. a.	*Narash shaknoti* *Narāsh shaknuvanti* *Harish shaknoti* } B. b.	*Naro bravīti* C. a. *Narā bruvanti* E. b. *Harir bravīti* D. a.	*Nara edhate* E. a. *Narā edhante* E. b. *Harir edhate* D. a.
Similarly before *kh*, *ph*, *th*, *chh*.		*Naro yāchati* C. a. *Narā yāchanti* E. b. *Harir yāchati* D. a.	Similarly before the other vowels and diphthongs.
		Similarly before the nasals, and before *h*, *l*, *v*: and before *r*, except in the last case; as,	Visargah before a pause.
		Naro rakshati C. a. *Narā rakshanti* E. b. *Harī rakshati* D. b.	*Atti narah* *Adanti narāh* *Atti Harih* } A. b.

CHANGES OF FINAL स् *s*.

29. The rules for the changes of Visargah apply equally to final sibilants. Thus, *manas hara* becomes *manohara* (as in C. a.); and *chakshus vishaya*, *chakshur vishaya* (as in D. a.);* and *chetas*, standing alone, is written *chetah* (A. b.).

* In a few compound words a final sibilant takes the cerebral form before *k*, as *prādus kṛita* become *prāduṣhkṛita*. Similarly, a final *r* before *k* or *p*: as, *nir* with *krānta*, *niṣhkrānta*; with *putra*, *niṣhputra*. See also r. 42, 43, and 131. 1.

30. स् *s* is changed to ष् *ṣh* when any other vowel except *a* or *ā* immediately precedes in the same word. Thus, *bhavasi*, "thou art"; but *karoṣhi*, not *karosi*, "thou doest."*

CHANGES OF FINAL *r*.

31. Again, rules A, B, D, apply equally to final *r*. Thus, *prātar kāla* becomes *prātaḥ kāla*; *prātar cha*, *prātash cha*; and the preposition *nir* before *ukta* remains unchanged, and before *rasa* is changed to *nī*; thus, *nirukta*, *nīrasa*.

32. But final *ar*, unlike *aḥ*, remains unchanged before *any* sonant (consonant or vowel); as, *prātar āsha*: and before the sonant *r* itself, drops the *r* and lengthens the preceding *a*; as, *punar rakshati* becomes *punā rakshati*.

33. It is to be observed further of *r*, that it may optionally double any consonant (except ह) that immediately follows it. Thus, निर् द्य may be written निर्द्दय.

Hence it appears that the symbol Visargah (:) may be considered as much a representative of final *s* and *r*, when these letters are imperceptible, as of final *ḥ*. Indeed, all those inflections of nouns and persons of verbs which are said to end in Visargah, might be said to end in *s*; only that, in such cases, the *s* is silent, or pronounced with an imperceptible breathing, as in the French *les*, or the English, *island*, *viscount*. So again, in many French words, such as *parler*, the final *r* is silent; and in some English, such as *card*, the sound of *r* is very indistinct; and in all these cases, *s* and *r* would be represented in Sanscrit by Visargah (ले: पार्ले: &c.).

The following Table exhibits the more common combinations of consonants at one view. Observe, that in the top line of initial letters the aspirated consonants have been omitted, because it is an universal rule, that whatever change takes place before any consonant, the same holds good before its aspirate. Final *s* has also been omitted, as undergoing precisely the same changes with final *ḥ*.

---

* Also when *k* precedes: as, *vid* with *su* is *vitsu*; but *bhuk*, *bhukshu*. Cf. r. 112. c.

INITIAL VOWELS AND CONSONANTS.	a	ā, i, &c.	k	g	ch	j	t	d	n	p	b	m	y	r	l	v	sh	s	h
FINAL CONSONANTS.																			
t, d	d a	d ā &c.	t k	d g	ch ch	j j	t t	d d	n n	t p	d b	n m	d y	d r	l l	d v	ch chh	t s	d dh
न् n	nn* a	nn* ā &c.	n k	n g	nsh ch	n† j	ns t	n d	n n	n p	n b	n m	n y	n r	l l	n v	n sh or ṅ sh or ṅ chh	n s	n h
ah	o 'a	a ā &c.	ah k	o g	ash ch	o j	as t	o d	o n	ah p	o b	o m	o y	o r	o l	o v	ah sh	ah s	o h
āh	ā a	ā ā &c.	āh k	ā g	āsh ch	ā j	ās t	ā d	ā n	āh p	ā b	ā m	ā y	ā r	ā l	ā v	āh sh	āh s	ā h
ih, īh	ir a	ir ā	ih k	ir g	ish ch	ir j	is t	ir d	ir n	ih p	ir b	ir m	ir y	ī r	ir l	ir v	ih sh	ih s	ir h
uh, ūh, eh, aih, oh, auh	ur a &c.	ur ā &c. &c.	uh k	ur g	ush ch	ur j	us t	ur d	ur n	uh p	ur b	ur m	ur y	ū r	ur l	ur v	uh sh	uh s	ur h
r, preceded by *any* vowel.	r a	r ā &c.	h k	r g	sh ch	r j	s t	r d	r n	h p	r b	r m	r y	r	r l	r v	h sh	h s	r h

* *n* is only doubled if preceded by a short vowel.

† A final *n* before *j* is very rarely written in the palatal form ञ *ñ*.

CHAPTER III.

ON SANSCRIT ROOTS, AND THE CRUDE FORM OF NOUNS.

35. Before treating of Sanscrit nouns, it will be advisable to point out in what respect the peculiar system adopted in their formation requires an arrangement of the subject different from that to which we are accustomed in other languages.

In Sanscrit nouns, then, there is this great peculiarity, that every one of them has two distinct states prior to the formation of the nominative case: viz. 1st, *a root;* 2dly, *a crude form,* coming from this root.

In the first place, therefore, let us inquire, what is the root. There are, in Sanscrit, a number of monosyllabic sounds, which are called roots. These are mere artificial inventions, having only an ideal existence; mere blocks, so to speak, of themselves quite useless;* from which, however, are carved out and fashioned all the varieties of nouns and verbs which exist in the language. Every one of these roots conveys some simple idea, which appears under different modifications in the derivatives from it. Thus, to mention a few of the most common: the root *kship* conveys the idea of "throwing"; *kṛi* of "doing," "making"; *hṛi* of "seizing"; *yuj*, "joining"; *as*, *vṛit*, "being"; *bhū*, "becoming"; *jīv*, "living"; *nī*, "leading"; *ji*, "conquering"; *gam*, *yā*, *char*, *kram*, *i*, *sṛi*, "going"; *vad*, *vach*, *brū*, "speaking"; *budh*, *gyā* (ज्ञा), "knowing"; *dṛish* (दृश्), "seeing"; *iṣh*, *kam*, "wishing"; *mṛi*, "dying"; *dā*, "giving"; *jan*, "producing"; *dhā*, "placing"; *ad*, *bhaksh*, *bhuj*, "eating"; *pā*, "drinking"; *pach*, "cooking"; *han*, "killing"; *pat*, "falling"; *vas*, "dwelling"; *vish* (विश्), "entering"; *sthā*, "standing"; *shru* (श्रु), "hearing"; *spṛish* (स्पृश्), "touching"; *sidh*, *sādh*, "accomplishing"; *krī* (क्री), "buying"; *kup*, *krudh*, "being

* Except in a few cases, where they are used by themselves as nouns.

angry"; *chi*, "collecting"; *ghrā*, "smelling"; *khyā*, "relating"; *nash* (नश्), "perishing"; *tyaj*, *rah*, "quitting"; *dwiṣh* (द्विष्), "hating"; *nind*, "blaming"; *dru*, "running"; *dyut*, *dīp*, *bhā*, *shubh*, "shining"; *pū*, "purifying"; *prachchh* (प्रच्छ्), "asking"; *āp*, *labh*, "obtaining"; *stu*, *shans*, "praising"; *yat*, "striving"; *yam*, "restraining"; *shak* (शक्), "being able"; *tap*, "heating"; *dah*, "burning"; *much*, "liberating"; *muh*, "being foolish"; *yudh*, "fighting"; *ruh*, "growing"; *has*, laughing"; *swap*, "sleeping"; *hriṣh* (हृष्), *nand*, *hlād*, "being glad"; *snā*, "bathing"; *rabh*, "beginning"; *swar*, "sounding"; *sah*, *vah*, "bearing"; *smri*, "remembering."

The student is recommended to commit to memory the commonest of these roots or elementary sounds, as here given. For it will appear in the sequel, that from each of them may be drawn out, with great regularity, 1st, a set of simple substantives; 2dly, of simple adjectives; 3dly, of simple verbs. To take, for example, the root *budh*, "to know."* From this root are formed, on fixed principles, the following substantives and adjectives; *bodha* or *bodhana*, "knowledge"; *buddhi*, "intellect"; *bodhaka*, "an informer"; *bauddha*, "a Buddhist"; *budha*, "wise"; *buddhimat*, "intellectual"; and the verbs, *bodhati*, "he knows"; *bodhayati*, "he informs"; *budhyate*, "it is known"; *bubhutsate*, or *bubodhishati*, "he wishes to know"; *bobudhyate*, "he knows well." And the simple idea contained in the root may be endlessly extended by the prefixing of prepositions; as, *prabodha*, "vigilance"; *prabudhyate*, "he awakes."

36. In the second place, it has been said that the Sanscrit noun, substantive and adjective, makes its first appearance in a state called *the crude form*.† The same may be said of the pronouns,

---

* It will be convenient, in the following pages, to express the idea contained in the root by prefixing to it the infinitive sign *to*. But the Student must not suppose that the sound *budh* denotes any thing more than the mere *idea* of "knowing"; nor must he imagine that in deriving nouns from it, we are deriving them from the infinitive, or from any part of the verb, but rather from a simple original sound, a mere imaginary word, which is the common source of both nouns and verbs.

† This state of the noun will, in the following pages, be called *the crude*.

numerals, and participles. Thus, *bodha, bodhana, tad, pañchan, bhavat,* are the crudes of the nominative cases *bodhah, bodhanam, sah, pañcha, bhavan,* respectively. The student should endeavour to understand, at the outset, the meaning and use of this crude form. It is an intermediate state between the root and nominative case, the naked form of the noun, which serves as the basis on which to construct its eight cases, beginning with the nominative. In a Greek or Latin dictionary we look for the noun under the nominative case, but in Sanscrit we look for it under its crude state; as, for example, *sah,* "he," is found under *tad.* And here let it be distinctly understood, that the crude form of a noun is very far from having a mere ideal existence, like the root. It is of the utmost practical utility. It is that form of the noun which is always used in the formation of compound words; and as every Sanscrit sentence contains, perhaps, more compound words than simple ones, it may with truth be said, that the crude state of the noun is not only that form under which it appears in the dictionary, but is also the most usual form under which it appears in books.

We may conceive it quite possible that Greek and Latin grammarians might have proceeded on a similar plan, and that they might have supposed a root λεγ, from which was drawn out the nouns λέξις, λεξικὸς, λεκτὸς, καταλογὴ, ἔλλογος, and the verbs λέγω, καταλέγω, ἐλλογέω: so also, a root *ag,* from which was derived the nouns *agmen, actio, actus;* and the verbs *ago, perago:* or a root *nau,* from which would come *nauta, navis, nauticus, navalis, navigo.* Again, they might have supposed a crude form to each of these nouns, as well as a root; as, for instance, λεξικο of λεξικὸς, and *navi* of *navis;* and they might have required the student to look for the noun *navis* under *navi,* and the verb *navigo* under *nau.* Further than this, they might have shewn that this crude form was the form used in the formation of compound words, as in λεξικογράφος, *naviger.* But Greek and Latin are too uncertain in their construction to admit of such a method of arrangement being extensively applied: such, however, is the artificial character of the Sanscrit language, that here it has been done throughout with great regularity and precision.

FORMATION OF THE CRUDES OF SIMPLE NOUNS.

37. Nouns substantive and adjective are of two kinds, simple and compound. *Simple* nouns are those which stand alone, and uncompounded with any other. *Compound*, are those made up of two or more nouns, the last only receiving inflection.*

It may be easily understood, from the preceding remarks, that the consideration of simple nouns divides itself into two heads: 1st, The formation of their crudes; 2dly, The formation of their cases; or, in other words, the enumeration of the different systems of declension which belong to each variety of crude form.

Observe, that it is not intended that the student should dwell long, *at first*, on the following pages, printed in small type. It will be essential for him, however, to read them over with attention, as a necessary introduction to the subject of declension in Chapter IV. Their importance will not be fully appreciated till he arrives at a more advanced period of his studies.

The crudes of nouns are formed in two ways, either by adding certain affixes to the ROOT, the vowel of which is liable, at the same time, to be changed to its Guna or Vṛiddhi substitute, or by adding certain affixes to CRUDES OF NOUNS already formed. It must be remembered, however, that, although every single word in the Sanscrit language is derived from some root, there are many in which the connection between the noun and its source, either in sense or form, is by no means obvious.† With the derivation of all such we shall not concern ourselves; and the following rules have only reference to those classes of nouns whose formation proceeds on clear and intelligible principles.

38. FIRST CLASS.—*Crudes in a, Masculine and Neuter; in ā and ī, Feminine.*

Formed by adding to ROOTS—

1. *a*, forming, 1st (nom. *-ah*), after the Vriddhi of medial *a* of a root, and the Guna of any other vowel, a large class of substantives masculine: as, from the root *div*, "to sport," *deva*, "a deity." If a root end in *ch* or *j*, these letters

* Compound nouns are treated of in Chapter IX. on Compound Words.

† Thus, पुरुष, "a man," is said to come from *pur*, "to precede"; *shṛigāla*, "a jackal," from *sṛij*, "to create"; *shiva*, "the god Shiva," from *shī*, "to sleep."

are changed to *k* and *g* respectively: as, from *pach*, "to cook," *pāka*, "cooking"; from *yuj*, "to join," *yoga*, "joining."

Forming, 2dly (nom. masc. *-ah*, fem. *-ā*, neut. *-am**), after Guna of a final, and sometimes Guna of a medial vowel, nouns of agency: as, from *plu*, "to swim," *plava*, "what swims"; from *sṛip*, "to creep," *sarpa*, "what creeps" (see r. 131. 1.).

Forming, 3dly (nom. *-ah -ā -am*), adjectives: as, from *shubh*, "to shine," *shubha*, "beautiful." Sometimes there is great change of the root: as in *shiva*, "propitious," *sundara*, "beautiful; and sometimes the feminine may be formed in *ī*: as, *sundarī*. There are very few adjectives formed with this affix.

II. *aka* (nom. *-akah*, *-akā* or *-ikā*, *-akam*), after Vriddhi of a final vowel or medial *a*, and Guna of any other vowel. Still more common than *a* to form adjectives and nouns of agency: as, from *tap*, "to burn," *tāpaka*, "inflammatory"; from *kṛi*, "to do," *kāraka*, "a doer" (r. 131. 3. *b*.); OBS. *-akā* is the feminine of the adjectives, and *-ikā* of the agents: as, *tāpakā*, *kārikā*.

III. *ana* (nom. *-anam*), after Guna of the root, forming, 1st, a large class of neuter substantives: as, from *nī*, "to guide," *nayana*, "guidance"; from *dā*, "to give," *dāna*, "a gift."

Forming, 2dly (nom. *-anah*, *-anā*, *-anam*), nouns of agency and adjectives: as, from *nṛit*, "to dance," *nartana*, "a dancer" (r. 131. 3. *c*.); from *shubh*, "to shine," *shobhana*, "bright." The feminine of the agents may be in *anī*.

IV. *tra* (nom. *-tram*), after Guna of the root: as, from *pā*, "to drink," *pātra*, "a vessel"; from *shru*, "to hear," *shrotra*, "the organ of hearing." This affix is used to form neuter nouns denoting some instrument or organ, and corresponds to the Latin *trum* in *aratrum*, *plectrum*, &c.

V. There are other uncommon affixes to roots to form adjectives in *a* (nom. *-ah*, *-ā*, *-am*): as, *ala*, *vara*, *ra*, *ura*, *ira*, *uka*, *tra*, *ma*, *ūka*. The following are examples of adjectives formed with these affixes; *chapala*, *jitwara*, *namra*, *bhidura*, *ruchira*, *varshuka*, *chitra*, *bhīma*, *jāgarūka*.

Formed by adding to NOUNS,

VI. *twa* (nom. *-twam*), forming neuter abstract substantives from any noun in the language: as, from *purusha*, "a man," *purushatwa*, "manliness." In adding this affix to crudes ending in nasals, the nasal is rejected: as, from *dhanin*, "rich," *dhanitwa*, "the state of being rich."

---

* OBS. When there are three genders, it will be sufficient, in future, to place the hyphen between them.

VII. *ya*, forming, 1st (nom. *-yam*), neuter abstract substantives and a few collectives, the first syllable of the noun taking Vṛiddhi: as, from *suhrid*, "a friend," *sauhṛidya*, "friendship." When the crude ends in a vowel, this vowel is rejected before *ya* is affixed: as, from *vichitra*, "various," *vaichitrya*, "variety."

Forming, 2dly (nom. *-ya*, *-yā*, *-yam*), adjectives expressing some relationship to the noun: as, from *dhana*, "wealth," *dhanya*, "wealthy." Sometimes Vṛiddhi takes place: as, from *soma*, "the moon," *saumya*, "lunar." In this case the fem. is *-yī*.

VIII. *a* (nom. *-ah*, *-ī*, *-am*), after Vṛiddhi of the first syllable of the noun, forming innumerable adjectives expressing some relationship to the noun. When the crude ends in *a*, no further affix is required, and the only change is the Vṛiddhi of the first syllable: as, from *purusha*, "a man," *paurusha*, "manly." When in *ā* or *i*, this *ā* or *i* must be rejected: as, from *sikatā*, "sand," *saikata*, "sandy." When in *u*, this *u* is changed to *av* before this and the three following affixes: as, from *Vishṇu*, "the god Vishṇu," *Vaishṇava*, "a worshipper of Vishṇu."

Sometimes the neuter form of this adjective is taken as an abstract substantive: as, nominative case, *paurusham*, "manliness"; or, as a collective: as, *kshaitram*, "fields," collectively, from *kshetra*. This applies to the two next affixes.

IX. *ika* (nom. *-ikah*, *-ikī*, *-ikam*), after Vṛiddhi of the first syllable of the noun, forming numerous adjectives. Before this affix is added, the final vowel of the crude must be rejected: as, from *dharma*, "religion," *dhārmika*, "religious."

X. *eya* (nom. *-eyah*, *-eyī*, *-eyam*), after Vṛiddhi of the first syllable of the noun, forming many adjectives. The final vowel of the crude must be rejected: as, from *purusha*, "a man," *paurusheya*, "manly"; from *agni*, "fire," *āgneya*, "fiery."

XI. *īya* (nom. *-īyah*, *-īyā*, *-īyam*), without any change of the noun, except the rejection of final *a*: as, from *parvata*, "a mountain," *parvatīya*, "mountainous." Sometimes there is Vṛiddhi: as, from *sukha*, "pleasure," *saukhīya*, "pleasurable." When the final of the crude remains, *k* is prefixed to the last two affixes.

XII. There are other uncommon affixes to nouns forming adjectives in *a* (nom. *-ah*, *-ā*, *-am*): as, *īna*, *vala*, *tana*; forming, from *grāma*, "a village," *grāmīna*, "rustic"; from *shikhā*, "a crest," *shikhāvala*, "crested"; from *shwas*, "to-morrow," *shwastana*, "future." This last corresponds to the Latin *tinus*, and has reference to *time*. *Ka* is sometimes added to words to form adjectives and collective nouns, and is often redundant. *Maya* (nom. *-mayah*, *-mayī*, *-mayam*) is a common affix added to any word to denote *made of*: as, from *loha*, "iron," *lohamaya*, "made of iron"; from *tejas*, "light," *tejomaya*, "consisting of light," "full of light."

By adding to ROOTS,

XIII. *ā* (nom. *-ā*), with no change of the root, forming feminine substantives: as, from *jīv*, "to live," *jīva*, "life." This affix is frequently added to the desiderative form of a root: as, from *pipās*, "to desire to drink," *pipāsā*, "thirst"; and rarely to the intensive: as, from *lolūy*, "to cut much," *lolūyā*, "cutting much."

By adding to NOUNS,

XIV. *tā* (nom. *-tā*), forming feminine abstract substantives: as, from *purusha*, "a man," *purushatā*, "manliness." This affix may be added to any noun in the language, and corresponds to the Latin *tas* in *celeritas*, &c.

XV. *ī* (nom. *-ī*), forming a large class of feminine substantives, usually derived from masculines in *a*, by changing *a* to *ī*: as, from *nada*, "a river," fem. *nadī*; from *putra*, "a son," fem. *putrī*; from *nartaka*, "a dancer," fem. *nartakī*.

---

39. SECOND CLASS.—*Crudes in* i, *Masculine, Feminine, and Neuter.*

Formed by adding to ROOTS,

I. *i*, forming, 1st (nom. *-ih*), a few masculine substantives, often not connected with their roots either in form or sense: as, from *ank*, "to mark", *agni*, "fire." When this affix is added to the root *dhā*, *ā* is dropped, and various prepositions are prefixed; as *sandhi*, *vidhi*, *nidhi*.

Forming, 2dly (nom. *-i*), one or two neuter substantives: as, from *vṛi*, "to surround"; *vāri*, "water."

Forming, 3dly (nom. *-ih*, *-ih*, *-i*), a few adjectives: as, from *shuch*, "to be pure"; *shuchi*, "pure."

II. *ti* (nom. *-tih*), forming an useful class of abstract substantives feminine. This affix bears a great analogy to the passive participle (r. 125.). The same changes of the root are required before it as before this participle; and, in fact, provided the passive participle does not insert *i*, this substantive may always be formed from it, by changing *ta* into *ti*. But if *i* is inserted before *ta*, no such substantive can be formed. Thus, from *vach*, "to speak," *ukta*, "spoken," *ukti*, "speech"; from *man*, "to imagine," *mata*, "imagined," *mati*, "the mind." And where *na* is substituted for *ta* of the passive participle, *ni* is substituted for *ti*; as, from *glai*, "to be weary," *glāna*, "wearied," *glāni*, "weariness." This affix corresponds to the *tio* of the Latin, added, in the same way, to passive participles: as *actus*, *actio*.

---

40. THIRD CLASS.—*Crudes in* u, *Masculine, Feminine, and Neuter.*

Formed by adding to ROOTS,

I. *u*, forming, 1st (nom. *-uh*), often with considerable change of the root, a few substantives of the masculine, and one or two of the feminine gender: as, from *bhā*, "to shine," *bhānu*, m. "the sun"; from *dhe*, "to drink," *dhenu*, f. "a cow."

Forming, 2dly (nom. *-u*), one or two neuter substantives: as, *madhu*, "honey."

Forming, 3dly (nom. *-uh-uh* or *-vī-u*), a few adjectives: as, from *tan*, "to stretch," *tanu*, "thin" (fem. *tanuh* or *tanwī*). This affix is often added to desiderative roots to form adjectives: as, from *pipās*, "to desire to drink," *pipāsu*, "thirsty."

II. *ishṇu* (nom. *-ishṇuh*, *-ishṇuh*, *-ishṇu*), with Guna of the root, forming adjectives: as, from *kshi*, "to perish," *kshayishṇu*, "perishing."

III. There are many other affixes to roots, forming nouns in *u* (nom. *-uh*, *-uh*, *-u*): as, *ru*, *nu*, *ālu*, *snu*, *āru*, *itnu*, *tu*. The following adjectives afford examples of these affixes: *bhīru*, *trasnu*, *shayālu*, *sthāsnu*, *sharāru*, *gadayitnu*; and the substantive *gantu*.

---

41. Fourth Class.—*Crudes in* ṛi (ऋ), *Masculine, Feminine, and Neuter.*

Formed by adding to roots,

tṛi, forming 1st (nom. *-tā*, *-trī*, *-tṛi*), nouns of agency of three genders, the same change of the root being required which takes place in the first future (r. 131. 2.). Thus, from *kship*, "to throw," *ksheptṛi*, "a thrower; from *dā*, "to give," *dātṛi*, "a giver." This corresponds to the Latin affix *tor*.

Forming 2dly (nom. *-tā*), a few nouns of relationship, masculine and feminine: as, *pitṛi*, "a father," *mātṛi*, "a mother."

---

42. Fifth Class.—*Crudes in* t *and* d, *Masculine, Feminine, and Neuter.*

Formed by adding to roots,

t (nom. *-t*, in all genders), if the root end in a *short vowel*: forming nouns of agency of three genders: as, from *kṛi*, "to do," *kṛit*, "a doer"; from *ji*, "to conquer," *jit*, "a conqueror." This class of nouns are never used, except as the last member of a compound: thus, *karmakṛit*, "a doer of work." Roots already ending in *t* or *d*, taken to form nouns of agency, fall under this class: as, from *vid*, "to know," *dharmavid*, "one who knows his duty." There are also a few nouns falling under this class, formed by prefixing prepositions to roots ending in *t* or *d*: as, from *dyut*, "to shine," *vidyut*, "lightning"; from *pad*, "to go," *sampad*, "success.

By adding to NOUNS,

I. *vat* (nom. *-vān*, *-vatī*, *-vat*), if the crude end in *a* or *ā*,* forming innumerable adjectives: as, from *dhana*, "wealth," *dhanavat*, "possessed of wealth." This and the next affix are universally applicable, and are of the utmost utility to form adjectives of possession. Sometimes *vat* is added to crudes in *s* and *t*: as in *tejaswat*, *vidyutwat* (violating r. 26. 29. and 14.).

II. *mat* (nom. *-mān*, *-matī*, *-mat*), if the crude end in *i*, *ī*, or *u*, to form adjectives like the preceding: as, from *dhī*, "wisdom," *dhīmat*, "wise"; from *anshu*, "a ray," *anshumat*, "radiant."

---

43. SIXTH CLASS.—*Crudes in* an *and* in, *Masculine, Feminine, and Neuter.*

Formed by adding to ROOTS,

I. *man* (nom. *-ma*), after Guna of the root, forming substantives of the neuter gender: as, from *kṛi*, "to do"; *karman*, "a deed." This affix corresponds to the Latin *men*, in *regimen*, *stamen*, &c. One or two nouns in *man* are masculine: as, *ātman*, "soul" (nom. *-mā*); and a few masculine nouns are formed with *an* instead of *man*: as, *rājan*, "a king" (nom. *-jā*), from *rāj*, "to shine." A few adjectives are formed with *van*: as, *dṛishwan*, "seeing" (nom. *-vā*, *-vā*, *-va*).

By adding to NOUNS,

II. *iman* (nom. *-imā*), forming masculine abstract substantives. If the noun ends in *a* or *u*, these vowels are rejected: as, from *kālo*, "black," *kāliman*, "blackness"; from *laghu*, "light," *laghiman*, "lightness"; from *mṛidu*, "soft," *mradiman*.† If it end in a consonant, this consonant, with its preceding vowel, is rejected: as, from *mahat*, "great," *mahiman*, "greatness."

By adding to ROOTS,

III. *in* (nom. *-ī*, *-inī*, *-i*), after Vriddhi of a final vowel and medial *a*, and Guna of

---

* *Vat* is not often found added to feminine crude forms. It occurs, however, occasionally; as, कान्तावत्, "having a wife," शिखावत्, "crested."

† A medial *ṛi* before a simple consonant is changed to *ra*, but not before a double consonant: as, from कृष्ण, "black," कृष्णिमन्, "blackness." This affix, *iman*, is generally added to *adjectives*, and the same changes take place before it, that take place before the affixes *īyas* and *ishṭha* (see r. 71. †). Thus, *gariman*, *preman*, *drāghiman*, *bhūman*, &c.

any other medial vowel, forming nouns of agency of three genders (r. 131. 3.): as, from *kṛi*, "to do," *kārin*, "a doer."

By adding to NOUNS,

IV. *in* (nom. *-ī*, *-inī*, *-i*), forming innumerable adjectives of possession. The final of a crude is rejected before this affix: as, from *dhana*, "wealth," *dhanin*, "wealthy"; from *mālā*, "a garland," *mālin*, "garlanded"; from *vrīhi*, "rice," *vrīhin*, "having rice."

V. *vin* (nom. *-vī*, *-vinī*, *-vi*), if the crude end in *ā* or *as*, forming a few adjectives: as, from *medhā*, "intellect," *medhāvin*, "intellectual"; from *tejas*, "splendour," *tejaswin*, "splendid." This last example violates r. 26. and 29.

---

44. SEVENTH CLASS.—*Crudes in* as, *Masculine, Feminine, and Neuter.*

Formed by adding to ROOTS,

as (nom. *-aḥ*), after Guna, forming neuter substantives: as, from *man*, "to think," *manas*, "the mind"; from *sṛi*, "to go," *saras*, "water." But in *vedhas*, "Brahmā," and *chandramas*, "the moon," masc., and *apsaras*, "a nymph," fem., the nominative is *-āḥ*. In place of *as*, the neuter affixes *is* or *us* are occasionally added: as, from *hu*, "to offer," *havis*, "ghee"; from *chaksh*, "to speak," *chakshus*, "the eye."

---

45. EIGHTH CLASS.—*Crudes in* any Consonant, except t, d, n, s, *Masculine, Feminine, and Neuter.*

Formed by using ROOTS as nouns of agency.

Any root may be used to form a noun of agency, provided it be compounded with another word. Thus, from *shak*, "to be able," *sarvashak*, "omnipotent." Those roots which end in *t* or *d*, or in a short vowel, having *t* affixed, have been already noticed as falling under the fifth class. This eighth class is intended to comprise all other roots, ending in *any consonant*: as, *bhuj* (nom. *bhuk*); *rāj* (nom. राट्); *prāchchh* (nom. प्राट्); *budh* (nom. *bhut*); *pur* (nom. *pūḥ*); *gir* (nom. *gīḥ*); *div* (nom. *dyauḥ*); *spṛish* (nom. *spṛik*); *vish* (nom. *viṭ*); *twish* (nom. त्विट्); *lih* (nom. लिट्); *duh* (nom. *dhuk*); *pipaksh* (nom. *pipuk*). There are also one or two other nouns derived from roots falling under this class: as, तृष्णज्, "thirsty" (nom. तृष्णक्); ऋत्विज्, "a priest" (nom. ऋत्विक्); वाच्, f. "speech" (nom. वाक्); असृज्, n. blood" (nom. असृक्).

CHAPTER IV.

DECLENSION.

THE ARTICLE.

46. There is no indefinite article in Sanscrit.* Thus, "a man" can only be expressed by the simple noun पुरुषः *purushah.* The definite article is usually expressed by the pronoun *sa,* as स पुरुषः *sa purushah,* "the man." The indefinite pronoun कश्चित् *kashchit* may be used like the English expression "a certain"; thus, कश्चित् पुरुषः "a certain man."

General Observations.

As, in the last chapter, nouns substantive and adjective were arranged under eight classes, according to the final of their crudes (the first four classes comprising those ending in vowels, the last four those ending in consonants), so it will be the object of the present chapter to give the eight systems of declension arising out of this arrangement. Moreover, as every class of crudes comprised adjectives as well as substantives, so it is intended that the examples of a masculine, feminine, and neuter substantive, exhibited under each system of declension, shall serve as the model for the masculine, feminine, and neuter of adjectives coming under the same class.

The learner will have already gathered that the noun has three genders, and that the gender is, in many cases, determinable from the termination of the crude. Thus, all crudes in *ā, ī,* and those formed with the affix *ti* (r. 39.), are feminine: nearly all nouns whose crudes end in *ana, twa, ya, tra, as, is, us,* and *man,* are neuter; all in *iman* are masculine; but those in *a, i, u,* and *ṛi,* are not reducible to rule. The nominative case is, however, in the first of these instances a guide to the gender: as, *devah,*

* In modern Sanscrit *eka* is very commonly used as an indefinite article, as *ekah purushah,* "a man."

"a deity," is masculine; but *dānam*, "a gift," neuter. And in other cases the meaning of the word: as, *pitṛi*, "a father," is masculine; and *mātṛi*, "a mother," feminine.

In Sanscrit, all the relations between the words in a sentence are expressed by inflections. A great many prepositions exist in the language, but these are very rarely used alone in government with any case, their chief use being as prefixes to verbs and nouns. This absence of syntactical auxiliaries leads to the necessity for eight cases. These are called, 1. nominative; 2. accusative; 3. instrumental; 4. dative; 5. ablative; 6. genitive; 7. locative; 8. vocative.* Of these, the third and seventh are new to the classical student. The *instrumental* denotes generally the instrument by which a thing is done; as, *tena kṛitam*, "done by him." The *locative* generally refers to the place or time in which any thing is done; as, *Ayodhyāyām* "in *Ayodhyā*"; *pūrvakāle*, "in former time"; *bhūmau*, "on the ground."† Hence it follows that the *ablative* is restricted to the sense *from*, and cannot be used, as in Latin and Greek, to express *by*, *with*, *in*, *at*, *on*, &c.

The noun has three numbers, singular, dual, and plural.

SECT. I.—DECLENSION OF CRUDES ENDING IN VOWELS, OR OF THE FIRST FOUR CLASSES OF NOUNS.

FIRST CLASS.—CRUDES IN *a*, MASCULINE AND NEUTER; IN *ā* AND *ī*, FEMININE.

Declined like देव *deva*, mas. "*a deity*"; जीवा *jīvā*, fem. "*life*"; नदी *nadī*, fem. "*a river*"; *and* दान *dāna*, neuter, "*a gift.*"

47. By far the greatest number of masculine and neuter nouns, in Sanscrit, end in *a* in the crude form; and by far the greatest number of feminine nouns end in either *ā* or *ī*. These we have arranged under the first class, and the examples we are about to give will serve as the model, not only for substantives, but also

* Obs. That these cases will sometimes be denoted by their initial letters. Thus, N. will denote nominative, I. instrumental.

† Both these cases are used to denote various other relations. See the Chapter on Syntax.

for all the adjectives given at r. 38. as falling under this class. For all adjectives which make *a* in the crude form of the masculine and neuter make *ā* or *ī* in the feminine. Thus, taking the adjective *sundara*, "beautiful." The masculine is declined like *deva* (nom. *sundarah*); the feminine like *jīvā* or *nadī* (nom. *sundarā* or *sundarī*); the neuter like *dāna* (nom. *sundaram*).

So great is the importance of this first class of nouns, that, to make its declension clearer, it will be advisable to give, in the first place, the following general scheme of its terminations.

MASCULINE.				THE TWO FEMININE FORMS.					
SING.		DUAL.	PLUR.	SING.		DUAL.		PLUR.	
Nom.	*ah*	*au*	*āh*	*ā*	*ī*	*e*	*yau*	*āh*	*yah*
Acc.	*am*	*au*	*ān*	*ām*	*īm*	*e*	*yau*	*āh*	*īh*
Ins.	*ena*	*ābhyām*	*aih*	*ayā*	*yā*	*ābhyām*	*ībhyām*	*ābhih*	*ībhih*
Dat.	*āya*	—	*ebhyah*	*āyai*	*yai*	—	—	*ābhyah*	*ībhyah*
Abl.	*āt*	—	—	*āyāh*	*yāh*	—	—	—	—
Gen.	*asya*	*ayoh*	*ānām*	—	—	*ayoh*	*yoh*	*ānām*	*īnām*
Loc.	*e*	—	*eṣhu*	*āyām*	*yām*	—	—	*āsu*	*īṣhu*
Voc.	*a*	*au*	*āh*	*e*	*i*	*e*	*yau*	*āh*	*yah*

NEUTER.			
SING.		DUAL.	PLUR.
Nom. Acc.	*am*	*e*	*āni*
Voc.	*a*	*e*	*āni*

The rest of the neuter terminations are like the masculine.

The classical student will recognise in this scheme many resemblances to the terminations of nouns in Latin and Greek, when it is remembered that the Sanscrit *a* corresponds to the Latin *u* and the Greek *ο*; the Sanscrit *m* to the Latin *m* and the Greek *ν*; the Sanscirt *ā* or *ī* to the Latin *a* and the Geek *η*, or *εια*, or *α*, or in the gen. plur. *ω*; the Sanscrit *bh* or *bhy* to the Latin *b*; and that the Sanscrit Visargah, or final *h*, is equivalent to *s*.

In the application of the above terminations, the finals of the crudes must first be rejected. Thus, taking *deva*, and rejecting the final, we have *dev;* and adding the terminations, we have the nom. *devah*, &c. The four examples are now declined in full.

48. *Masculine Crudes in* a, *like* देव, "*a deity*" (*deus*).

N.	देवः *devah*,	देवौ *devau*,	देवाः *devāh*.
Ac.	देवं *devam*,	— *devau*,	देवान् *devān*.
I.	देवेन *devena*,	देवाभ्यां *devābhyām*,	देवैः *devaih*.
D.	देवाय *devāya*,	— *devābhyām*,	देवेभ्यः *devebhyah*.
Ab.	देवात् *devāt*,	— *devābhyām*,	— *devebhyah*.
G.	देवस्य *devasya*,	देवयोः *devayoh*,	देवानां *devānām*.
L.	देवे *deve*,	— *devayoh*,	देवेषु *deveṣhu*.
V.	देव *deva*,	देवौ *devau*,	देवाः *devāh*.

In accordance with r. 21, such words as नर, "a man," पुरुष, "a man," मृग, "a deer," are written in the ins. sing. नरेण, पुरुषेण, मृगेण, and in the gen. plur. नराणां, पुरुषाणां, मृगाणां, the cerebral nasal taking the place of the dental.

49. *Feminine Crudes in* ā *and* ī, *like* जीवा, "*life*," *and* नदी, "*a river*."

N.	जीवा *jīvā*,	जीवे *jīve*,	जीवाः *jīvāh*.
Ac.	जीवां *jīvām*,	— *jīve*,	— *jīvāh*.
I.	जीवया *jīvayā*,	जीवाभ्यां *jīvābhyām*,	जीवाभिः *jīvābhih*.
D.	जीवायै *jīvāyai*,	— *jīvābhyām*,	जीवाभ्यः *jīvābhyah*.
Ab.	जीवायाः *jīvāyāh*,	— *jīvābhyām*,	— *jīvābhyah*.
G.	— *jīvāyāh*,	जीवयोः *jīvayoh*,	जीवानां *jīvānām*.
L.	जीवायां *jīvāyām*,	— *jīvayoh*,	जीवासु *jīvāsu*.
V.	जीवे *jīve*,	जीवे *jīve*,	जीवाः *jīvāh*.

N.	नदी *nadī*,	नद्यौ *nadyau*,	नद्यः *nadyah*.
Ac.	नदीं *nadīm*,	— *nadyau*,	नदीः *nadīh*.
I.	नद्या *nadyā*,	नदीभ्यां *nadībhyām*,	नदीभिः *nadībhih*.
D.	नद्यै *nadyai*,	— *nadībhyām*,	नदीभ्यः *nadībhyah*.
Ab.	नद्याः *nadyāh*,	— *nadībhyām*,	— *nadībhyah*.
G.	— *nadyāh*,	नद्योः *nadyoh*,	नदीनां *nadīnām*.
L.	नद्यां *nadyām*,	— *nadyoh*,	नदीषु *nadīṣhu*.
V.	नदि *nadi*,	नद्यौ *nadyau*,	नद्यः *nadyah*.

50. *Neuter Crudes in* a, *like* दान, "*a gift*" (*donum*, δῶρον).

N. Ac.	दानं *dānam*,	दाने *dāne*,	दानानि *dānāni*.
Voc.	दान *dāna*,	दाने *dāne*,	दानानि *dānāni*.

The rest like the masculine *deva*.

Observe, that since the voc. dual and plural of the Sanscrit noun coincides with the nom., it will, in future, be omitted.

† When a feminine noun, like *jīvā*, is taken to form the last member of a compound adjective, it is declined like *deva* for the masculine, and *dāna* for the neuter. Thus, taking the feminine noun *vidyā*, "learning;" from this is formed the compound *alpavidyā*, "little learning:" and when this is used as a compound adjective it becomes, in the nom. masc. fem. and neut., *alpavidyaḥ*, *alpavidyā*, *alpavidyam*, "possessed of little learning." On the same principle, a masculine noun takes the feminine and neuter terminations when forming the last member of a compound adjective; and a neuter noun, the masculine and feminine.

To convince the student of the absolute necessity of studying attentively the declension of this first class of nouns, he is recommended to turn back to r. 38. He will there find given, under fifteen heads, the various forms of nouns, substantive and adjective, which follow this declension. All the masculine substantives in this list are declined like *deva;* all the feminine either like *jīvā* or *nadī;* all the neuter like *dāna*. Again, all the adjectives in this list follow the same three examples for their three genders. Again, according to *deva* masculine, *jīvā* feminine, and *dāna* neuter, are declined all regular comparative and superlative degrees of the form *puṇyatara*, *puṇyatama* (r. 71.); all irregular superlatives of the form *balishṭha* (r. 71.); all present participles of the forms *kurvāṇa*, *kriyamāṇa* (r. 124.); all passive past participles of the form *kṛita*, &c., which are the most common and useful of all verbal derivatives (r. 125. 1. 2. 3. 4.); all indefinite future participles, which are of constant occurrence, of the forms *kārya*, *karaṇīya*, *kartavya* (r. 129.); all participles of the second future, of the form *karishyamaṇa* (r. 130.); many ordinals, like *prathama* (r. 74.). Lastly, according to *nadī* feminine, are also declined the *feminines* of adjectives like *tanu* (r. 40.); the *feminines* of innumerable adjectives like *dhanavat, dhīmat* (r. 42.), *dhanin,* and *medhāvin* (r. 43.); the *feminines* of nouns of agency like *kārin* (r. 131. 3.); the *feminines* of nouns of agency like *kartṛi* (r. 131. 2.); the *feminines* of irregular comparative degrees like *balīyas* (r. 72. 69.†); the *feminines* of present participles like *kurvat* (r. 123. and 63.); the *feminines* of active participles of the third preterite like *kṛitavat* (r. 127. and 62.); the *feminines* of active participles of the second preterite like *vividvas* (r. 127. and 69.†); the *feminines* of many ordinals like *pañchama* (r. 74.).

Hence it is evident, that although we have arranged Sanscrit nouns under eight classes, the last seven classes contain but a small proportion of nouns and participles compared with the almost innumerable number embraced by the first. The student, therefore, ought not to advance a step further in the Grammar till he has made himself thoroughly master of this declension.

† There are a few useful words (*originally* feminine, and not derived from masculines like *nadī* and *putrī,* in r. 38. xv.), such as श्री, "prosperity," भी, "fear," ह्री, "shame," which vary from the declension of नदी *nadī;* thus, sing. nom. श्रीः, acc. श्रियं, ins. श्रिया, dat. श्रिये or श्रियै, abl. and gen. श्रियः or श्रियाः, loc. श्रियि or श्रियां. So again, स्त्री, "a woman," nom. sing. dual and plur. स्त्री, स्त्रियौ, स्त्रियः, acc. स्त्रियं or स्त्रीं, स्त्रियौ, स्त्रियः or स्त्रीः, ins. स्त्रिया, स्त्रीभ्यां, स्त्रीभिः, dat. स्त्रियै, &c., abl. and gen. स्त्रियाः &c., loc. स्त्रियां &c., voc. स्त्रि &c. लक्ष्मी, "fortune," agrees with श्री &c. in making its nom. लक्ष्मीः.

SECOND CLASS.—CRUDES IN *i*, MASCULINE, FEMININE, AND NEUTER.

Declined like कवि *kavi*, masc. "*a poet*"; मति *mati*, fem. "*the mind*"; वारि *vāri*, neut. "*water*."

51. *Masculine Crudes in* i, *like* कवि, "*a poet.*"

N.	कविः *kaviḥ,*	कवी *kavī,*	कवयः *kavayaḥ.*
Ac.	कविं *kavim,*	— *kavī,*	कवीन् *kavīn.*
I.	कविना *kavinā,*	कविभ्यां *kavibhyām,*	कविभिः *kavibhiḥ.*
D.	कवये *kavaye,*	— *kavibhyām,*	कविभ्यः *kavibhyaḥ.*
Ab.	कवेः *kaveḥ,*	— *kavibhyām,*	— *kavibhyaḥ.*
G.	— *kaveḥ,*	कव्योः *kavyoḥ,*	कवीनां *kavīnām.*
L.	कवौ *kavau,*	— *kavyoḥ,*	कविषु *kavishu.*
V.	कवे *kave,*		

So also, *agni*, "fire" (*ignis*); and nouns formed from *dhā*, "to hold"; as, *sandhi*, "union."

52. *Feminine Crudes in* i, *like* मति, "*the mind.*"

N.	मतिः *matih,*	मती *matī,*	मतयः *matayah.*
Ac.	मतिं *matim,*	— *matī,*	मतीः *matīh.*
I.	मत्या *matyā,*	मतिभ्यां *matibhyām,*	मतिभिः *matibhih.*
D.	मतये *mataye,**	— *matibhyām,*	मतिभ्यः *matibhyah.*
Ab.	मतेः *mateh,**	— *matibhyām,*	— *matibhyah.*
G.	— *mateh,**	मत्योः *matyoh,*	मतीनां *matīnām.*
L.	मतौ *matau,**	— *matyoh,*	मतिषु *matiṣhu.*
V.	मते *mate,*		

53. *Neuter Crudes in* i, *like* वारि, "*water*" (*mare*).

N.	वारि *vāri,*	वारिणी *vāriṇī,*	वारीणि *vārīṇi.*
Ac.	— *vāri,*	— *vāriṇī,*	— *vārīṇi.*
I.	वारिणा *vāriṇā,*	वारिभ्यां *vāribhyām,*	वारिभिः *vāribhih.*
D.	वारिणे *vāriṇe,*	— *vāribhyām,*	वारिभ्यः *vāribhyah.*
Ab.	वारिणः *vāriṇah,*	— *vāribhyām,*	— *vāribhyah.*
G.	— *vāriṇah,*	वारिणोः *vāriṇoh,*	वारीणां *vārīṇām.*
L.	वारिणि *vāriṇi,*	— *vāriṇoh,*	वारिषु *vāriṣhu.*
V.	वारि *vāri* or वारे *vāre,*		

Although there are few substantives declined like *kavi* and *vāri*, yet adjectives like *shuchi* (r. 39.), and compound adjectives ending in *i*, are declined like *kavi* in the masc.; like *mati* in the fem.; and like *vāri* in the neuter.

† When a feminine noun ending in *i* is taken to form the last member of a compound adjective, it must be declined like *kavi* in the masc., and *vāri* in the neut. Thus the compound adjective *alpamati* in the acc. plur. masc. would be *alpamatīn*;

---

* The dat. may also be *matyai*; the ab. and gen. *matyāh*; the loc. *matyām*.

fem. *alpamatīḥ*; neut. *alpamatīni*. The same holds good if a masc. or neut. noun be taken to form the last member of a compound.

The declension of the neuter of this class follows the analogy of nouns in *in*. Hence, *vāri* serves also as the model for the neuters of adjectives and nouns of agency in *in*, like *dhanin* and *kārin* (r. 66.); and the neuters of nouns of agency in *ṭri*, like *kartṛi* (r. 57.).

† There are two useful irregular masculine nouns in *i*; viz. सखि *sakhi*, "a friend," nom. sing. dual and plur. *sakhā*, *sakhāyau*, *sakhāyah*; acc. *sakhāyam*, *sakhāyau*, *sakhīn*; ins. *sakhyā*, *sakhibhyām*, *sakhibhiḥ*; dat. *sakhye*, &c.; abl. and gen. *sakhyuh*, &c.; loc. *sakhyau*, &c.; voc. *sakhe*, &c. And पति *pati*, "a master," which, when not used in a compound word, follows *sakhi* in the five last cases sing. (thus, ins. *patyā*, &c.): in the other cases, *kavi*. But this word is almost always found as the last member of a compound, and is then regularly declined like *kavi*; thus, ins. *bhūpatinā*, "by the king." The noun अस्थि *asthi*, neut. "a bone," drops the final vowel in some of its cases; as, ins. sing. *asthnā*; dat. *asthne*; abl. *asthnah*, &c.

THIRD CLASS.—CRUDES IN *u*, MASCULINE, FEMININE, AND NEUTER.

Declined like भानु *bhānu*, masc. "*the sun*"; धेनु *dhenu*, fem. "*a milch cow*"; मधु *madhu*, neut. "*honey*."

54. *Masculine Crudes in* u, *like* भानु *bhānu*, "*the sun*."

N.	भानुः *bhānuh*,	भानू *bhānū*,	भानवः *bhānavaḥ*.
Ac.	भानुं *bhānum*,	— *bhānū*,	भानून् *bhānūn*.
I.	भानुना *bhānunā*,	भानुभ्यां *bhānubhyām*,	भानुभिः *bhānubhiḥ*.
D.	भानवे *bhānave*,	— *bhānubhyām*,	भानुभ्यः *bhānubhyah*.
Ab.	भानोः *bhānoh*,	— *bhānubhyām*,	— *bhānubhyah*.
G.	— *bhānoh*,	भान्वोः *bhānvoh*,	भानूनां *bhānūnām*.
L.	भानौ *bhānau*,	— *bhānvoh*,	भानुषु *bhānuṣhu*.
V.	भानो *bhāno*,		

55. *Feminine Crudes in* u, *like* धेनु *dhenu,* "*a milch cow.*"

N.	धेनुः *dhenuh,*	धेनू *dhenū,*	धेनवः *dhenavah.*
Ac.	धेनुं *dhenum,*	— *dhenū,*	धेनूः *dhenūh.*
I.	धेन्वा *dhenwā,*	धेनुभ्यां *dhenubhyām,*	धेनुभिः *dhenubhih.*
D.	धेनवे *dhenave,**	— *dhenubhyām,*	धेनुभ्यः *dhenubhyah.*
Ab.	धेनोः *dhenoh,**	— *dhenubhyām,*	— *dhenubhyah.*
G.	— *dhenoh,**	धेन्वोः *dhenwoh,*	धेनूनां *dhenūnām.*
L.	धेनौ *dhenau,**	— *dhenwoh,*	धेनुषु *dhenuṣhu.*
V.	धनो *dheno,*		

56. *Neuter Crudes in* u, *like* मधु *madhu,* "*honey,*" "*wine*" (μέθυ).

N.	मधु *madhu,*	मधुनी *madhunī,*	मधूनि *madhūni.*
Ac.	— *madhu,*	— *madhunī,*	— *madhūni.*
I.	मधुना *madhunā,*	मधुभ्यां *madhubhyām,*	मधुभिः *madhubhih.*
D.	मधुने *madhune,*	— *madhubhyām,*	मधुभ्यः *madhubhyah.*
Ab.	मधुनः *madhunah,*	— *madhubhyām,*	— *madhubhyah.*
G.	— *madhunah,*	मधुनोः *madhunoh,*	मधूनां *madhūnām.*
L.	मधुनि *madhuni,*	— *madhunoh,*	मधुषु *madhuṣhu.*
V.	मधु *madhu* or मधो *madho.*		

Although there are but few substantives declined like *dhenu* and *madhu,* yet it is important to study their declension, as well as that of the masc. noun *bhānu;* for all simple adjectives like *tanu,* and all like *pipāsu* (r. 40.), and all other simple adjectives in *u,* and all compound adjectives ending in *u,* are declined like *bhānu* in the masc.; *dhenu* in the fem.; and *madhu* in the neut. Many adjectives in *u,* however, optionally follow the declension of *nadī,* in the fem.; as, *tanu* makes its nom. fem. either *tanuh* or *tanwī.*

† There are one or two feminine nouns in *ū* long, whose declension must be noticed here: as, वधू, "a wife," declined analogously to *nadī.* Nom. sing. dual. and plur. *vadhūh, vadhwau, vadhwah;* acc. *vadhūm, vadhwau, vadhūh;* ins. *vadhwā, vadhūbhyām, vadhūbhih;* dat. *vadhwai, vadhūbhyām, vadhūbhyah;* abl. *vadhwāh, &c.;*

* The dat. may also be *dhenwai;* the ab. and gen. *dhenwāh;* the loc. *dhenwām.*

gen. *vadhwāh, vadhwoh, vadhūnām;* loc. *vadhwām, vadhwoh, vadhūshu;* voc. *vadhu.* So again, भू, "the earth," declined analogously to श्री. Nom. sing. dual. and plur. *bhūh, bhuvau, bhuvah;* acc. *bhuvam, bhuvau, bhuvah;* ins. *bhuvā, bhūbhyām, bhūbhih;* dat. *bhuve* or *bhuvai, &c.;* abl. and gen. *bhuvah* or *bhuvāh, &c.;* loc. *bhuvi* or *bhuvām, &c.*

FOURTH CLASS.—CRUDES IN *tri* ऋ, MASCULINE, FEMININE, AND NEUTER.

Declined like दातृ *dātri*, m. f. n. "*a giver*, पितृ *pitri*, m. "*a father.*"

57. *Masculine form of Crudes in tri, like* दातृ (*dator,* δοτήρ), *and* पितृ (*pater*).

N.	दाता *dātā,* पिता *pitā,*	दातारौ *dātārau,* पितरौ *pitarau,*	दातारः *dātārah.* पितरः *pitarah.*
Ac.	दातारं *dātāram,* पितरं *pitaram,*	— *dātārau,* — *pitarau,*	दातॄन् *dātṝn.* पितॄन् *pitṝn,* &c.
I.	दात्रा *dātrā,*	दातृभ्यां *dātribhyām,*	दातृभिः *dātribhih.*
D.	दात्रे *dātre,*	— *dātribhyām,*	दातृभ्यः *dātribhyah.*
Ab.	दातुः *dātuh,*	— *dātribhyām,*	— *dātribhyah.*
G.	— *dātuh,*	दात्रोः *dātroh,*	दातॄणां *dātṝṇām.*
L.	दातरि *dātari,*	— *dātroh,*	दातृषु *dātrishu.*
V.	दातर् *dātar,*		

Obs. Nouns of relationship like *pitri* only differ from nouns of agency like *dātri* in the nom. dual and plural, and the acc. sing. and dual, where the former has the penultimate short, the latter, long. Feminine nouns of relationship like *mātri*, "a mother," are declined like *pitri*, except in the acc. plural मातॄः.

† नृ *nri*, "a man," is declined like *pitri* (nom. *nā, &c.*), but usually makes नृणां in the gen. plural.

The feminine form of nouns of agency in *tri* is declined like *nadī;* as, nom. दात्री, &c. (see r. 49.).

The neuter form follows the declension of *vāri;* as, nom. acc. दातृ, दातृणी, दातॄणि (see r. 53.).

SECT. II.—DECLENSION OF CRUDES ENDING IN CONSONANTS, OR OF THE LAST FOUR CLASSES OF NOUNS.

General Observations.

58. The first four classes of nouns, whose declension has just been considered, comprise nearly all the substantives in the language. If we except substantives ending in *man* and *as*, the last four classes of nouns consist almost entirely of adjectives, participles, and roots, taken to form the last member of compound words. There is one general scheme of terminations applicable to all nouns ending in consonants. It is as follows:—

	SING.	DUAL.	PLURAL.
Nom.	..	*au*	*ah*
Acc.	*am*	—	—
Inst.	*ā*	*bhyām*	*bhih*
Dat.	*e*	—	*bhyah*
Abl.	*ah*	—	—
Gen.	—	*oh*	*ām*
Loc.	*i*	—	*su*
Voc.	..	*au*	*ah*

This scheme applies without exception to the few substantives, and to the masculine of the many adjectives and participles, whose crudes end in consonants. It also applies, with the exception of the nom. and acc. cases, to the neuter of these same adjectives and participles; but their feminine generally follows the declension of *nadī* (r. 49.). The nominative singular admits of so much variation, that no one termination is general enough to be inserted in the scheme.

Many of the terminations will be already familiar to the learner, especially those of the dual and plural. Indeed, certain terminations prevail, with various modifications, in *all* Sanscrit nouns: and this prevalence of certain sounds, as characteristic of certain cases, has led native grammarians into the error of constructing a technical scheme of terminations, which they apply universally in the declension of *every noun* in the language. This technical scheme does, in point of fact, correspond with the scheme we have given above, as applicable to the last four classes; but when, on comparing this with the scheme belonging to the first class (r. 47.), it is seen how very great is the dissimilarity between the two; and when it is remembered that the first class embraces a much larger number of nouns than all the other seven classes combined, there seems but little reason for any such process of generalization. For surely if any general scheme is given at all, it should be that which is most universally applicable; and if any system of adaptation is to be adopted, it should consist in an adaptation of the smaller number to the larger, rather than the larger to the smaller; or we are led into endless alteration and substitution, and very unnecessary perplexity and confusion.

† There are two or three useful words in the language ending in *ai*, *o*, and *au*, which conform to the scheme of nouns ending in consonants. Thus, *rai*, m. "wealth." N. *rāh*, *rāyau*, *rāyah*; A. *rāyam*, *rāyau*, *rāyah*; I. *rāyā*, *rābhyām*, *rābhih*, &c. (cf. *rebus*). *Go*, m. f. "an ox or cow." N. *gauh*, *gāvau*, *gāvah*; ac. *gām*, *gāvau*, *gāh*; ins. *gavā*, *gobhyām*, *gobhih*, &c. And *nau*, f. "a ship." N. *nauh*, *nāvau*, *nāvah*; acc. *nāvam*, *nāvau*, *nāvah*; ins. *nāvā*, &c. (Cf. ναῦς, *navis*).

FIFTH CLASS.—CRUDES IN *t* AND *d*, MASCULINE, FEMININE, AND NEUTER.

Declined like कर्म्मकृत् *karmmakṛit*, m. f. n. "*a doer of work*"; धर्म्मविद् *dharmmavid*, m. f. n. "*one who knows his duty*"; धनवत् *dhanavat*, m. f. n. "*wealthy*."

59. *Masculine and Feminine form of Crudes in* t *and* d, *declined like* कर्म्मकृत् *and* धर्म्मविद्.

N.	कर्म्मकृत् *karmakṛit*,*	कर्म्मकृतौ *karmakṛitau*,	कर्म्मकृतः *karmakṛitah*.
Ac.	कर्म्मकृतं *karmakṛitam*,	— —	— —
I.	कर्म्मकृता *karmakṛitā*,	कर्म्मकृद्भ्यां *karmakṛidbhyām*,	कर्म्मकृद्भिः *karmakṛidbhih*.
D.	कर्म्मकृते *karmakṛite*,	— —	कर्म्मकृद्भ्यः *karmakṛidbhyah*.
Ab.	कर्म्मकृतः *karmakṛitah*,	— —	— —
G.	— —	कर्म्मकृतोः *karmakṛitoh*,	कर्म्मकृतां *karmakṛitām*.
L.	कर्म्मकृति *karmakṛiti*,	— *karmakṛitoh*,	कर्म्मकृत्सु *karmakṛitsu*.
V.	Like the nominative.		

* Although *r* has the effect of doubling the letter immediately under it in the Sanscrit character (r. 33.), it is unnecessary always to double the letter in the Roman type. Strictly, however, this word should be written *karmmakṛit*.

N. धर्म्मविद् *dharmavid*, धर्म्मविदौ *dharmavidau*, धर्म्मविदः *dharmavidah*.
Ac. धर्म्मविदं *dharmavidam*, &c.
Loc. plur. धर्म्मवित्सु *dharmavitsu*, by r. 14.

The neuter form of nouns like *karmakṛit* and *dharmavid* is, in the nom. and acc. कर्म्मकृत्, कर्म्मकृती, कर्म्मकृन्ति, धर्म्मविद्, धर्म्मविदी, धर्म्मविन्दि. In the other cases it resembles the masc. and fem.

60. All substantives like मरुत् *marut*, m. "wind," सम्पद् *sampad*, f. "success," and कुमुद् *kumud*, n., "a lotus," follow the declension of *karmakṛit* and *dharmavid*: thus, nom. *marut, marutau, marutah; sampad, sampadau, sampadah; kumud, kumudī, kumundi*, &c.

61. The masculine form of crudes formed with the affixes *vat* and *mat*, is declined like धनवत्.

N. धनवान् *dhanavān*, धनवन्तौ *dhanavantau*, धनवन्तः *dhanavantah*.
Ac. धनवन्तं *dhanavantam*, — *dhanavantau*, धनवतः *dhanavatah*.
Voc. धनवन् *dhanavan*,

The other cases are like *karmakṛit*; as, ins. धनवता *dhanavatā*, &c.

The feminine form of nouns like *dhanavat* is declined like *nadī*: thus, nom. *dhanavatī, dhanavatyau, dhanavatyah*, &c. (see r. 49.).

The neuter form is, in the nom. and ac., *dhanavat, dhanavatī, dhanavanti*; and in the other cases like the masculine.

62. So, also, all adjectives like धीमत् *dhīmat*, "wise," and all active past participles like कृतवत् *kṛitavat*, "he did" (r. 127,): thus, nom. masc. *dhīmān*, &c., *kṛitavān*, &c.; acc. *dhīmantam*, &c., *kṛitavantam*, &c.; voc. *dhīman*, &c. So, also, the nom. fem. *dhīmatī*, &c., *kṛitavatī*, &c.; and nom. neut. *dhīmat*, &c., *kṛitavat*, &c.

63. After *dhanavat* may also be declined present participles like पचत् *pachat*, "cooking" (r. 123.), except in the nom. sing., which is *pachan* instead of *pachān*. Many of these participles also differ from *dhanavat*, by inserting a nasal throughout all the cases of the feminine. Thus, nom. *pachantī, pachantyau, pachantyah*; acc. *pachantīm, pachantyau, pachantīh*; ins. *pachantyā*, &c.

The adjective महत् *mahat*, "great," is declined like *dhanavat*, but makes the penultimate long before the nasal; thus, nom. *mahān, mahāntau, mahāntah*; acc. *mahāntam, mahāntau, mahatah*: nom. fem. *mahatī*, &c.: nom. neut. *mahat, mahatī, mahānti*.

SIXTH CLASS.—CRUDES IN *an* AND *in*, MASCULINE, FEMININE, AND NEUTER.

Declined like आत्मन् *ātman*, m. "*soul*"; राजन् *rājan*, m. "*a king*"; कर्मन् *karman*, n. "*a deed*"; नामन् *nāman*, n. "*a name*"; *and* धनिन् *dhanin*, m. f. n. "*rich.*"

64. *Masculine and Feminine form of Crudes in* an, *declined like* आत्मन् *and* राजन्. (Cf. *rex, regis*).

N.	आत्मा *ātmā*, राजा *rājā*,	आत्मानौ *ātmānau*, राजानौ *rājānau*,	आत्मानः *ātmānah*. राजानः *rājānah*.
Ac.	आत्मानं *ātmānam*, राजानं *rājānam*,	— *ātmānau*, — *rājānau*,	आत्मनः *ātmanah*. राज्ञः *rājnah*.*
I.	आत्मना *ātmanā*, राज्ञा *rājnā*,	आत्मभ्यां *ātmabhyām*, राजभ्यां *rājabhyām*,	आत्मभिः *ātmabhih*. राजभिः *rājabhih*.
D.	आत्मने *ātmane*, राज्ञे *rājne*,	— *ātmabhyām*, — *rājabhyām*,	आत्मभ्यः *ātmabhyah*. राजभ्यः *rājabhyah*.
Ab.	आत्मनः *ātmanah*, राज्ञः *rājnah*,	— *ātmabhyām*, — *rājabhyām*,	— *ātmabhyah*. — *rājabhyah*.
G.	— *ātmanah*, — *rājnah*,	आत्मनोः *ātmanoh*, राज्ञोः *rājnoh*,	आत्मनां *ātmanām*. राज्ञां *rājnām*.
L.	आत्मनि *ātmani*, राज्ञि *rājni*,†	— *ātmanoh*, — *rājnoh*,	आत्मसु *ātmasu*. राजसु *rājasu*.
V.	आत्मन् *ātman*, राजन् *rājan*,		

65. Observe, that it is necessary to give two examples of nouns in *an*, because if *an* be preceded by *m* or *v*, and this *m* or *v* be conjunct with a preceding consonant, the noun is then declined like *ātman*. Hence, अध्वन् *adhwan*, m. "a road," and दृश्वन् *drishwan*, m. "a looker," make in the ins. *adhwanā*, *drishwanā*. But if this *m* or *v* be not conjunct, then the noun follows *rājan*; as, *laghiman*, m. "lightness"; ins. *laghimnā*. And if *an* be preceded by any other consonant than *m* or *v*, even although it be conjunct,

* As remarked in p. 3., this word is usually pronounced *rāgyah*; but, for the better illustration of the present subject, ज्ञ is represented by *jn* throughout the declension of this noun.

† Or *rājani*.

the noun then also follows *rājan*; as, मूर्द्धन् *mūrddhan*, m. "the head"; ins. मूर्द्ध्ना *mūrddhnā*.

There are no simple feminine nouns in *an*; but when masculine nouns are taken to form the last member of a compound adjective they take a feminine and neuter form; as in *mahātman*, "magnanimous."* The feminine form, however, is declined precisely like the masculine, and the neuter follows the declension of *karman* below.

66. *Neuter Crudes in* man, *declined like* कर्म्मन् *and* नामन् (*nomen*).

In the former the *m* is conjunct, in the latter, not.

N. and Ac.	कर्म्म *karma*,	कर्म्मणी *karmaṇī*,	कर्म्माणि *karmāṇi*.
	नाम *nāma*	नाम्नी *nāmnī*,	नामानि *nāmāni*.
Ins.	कर्म्मणा *karmaṇā*	The other cases like the masc.; as, gen. plur.	
	नाम्ना *nāmnā*.	*karmaṇām*, *nāmnām*; loc. *karmasu*, *nāmasu*.	

So also the neuter nouns, *janman*, *veshman*, *ashman*, *varman*, *vartman*, *charman*, *chhadman*, follow the declension of *karman*; but *dāman*, *sāman*, *dhāman*, *vyoman*, *roman*, *preman*, that of *nāman*. When neuters in *an* compose the last member of compound adjectives, they may take the masc. or fem. form.†

† Anomalies in *an*: श्वन्, m. (cf. κυων), "a dog." Nom. श्वा, श्वानौ, श्वानः; acc. श्वानं, श्वानौ, शुनः. In all these anomalies the acc. c. plur. is generally the clue to the form assumed by the noun before the terminations beginning with vowels. Thus, instr. is शुना, श्वभ्यां, &c. So again, युवन्, m. f. n. (cf. *juvenis*) "young"; nom. *yuvā*, *yuvānau*, *yuvānah*; acc. *yuvānam*, *yuvānau*, *yūnah*; inst. *yūnā*, *yuvabhyām*, &c. ब्रह्महन्, "a Brahmicide"; nom. -हा, -हणौ, -हणः; acc. -हणं, -हणौ, -घ्नः; instr. घ्ना &c. अहन्, n. "a day"; nom. and acc. अहः, अह्नी, or अहनी, अहानि; instr. अह्ना, अहोभ्यां, अहोभिः; dat. अह्ने &c.

---

* When *rājan* is taken to form a compound of this kind, it is declined like *deva* (r. 48.); as, nom. *mahārājah*; acc. *mahārājam*, &c.

† As in the sentence, *Vedogarbhanāmā Brāhmaṇa āsīt*, "There was a Brahmin named Vedagarbha."

67. *Masculine form of Crudes in* in, *declined like* धनिन्, "*rich.*"

N.	धनी *dhanī,*	धनिनौ *dhaninau,*	धनिनः *dhaninah.*
Ac.	धनिनं *dhaninam,*	— *dhaninau,*	— *dhaninah.*
I.	धनिना *dhaninā,*	धनिभ्यां *dhanibhyām,*	धनिभिः *dhanibhih.*
D.	धनिने *dhanine,*	— *dhanibhyām,*	धनिभ्यः *dhanibhyah.*
Ab.	धनिनः *dhaninah,*	— *dhanibhyām,*	— *dhanibhyah.*
G.	— *dhaninah,*	धनिनोः *dhaninoh,*	धनिनां *dhaninām.*
L.	धनिनि *dhanini,*	— *dhaninoh,*	धनिषु *dhanishu.*
V.	धनिन् *dhanin,*		

So also nouns of agency like *kārin.* The fem. form of nouns in *in* is declined like *nadī*; as, nom. *dhaninī, kāriṇī* (see r. 49.).

The neuter form follows the declension of *vāri;* as, nom. धनि, धनिनी, धनीनि (see r. 53.).

† *Pathin*, m. "a path," is declined irregularly; thus, sing. *panthāh, panthānam, pathā, pathe, pathah, pathi, pathin;* dual, *panthānau, pathibhyām, pathoh;* plur. *panthānah, pathah, pathibhih, pathibhyah, pathām, pathishu.*

SEVENTH CLASS.—CRUDES IN *as*, MASCULINE, FEMININE, AND NEUTER.

Declined like चन्द्रमस् chandramas, m. "*the moon*"; and मनस् manas, n. "*the mind.*"

68. *Masculine and Feminine form of Crudes in* as, *declined like* चन्द्रमस्.

N.	चन्द्रमाः *chandramāh,*	चन्द्रमसौ *chandramasau,*	चन्द्रमसः *chandramasah.*
Ac.	चन्द्रमसं *chandramasam,*	— *chandramasau,*	— *chandramasah.*
I.	चन्द्रमसा *chandramasā,*	चन्द्रमोभ्यां *chandramobhyām,*	चन्द्रमोभिः *chandramobhih.*
D.	चन्द्रमसे *chandramase, &c.*		

The other cases are like the neuter below, excepting the voc. dual and plur. (r. 50.).

69. *Neuter Crudes in* as, *declined like* मनस् (*μένος, mens*).

N. V.	मनः *manah,*	मनसी *manasī,*	मनांसि *manānsi.*
Ac.	— *manah,*	— *manasī,*	— *manānsi.*
I.	मनसा *manasā,*	मनोभ्यां *manobhyām,*	मनोभिः *manobhih.*
D.	मनसे *manase,*	— *manobhyām,*	मनोभ्यः *manobhyah.*
Ab.	मनसः *manasah,*	— *manobhyām,*	— *manobhyah.*
G.	— *manasah,*	मनसोः *manasoh,*	मनसां *manasām.*
L.	मनसि *manasi,*	— *manasoh,*	मनस्सु *manassu* (or -ःसु).

Observe, that the masculine noun *chandramas* is also the model for the fem. noun *apsaras*, "a nymph," and for the fem. form of compound adjectives, and that it only differs from the neuter in the nom. and acc. cases.

Nearly all simple substantives in *as* are neuter; but when these substantives are taken to form a compound adjective, they are declinable also in the masculine and feminine like *chandramas*. Thus, when *manas* is taken to form the compound adjective *mahāmanas*, "magnanimous," it makes in the nom. (masc. and fem.) *mahāmanāḥ, mahāmanasau, mahāmanasaḥ*. In the same way is formed *durmanas*, "evil-minded" (nom. *durmanāḥ*, &c.), to which a very remarkable analogy is presented by the Greek δυσμενὴς, m. and f., making in the neut. δυσμενές, derived from μένος. (Prof. Eastwick's transl. of Bopp's Comp. Gram. §. 146.).

† There are a few neuter nouns in *is* and *us*, which are declined exactly like *manas*, substituting *i* and *u* for *a* throughout, and therefore *sh* for *s*, and *r* for *o* (r. 30. 27.). Thus, *Havis*, "ghee"; nom. and acc. *Haviḥ, Havishī, Havīnshi;* ins. *Havishā, Havirbhyām, Havirbhiḥ, &c.;* and *chakshus*, "the eye"; nom. and acc. *chakshuḥ, chakshushī, chakshūnshi;* ins. *chakshushā, chakshurbhyām, chakshurbhiḥ, &c.* *Āshis*, f. "a blessing," makes in the nom. *āshīḥ, āshishau, āshishaḥ;* acc. *āshisham, āshishau, āshishaḥ, &c.* Similarly, *dos*, m. "the arm"; but this last is in the ins. either *doshā* or *doshṇā;* dat. *doshe* or *doshṇe, &c.* *Puns*, "a male"; nom. *pumān, pumānsau, pumānsaḥ;* acc. *pumānsam, pumānsau, punsaḥ;* ins. *punsā pumbhyām, &c.*

Adjectives in the comparative degree, formed by the affix *īyas* (r. 71.), follow the declension of *manas*, except in the nom. and acc. Thus, *balīyas*, "more powerful"; nom. *balīyān, balīyānsau, balīyānsaḥ;* acc. *balīyānsam, balīyānsau, balīyasaḥ;* ins. *balīyasā, balīyobhyām, &c.* The voc. sing is *balīyan*. The fem. form is declined like *nadī* (r. 49.). The neut. form is declined like *manas* throughout.

Participles of the 2d preterite (r. 127.), like *vividwas* (from *vid*, "to know") and *jagmivas* (from *gam*, "to go") are declined in some of their cases as if they were written *vividus, jagmyus;* and in others as if written *vividwat, jagmivat*. Thus, nom. *vividwān, -wānsau, -wānsaḥ;* acc. *vividwānsam, -wānsau, vividushaḥ;* ins. *vividushā, vividwadbhyām, vividwadbhiḥ*. The root *vid*, "to know," has an irregular pres. part. *vidwas*, used often as an adjective ("learned"), and declined exactly like *vividwas*. These participles are declined like *nadī* in the fem. (r. 49.), and in the neut. like the masc., except in the nom. and acc., which are *vividwah, vividushī, vividwānsi*. The advanced student will here observe, that as the 2d preterite of *vid*, "to know," is used as a present tense, so the participle of the 2d preterite is used as a present participle, the reduplicated syllable only being rejected.

EIGHTH CLASS.—CRUDES IN *any Consonant except t, n, s*, MASCULINE, FEMININE, AND NEUTER.

70. This class consists principally of roots taken to form the last member of compound words. They are not of very common occurrence, except as ending in *t* or *d* (see *karmakṛit*, r. 59.). The only difficulty in their declension arises from their combination with those terminations in the scheme at r. 58., which begin with consonants, viz. three cases in the dual, and four in the plural. Whatever change, however, takes place in the nominative, is preserved before these consonantal terminations. Thus, masc. and fem. *bhuj*, "an eater": nom. *bhuk*; ins. dual *bhugbhyām*; ins. plur. *bhugbhih*; loc. *bhukshu*. So again *spṛish*, nom. *spṛik*;* and in the other cases, *spṛigbhyām, spṛigbhih, spṛikshu*. So again *rāj*, nom. *rāṭ* (राट्); and the other cases, *rāḍbhyām, rāḍbhih, rāṭsu*. And *lih*, "a licker," nom. *liṭ* (लिट्); and the other cases, *liḍbhyām, liḍbhih, liṭsu*. And *duh*, nom. *dhuk*;* and the other cases, *dhugbhyām, dhugbhih, dhukshu*. Before the terminations which begin with vowels, the final consonant of the root, whatever it may be, is always preserved. Thus, acc. *bhujam, spṛisham, rājam, liham, duham*, &c.; ins. *bhujā, spṛishā, rājā, lihā, duhā*, &c. The neuter is as follows: nom., acc., voc. (sing., dual, and plur.), *bhuk, bhujī, bhuñji*; *rāṭ, rājī, rāñji*; *liṭ, lihī, linhi*; *dhuk, duhī, dunhi*.

† The few simple nouns which fall under this class are declined on a similar principle. But *asṛij*, n. "blood" (nom. *asṛik*), makes in the ins. *asṛijā* or *asnā*; dat. *asṛije* or *asne*; acc. pl. *asṛiñji* or *asāni*: *ap*, f. "water," is declined in the plural only; thus, *āpah, apah, adbhih, adbhyah, apām, apsu, āpah*: *div*, f. "the sky," sing. nom. *dyauh*; acc. *divam* or *dyām*; ins. *divā, &c.*; dual. *divau, dyubhyām, divoh*; plur. nom. acc. *divah*; ins. *dyubhih, &c.*

---

* श् *sh* and ह् *h* appear to be nearly allied to *k*, and often pass into *k* in Greek and Latin words. Thus, from *dasha*, "ten," δεκα, "decem"; from हृदय, καρδια, "cor."

Sect. III.—ADJECTIVES.

The declension of substantives involves that of adjectives; and, as already seen, the three examples of substantives, given under each class, serve as the model for the three genders of adjectives falling under the same class. Adjectives, *in their simplest form,* not derived from substantives, are very rarely found in Sanscrit. Such as do occur belong chiefly to the first and third classes of nouns; as, *priya,* "dear" (nom. m. f. n. *priyaḥ, priyā, priyam,** r. 48. 49. 50.); *sādhu,* "good" (nom. m. f. n. *sādhuḥ, sādhuḥ* or *sādhwī, sādhu,* r. 54. 55. 49. 56.).

Adjectives *formed from substantives* are very numerous, as may be seen by a reference to r. 38. 42. and 43. IV. They belong chiefly to the first, fifth, and sixth classes of nouns. The following examples may be added to those already given; *mānuṣha,* "human" (nom. m. f. n. *mānuṣhaḥ, mānuṣhī, mānuṣham,* r. 48. 49. 50.); *shrīmat,* "prosperous" (nom. m. f. n. *shrīmān, shrīmatī, shrīmat,* r. 62.); *balin,* "strong" (nom. m. f. n. *balī, balinī, bali,* r. 67.).

Compound adjectives are most abundant. The following are examples: *phalopeta,* "possessed-of-fruit"; *durbuddhi,* "evil-minded"; *alpatanu,* "small-bodied"; *sarvajit,* "all-conquering"; *sujanman,* "well-born"; *gatachetas,* "bereft-of-sense"; which are thus referrible to their respective classes.

	1st class.	2d class.	3d class.	5th class.	6th class.	7th class.
Nom. m.	*phalopetaḥ*	*durbuddhiḥ*	*alpatanuḥ*	*sarvajit*	*sujanmā*	*gatachetāḥ*
Nom. f.	*phalopetā*	*durbuddhiḥ*	*alpatanuḥ*	*sarvajit*	*sujanmā*	*gatachetāḥ*
Nom. n.	*phalopetam*	*durbuddhi*	*alpatanu*	*sarvajit*	*sujanma*	*gatachetaḥ*

71. The degrees of comparison are formed in two ways; 1st, by adding to the crude तर *tara* (nom. *-taraḥ, -tarā, -taram,* cf. Greek τερος) for the comparative; and तम *tama* (nom. *-tamaḥ,*

---

* When it is remembered that final *ḥ* often becomes *s*, and that *a* is equivalent in pronunciation to *u*, the three genders of this adjective might be written *priyus priyā, priyum;* thus offering a perfect similarity to Latin adjectives in *us*.

-tamā, -tamam, cf. Greek τατος) for the superlative. Thus, *puṇya*, "holy," पुण्यतर *puṇyatara*, "more holy," पुण्यतम *puṇyatama*, "most holy," declined like nouns of the first class (r. 48. 49. 50.). So, also, *dhanavat*, "wealthy," *dhanavattara*, "more wealthy," *dhanavattama*, "most wealthy"; and *dhanin*, *dhanitara*, *dhanitama* (r. 20.†).

2dly, by adding ईयस् *īyas* (nom. *-īyān*, *-īyasī*, *-īyah*, cf. Greek ιων) for the comparative, and इष्ठ *ishṭha* (nom. *-ishṭhah -ishṭhā*, *-ishṭham*, cf. Greek ιστος) for the superlative. In general, the only change that takes place before these affixes is the rejection of a final vowel, or of an affix. Thus, *balin*, "strong," becomes *bal*, making बलीयस् *balīyas*, "stronger" (see r. 69.†), बलिष्ठ *balishṭha* "strongest" (declined like nouns of the first class); *laghu*, "light," becomes *lagh*, making *laghīyas*, "lighter," *laghishṭha*, "lightest." Observe, however, that these affixes do not often imply comparison, but simply *excess*: thus, *balīyas* and *balishṭha* more usually signify "very strong."

† But besides the rejection of the final, the crude often undergoes considerable change, as in Greek; and its place is sometimes supplied by a substitute. Thus, *mridu*, "soft," becomes *mrad*, making *mradīyas*, *mradishṭha*; *guru*, "heavy," *gar*, making *garīyas* (cf. Latin *gravius*), *garishṭha*; *priya*, "dear," *pra*, making *preyas*, *preshṭha*; *bahu*, "many," *bhū*, making *bhūyas*, *bhuyishṭha*; *dīrgha*, "long," *drāgh*; *dūra*, "far," *dav*; *antika*, "near," *ned*; *kshudra*, "small," *kshod*; *yuvan*, "young," *yav*; *prashasya*, "good," *shra*;* *alpa*, "small," *kan*; *uru* (εὐρύς), "large," *var*, making *varīyas*, *varishṭha* (Ϝάριστος). See Prof. Eastwick's translation of Bopp's Comp. Gram. §. 298.

Sect. IV.—NUMERAL ADJECTIVES.

72. *Cardinals.*

एक *eka*, 1; द्वि *dwi*, 2; त्रि *tri*, 3; चतुर् *chatur*, 4; which are thus declined.

Eka, "one" (singular only), follows the declension of pronominals: nom. m. *ekah*; dat. m. *ekasmai*; nom. f. *ekā*; dat. f. *ekasyai*; nom. n. *ekam* (see *sarva*, r. 87.).

* Prof. Bopp derives *shreyas* and *shreshṭha* from *shrīmat*, "fortunate," the affix being rejected.

Dwi, "two" (dual only), is declined as if the crude were *dwa*: nom., acc., voc. m. *dwau*, f. n. *dwe*; ins., dat., ab. m. f. n. *dwābhyām*; gen., loc. *dwayoh*.

Tri, "three," and *chatur*, "four" (plural only), declined—

	MASC.	FEM.	NEUT.	MASC.	FEM.	NEUT.
N. V.	*trayah*,	*tisrah*,	*trīṇi*,	*chatwārah*,	*chatasrah*,	*chatwāri*.
Ac.	*trīn*,	—	—	*chaturah*,	—	—
I.	*tribhih*,	*tisṛibhih*,		*chaturbhih*,	*chatasṛibhih*,	
D. A.	*tribhyah*,	*tisṛibhyah*,		*chaturbhyah*,	*chatasṛibhyah*,	
G.	*trayāṇām*,	*tisṛiṇām*,		*chaturṇām*,	*chatasṛiṇām*,	
L.	*triṣhu*,	*tisṛiṣhu*,		*chaturṣhu*,	*chatasṛiṣhu*,	

The neuter only differs from the masc. in the nom., voc., and acc. cases.

पञ्चन् *pañchan*, 5; षष् *ṣhaṣh*, 6; सप्तन् *saptan*, 7; अष्टन् *aṣhṭan*, 8; नवन् *navan*, 9; दशन् *dashan*, 10.

73. *Pañchan*, "five"; *ṣhaṣh*, "six"; *aṣhṭan*, "eight" (plural only); declined—

	M. F. N.	M. F. N.	M. F. N.
N. Ac. V.	*pañcha*,	*ṣhaṭ*,	*aṣhṭa* or *aṣhṭau*.
Ins.	*pañchabhih*,	*ṣhaḍbhih*,	*aṣhṭabhih* or *aṣhṭābhih*.
D. Ab.	*pañchabhyah*,	*ṣhaḍbhyah*,	*aṣhṭabhyah* or *aṣhṭābhyah*.
Gen.	*pañchānām*,	*ṣhaṇṇām*,	*aṣhṭānām*.
Loc.	*pañchasu*,	*ṣhaṭsu*,	*aṣhṭasu* or *aṣhṭāsu*.

Saptan, *navan*, and *dashan*, and all other numerals ending in *an*, follow the declension of *pañchan*.

Ekādashan, 11; *dwādashan*, 12; *trayodashan*, 13; *chaturdashan*, 14; *pañchadashan*, 15; *ṣhoḍashan* (षोडशन्), 16; *saptadashan*, 17; *aṣhṭādashan*, 18; *navadashan* or *ūnavinshati*, 19; *vinshati* (विंशति), 20; *trinshat* (त्रिंशत्), 30; *chatwārinshat* (चत्वारिंशत्), 40; *pañchāshat* (पञ्चाशत्), 50; *ṣhaṣhṭi* (षष्टि), 60; *saptati* (सप्तति), 70; *ashīti* (अशीति), 80; *navati* (नवति), 90; *shata*, n. (शत), 100; *sahasra*, n. (सहस्र), 1000. As from *dashan*, "ten," are formed *ekādashan*, *dwādashan*, *trayodashan*, &c., so from *vinshati*, "twenty," are formed *ekavinshati*, "twenty-one"; *dwāvinshati*, "twenty-two"; *trayovinshati*, "twenty-three," &c. But due regard must be paid to the laws of combination; thus, *ṣhaḍvinshati* (षड्विंशति), 26; *trayastrinshat*, 33; *ṣhaṭtrinshat*, 36; *chatushchatwārinshat*, 44; *chatuhpañchāshat* (चतुःपञ्चाशत्), 54; *trayahsaptati* (त्रयःसप्तति), 73; *tryashīti* (त्र्यशीति), 83; *pañchāshīti*, 85; *ṣhaṇṇavati* (षण्णवति), 96.

Vinshati (20), and *trinshat* (30), are declined like fem. nouns of the third and fifth classes, usually in the singular. As, शायकान् विंशतिं निचखान, "he infixed twenty arrows." *Shata* (100), *sahasra* (1000), are neut. nouns of the first class, usually declined in the sing.; as, सहस्रं पितरः, "a thousand ancestors": or they may govern a genitive case; as, सहस्रं पितॄणां (cf. the use of the Latin *mille*).

74. *Ordinals.*

Prathama, "first"; *dwitīya*, "second"; *tṛitīya*, "third"; are declined as pronominals (see r. 87.).

Chaturtha, "fourth" (cf. τέταρτος); *pañchama*, "fifth"; *ṣhaṣhṭha* (षष्ठ), "sixth"; *saptama*, "seventh"; *aṣhṭama*, "eighth"; *navama*, "ninth"; *dashama*, "tenth"; like nouns of the first class (nom. *-ah*, *-ī*, *-am*).

The ordinals from "eleventh" to "twentieth," are formed from the cardinals, by rejecting the final *n*; thus, *ekādasha* (nom. *-ah*, *-ī*, *-am*).

"Twentieth" is formed, either by adding the superlative affix *tama* to the cardinal, as *vinshatitama*; or by rejecting the final, and leaving *vinsha* (nom. *-ah*, *-ī*, *-am*). So also *trinshattama* or *trinsha*, "thirtieth." Similarly "fortieth" and "fiftieth." The other decimal cardinals form the ordinals either by adding *tama*, or by changing *ti* to *ta*; as, *saptatitama* or *saptata*, "seventieth."

Numerical Symbols.

१	२	३	४	५	६	७	८	९	१०
1	2	3	4	5	6	7	8	9	10

CHAPTER V.

PRONOUNS.

FORMATION OF THE CRUDE.

PRONOUNS have no crude state analogous to that of nouns, that is, no state distinct from all inflexion, serving as the basis on which all the cases are constructed.

The question then arises, what form of the pronoun is used in the formation of compound words. In the pronouns of the first and second persons, the ablative cases, singular and plural, and in the other pronouns, the nominative and accusative cases neuter, are considered as expressive of the most general and comprehensive state of the pronoun. These cases, therefore, discharge the office of a crude, and are constantly found at the commencement of compound words.

DECLENSION OF THE PERSONAL PRONOUNS.

75. मत् *mat*, "I," is taken for the crude of the sing.; and अस्मत् *asmat*, "we," for the crude of the plur. of the first personal pronoun.

N. अहं *aham*, "I."	आवां *āvām*, "we two,"	वयं *vayam*, "we."
Ac. मां *mām*, "me,"*	— *āvām*, "us two,"*	अस्मान् *asmān*, "us."*
I. मया *mayā*,	आवाभ्यां *āvābhyām*,	अस्माभिः *asmābhih*.
D. मह्यं *mahyam*,*	— *āvābhyām*,*	अस्मभ्यं *asmabhyam*.*
Ab. मत् *mat*,	— *āvābhyām*,	अस्मत् *asmat*.
G. मम *mama*,*	आवयोः *āvayoh*,*	अस्माकं *asmākam*.*
L. मयि *mayi*,	— *āvayoh*,	अस्मासु *asmāsu*.

76. त्वत् *twat*, "thou," is taken for the crude of the sing.; and युष्मत् *yushmat*, "you," for the crude of the plural of the second personal pronoun.

---

* The acc. sing. may also be मा; the dat., gen. मे; the acc., dat., gen. dual नौ; the acc., dat., gen. plur. नः (cf. Lat. *nos*).

N. त्वं *twam*, "thou,"	युवां *yuvām*, "you two,"	यूयं *yūyam*, "you."
Ac. त्वां *twām*,*	— *yuvām*,	युष्मान् *yushmān*.*
I. त्वया *twayā*,	युवाभ्यां *yuvābhyām*,	युष्माभिः *yushmābhih*.
D. तुभ्यं *tubhyam*,*	— *yuvābhyām*,*	युष्मभ्यं *yushmabhyam*.*
Ab. त्वत् *twat*,	— *yuvābhyām*,	युष्मत् *yushmat*.
G. तव *tava*,*	युवयोः *yuvayoh*,*	युष्माकं *yushmākam*.*
L. त्वयि *twayi*,	— *yuvayoh*,	युष्मासु *yushmāsu*.

77. तत् *tat* or तद् *tad*, "he," is taken as the crude of the sing. and plur. of the third personal pronoun. With this pronoun cf. the Greek article.

MASCULINE.

N. सः *sah*, "he,"	तौ *tau*, "they two,"	ते *te*, "they."
Ac. तं *tam*,	— *tau*,	तान् *tān*.
I. तेन *tena*,	ताभ्यां *tābhyām*,	तैः *taih*.
D. तस्मै *tasmai*,	— *tābhyām*,	तेभ्यः *tebhyah*.
Ab. तस्मात् *tasmāt*,	— *tābhyām*,	— *tebhyah*.
G. तस्य *tasya*,	तयोः *tayoh*,	तेषां *teshām*.
L. तस्मिन् *tasmin*,	— *tayoh*,	तेषु *teshu*.

FEMININE.

N. सा *sā*, "she,"	ते *te*,	ताः *tāh*.
Ac. तां *tām*,	— *te*,	— *tāh*.
I. तया *tayā*,	ताभ्यां *tābhyām*,	ताभिः *tābhih*.
D. तस्यै *tasyai*,	— *tābhyām*,	ताभ्यः *tābhyah*.
Ab. तस्याः *tasyāh*,	— *tābhyām*,	— *tābhyah*.
G. — *tasyāh*,	तयोः *tayoh*,	तासां *tāsām*.
L. तस्यां *tasyām*,	— *tayoh*,	तासु *tāsu*.

Neuter, nom. acc. तत् *tat*, ते *te*, तानि *tāni*; the rest like the masculine.

This pronoun is sometimes used *emphatically* with the other pronouns, like *ille* and *ipse*. Thus, सोऽहं, "*ille ego*"; ते वयं, "*illi nos*"; स त्वं, "*ille tu*"; ते यूयं, "*illi vos*"; स एषः, "*ille ipse*"; तद् एतत्, "*id ipsum*."

---

* The acc. sing. may also be त्वा; the dat. gen. ते; the acc., dat., gen. dual वां; the acc., dat., gen. plur. वः (cf. Lat. *vos*).

REFLEXIVE PERSONAL PRONOUNS.

78. The oblique cases of आत्मन्, "soul," "self" (declined p. 41.), are used reflexively in place of the three personal pronouns, like the Latin *ipse*. Thus, *ātmānam* (*me ipsum*) *anāhāreṇa hanishyāmi*, "I will kill myself by fasting"; *ātmānam* (*te ipsum*) *mṛitavad darshaya*, "show thyself as if dead"; *ātmānam* (*se ipsum*) *nindati*, "he blames himself."

DEMONSTRATIVE PRONOUNS DECLINED.

79. The third personal pronoun तत् *tat*, "he," declined above, is constantly used in a demonstrative sense, to signify "that" or "this"; and by prefixing *e* to it, another common pronoun is formed still more strongly demonstrative; as, nom. एष: *eshah* (r. 30.), एतौ *etau*, एते *ete*"; acc. एतं *etam*, &c.; ins. एतेन *etena*, &c.

There is another very common demonstrative pronoun, of which इदं *idam*, "this," the nom. case neuter, is considered to be the crude, but is never used as such.

MASCULINE.

N.	अयं *ayam*, "this,"	इमौ *imau*, "these two,"	इमे *ime*, "these."
Ac.	इमं *imam*,*	— *imau*,	इमान् *imān*.
I.	अनेन *anena*,	आभ्यां *ābhyām*,	एभि: *ebhih*.†
D.	अस्मै *asmai*,	— *ābhyām*,	एभ्य: *ebhyah*.
Ab.	अस्मात् *asmāt*,	— *ābhyām*,	— *ebhyah*.
G.	अस्य *asya*,	अनयो: *anayoh*,	एषां *eshām*.
L.	अस्मिन् *asmin*,	— *anayoh*,	एषु *eshu*.

FEMININE.

N.	इयं *iyam*,	इमे *ime*,	इमा: *imāh*.
Ac.	इमां *imām*,*	— *ime*,	— *imāh*.
I.	अनया *anayā*,	आभ्यां *ābhyām*,	आभि: *ābhih*.
D.	अस्यै *asyai*,	— *ābhyām*,	आभ्य: *ābhyah*.
Ab.	अस्या: *asyāh*,	— *ābhyām*,	— *ābhyah*.
G.	— *asyāh*,	अनयो: *anayoh*,	आसां *āsām*.
L.	अस्यां *asyām*,	— *anayoh*,	आसु *āsu*.

* The acc. m. may be एनं, the acc. f. एनां.

† This pronoun affords the only example of the old form for the instr. plur. of masculine

Neut., nom. acc. इदं *idam*, इमे *ime*, इमानि *imāni;* the rest like the masculine.

There is another demonstrative pronoun rarely used except in the nom., of which *adas* is taken as the crude: nom. m. *asau*, "this" or "he," *amū*, *amī;* acc. *amum;* ins. *amunā*, *&c.*

RELATIVE PRONOUN—"*who*," "*which*."

80. The relative may be formed by simply substituting *y* for *s* and *t*, in the pronoun *tad*. Thus, crude form *yad:* nom. m. यः *yah*, "who," यौ *yau*, ये *ye;* acc. यं *yam*, "whom," &c.

INTERROGATIVE PRONOUN—"*who?*" "*what?*"

81. As the relative is formed by substituting *y*, so the interrogative by substituting *k* for *s* and *t*, in the pronoun *tad*. Thus, nom. m. कः *kah*, "who?" कौ *kau*, के *ke*. In the nom. neut., however, the interrogative is किं *kim* and not *kad*.* *Kim* is also the crude, and occurs in a few compounds; as, किमर्थं, "on what account?"

POSSESSIVE PRONOUNS.

82. These are formed by adding the affix *īya* (r. 38. XI.) to the crude of the personal pronouns; as, *madīya*, "mine" (nom. *-ah*, *-ā*, *-am*); *twadīya*, "thine"; *asmadīya*, "our." Observe, however, that the gen. case of the personal pronouns is more usually taken to express the possessive; as, तस्य पुत्रः, "his son."

REFLEXIVE POSSESSIVE PRONOUNS.

83. स्व *swa* (cf. *suus*), declined like *sarva*, r. 87. (nom. स्वः, स्वौ, स्वे†), is used reflexively, in reference to all three persons, and may stand for "my own," "thy own," "his own," "our own," &c. It often occupies the first place in a compound; thus, स्वगृहं गच्छति,

---

masculine nouns of the first class. This form is still preserved in the Vedas, and in accordance with this, the instr. plur. of *deva* (r. 48.) would be *devebhih*.

* *Kad*, however, was the old form, and is retained in a few words; such as *kachchit*, "perhaps"; *kadartha*, "useless" ("of what use?"); *kadadhwan*, "a bad road" ("what a road!").

† But the abl. and loc. sing. m., and nom. pl. m. may follow *deva*, r. 48.

"he goes to his own house."* The gen. case of *ātman* (p. 41.), or often the crude, is used with the same signification; as, आत्मनो गृहं or आत्मगृहं गच्छति.†

HONORIFIC PRONOUN.

84. भवत् *bhavat*, "your honour," requiring the 3d person of the verb, is declined like *dhanavat* (r. 61.). Thus, nom. *bhavān, bhavantau, bhavantah*. It is used respectfully in place of the second personal pronoun; as, *bhavān dharmam karotu*, "let your honour practise virtue."

INDEFINITE PRONOUNS.

85. The indeclinable affixes *chit, api*, and *chana*, added to the several cases of the interrogative pronoun, give them an indefinite signification. Thus, nom. sing. masc. कश्चित् *kashchit*, "somebody," "any body"; acc. कञ्चित् *kañchit*; ins. *kenachit*; dat. *kasmaichit*; loc. कस्मिंश्चित् *kasminshchit* (r. 20.); nom. plur. masc. *kechit*. So also nom. कोऽपि *ko'pi*, कश्चन *kashchana*, "somebody"; ins. *kenāpi*, &c. By prefixing न, is formed the negative न कश्चित्, "nobody."

† In the same way interrogative adverbs are made indefinite. Thus, from *kati*, "how many?" *katichit*, "a few"; from *kadā*, "when?" *kadāchit*, "at some time"; from *katham*, "how?" *kathañchana*, "some how."

WHOSOEVER, WHATSOEVER.

86. This is expressed by prefixing the relative pronoun to the interrogative. Thus, यः कश्चित्, "whosoever"; यत् किञ्चित्, "whatsoever." Or by repeating the relative; as, यो यः, यद् यद्.

PRONOMINALS.

87. There are certain common adjectives which partake of the nature of pronouns, and follow the declension of *tad* (r. 77.). Thus,

* In modern Sanscrit *nija* often takes the place of *swa*; as, निजगृहं गच्छति.

† Prof. Lassen cites a remarkable example from the *Rāmāyana*, in which आत्मन् refers to the dual number. *Putram ātmanah sprishtwā nipetatuh*, "they two fell down after touching their son." Anthol. p. 171.

सर्व *sarva*, "all": nom. masc. *sarvah, sarvau, sarve;* dat. *sarvasmai;* nom. fem. *sarvā,* &c.; dat. *sarvasyai,* &c. But the nom. neut. is *sarvam,* &c., not *sarvad.* The following are the most useful of these pronominals. *Eka,* "one"; *prathama,* "first"; *dwitīya,* "second"; *tritīya,* "third"; *alpa,* "few"; *ubha,* "both"; *anya,* "other"; *itara,* "other"; *katara,* "which of the two?" (the three last also follow *tad* in the nom. and acc. neut. *anyat, itarat, katarat*). But some of these are optionally declined like nouns of the first class; thus, *alpa,* nom. plur. *alpāh* or *alpe.*

CHAPTER VI.

VERBS.

General Observations.

ALTHOUGH the Sanscrit verb will be found somewhat intricate by one who follows it through all its windings, yet such a general view of its structure as will be sufficient to answer the practical wants of the general reader may be easily given, and as easily apprehended. There is no part of the grammar so capable as this of plain exoteric explanation, whilst there is none so obscured by the *esoteric* and mystical teaching of native grammarians; none, of which the general principles are so few and so close to the surface, whilst the abstruser truths, the niceties and refinements, are multiplied to an extent that tends to discourage, or even disgust the uninitiated learner. Hence it happens that the expounder of Sanscrit Grammar, who wishes to exhaust his subject, is here not only compelled to embarass and perplex an otherwise simple statement, by the diffuse exhibition of various forms, and tenses, and exceptions, which are of little utility to the ordinary student, but is forced, moreover, to bewilder the beginner by a complication of technical phrases, conventional abbreviations, and symbolical letters, which are as puzzling at the first stage of his studies, as they may be useful in assisting his memory at a later period. And thus it is that a very false impression is formed of the difficulty of a language, the broad and useful principles of which lie wholly within the reach of the most moderate capacity. It will be the aim of the following pages to disentangle the subject, as much as possible, from this superabundant weight of mystical symbols and unusual tenses and forms, many of which exist more in the theory of grammarians than in the practice of approved writers; and although no part of the verb will be left unnoticed, the larger print will serve to attract the eye of the student to those points which are of general utility and real importance, whilst the smaller will indicate those portions of the subject which are to be reserved for after-consideration.

Although the Sanscrit verb offers the most striking and interesting analogies to the Greek, nevertheless, so peculiar and artificial is the process by which it is formed, that it would be impossible, in treating of it, to adopt an arrangement which would be likely to fall in with the preconceived notions of the classical student.

There are ten tenses. Seven of them are of common occurrence; viz. 1. the present, 2. the first preterite, 3. the potential, 4. the imperative, 5. the second preterite, 6. the first future, 7. the second future. Three are of rare occurrence; viz. 8. the third preterite, 9. the benedictive, 10. the conditional. There is also an infinitive mood, and several participles. Of these tenses the present, the three preterites, and the two futures, belong properly to the indicative mood; and the imperative, potential, benedictive, and conditional, are more properly moods than tenses. Since, however, these moods do not comprehend other tenses under them, but are susceptible of all times, present, past, and future, it can lead to no embarassment to consider them as tenses, and to arrange them indiscriminately with the others in the manner proposed above.

† Although the three preterites are used without much distinction, yet it should be observed that they properly express different degrees of past time. The first pre-

terite corresponds to the imperfect of Greek and Latin verbs, and properly has reference to an event doing at some time past, and not ended. The second preterite has reference to an event done and past at some definite period. The third preterite, to an event done and past at some indefinite period, thus corresponding to the Greek aorist. So, also, the two futures properly express, the first definite, the second indefinite futurity. The potential may generally be rendered in English by some one of the auxiliaries "may," "can," "would," "should," "ought." The conditional is used after the conjunction *yadi*, "if": it occurs, however, but very rarely, and the potential usually supplies its place in conditional sentences. The benedictive is a tense sometimes used in praying and blessing.

The infinitive mood generally has an active, but is capable of a passive signification.

Every tense has three numbers, singular, dual, and plural.

There are two voices or systems of inflection, the one called Parasmaipada, the other Ātmanepada.* The former is supposed to convey a transitive sense, the action passing *parasmai*, "to another"; the latter, a reflexive sense, corresponding to that conveyed by the Greek middle voice, the action reverting *ātmane*, "to one's self."† This distinction, however, is very rarely preserved; and we find verbs, transitive or intransitive, conjugated indifferently in the parasmaipada or ātmanepada, or both. When, however, the verb is conjugated in both, the ātmane may then sometimes yield its appropriate meaning, and give a kind of reflexive sense, or a sense directing the action in some way to the advantage of the agent.

Passive verbs are invariably conjugated in the ātmanepada.

From every root five kinds of verbs may, in theory, be elicited—a primitive, a causal, a passive, a desiderative, and intensive.

* If the term *voice* has reference to the system of inflection, it is obvious that there can only be two voices in Sanscrit; and although the *ātmanepada*, in one or two instances, has a middle sense, yet it cannot be said to correspond with the Greek middle voice, the chief characteristic of which is, that it takes a middle inflection, partly active, partly passive.

† The words *parasmaipada* and *ātmanepada* will often be contracted into *par.*, *ātm.*

Of these, the two last forms are very rarely met with, except in the nouns and participles derived from them; and will therefore be but slightly noticed in these pages. So, also, from every noun, certain nominal verbs may, in theory, be elicited. Very few of these, however, are in frequent use. There are ten conjugations. Primitive verbs may belong to any one of the first nine conjugations, but by far the greatest number belong either to the 1st, 4th, or 6th, the other six conjugations comprising so few verbs that they may be regarded rather as exceptions. These nine conjugations apply to the first four tenses only. The other tenses of the primitive are formed according to one rule. Causal verbs form the 10th conjugation. Every root has a passive form, entirely independent of the conjugational form assumed by the root; and the student will observe, that the passive cannot, in Sanscrit, be considered a *voice*, according to the usual acceptation of the term. For, in that case, he would expect a verb in the passive voice to correspond in form with a verb in the active, in the way that *audior* corresponds with *audio*, and *ἀκούομαι* with *ἀκούω*, the terminations or system of inflection only being changed. But, in Sanscrit, the passive often varies entirely in form from the active verb, whilst the terminations may in both cases be the same, viz. those of the ātmanepada. It is rather a distinct derivative from the root, formed on one invariable principle, without the least community with the conjugational structure of the active verb. Thus, the root *bhid*, "to divide," is of the 7th conjugation, and makes *bhinatti* or *bhinte*, "he divides"; *dwiṣh*, "to hate," is of the 2d conjugation, and makes *dweṣhṭi* or *dwiṣhṭe*, "he hates"; but the passive of both is formed according to one invariable rule, by the simple insertion of *y*, without the least reference to the conjugational form of the active: thus, *bhidyate*, "he is divided"; *dwiṣhyate*, "he is hated."

From these observations it is evident that the difficulty of the Sanscrit verb is as nothing when compared with the Greek. The Greek verb has three voices, and about ninety tenses and moods: the Sanscrit has only two voices, and not more than twenty-one tenses and moods. Besides which, a far greater number of verbs are susceptible of the three voices in Greek, than of the two in Sanscrit.

Moreover, in Sanscrit, there are no contracted verbs, and no difficulties resulting from difference of dialect; and although there are ten conjugations, yet these have reference to four tenses only, and, under some of these conjugations, only two or three common verbs are contained.

Verbs primitive, causal, and passive, may, like nouns, be divided into simple and compound. *Simple verbs* may be regarded as falling under two heads, either as derived from uncompounded roots, or as derived from nouns. *Compound verbs* are those formed by combining roots with prepositions or other adverbial prefixes.*

SIMPLE VERBS DERIVED FROM ROOTS.

It has been already shown that there are a large number of monosyllabic sounds in Sanscrit, called *roots*, which, having a mere ideal existence, are the source of verbs as well as nouns. These roots are in number about two thousand, and the theory of grammarians is, that each of them may serve as the basis on which to construct five kinds of verbs; 1. a primitive, transitive or intransitive; 2. a causal, having often a causal and often merely a transitive signification; 3. a passive; 4. a desiderative, giving a sense of wishing to the root; and 5. an intensive (or frequentative), heightening the idea contained in the root. It will be found, however, in practice, that the greater number of these two thousand roots never occur at all in the form of verbs, nor, indeed, in any other form but that of the nouns to which they give origin; and that the roots in real use as the source of verbs are comparatively very few. Of these few, moreover, certain particular roots (such, for example, as *kṛi*, "to do"), as if to compensate for the inactivity of the others, are kept in constant employment, and, by compounding them with prepositions and other prefixes, applied to the expression of the most various and opposite ideas.

Nevertheless, theoretically, from every root in the language may be elicited five kinds of verbs. The first, or primitive verb,

* Compound verbs will be treated of in the chapter on compound words.

is formed from the root, according to the nine different rules for the changes of the root, required by the first nine conjugations; the second, or causal, is formed according to the rule for the change of the root, required by the 10th conjugation; viz. the addition of *ay* to the root, the vowel of which has taken the Guna change. The third, or passive, is formed according to the rule for the change of the root, required by the 4th conjugation, viz. the addition of *y* in the first four tenses. The fourth, or desiderative, is formed by the addition of *iṣh* or *s*, the root also undergoing reduplication. The fifth, or intensive, is formed like the passive, according to the rule required by the 4th conjugation, and is, in fact, a reduplicated passive verb. It may also be formed analogously to the rule for the 3d conjugation. Thus, take the root *shubh*, conveying the idea of "shining"—from this are elicited, 1. the primitive, *shobh*, "to shine"; 2. the causal, *shobhay*, "to cause to shine" or "illuminate"; 3. the passive, *shubhy*, "to be bright"; 4. the desiderative, *shushobhiṣh*, "to desire to shine"; 5. the intensive, *shoshuby*, "to shine very brightly." See also p. 19.

Of these five forms of verbs, the primitive, causal, and passive, are the only three used by the best writers, and to these alone the attention of the reader will now be directed. The subject, therefore, will divide itself into two heads. In the first place, the *formation* of the base: 1st, of primitive; 2dly, of causal; 3dly, of passive verbs. In the second place, the *inflection* of the base of these same forms respectively. But here it may be asked, what is the base?

THE BASE OF THE VERB.

The base of the verb is that changed form of the root to which the terminations are immediately affixed, and holds exactly that intermediate position between the root and the inflected verb itself, which the crude form holds between the root and the inflected noun. This great peculiarity, therefore, cannot be too often or too forcibly impressed upon the attention of the learner, that, in the treatment of Sanscrit verbs, two perfectly distinct subjects offer themselves for consideration: 1st, the *formation* of the base, or, in other words, an investigation into the changes which the root undergoes before the terminations are affixed; 2dly, the *inflection* of the base, or the union of the base with its terminations.

The first of these two subjects of inquiry will be found to be that in which consists all the difficulty of the subject; for, as far as the terminations are concerned, no dead language conforms more systematically to one general scheme, than the one with which we are concerned.

There are ten rules or conjugations, according to which the bases of verbs may be formed. But in these we have already noted a great peculiarity, and one which has much weight in a comparison between the difficulties of a Greek and Sanscrit verb. Of these ten conjugations, the first nine have reference only to the first four tenses; viz. the present, first preterite, potential, and imperative. Hence these are called the conjugational tenses. After passing these four tenses the conjugational structure of the base is entirely forgotten; and in the formation of the bases of the six remaining tenses all roots conform to one general rule, and are as if they belonged to one general conjugation. Hence these tenses are called non-conjugational. The tenth alone retains the conjugational structure of the base throughout *all the tenses* of the verb; but as this conjugation has no reference to primitives, but to causals only, no confusion can arise from this apparent inconsistency. Of the 2000 roots, about one half follow the 1st conjugation, about 130 follow the 4th, and about 140 the 6th. Of the remaining roots, not more than 20 *in common use* follow the 2d; not more than 5 follow the 3d; not more than 6 the 7th; not more than 4 the 5th; not more than 1 the 8th; not more than 12 the 9th.

Primitive verbs, therefore, which constitute the first nine conjugations, will be divided into *two grand classes*, according as they fall under one or other of these nine conjugations. Regular primitive verbs will be those of the 1st, 4th, and 6th conjugations. Irregular primitives those of the 2d, 3d, 5th, 7th, 8th, and 9th conjugations. The first class we call regular, because under it are contained nearly all the common verbs in the language; the second irregular, as comprehending only fifty or sixty useful verbs in all.

All causal verbs follow the 10th conjugation, and, in point of fact, constitute this conjugation; for all those primitive verbs which are said by grammarians to belong to the 10th conjugation, may be regarded as causal verbs.

All passive verbs are ātmanepada verbs of the 4th conjugation. The parasmaipada of the 4th conjugation is constituted of certain primitive verbs, which have a neuter signification.

† There seems no necessity for creating a tenth conjugation as distinct from the causal. So that it would greatly simplify the subject, if this conjugation were expunged altogether from the Grammar, and the addition of *ay* to the root considered, in all cases, as the mark of a causal verb. And it is plain that *ay* is not the sign of a separate conjugation, in the way that *nu* is the sign of the 5th conjugation, or in the way of any other conjugational sign, for it is retained throughout the other tenses of the verb, not only in the first four, just as the desiderative *iṣh* is retained throughout. And although there are many verbs given under the 10th conjugation, which have rather a transitive than a causal signification, yet there are also many causal verbs which are used only in a transitive sense. It will therefore make the subject less complex to consider that the affix *ay* is always the sign of the causal form, merely bearing in mind that causal forms do not necessarily imply causality.

It may also be questioned whether there be any necessity for creating a 4th conjugation as distinct from the passive. For since it is found that either a neuter or passive signification attaches to nearly all the verbs placed under the 4th conjugation, and that passive verbs are identical with its *ātmanepada* inflection, it may with reason be suspected that the occasional assumption of a neuter signification and a *parasmaipada* inflection by a passive verb, was the only cause which gave rise to the creation of this conjugation. And this theory is supported by the fact that many passive verbs (as, for example, *jāyate*, "he is born," from the root *jan*; and *pūryate*, "he is filled," from the root *pṛī*) are confounded with verbs of this conjugation. So that it seems not unlikely, that, by making this 4th conjugation, Grammarians only meant to say that the passive form of verbs, or the addition of *y* to the root, is also the form that may be used to express a neuter or intransitive signification; the only difference requisite to be made between the two forms being exactly that which might be expected to exist between them; viz. that the one should take the *ātmanepada;* the other, the *parasmaipada* inflection. At any rate this fact is clear that the *par.* of the 4th conjugation is the form used in numerous roots to yield a neuter signification; and that the *ātm.* is identical with the form used to yield a passive sense. Hence it arises, that many roots appear in the 4th conjugation as neuter verbs, which also appear in some one of the other nine as transitive. For example, *yuj,* "to join," when used in an active sense is conjugated either in the 7th conjugation, or in the causal; when in a neuter, in the 4th. So also, *push,* "to nourish"; *kshubh,* "to agitate"; *klish,* "to vex"; *sidh,* "to accomplish."

Sect. I.—REGULAR PRIMITIVES, OR VERBS OF THE 1st, 4th, AND 6th CONJUGATIONS.

TERMINATIONS OF THE CONJUGATIONAL TENSES.

PARASMAIPADA.			ATMANEPADA.		
Sing.	Dual	Plur.	Sing.	Dual	Plur.
Present Tense.					
āmi	*āvah*	*āmah*	*e*	*āvahe*	*āmahe*
asi	*athah*	*atha*	*ase*	*ethe*	*adhwe*
ati	*atah*	*anti*	*ate*	*ete*	*ante*
First Preterite.					
am	*āva*	*āma*	*e*	*āvahi*	*āmahi*
ah	*atam*	*ata*	*athāh*	*ethām*	*adhwam*
at	*atām*	*an*	*ata*	*etām*	*anta*
Potential.					
eyam	*eva*	*ema*	*eya*	*evahi*	*emahi*
eh	*etam*	*eta*	*ethāh*	*eyāthām*	*edhwam*
et	*etām*	*eyuh*	*eta*	*eyātām*	*eran*
Imperative.					
āni	*āva*	*āma*	*ai*	*āvahai*	*āmahai*
a	*atam*	*ata*	*aswa*	*ethām*	*adhwam*
atu	*atām*	*antu*	*atām*	*etām*	*antām*

Obs., the terminations read downward; thus, *āmi* is the 1st pers. sing.; *asi* the 2d sing.; *ati* the 3d.

FORMATION OF THE BASE OF THE CONJUGATIONAL TENSES OF REGULAR PRIMITIVE VERBS.

88. Obs., that it is an universal rule in every conjugation that the augment *a* is prefixed to the base of the first pret.; and that when this is prefixed to bases beginning with the vowels *i, u,* and *ṛi,* short or long, it blends with them into *ai, au, ār* (instead of *e, o, ar,* by r. 5.). Thus the base इच्छ् becomes in the first pret. *aichchham,* and *ṛidhno, ārdhnot.*

First Conjugation.

a. If a root be of the 1st conjugation, the rule for the formation of the base in the conjugational tenses is, that the Guna be substituted for the vowel of the root throughout *every person of every tense.* Thus, from बुध् *budh,* "to know," is formed the base बोध् *bodh** (बोधामि, *bodhāmi,* &c.). From *bhū,* "to be," *bho* (*bhavāmi,* &c., r. 10.†). From *nī,* "to lead," *ne* (*nayāmi,* &c., r. 10.†). From *sṛip, sarp;* from *klṛip, kalp* (p. 2.†). In the first preterite the only difference in the base will be that *a* is prefixed; thus, *abodh, abho, ane* (*abodham,* &c., *abhavam,* &c., *anayam,* &c.). In the potential and imperative the base is exactly the same as in the present (*bodheyam,* &c., *bodhāni,* &c.).

b. Since there is no Guna of *a,* roots like पच् *pach,* "to cook," do not change (*pachāmi,* &c.). Nor does any change take place if the root ends in two consonants; as, *nind,* "to blame": nor if the root contain a long vowel, *not final;* as, *jīv,* "to live." Obs. It will be hereafter seen that this prohibition of Guna extends to the other tenses as well as to the conjugational.†

c. Some roots of the 1st conjugation form their bases in the first four tenses by a change peculiar to themselves, which change is of course discarded in the other tenses. Thus, from स्था *sthā,* "to stand," comes the base तिष्ठ् *tishṭh* (*tishṭhāmi, &c.*); from गम् *gam,* "to go," गच्छ् *gachchh;* from सद् *sad,* ātm. "to sink," *sīd;* from

---

* Bopp has shewn that an analogous change takes place in Greek. Thus, the root φυγ (ἔφυγον) becomes φεύγω in the present.

† Thus, *nind* is in the 2d pret. *nininda;* in the 1st fut. *ninditā;* in the 3d pret. *anindīt;* in the causal, *nindayati.*

घ्रा *ghrā*, "to smell," जिघ्र् *jighr;* from *pā*, "to drink," *piv;* and from दृश् *dṛish*, "to see," the substituted base पश्य् *pashy;* from *yam*, "to restrain," *yachchh;* from *gup*, "to protect"; *gopāy*.

Fourth Conjugation.

89. If a root be of the 4th conjugation, no Guna takes place, but the base is formed by the simple addition of *y* to the root. Thus, from सिध् *sidh*, "to succeed," is formed the base *sidhy* (*sidhyāmi*, &c.); from नृत् *nṛit*, "to dance," the base *nṛity*.

a. The following are anomalous changes. From जॄ, "to grow old," is formed the base, *jīry;* from *div*, "to sport," *dīvy;* from *kram*, "to go," *krāmy;* from *bhram*, "to whirl," *bhrāmy;* from भ्रंश् *bhransh*, "to fall," भ्रश्य *bhrashy;* from *jan*, ātm. "to be born," *jāy;* from *vyadh*, par. "to pierce," *vidhy*. See the remarks, p. 62.†.

Sixth Conjugation.

90. If a root be of the 6th conjugation, the general rule is, that no change at all takes place, and that the root stands also for the base. Thus, the root *kship*, "to throw," is also the base (*kshipāmi*, &c.). So also दिश् *dish*, "to point out" (*dishāmi*, &c.).*

a. Some roots, however, take a change peculiar to themselves; as, from इष् *ish*, "to wish," the base इच्छ्; from प्रच्छ्, "to ask," पृच्छ्; and a final *u* or *ū* is changed to *uv*, and *ṛi* to *riy;* and *ṛī* to *ir*. As, from *dhū*, "to shake," *dhuv;* from मृ *mṛi*, ātm. "to die," *mriy* (म्रिये, &c.); from धृ *dhṛi*, ātm. "to exist," *dhriy;* from कॄ *kṛī*, "to scatter," *kir* (*kirāmi*, &c.).

b. Some insert a nasal; as, from *much*, "to let go," the base *muṅch* (मुञ्चामि, &c.); from *lip*, "to anoint," *limp;* from *sich*, "to sprinkle," *siṅch;* from कृत्, "to cut," कृन्त्.

Having thus explained the formation of the base in the conjugational tenses of the regular primitive, it will be necessary to exhibit the irregularities presented in these same tenses by about

---

* Roots ending in consonants in the 6th conj. generally contain either *i*, *u*, or *ṛi;* and these vowels would have taken Guna had the root fallen under the 1st.

fifty common roots belonging to the 2d, 3d, 5th, 7th, 8th, and 9th conjugations, before we proceed to the remaining six tenses of the verb, the rules for the formation of which are common to all.

The student, however, who wishes for a continuous survey of all the tenses of the verb will pass over the next section, and proceed at once to Sect. III.

Sect. II.—CERTAIN IRREGULAR PRIMITIVES, OR VERBS OF THE 2d, 3d, 5th, 7th, 8th, AND 9th CONJUGATIONS.

TERMINATIONS OF THE CONJUGATIONAL TENSES.*

PARASMAIPADA.			ATMANEPADA.		
			Present Tense.		
mi P	*vah*	*mah*	*e*	*vahe*	*mahe*
si or *ṣhi* P	*thah*	*tha*	*se* or *ṣhe*	*āthe*	*dhwe*
ti P	*tah*	*anti* or *ati*	*te*	*āte*	*ate*
			First Preterite.		
am P	*va*	*ma*	*i*	*vahi*	*mahi*
h P	*tam*	*ta*	*thāh*	*āthām*	*dhwam*
t P	*tām*	*an* or *uh*	*ta*	*ātām*	*ata*
			Potential.		
yām	*yāva*	*yāma*	*īya*	*īvahi*	*īmahi*
yāh	*yātam*	*yāta*	*īthāh*	*īyāthām*	*īdhwam*
yāt	*yātām*	*yuh*	*īta*	*īyātām*	*īran*
			Imperative.		
āni P	*āva* P	*āma* P	*ai* P	*āvahai* P	*āmahai* P
hi or *dhi*	*tam*	*ta*	*swa* or *ṣhwa*	*āthām*	*dhwam*
tu P	*tām*	*antu* or *atu*	*tām*	*ātām*	*atām*

Obs. The terminations read downwards; thus, *mi* is the 1st pers. sing., *si* the 2d sing., *ti* the 3d. The mark P placed after certain terminations indicates that certain peculiar changes, to be afterwards explained, take place in the root before these terminations.

* This *irregular* scheme of terminations corresponds to the technical scheme given by native Grammarians, as applicable to all verbs. Let the reader compare this

FORMATION OF THE BASE OF THE CONJUGATIONAL TENSES.

These irregular primitives cause the chief difficulty of Sanscrit conjugation; for they not only present an ever-varying form of base throughout the different persons of each tense, but also require a scheme of terminations which differs, in many important points from the regular scheme, and more especially in this, that the terminations begin generally with *consonants* instead of vowels.

In this last respect the above scheme resembles that of the first and second future, p. 73, and all the other non-conjugational tenses, p. 81. Hence the combination of the final consonants of a base with the initial *s* or *t* of these terminations, and of those of the non-conjugational tenses, requires an acquaintance with the following rules.

Combination of final ch *and* j, *with* t, th, *and* s.

91. Final *ch* and *j*, before *t*, *th*, and *s*, are changed to *k*, the *k* blending with *s* into क्ष *ksh* (r. 30. note): thus, *vach* with *ti*, *vakti*; with *thah*, *vakthah*; with *si*, *vakshi*: *moch* with *syāmi*, *mokshyāmi*; *much* with *ta*, *mukta*: *tyaj* with *ta*, *tyakta*; with *syāmi*, *tyakshyāmi*. But a final palatal is, in a few cases, changed to ष् *ṣh* before *t*, *th*; and *t*, *th* then become ट्, ठ्: thus, *mārj* with *ti*, मार्ष्टि; मृज् with *thah*, मृष्ठः; सृज् with *ta*, सृष्ट; प्रच्छ् with *tā*, प्रष्टा.

Combination of final dh *and* bh, *with* t, th, *and* s.

a. Final ध् *dh* and भ् *bh*, before *t* and *th*, are changed, the one to *d*, the other to *b*, and both *t* and *th* then become *dh*. Thus,

---

this with the *regular* scheme at p. 63, and observe how essentially they differ. Let him also bear in mind that the total number of verbs, primitive and derivative (exclusive of Intensives and innumerable Nominals), that follow the regular scheme, would amount to about eight thousand, whilst the total number that follow this irregular scheme would hardly exceed two hundred; he will then understand that if any general scheme is to be propounded at all, it should rather be that at p. 63. This is another proof that native Grammarians are altogether wanting in clear logical arrangement of their subject.

rundh with *tah* or *thah* becomes equally *runddhah* (रुन्द्धः); *labh* with *tāhe*, *labdhāhe* (लब्धाहे).

b. Final *dh* and *bh*, before *s*, are changed (by r. 13.), the one to *t* the other to *p*. Thus, *ruṇadh* with *si* becomes *ruṇatsi; sedh* with *syāmi*, *setsyāmi; labh* with *sye*, *lapsye*. And if the initial of the root be *d* or *b*, the aspirate, which has been rejected in the final, is thrown back on the initial; as, *bodh* with *sye*, *bhotsye*.*

Combination of final श् sh, ष् ṣh, स् s, *with* t, th, s, dh.

c. Final श् *sh*, before *t* and *th*, is changed to ष् *ṣh;* and the *t*, *th*, take the cerebral form ट्, ठ्: thus, ईश् with *te*, ईष्टे; and रेश् with *thāh*, रेष्ठाः.

d. Similarly, final ष् *ṣh*, before *t* and *th*, requires the change of *t*, *th*, to ट् ठ्. Thus, द्वेष् with *ti*, द्वेष्टि; and द्विष् with *thah*, द्विष्ठः.

e. Final श् *sh* or ष् *ṣh*, before *s*, are changed to *k*, the *s* then becoming *ṣh* (r. 30. note): thus, वश् with *si*, वक्षि; द्वेष् with *si*, द्वेक्षि; दृश् with *syāmi*, द्रक्ष्यामि.

f. Final श् or ष्, before the termination *dhi* of the imperat., are changed to ड् *ḍ*, the *dhi* becoming ढि *ḍhi*. Thus, द्विष् with *dhi*, द्विड्ढि. Similarly with *dhwam*, द्विड्ढ्वं.

g. Final स् *s*, before the termination *dhi* of the imperat., is either dropped, or changed to *d*. Thus, *chakās* with *dhi*, either *chakādhi* or *chakāddhi;* शास् with *dhi*, शाधि; हिंस् with *dhi*, हिंद्धि.

Combination of final ह् h *with* t, th, *and* s.

h. Final ह् *h*, before *t* and *th*, is changed to *g*, and both *t* and *th* then become ध् *dh*. Thus, *duh* (दुह्) with *tah* or *thah* becomes equally *dugdhah; dah* (दह्) with *tāsmi*, *dagdhāsmi*. But if the root begin with any other letter but *d* or *n*, then its final ह् coalesces with the *t* or *th* of the termination into ढ् *ḍh;* and the radical vowel, if short, is lengthened: as, मुह् with *ta*, मूढ; रुह् with *ta*, रूढ; *leh* (लेह्) with *ti*, *leḍhi* (लेढि); and रोह् with *tāsmi*, रोढास्मि. Similarly the final of दुह्, before the termination *dhi* of the imperat.,

* There is a very remarkable parallel to this in the Greek τρεφω, making in the future θρεψω, noticed by Prof. Bopp.

becomes *dugdhi* (दुग्धि); and the final of लिह् blends with the same termination into *ḍh* (लीढि).

i. Final ह् *h* before *s*, follows the analogy of final श् and ष्, and is changed to *k*, which blends with *s* into क्ष् *ksh*. Thus, *leh* with *si* becomes *lekshi;* रोह् with *syāmi*, रोक्ष्यामि. And if the initial of the root be *d* or *g*, the aspirate which has been changed to *k* is thrown back on the initial. Thus, *doh* (दोह्) with *si*, *dhokshi;* दह् with *syāmi*, धक्ष्यामि; अगुह् with *sam*, अघुक्षं.

Second Conjugation.

92. If the root be of the 2d conjugation, the base is formed by substituting the Guna vowel for the vowel of the root, before those terminations only that are marked with P: before all the other terminations the original vowel of the root is retained.* Thus, from *vid*, "to know," is formed the base of the singular present, *ved* (*vedmi*, &c.), the base of the dual and plur. *vid* (*vidwah*, &c.): from *dwiṣh*, "to hate," the bases *dweṣh* and *dwiṣh*†: from *i*, "to go," the bases *e* and *i* (1st sing. *emi*, cf. εἶμι; 1st pl. *imah*, cf. ἴμεν): from जागृ, "to awake," *jāgar* and *jāgṛi* (3d sing. du. pl. *jāgarti*, *jāgṛitah*, *jāgrati*,‡ r. 7.).

a. Those roots of this and the 3d and 7th conj. whose bases end in consonants reject the terminations of the 2d and 3d pers. sing. 1st pret. (excepting *ad*, "to eat," which inserts *a* before *h* and *t*). But the final of the base is changed analogously to crudes of the 8th class in the nom. case (see p. 27. r. 45.). Thus, sing. *avedam*, *avet*, *avet*. *Adweṣham*, *adweṭ* (अद्वेट्), &c. They also take *dhi* for *hi* in the imperative.§

---

* Bopp has noticed a corresponding lengthening of the vowel of the root before certain terminations in Greek. Cf. δίδωμι, δίδομεν, εἶμι, ἴμεν.

† The other forms of the base of *dwiṣh* are seen in r. 91. *e. f.*

‡ Roots of more than one syllable, and *jaksh*, "to eat," and *shās*, "to rule," and all roots of the 3d conjugation, necessarily reject the nasal of the 3d plur., of the pres., and imp. paras., and take *uh* for *an* in the 3d plur. 1st pret. Some other roots in the 2d conj. optionally take *uh* for *an*; as, *vid*, *dwiṣh*, *pā*, *yā*.

§ *Dhi* was originally the *only* form. Hence in the Vedas श्रुधि (κλῦθι).

b. Roots like *ad*, "to eat"; *pā*, "to protect"; *yā*, "to go," having no Guna substitute, do not change at all (*admi, &c.; pāmi, &c.; yāmi, &c.*). But *daridrā*, par. "to be poor," makes its base *daridri* before the consonantal terminations not marked with **P**, and *daridr* before *ati, uh, atu* (3d pers. sing. dual, plur. *daridrāti, daridritah, daridrati*), see note marked ‡, p. 69.

c. The root *stu*, "to praise," and some others in *u*, take Vriddhi before the consonantal **P** terminations,* changing *u* to *uv* before the vowel terminations. Hence, the three bases, *stau, stu, stuv* (*stauti, stutah, stuvanti*). Similarly, *sū*, ātm. "to bring forth," makes *suv* before the vowel terminations (*sūte, suvāte, suvate*); ब्रू *brū*, "to speak," makes *bravī* before the consonantal **P** terminations, and *bruv* before the vowel terminations. Hence, in the par., the three bases, *bravī, brū, bruv* (*bravīti, brūtah, bruvanti*); and in the ātm. the two bases *brū, bruv* (*brūte, bruvāte, bruvate*).

d. Rud, "to weep," besides the usual Guna change, adds *i* to the root before all the consonantal terminations except *y*. Hence the three bases *rodi, rudi, rud* (*roditi, ruditah, rudanti*). Similarly, but without Guna, the roots *swap*, "to sleep," *shwas* and *an*, "to breathe," *jaksh*, "to eat." *Han*, "to kill," makes its base *ha* before *t* or *th*; *ghn* before *anti, an, antu*; and *ja* before *hi* (*hanti, hatah, ghnanti*; 2d pers. imp. *jahi*).

e. शास्, "to rule," makes its base शिष् before *t, th* (which then become *ṭ, ṭh*) and *y*, and changes its final to *t* in the 2d and 3d sing. 1st pret. (*ashāt*).

f. अस् *as*, "to be," rejects its initial *a*, except in the 1st pret., and except before the **P** terminations of the other tenses.

दुह्, "to milk," and लिह्, "to lick," form their bases as seen at r. 91. *h, i*.

Third Conjugation.

93. If a root be of the 3d conjugation, the base is formed by the reduplication of the initial consonant and vowel of the root, *a* being the reduplicated vowel for *ā*, *i* for *ī* or *ṛi*, and *u* for *ū*; and in the reduplication of the consonant, an unaspirated letter being substituted for an aspirated, and *j* for *h*. Besides the reduplication of the root, the *radical syllable* is subjected to the Guna change, but only before the **P** terminations, as in the 2d conj.

* By "the consonantal **P** terminations" is meant those terminations marked with **P** which begin with consonants.

Thus, from भृ *bhṛi*, "to bear," are formed the two bases *bibhar* and *bibhṛi* (3d sing. du. pl. *bibharti*, *bibhṛitah*, *bibhrati*, r. 7.); from *hu*, "to sacrifice," the two bases *juho* and *juhu* (*juhoti*, *juhutah*, *juhwati*, r. 7.); from *bhī*, "to fear," *bibhe* and *bibhī* (*bibheti*, *bibhītah*, *bibhyati*). The 3d conj. is the only one which *invariably* drops the nasal in the 3d pl. of the pres. and imp. par., and takes *uh* for *an* in the 3d pl. of the 1st pret. Before this *uh* Guna is required.

a. दा, "to give," in the par. drops the *ā* before all except the P terminations, making its base *dad*, changeable to *dat* (*dadāti*, *dattah*, *dadati*), and *de* before the *hi* of the imperat. Similarly, धा, "to place," makes its base *dadh* before *v*, *m*, *y*, or a vowel, and *dhe* before *hi*; but *dhat* before *t*, *th*, or *s* (*dadhāti*, *dhattah*, *dadhati*).

Fifth Conjugation.

94. If a root be of the 5th conjugation, the base is formed by adding *nu* to the root, which is converted to the Guna *no* before the P terminations. Thus, from *chi*, "to gather," are formed the two bases *chino* and *chinu** (*chinoti*, *chinutah*, *chinwanti*, r. 7.) In roots ending in vowels, the *u* of *nu* may be dropped before *v* and *m*. The roots *āp*, "to obtain"; शक्, "to be able"; तृप्, "to satisfy"; and ऋध्, "to increase"; ending in consonants, add *nuv* instead of *nu* before the vowel terminations (*shaknoti*, *shaknutah*, *shaknuvanti*). श्रु *shru*, "to hear" (sometimes placed under the 1st conj.), substitutes शृ *shṛi* for the root (शृणोति, r. 21., शृणुतः शृण्वन्ति).

Roots ending in vowels reject the termination *hi* of the imperative: as, *shṛinu*, "do thou hear"; but *āpnuhi*, "do thou obtain."

Seventh Conjugation.

95. If a root be of the 7th conjugation, the base is formed by inserting *na* between the vowel and final consonant† of the root, before

---

* This change of *nu* to *no* is supplied in the corresponding Greek affix νυ, by lengthening the υ, as in ζεύγνῡμι, ζεύγνυμεν; δείκνυμι, δείκνυμεν. Bopp.

† All the roots in this conjugation end in consonants.

the P terminations, and *n* before all the other terminations.* Thus, from *bhid*, "to divide," are formed the two bases *bhinad* and *bhind*, changeable to *bhint* (*bhinatti*, *bhinttah*,† *bhindanti*); from *rudh*, "to restrain," *ruṇadh* and *rundh*, changeable to *rund* (*ruṇaddhi*, *runddhah*, r. 91. *a.*, *rundhanti*); from *hins*, "to injure," *hinas* and *hins*; from *bhuj*, "to eat," *bhunaj*, changeable to *bhunak*, and *bhuñj*, changeable to *bhuṅk* (r. 91.). Similarly *yuj*, "to join."

Bhañj, "to break," rejects its nasal before *na* is inserted. Hence the bases *bhanaj* and *bhañj* (*bhanakti*, *bhaṅ·ktah*, *bhañjanti*).

Eighth Conjugation.

96. The base in this conjugation is formed by the addition of *u* to the root, converted to the Guna *o* before the P terminations. There are only ten roots in this conjugation, nine of which are not in common use. Moreover, these nine all end in *n*, and therefore the addition of *o* and *u* will have the same effect as the addition of *no* and *nu* in the 5th conjugation. Thus, *tano* and *tanu*, from *tan*, "to extend" (1st sing. pl. *tanomi*, *tanumah*, cf. τάνυμι, τάνυμες). But the tenth root in this class is कृ *kṛi*, "to do," by far the most common and useful root in the language. This root not only converts the conjugational affix *u* to the Guna *o* before the P terminations, but also changes the radical vowel *ṛi* to the Guna *ar* before these same terminations, and before the other terminations to *ur* (*karoti*, *kurutah*, *kurvanti*), and rejects the conjugational *u* before *v*, *m*, *y* (1st plur. *kurmah*).

Ninth Conjugation.

97. If a root be of the 9th conjugation, the base is formed by

---

* Similarly, *n* is inserted in certain Greek and Latin roots; as, μαθ, μανθανω; λαβ, λαμβανω; θιγ, θιγγανω; *scid*, *scindo*; *fid*, *findo*; *tag*, *tango*; *liq*, *linquo*, *&c.*

† The final *t* of the base may be dropped, *bhintah*; so, also, *rundhah* for *runddhah*.

adding *nū* to the root before the P terminations, and *nī* before all the others, excepting those beginning with vowels, where only *n* is added. Thus, from *pū*, "to purify," are formed the three bases *punā*, *punī*, and *pun* (*punāti*, *punītah*, *punanti*). This root, with some others ending in long vowels (as, *dhū*, "to shake"; *lū*, "to cut"; स्तॄ, "to spread"), shortens its vowel in forming the base. ग्रह्, "to take," makes its bases गृह्णा, गृह्णी, गृह्ण् (r. 21.*); and ज्ञा, "to know"; जाना, जानी, जान् (*jānāti*, *jānītah*, *jānanti*).

Roots ending in consonants substitute *āna* for *nīhi*, the proper termination of the 2d pers. of the imperat. As, गृहाण, "take thou"; and अशान, "eat thou," from अश्, "to eat."

SECT. III.—PRIMITIVE VERBS OF ALL CONJUGATIONS IN THE NON-CONJUGATIONAL TENSES.

TERMINATIONS OF THE NON-CONJUGATIONAL TENSES.

PARASMAIPADA.			ATMANEPADA.		
		Second Preterite.			
a	**iva*	**ima*	*e*	**ivahe*	**imahe*
itha or *tha*	*athuh*	*a*	**iṣhe*	*āthe*	**idhwe*
a	*atuh*	*uh*	*e*	*āte*	*ire*

* The roots श्रु, स्तु, द्रु, स्रु, कृ, भृ, सृ, वृ reject the initial *i* from these terminations.

		First Future.			
tāsmi	*tāswah*	*tāsmah*	*tāhe*	*tāswahe*	*tāsmahe*
tāsi	*tāsthah*	*tāstha*	*tāse*	*tāsāthe*	*tādhwe*
tā	*tārau*	*tārah*	*tā*	*tārau*	*tārah*

		Second Future.			
syāmi	*syāvah*	*syāmah*	*sye*	*syāvahe*	*syāmahe*
syasi	*syathah*	*syatha*	*syase*	*syethe*	*syadhwe*
syati	*syatah*	*syanti*	*syate*	*syete*	*syante*

Observe, that by reason of r. 30. (with note), the most frequent form of the terminations of the second future is *ṣhyāmi*, &c.

* The letter ह although compounded with the nasal does not prevent the opera- tion

FORMATION OF THE BASE OF THE NON-CONJUGATIONAL TENSES.

Second Preterite.

98. The first step in the formation of the base of this tense is the reduplication of the initial consonant of the root with its vowel, or of the initial vowel: thus, from *budh*, "to know," *bubudh*; and if the root end in a consonant, the radical vowel takes Guna before the terminations of the sing. par., but before all the other terminations reverts to its original form; hence, the two bases *bubodh*, *bubudh* (*bubodha*, *bubodhitha*, *bubodha*, dual *bubudhiva*, *bubudhathuh*, &c., ātm. *bubudhe*, &c.): if in a vowel, this vowel takes Vṛiddhi in the 1st* and 3d sing. par., and Guna in the 2d, and before all the other terminations, both par. and ātm., reverts to its original form: thus, from *nī*, "to lead," the bases *ninai*, *nine*, *ninī* (*nināya*, r. 8., *ninayitha* r. 10. or *ninetha*, *nināya*, *ninyiva*,† *ninyathuh*, &c., ātm. *ninye*, &c.); so also from *kṛi*, the bases *chakār*, *chakar*, *chakṛi*, (*chakāra*, *chakartha*, dual *chakṛiva*); and from *dhū*, the bases *dudhau*, *dudho*, but in dual, plur. &c. *dudhuv*‡ (*dudhāva*, r. 8., *dudhavitha* r. 10. or *dudhotha*, *dudhāva*, *dudhuviva*, &c., ātm. *dudhuve*, &c.). *Bhū*, "to be," is anomalous, making its base *babhūv* beṣfore all the terminations.

Observe, that all the terminations of this tense begin with vowels. It is indicated, however, in the scheme, that an initial *i* is sometimes rejected in the 2d pers. sing. This *i* may be optionally rejected in those roots only in which (as we shall afterwards see)

---

tion of r. 21., and according to the same rule, *krī*, "to buy," 9th conj., makes its bases *krīṇā*, *krīṇī*, *krīṇ* (क्रीणाति, क्रीणीतः, क्रीणन्ति).

* All Grammarians assert that there is an optional change to Guna in the 1st pers., but this is never found.

† By a special rule, the *ī* of the base is here changed to the semi-vowel instead of following r. 4. But roots ending in *i* or *ī*, of which the initial consonant is *double*, change *i* or *ī* to *iy* before these same vowel terminations, that is, before all excepting the sing. par.: hence, from श्रि come the three bases *shishrai*, *shishre*, and *shishriy*.

‡ *All roots* ending in *u* or *ū* change *u* or *ū* to *uv* before these vowel terminations; excepting, of course, the roots श्रु, स्तु, द्रु, स्रु, in the persons marked with *.

it is necessarily rejected in the futures.* In the other persons the *i* marked with * is retained in every root in the language, except eight, viz. कृ, "to do"; भृ, "to bear"; श्रु, "to hear"; स्तु, "to praise," सृ, "to go," &c., all ending in vowels. Hence it happens that consonants can never come into coalition, except in the 2d pers. sing. of this tense. Its formation, therefore, is not attended with any difficulties of consonantal combination. There are certain rules, however, to be acquired, relative to the reduplication of an initial consonant with its vowel, and an initial vowel. With regard to the vowel belonging to the initial consonant, *a* is reduplicated for *a, ā, ṛi*, or *ṛī*; *i* for *i, ī*, or *e*; *u* for *u, ū*, or *o*: as, from *dā, dadau*; from *ṭri, tatāra*; from *sev, sisheva*; from *pū, pupāva*.

99. *Rules for the Reduplication of an Initial Consonant.*

a. If a root begin with an aspirated consonant, its corresponding unaspirated form is reduplicated; as, from *bhid, bibheda* (बिभेद).†

b. If with *k* or *kh*, the reduplicated letter is *ch*: as, from *kṛi, chakāra* (चकार); from *khan, chakhāna* (चखान).

c. If with *g, gh*, or *h*, the reduplicated letter is *j*: as, from *gam, jagāma*; from *ghrā, jaghrau* (जघ्रौ); from *hṛi, jahāra* (जहार).

d. If with a double consonant, the first only is reduplicated: as, from *tyaj, tatyāja* (तत्याज); from *kship, chikshepa* (चिक्षेप).

e. If with a double consonant, whose first is a sibilant and the second a hard consonant, the second only is reduplicated: as, from *spṛish, pasparsha* (पस्पर्श); from *skand, chaskanda* (चस्कन्द).

Reduplication of an Initial Vowel.

f. If a root ending in a single consonant begin with *a, i*, or *u*, these vowels are repeated, and the two similar vowels blend into one long one. Thus, *āsa* from *a* and *as*, "to be"; *āpa* from *a* and *āp*, r. 4.; the dual *īshatuh* from *i* and *iṣh*; *ūkhatuh* from *u* and *ukh*: but in the sing. of the last two cases, the radical *i* or *u* taking

* Thus, *pach*, "to cook," forbids *i* in the future; therefore the 2d sing. is either *papaktha* or *pechitha*. So also *nī*, "to lead," *ninayitha* or *ninetha*, as above.

† So in the Greek, τέθαπται from θαπτω; πεφίληκα from φιλεω.

‡ Grammarians assert that the short *a* is optionally retained in the first person.

Guna, the reduplicated *i* becomes *iy* before *e* (*iyesha*), and *uv* before *o* (*uvokha*). If a root ending in a *double* consonant begin with *a*, or, ending in a single consonant, begin with *ṛi*, the reduplicated syllable is *ān:* thus, आनर्च, 3d sing. of अर्च; *ānardha*, of *ṛidh*. The root इ *i* is in the sing. *iyāya*, *iyayitha*, *&c.*, dual *īyiva*, *&c.*

Anomalous Modes of forming the Second Preterite.

There are many anomalous ways of forming the base of the 2d pret.

a. Roots ending in *ā* (as, *dā*, "to give"; *sthā*, "to stand"; *yā*, "to go," &c.) drop the *ā* before all the terminations, except *tha*, and substitute *au* for that of the 1st and 3d sing. par. Hence, the bases *dad*, *tasth*, *yay* (ददौ *dadau*, तस्थौ *tasthau*, ययौ *yayau;* dual, *dadiva*, *tasthiva*, *yayiva*). Similarly roots in *ai*, as *gai* (*jagau*).

b. Roots ending in the vowel *ṛi*, in accordance with r. 98, change *ṛi* to *ār* in the 1st and 3d sing., and to *ar* in the 2d sing., and before the other terminations *retain* the vowel *ṛi* changeable to *r*; but roots in which *ṛi* is preceded by a *double* consonant, and most roots in long *ṛī*, instead of retaining this vowel, change it to *ar* in the dual and plur. par., and consequently throughout the ātm. Thus, from *smṛi*, sing. *sasmāra*, *sasmaritha*, *sasmāra*, dual *sasmariva*, &c.; ātm. *sasmare*, *&c.*

c. Roots beginning with any consonant, and ending with a single consonant, and inclosing a short *a*, lengthen the *a* in the 1st and 3d sing.: as, from *pach*, "to cook," *papāch;* from *tyaj*, "to quit," *tatyāj* (*tatyāja*, *tatyajitha*, *tatyāja*, *tatyajiva*, *&c.*). Moreover, before *itha* and in the dual and plur. par., and all the persons of the ātm., if the initial as well as the final consonant of the root be single, the *a* is changed to *e*, and, to compensate for this, the reduplication suppressed. Thus, from *pach* come the two bases *papāch* and *pech* (*papācha*, *pechitha* or *papaktha*, *papācha*, *pechiva;* ātm. *peche*, *&c.*); from *labh*, ātm. "to obtain" (cf. λαμβανω, ἐλαβον), the base *lebh* throughout (*lebhe*, *lebhishe*, *lebhe*, *lebhivahe*, *&c.*).*

d. Roots of this last kind, that require a substituted consonant in the reduplication, are excepted from the rule (but not *bhaj* and *phal*). So, also, certain roots beginning with *v* are excepted. These require that the reduplicated syllable be *u*, or the corresponding vowel of the semi-vowel, and change *va* of the root to *u* before every termination, except those of the sing. par., the two *u*'s then blending into one long one. Thus, from *vach*, "to speak," come the two bases *uvāch* and *ūch* (*uvācha*, *ūchatuh*, *ūchuh*). A similar rule is applied in *yaj*, "to sacrifice" (*iyāja*, *ījatuh*, *ījuh*).

---

* The roots *trap*, and *grath*, and *shrath*, and तॄ, "to pass" (*tatāra*, *teratuh*, *teruh*, as if the root were *tar*), and *bhram*, *swan*, *rāj*, *rādh*, *bhrāj* (*bhreje*, *bhrejāte*, *bhrejire*), *bhrāsh*, and *vam* may follow this rule, although not answering the above conditions.

e. Gam, "to go"; *han*, "to kill" (which forms its 2d pret. as if the root were *ghan*); *jan*, "to be born"; and *khan*, "to dig"; drop the medial *a* before all the terminations except those of the sing. par. Hence, from *gam* come the two bases *jagām*, *jagm* (*jagāma*, *jagmatuh*, *jagmuh*).

f. ग्रह्, "to siege," and प्रच्छ्, "to ask," make their bases जग्राह् and जगृह्, पप्रच्छ् and पपृच्छ् (जग्राह, जगृहतुः, जगृहुः); स्वप्, "to sleep," makes सुष्वाप् and सुषुप्; ह्वे, "to call," forms its base like roots in *u* (*juhāva*, *juhuvatuh*, *juhuvuh*); जि, "to conquer," forms its base as if from *gi* (*jigāya*, *jigyatuh*, &c.).

g. Roots which begin with a vowel, long by nature or position,* and all roots of more than one syllable, form their bases by adding *ām* to the root, and affixing the 2d pret. of some one of the auxiliaries, *as*, "to be"; *bhū*, "to become"; कृ *kri*, "to do." Thus, from ईश् comes the base ईशां (ईशामास, or ईशाम्बभूव, or ईशाञ्चकार).

100. *The First and Second Future.*

The first future (as noticed by Bopp) results from the union of the nom. case of the noun of agency (formed with the affix तृ *tri*, r. 41.) with the present tense of the verb, *as*, "to be." Thus, taking *dātri*, "a giver" (declined p. 37.), and combining its nom. case with *asmi* and *he*, we have *dātāsmi* and *dātāhe*, "I am a giver," identical with the 1st pers. sing. par. and ātm. of the 1st fut., "I will give." So also *dātāsi* and *dātāse*, "thou art a giver," or "thou wilt give." In the 1st and 2d persons dual and plur. the sing. of the noun is joined with the dual and plur. of the auxiliary. In the 3d person the auxiliary is omitted, and the 3d pers. sing. dual and plur. of the 1st future in both voices is then identical with the nom. case sing. dual and plur. of the noun of agency. Thus, *dātā*, "a giver," or "he will give"; *dātārau*, "two givers," or "they two will give," &c.†

The second future, in its terminations, stands in close relationship with the present tense, the only difference being that *sy* is prefixed.

---

* Except *āp*, "to obtain," and roots having an initial *a* before two consonants.

† The future signification inherent in the noun of agency *dātā*, seems implied in Latin by the relation of *dator* to *daturus*.

The invariable rule for the formation of the base of both future tenses is, that the Guna be substituted for the vowel of the root*: thus, from *jī*, "to conquer," the base *je* (*jetāsmi, jeṣhyāmi*); from *shru*, "to hear," the base *shro* (श्रोतास्मि, श्रोष्यामि). And the general rule, moreover, is, that if the root end in a *consonant*, the vowel *i* be inserted between the base and terminations. Thus, from *budh* comes the base *bodhi* (बोधितास्मि *bodhitāsmi*, &c.; बोधिष्यामि *bodhiṣhyāmi*, &c.). This insertion of *i*, the manifest object of which is to prevent the coalition of consonants, is unfortunately, however, forbidden in about one hundred roots, some of which are of very common occurrence; and the combination of the radical consonant with the initial *t* and *s* of the terminations, will require an acquaintance with the rules already laid down at p. 67. When these rules are acquired, there will be no difficulty in the formation of these tenses. The only question is, how are we to distinguish between those roots which insert *i*, and those which do not?

The laws about to be laid down will determine this point, and it is of the utmost importance that the attention of the student be directed towards them, as the assumption or rejection of this inserted vowel is not confined to the two futures, but extends to many other parts of the verb; insomuch, that if the first future reject *i*, it is, as a necessary consequence, rejected in the third preterite, the ātm. of the benedictive, the conditional, the infinitive mood, the passive past participle, the indeclinable past participle, the future participle formed with the affix *tavya*, and the noun of agency formed with the affix *tṛi*; and is, moreover, optionally rejected in the 2d pers. sing. of the 2d pret., and decides the formation of the desiderative form of the root by *s* instead of *iṣh*. So that the learner, if he know the first future, will pass on with great ease to the formation of these other parts of the verb, and should always look to this tense as his guide. For example, taking the root *kship*, "to throw," and finding the 1st fut. to be *kshептāsmi*, he knows that *i* is rejected. Therefore he knows the

---

* Unless such substitution be forbidden according to r. 38. *a*.

2d future to be *kshepsyāmi;* the 3d pret. to be *akshaipsam;* the ātm. of the benedictive, *kshipsīya;* the conditional, *akshepsyam;* the infinitive, *ksheptum;* the passive past participle, *kshipta;* the indeclinable part. *ksheptwā;* the future part. *ksheptavya;* the noun of agency, *ksheptṛi;* the 2d pers. sing. of the 2d pret. optionally *chikshepṭha;* the desiderative, *chikshipsāmi.* On the other hand, taking the root *yāch,* "to ask," and finding the 1st future to be *yāchitā,* he knows that *i* is inserted, and therefore the same parts of the verb will be *yāchiṣhyāmi, ayāchiṣham, yāchiṣhīya, ayāchiṣhyam, yāchitum, yāchita, yāchitwā, yāchitavya, yāchitṛi, yayāchitha, yayāchiṣhāmi,* respectively.

It is evident that roots ending in vowels do not require *i,* and it may be taken as a general rule that they do not insert it: there are only a few exceptions, as follows:

101. *Roots ending in Vowels,* inserting i *in the Primitive.*

Obs. In the following lists the 3d pers. sing. of the 1st and 2d future is given after each root.

a. Roots ending in *ū;* as, *bhū,* "to be" (*bhavitā, bhaviṣhyati*).

b. Roots ending in *ṛī;* as, तॄ *tṛī,* "to pass" (*taritā, tariṣhyati*): and in these, inserted *i* is optionally lengthened (*tarītā, tarīṣhyati*).

c. Roots ending in *ṛi* short insert *i* in the 2d future, although rejecting it in the first; as, कृ (*kariṣhyāmi*), हृ (*hariṣhyāmi*).

Roots ending in Consonants, inserting i *in the Primitive.*

d. All roots, without exception, ending in *kh, g, gh, ṭ, ṭh, ḍ, ṇ, t, th, b, y, r, l, v,* insert *i;* in *k* there is one exception; in *ch,* four; in *chh,* one; in *j,* ten common exceptions; in *d,* eight; in *dh,* eleven; in *n,* two; in *p,* twelve; in *bh,* three; in *m,* five; in श् *sh,* seven; in ष् *ṣh,* nine; in *s,* one; in ह् *h,* twelve.

Roots ending in Vowels, rejecting i *in the Primitive.*

e. All roots in *ā* reject *i;* as, *dā* (*dātā, dāsyati*): all common roots in *i* and *ī;* as, *je* (*jetā, jeṣhyati*).

f. All common roots in *u;* as, *shru* (*shrotā, shroṣhyati*): all in *ṛi* reject *i* in the 1st future; as, हृ *hṛi* (*hartā, hariṣhyati*).

102. *Roots ending in Consonants,* rejecting i *in the Primitive.*

Of roots ending in **K**, शक् (*shaktā, shakshyati*, r. 91.). In **CH**, *pach* (*paktā, pakshyati*), so *vach*; *sich* (*sektā, sekshyati*), *much* (*moktā, mokshyati*). In **CHH**; प्रच्छ् (*prashṭā*, r. 91., *prakshyati*). In **J**, *tyaj* (*tyaktā, tyakshyati*), so *bhaj*; *yaj* (*yashṭā*, r. 91., *yakshyati*); रञ्ज् (रङ्क्ता, रंक्ष्यति), so also *bhañj, sañj*; *yuj* (*yoktā, yokshyati*), so *bhuj*; सृज् *srij** (स्रष्टा, स्रक्ष्यति); मृज् (*mārshṭā*,† *mārkshyati*). In **D**, *ad* (*attā, atsyati*), so *pad, sad*; *bhid* (*bhettā, bhetsyati*), so *chhid, khid*; *tud* (*tottā, totsyati*), so *nud*. In **DH**, *bandh* (*banddhā*, r. 91. *a.*, *bhantsyati*, r. 91. *b.*), *vyadh* (*vyaddhā, vyatsyati*), *sādh* (*sāddhā, sātsyati*), so *rādh*; *sidh* (*seddhā, setsyati*), *budh*,† 4th conj. (*boddhā, bhotsyate*, r. 91. *b.*); *yudh* (*yoddhā, yotsyate*); so *rudh, krudh, kshudh, shudh*. In **N**, *man*† (*mantā, mansyate*), *han* (*hantā*, but *hanishyati*). In **P**, *tap* (*taptā, tapsyati*), so *vap, shap, swap*; *āp* (*āptā, āpsyati*), *kship* (*ksheptā, kshepsyati*), so *lip*; *lup* (*loptā, lopsyati*); सृप् *srip* (*sarptā* or *sraptā*,* *sarpsyati* or *srapsyati*), so *trip*,† *drip*;† *klrip* (*kalptā*,† *kalpsyati*). In **BH**, *labh* (*labdhā*, r. 91, *a.*, *lapsyate*, cf. λήψεται, r. 91. *b.*), so *rabh*; *lubh* (*lobdhā*,† but *lobhishyati*). In **M**, *gam* (*gantā*, but *gamishyati*), *nam* (*nantā, nansyati*), so *yam*; *ram* (*rantā, ransyate*), so *kram*.† In श् **SH**, *dansh* (दंष्टा, दंक्ष्यति), *vish* (वेष्टा, r. 91. *c.*, वेक्ष्यति, r. 91. *e.*), so *dish*; दृश् *drish* (द्रष्टा,* द्रक्ष्यति), so *sprish, mrish*; *krush* (क्रोष्टा, क्रोक्ष्यति). In ष् **SH**, *taksh* (*tashṭā*,† *taksyati*), *ish* (*eshṭā*,† but *eshishyati*), *dwish* (द्वेष्टा, द्वेक्ष्यति), so *shlish, pish*; *dush* (दोष्टा, दोक्ष्यति); so *push, shush, tush*; *krish* (*krashṭā** or *karshṭā*, *krakshyati* or *karkshyati*). In **S**, *vas* (*vastā, vatsyati*). In ह् **H**, *dah* (*dagdhā*, r. 91. *h.*, *dhakshyati*, r. 91. *i.*); *vah* (वोढा, r. 91. *h.*, *a* being changed to *o*, वक्ष्यति), *sah* (सोढा,† but *sahishyate*), *nah* (*naddhā, natsyati*, as if from *nadh*), *gāh* (गाढा,† घाक्ष्यते), *lih* (लेढा, लेक्ष्यति), *dih* (*degdhā, dhekshyati*, r. 91. *i.*), *snih* (*snegdhā*,† *snekshyati*), *ruh* (रोढा, रोक्ष्यति), *muh* (मोढा† or मोग्धा, मोक्ष्यति), *duh* (*dogdhā, dhokshyati*), *druh*† (द्रोढा or द्रोग्धा, ध्रोक्ष्यति), *guh*† (गोढा, घोक्ष्यति).

---

* In certain roots containing the vowel *ri*, the vowel passes into *ra* and *rā*, instead of the Guna *ar* or Vriddhi *ār*. Thus, the 1st future of *srij* is स्रष्टा for सर्ष्टा; and the 3d pret. असाक्षं for असार्क्षं.

† All these roots may optionally take *i* in the futures.

THIRD PRETERITE TENSE.

TERMINATIONS OF THE THIRD PRETERITE.

PARASMAIPADA — FORM I. — ATMANEPADA.

Terminations of Verbs inserting i.

iṣham	*iṣhwa*	*iṣhma*	*iṣhi*	*iṣhwahi*	*iṣhmahi*
īh	*iṣhṭam*	*iṣhṭa*	*iṣhṭhāh*	*iṣhāthām*	*idhwam* or *iḍhwam*
īt	*iṣhṭām*	*iṣhuh*	*iṣhṭa*	*iṣhātām*	*iṣhata*

FORM II.

Terminations of Verbs rejecting i.

sam	*swa*	*sma*	*si*	*swahi*	*smahi*
sīh	*stam* or *tam*	*sta* or *ta*	*sthāh* or *thāh*	*sāthām*	*dhwam* or *ḍhwam*
sīt	*stām* or *tām*	*suh*	*sta* or *ta*	*sātām*	*sata*

OBS. By reason of r. 30. (with note) the initial sibilant almost always takes the cerebral form *ṣh*.

FORM III.

Terminations corresponding to the First Preterite.

am	*āva*	*āma*	*e* or *i*	*āvahi*	*āmahi*
ah	*atam*	*ata*	*athāh*	*ethām* or *āthām*	*adhwam*
at	*atām*	*an*	*ata*	*etām* or *ātām*	*anta*

103. *Formation of the Base of the Third Preterite.*

This complex and "multiform" tense, the most troublesome and intricate in the whole Sanscrit verb, is not so much one tense, as an aggregation of several tenses, all more or less allied to each other, all bearing a manifest resemblance to the first preterite, but none of them exactly assignable to that tense, and none of them so distinct in its character or so universal in its application as to admit of segregation from the general group, under any separate title of its own.

Fortunately for the study of Sanscrit, the third preterite very rarely occurs in the earlier and better specimens of Hindu composition; and the student who contents himself with the Rāmāyaṇa, Mahābhārata, Hitopadesha, and Laws of Manu, and avoids the grammatical Poem of Bhaṭṭi, and the extravagant writings of more modern authors, will lose nothing by an almost total ignorance of this tense, or, at least, may satisfy himself with a very cursory survey of its character and functions.

All the varieties of this tense are reducible to three distinct forms, adapted to the three schemes of terminations given in the table above. The first form is that which belongs to those roots which insert *i* before the terminations of the non-conjugational tenses: the second belongs to those which reject *i*: and the third, which most nearly approximates to the 1st pret., belongs, in the first place, to certain roots, whose bases in the *first* pret. present some important variation from the root; in the second, to certain roots ending in श् *sh*, ष् *ṣh*, or ह् *h*, which have *i*, *u*, or *ṛi* for their radical vowel; and, in the third, to causals, or verbs of the 10th conjugation.

In all the modifications of this tense, the first step in the formation of the base is the prefixing of the augment *a*, a further indication of its community of character with the first preterite. But besides this there are changes of the base peculiar to each form.

Form 1. *Formation of the Base.*

a. In the first form, if a root end in a vowel, the base must be formed in the par. by the Vṛiddhi change, and in the ātm. by the Guna: thus, from *pū*, "to purify," come the two bases *apau* and *apo* (अपाविषं *apāviṣham*, *&c.* r. 8., अपविषि *apaviṣhi*, *&c.*, r. 10.†). Very few roots *ending in vowels* take the inserted *i*, and therefore very few follow this form.

ḅ. If a root end in a single consonant, Guna is required in both par. and ātm. (r. 88. *b.*). Thus, from *budh*, *abodh* (अबोधिषं *abodhiṣham*, *&c.*, अबोधिषि *abodhiṣhi*, *&c.*). Almost all roots ending in consonants, which insert *i*, follow this form.

c. A medial *a* is sometimes lengthened; as, from *vad*, *avād* (*avādiṣham*, *&c.*).

d. A few roots in *ā*, *e*, *o*, and *ai*, with three in *m*, viz. *yam*, *ram*, *nam*, insert *s* before the terminations of this form, the final *e*, *o*, and *ai*, being changed to *ā*. Thus, from *yā*, *ayās* (*ayāsiṣham*, *&c.*); from *so*, *asās* (*asāsiṣham*, *&c.*); from *yam*, *ayans* (*ayansiṣham*, *&c.*). In the ātm. they follow form 2. (*ayāsi*, *&c.*, *aransi*, *&c.*).

Form 2. *Formation of the Base.*

e. The greater number of roots rejecting *i* follow this form.

Observe that the initial *s* may often be rejected from those terminations in which it is compounded with *t*, *th*. This takes place when the base ends in any consonant except a nasal or a semi-vowel, or in any short vowel; and *ḍhwam* (ढ्वं) takes the place of *dhwam* when the base ends in any other vowel than *ā*.

f. If a root end in either a consonant or a vowel, Vṛiddhi takes place in the par.; as, from *kṛi*, *akār* (अकार्षं *akārṣham*, *&c.*), from *yuj*, *ayauj* (अयौक्षं *ayauksham*, *&c.*, dual *ayaukshwa*, *ayauktam*, *&c.*); from *rudh* (*arautsam*, *&c.*, dual *arautswa*, *arauddham*, r. 91. *a. b.*); from *dah* (*adhāksham*, *&c.*, dual *adhākshwa*, *adāgdham*, r. 91. *h. i.*).

g. But in the ātm. if a root end in any other vowel than *ṛi*, Guna takes place; as, from *chi*, *ache* (अचेषि *acheshi*, *&c.*); and if in *ṛi*, or any consonant, then the vowel is unchanged; as, from *kṛi*, *akṛi* (*akṛishi*, *akṛithāh*, *&c.*); from *yuj*, *ayuj* (*ayukshi*, *ayukthāh*, *&c.*); from *rudh*, *arudh* (*arutsi*, *aruddhāh*, *aruddha*, r. 91. *a. b.*).

*Form 3.** *Formation of the Base.*

h. Roots of any conjugation, making use of this form, in general attach the terminations directly to the root: thus, from *gam*, *agam* (*agamam*, *&c.*); from *bhid*, *abhid* (अभिदं *abhidam*, *&c.*). And no confusion can arise from this apparent identity with the 1st pret., as in all cases where these terminations are used for the 3d pret., the 1st pret. presents some difference in the form of its base; as in *agachchham*, *abhinadam*. So again, the sixth conjugation, which alone can ever shew a perfect identity of root and base, never makes use of this form for its 3d pret., unless by some special rule the base of its 1st pret. is made to differ from the root. Thus, *lip*, "to smear" (cf. ἀλείφω), which is *alipam* in the 3d pret., is *alimpam* in the first.

i. Certain roots ending in long vowels, as *dā*, "to give,"† make use of the terminations of this form, but reject the initial vowel throughout (*adām*, *adāh*, *adāt*; dual, *adāva*; 3d pl. *aduh*; ātm. *adishi*, *&c.*, form 2.‡). So *bhū*, "to be," except in the 1st sing. and 3d plur. (अभूवं *abhūvam*, *abhūh*, *&c.*; 3d plur. *abhūvan*; in the ātm. *abhavishi*, *&c.* form 2.).

j. The roots *vach*, "to speak," and *pat*, "to fall," follow this form; but, in contradistinction to the 1st pret., make their bases *avoch*, *apapt* (*avocham*, *apaptam*, cf. ἔπιπτον). *As*, "to throw," makes *āsth*; *shās*, *ashish*; *nash*, *anesh*.

k. Certain roots ending in श *sh*, ष *sh*, ह *h*, inclosing a medial *i*, *u*, or *ṛi*, form their 3d pret. according to this third scheme; but whenever confusion is likely to arise

---

* Bopp has noticed that this form of the 3d pret. corresponds very clearly with the 2d aorist of the Greek (cf. *asthām*, *asthās*, *asthāt* with ἔστην, ἔστης, ἔστη), and that the first two forms are more or less analogous to the 1st aorist.

† Bopp remarks that the 1st pret. of this root *adadām* bears the same relation to its 3d preterite *adām*, that ἐδίδων does to ἔδων. So also the relation of *adhām* (3d pret. of *dhā*) to *adadhām* (1st pret.) corresponds to that of ἔθην to ἐτίθην. Cf. also *abhavah* and *abhūh* with ἔφυες and ἔφυς.

‡ Roots like *dā*, in the ātm., change the radical *ā* to *i*, and follow form 2.: thus, *adishi*, *adithāh*, *adita*, *adishwahi*, *&c.*

between the 1st and 3d preterites, the base is formed by the addition of *ṣh* to the root, the final of the root being at the same time changed to *k* (r. 91. *e.*).

Thus from दिश् *dish*, "to point out," comes the base *adiksh* (अदिक्षं *adiksham*, *&c.*, cf. ἔδειξα, 1st pret. *adisham*); from *dwiṣh*, "to hate," *adwiksh* (*adwiksham*, *&c.*); from *duh*, "to milk," *adhuksh* (*adhuksham*, *&c.*, r. 91. *i.*). But this class of roots substitutes *i* for *e*, the termination of the 1st pers. sing. ātm. (*adikshi*, *adikshathāh*, *&c.*), and *āthām*, *ātām*, for *ethām*, *etām*, in the 2d and 3d dual (*adikshāthām*).*

Causal verbs make use of the terminations of this form, but the base assumes a very peculiar reduplication (analogous to the Greek pluperfect), to be afterwards explained. Thus, from *budh*, *abūbudh* (*abūbudham*, *&c.*).

BENEDICTIVE AND CONDITIONAL TENSES.

TERMINATIONS.

Benedictive.

PARASMAIPADA.			ATMANEPADA.		
yāsam	*yāswa*	*yāsma*	*sīya*	*sīvahi*	*sīmahi*
yāh	*yāstam*	*yāsta*	*siṣhṭhāh*	*sīyāsthām*	*sīdhwam* (*ḍhwam*)
yāt	*yāstām*	*yāsuh*	*siṣhṭa*	*sīyāstām*	*sīran*

Conditional.

syam	*syāva*	*syāma*	*sye*	*syāvahi*	*syāmahi*
syah	*syatam*	*syata*	*syathāh*	*syethām*	*syadhwam*
syat	*syatām*	*syan*	*syata*	*syetām*	*syanta*

OBS. The initial sibilant, in the terminations of both these tenses, almost always takes the cerebral form *ṣh*.

Formation of the Base of the Benedictive or Precative.

104. In forming the base of this tense the parasmaipada never admits inserted *i*, but those roots which take inserted *i* in the futures (see p. 79.) take it also in the ātmanepada of this tense; as from *bhū*, "to be," the two bases *bhū* and *bhavi* (भूयासं *bhūyāsam*, *&c.*, भविषीय *bhaviṣhīya*, *&c.*).

* A few roots of this kind optionally follow form 2. in the ātm.; as, लिह् may be अलिक्षि, अलीढाः, अलीढ, &c., and दुह, अधुक्षि, अदुग्धाः, अदुग्ध, &c., r. 91. *h. i.*

a. If a root end in *ā*, this vowel is changed to *e* in the par.; as, from *dā*, *de* (देयासं *deyāsam*, *&c.*), but not in the ātm. (दासीय *dāsīya*, *&c.*).

b. If in *i* or *u*, these vowels are lengthened in the par.; as, from *chi*, *chī*; from *hu*, *hū* (*chīyāsam*, *&c.*, *hūyāsam*, *&c.*), and changed to Guna in the ātm. (*cheshīya*, *hoshīya*). Similarly ह्वे and ज्ये (हूयासं, जयासं).

c. If in ऋ *ṛi*, this vowel is changed to रि *ri* in the par., but retained in the ātm.; thus, from कृ, the bases क्रि and कृ (क्रियासं, कृषीय). After a double consonant *ṛi* becomes *ar* in the par. As also before inserted *i* (*staryāsam*, *starishīya* from *stṛi*).

d. If in ॠ *ṝī*, this vowel is changed to *īr*, in both voices; as, from तॄ the base तीर् (*tīryāsam*, *tīrshīya*); but before inserted *i* in the ātm. to *ar* (*tarishīya* or *tarīshīya*).

e. If in a consonant, there is no change in the par., and no change in the ātm., unless the root take the inserted *i*, when Guna is required; as, from *budh* the bases *budh* and *bodhi* (*budhyāsam*, *bodhishīya*); from *dwish*, the base *dwish* (*dwishyāsam*, *dwikshīya*). But in the par. certain roots undergo changes analogous to those in the 2d pret. (r. 99. *d. f.*) and in the passive (r. 112. *d. f.*). Thus, from *grah*, *grihyāsam*, *&c.*; from *vach*, *uchyāsam*, *&c.*; from *swap*, *supyāsam*; from *yaj*, *ijyāsam*, *&c.*

It is to be remarked of this tense, that the changes of the base before the *y* of the par. terminations are analogous to those before the *y* which is the sign of neuter and passive verbs (r. 89. 112.). Observe, moreover, that the terminations resemble those of the potential of irregular primitives (p. 66.); the only difference being, that in most cases a sibilant, and in some, two sibilants, are either prefixed or inserted.

Formation of the Base of the Conditional.

105. This tense, in its formation, lies half way between the first preterite and the second future. It resembles the 1st pret. in prefixing the augment *a* to the base, and in the latter part of its terminations: it resembles the second future in inserting *i* in exactly those roots in which the future inserts *i*, and in the first part of its terminations. Thus, from *budh* comes the base *abodhi* (अबोधिष्यं *abodhishyam*, *&c.*); from *kship*, the base *akshep* (अक्षेप्स्यं *akshepsyam*, *&c.*).

INFINITIVE MOOD.

Termination *tum* (cf. the Latin supine).

Formation of the base.

106. The base of the infinitive is identical with the base of the first future, and where one inserts *i*, the other does also. Thus from *budh*, *bodhi* (बोधितुं *bodhitum*); from *kship*, *kshep* (क्षेप्तुं *ksheptum*). Moreover, all the rules for the change of the final consonant of a root before the *t* of the future terminations apply equally before

the *t* of the infinitive. Hence, by substituting *um* for the final *ā* of the 3d pers. sing. of the 1st future, the infinitive is at once obtained. See p. 80. Thus, *tyaktā, tyaktum; prashṭā, prashṭum* (प्रष्टुं); *soḍhā, soḍhum* (सोढुं), &c. &c.

CAUSALS, OR VERBS OF THE 10TH CONJUGATION.

107. Every root in the language may, in theory, take what is called a causal form; and, moreover, practically, this is a most useful form of the root, that may be used to give either a causal or active sense to a primitive verb. Thus the primitive verb *bodhati*, "he knows," becomes in the causal बोधयति *bodhayati*, "he causes to know," or "informs"; and the primitive *kshubhyati*, "he is shaken," becomes *kshobhayati*, "he shakes." This form, also, may sometimes give the sense of allowing or permitting, as *hārayati*, "he allows to take"; *nāshayati*, "he suffers to perish."

The Terminations of Causals.

a. These, in the conjugational tenses, are precisely those of regular primitive verbs, p. 63. Of the non-conjugational tenses, the second preterite necessarily conforms to the general scheme in its terminations, inasmuch as the tense itself results from the annexation of the 2d preterite of some one of the auxiliaries *as, bhū* or *kṛi*, to a particular form of the causal base. In the two futures, the benedictive and conditional, the terminations are precisely those of the general scheme. In the third preterite they are those of the third form (p. 81.).

Formation of the Base of Causals.

b. The first step in the formation of the base is the addition of *ay* to the root; and this affix is retained throughout all the tenses, conjugational and non-conjugational, excepting only the third preterite, and excepting the benedictive par.

Conjugational Tenses.

c. If a root end in a vowel, Vṛiddhi is required: as, from *nī, nai*, forming, with the affix *ay*, the base *nāyay*, r. 8. (pres. नाययामि

nāyayāmi, &c.; 1st pret. *anāyayam*, &c.); from *kṛi*, the base *kāray* (कारयामि *kārayāmi*, &c.).

d. Anomalies.—Roots in *ā* or in *e*, *ai*, changeable to *ā*, cannot take Vriddhi, but insert *p*, or sometimes *y*, between the root and the affix *ay*. Thus, from *dā*, the base *dāpay*; from *pā*, "to drink," *pāyay*; from *hwe*, *hwāyay*. But *pā*, "to preserve," inserts *l* (*pālayāmi*, &c.). The roots *i*, "to go"; *ji*, "to conquer"; *smi*, "to smile"; *chi*, "to collect"; and *bhī*, "to fear"; form their bases, *āpay*;* *jāpay*; *smāpay*; *chāpay* or *chapay*; *bhāpay*, ātm., or *bhīshay*, ātm., respectively. *Hrī*, "to be ashamed," and *ṛi*, "to go," take Guna, and form their bases *hrepay* and *arpay*.

e. If a root end in a consonant and contain the vowel *a*, this *a* is generally lengthened; as, from *pach*, *pāchay* (पाचयामि, &c.): but not always; as from *gam*, *gamay*† (गमयामि, &c.). If it contain any other vowel, Guna takes place (unless as prohibited, r. 88. *b*.): thus, from *budh*, *bodhay* (*bodhayāmi*, &c.); from *sṛip*, *sarpay*.

f. Anomalies.—*Ruh*, "to grow," forms *ropay*; *dush*, "to pollute," *dūshay*; *hān*, "to kill," *ghātay*; *shad*, "to perish," *shātay*; *sphur* (स्फुर्), "to quiver," *sphāray*; *sphāy* (स्फाय्), "to increase," *sphāvay*.

Non-conjugational Tenses.

The changes of the root requisite to form the base of the conjugational tenses are continued in all of these, the *ay* only being rejected in the 3d pret. and in the benedictive parasmai.

Second Preterite of Causals.

108. The second preterite is formed (according to r. 99. *g*.) by adding *ām* to the base of the conjugational tenses, and affixing to this the second preterite of some one of the auxiliaries *as*, *bhū* or *kṛi*; thus, from *budh*, *bodhayām* (बोधयामास *bodhayāmāsa* or *bodhayāmbabhūva*‡ or *bodhayāñchakāra*).

---

* Thus, from *adhī*, "to go over" or "read," comes *adhyāpayati*, "he causes to read" or "teaches."

† Few roots in *m* lengthen the *a*. Some, however, optionally do so.

‡ It may be questioned whether *bhū* is ever found added to causals.

The First and Second Future of Causals.

In these tenses the inserted *i* is invariably assumed between the base, as formed in the conjugational tenses, and the usual terminations. Thus, from *budh, bodhayi* (*bodhayitāsmi*, &c.; *bodhayishyāmi*, &c.).

The Third Preterite of Causals.

109. In the formation of the base of this tense, the affix *ay* is rejected; but any other change that may take place in the conjugational tenses, such as the insertion of *p* or *y*, is preserved. The base is a reduplicated form of this change, and to this reduplication the augment *a* is prefixed. Thus, taking the bases *bodhay* and *jāpay* (caus. bases of *budh*, "to know," and *ji*, "to conquer"), and rejecting *ay*, we have *bodh* and *jāp*; and from these are formed the bases of the 3d pret., *abūbudh* and *ajījap* (अबूबुधं *abūbudham*, *&c.*, अजीजपं *ajījapam*, *&c.*, cf. the Greek pluperfect). The rule for this reduplication is as follows:—The initial consonant of the root, with its vowel, are reduplicated, and the reduplicated consonant follows the rules given at r. 99.; but the reduplication of the vowel is peculiar.

Rules for the Reduplication of the Vowel of the Initial Consonant.

Causal bases, after rejecting *ay*, will end either in *āy*, *āv*, *ār*, or a consonant preceded by *a*, *ā*, *e*, *o*, or *ar*. The usual reduplicated vowel for all these vowels except *o*, is *i*. But *u* is reduplicated for *o*, and sometimes also for *āv*. In general, this reduplicated vowel is made long, and to compensate for this, the long vowel of the causal base shortened, or, if it be Guna, changed to its cognate short vowel. Thus, the causal base *nāy* (from *nī*, rejecting *ay*) makes the base of the 3d pret. *anīnay* (*anīnayam*, *&c.*); the causal base *bhāv* (from *bhū*) makes *abībhav*; the causal base *kār* (from *kṛi*), *achīkar*; *gam* (from *gam*), *ajīgam*; *pāch* (from *pach*), *apīpach*; *pāl* (from *pā*), *apīpal*; *ved* (from *vid*), *avīvid*; *vart* (from *vṛit*), *avīvṛit*. But *bodh* (from *budh*), *abūbudh*; and *sāv* (from *su*), *asūshav*. Sometimes the reduplicated vowel is only long by position before two consonants, the radical vowel being still made short; as, *shrāv* (from *shru*) makes *ashushrav*; *drāv* (from *dru*), *adudrav*; *bhrāj*, *abibhraj*. Sometimes the reduplicated vowel remains short, whilst the vowel of the causal base, which must be long either by nature or position, remains unchanged. Thus, the causal base *jīv* (from *jīv*) may make *ajijīv*; *chint*, *achichint*; *kalp*, *achikalp*. In such cases *a* may be reduplicated for *a* or *ā*; as, *laksh* makes *alalaksh*; *yāch*, *ayayāch*; *vart* (from *vṛit*) *avavart*, *&c.*†

† The following bases of the 3d preterite are formed anomalously from causal

Rules for the Reduplication of an Initial Vowel.

If a root begin with a vowel this vowel is not reduplicated, only coalescing with the augment *a* according to the rule, p. 64.; but the reduplicated form of the final consonant, with the vowel *i*, is inserted between the augment and vowel thus coalescing, and the final consonant. Thus the root *aksh* makes *āchiksh* p. 75. *b.* (*āchiksham, &c.*); *arh, ārjih; āp, āpip; īḍ* (ईड्), *aiḍiḍ; ūh, aujih; ṛidh, ārdidh.*

The Benedictive and Conditional of Causals.

110. The base of these tenses does not differ from that of the non-conjugational tenses; *ay* is retained, and after it the inserted *i* invariably assumed; excepting in the benedictive paras., where both *ay* and *i* are rejected. Thus, from *budh*, the bases *bodh, bodhayi, abodhayi* (*bodhyāsam, &c.; bodhayishīya, &c.; abodhayishyam, &c.*).

PASSIVE VERBS.

Every root in the language may take a passive form. It is a form, however, little used, except in the 3d person sing. and plural of the present and imperative; for although a passive construction is exceedingly common in Sanscrit syntax, yet almost all the tenses of the passive verb are expressed by participles.

Our reasons for denominating the passive a distinct derivative from the root rather than a voice of the primitive, and for considering that the 4th conjugation of primitives results from the occasional assumption of a parasmaipada form* by this passive verb, have been already given† (see pp. 58. 62.).

111. Passive verbs are conjugated with the regular ātmanepada

---

bases, *apīyy* from *pāy* (*pā*, "to drink"); *atishṭhip* from *sthāp* (*sthā*, "to stand"); *adhyajīgap* from *adhyāp* (*i*, "to go," with *adhi*); *ajighrip* from *ghrāp*.

* The 4th conjugation can hardly be said to possess an ātmanepada; or if so, then its ātmanepada is identical with the passive. And it seems probable that those ātmanepada verbs, such as *pad*, "to go," and *budh*, "to know," which are placed under the 4th conjugation, are in reality passive verbs; at any rate, the forms given for their 3d preterites (*apādi, abodhi*) can only belong to passives.

† That the passive does occasionally take the terminations of the parasmaipada is corroborated by Bopp, who gives several instances; as, *chhidyet* for *chhidyeta*. Nal. xiv. 6.; *mokshyasi* for *mokshyase*, "thou shalt be liberated." Other instances may be found in Westergaard; as, *vidyati* for *vidyate*.

inflections; that is, in the conjugational tenses they conform to the scheme for the ātm. at p. 63., and in the non-conjugational tenses to the general schemes at p. 73., p. 81., and p. 84.

In the third preterite they take the first two forms (p. 81.), according as the root may admit the inserted *i* or not; but require that, in the 3d pers. sing. of both forms, the termination be invariably *i* (इ) in place of *ishṭa* and *sta*.

Conjugational Tenses.

112. In the formation of these the passive verb is to be treated like a regular primitive of the 4th conjugation; that is, in general the only change made in the root is the affixing of *y*; but before this affix certain changes of a final vowel may take place, some of which are analogous to those of the 4th conj. A final *ā*, *e*, *ai*, or *o* are changed to *ī*: as, from *dā*, the base *dīy* (3d sing. दीयते); so also *dhā*, *pā*, *sthā*, *hā*, *mā*; so also *gai*, "to sing," (*gīy*).

a. If in *i* or *u*, or a semi-vowel preceded by *i* or *u*, these vowels are lengthened: as, from *ji*, *jīy*; from *hu*, *hūy*; from *div*, *dīvy*.

b. If in ऋ *ṛi*, this vowel becomes रि *ri*; as, from कृ, the base *kriy* (क्रियते); but *ar*, if two consonants precede; as from स्मृ *smṛi*, *smary*.

c. If in ॠ *ṝī*, this vowel becomes *īr*: as, from कॄ *kṝī*, "to scatter," *kīry* (कीर्यते, &c.). But from *pṝī*, *pūry*.

d. Roots ending in two consonants, of which the first is a nasal, usually reject the nasal: as, from *bandh*, *badhy*; from *stambh*, *stabhy*; from *sañj* (सञ्ज्), *sajy*. From शास् comes शिष्य् (p. 70. *e.*).

e. Jan, *khan*, and *tan*, may optionally reject the final nasal, but the *a* is then lengthened: as, from *jan*, *jāy* or *jany* (जायते or जन्यते).

f. From *vach*, *vad*, *vap*, *vas*, *swap*, come the bases *uchy*, *udy*, *upy*, *ushy*, *supy*: from *grah*, *prachh*, and *vyadh*, the bases *gṛihy* (गृह्यते, &c.), *pṛichhy*, *vidhy*: from *yaj*, *hwe*, *ve*, come *ijy*, *hūy*, *ūy*.

Non-conjugational Tenses.—Second Preterite of Passives.

The base of this tense in the passive verb is identical with that of all primitive verbs. The bases, therefore, as formed at p. 74., will serve equally well for the 2d preterite of the passive, provided only that they be restricted to the ātmanepada inflection.

The First and Second Future of Passives.

113. In these and the remaining tenses no variation can occur

from the bases of the same tenses in the primitive, unless the root end in a vowel. In that case the insertion of *i* may take place in the passive, although prohibited in the primitive, provided the final vowel of the root be first changed to its Vṛiddhi substitute. Thus, from *chi*, to gather," may come the base of the 1st and 2d fut. pass. *chāyi* (*chāyitāhe*, &c., *chāyiṣhye*, &c.), although the base of the same tenses in the primitive is *che* (*chetāhe*, &c., *cheṣhye*, &c.). Similarly from *hu* and *kṛi* may come *hāvi* and *kāri* (*hāvitāhe*, *kāritāhe*), although the bases in the primitive are *ho* and *kar*. In like manner *i* may be inserted when the root ends in long *ā*, provided that, instead of a change to Vṛiddhi (which is impossible), *y* be interposed between the final *ā* and inserted *i*. Thus, from *dā*, "to give," may come the base of the fut. pass. *dāyi* (*dāyitāhe*, &c.), although the base of the same tenses in the primitive is *dā* (*dātāhe*, &c.). But in all these cases it is permitted to take the base of the primitive for that of the passive, and *chetāhe* or *chāyitāhe* may equally stand for the 1st fut. pass.*

In the case of roots ending in consonants, the base of the two futures in the passive will be identical with that of the same tenses in the primitive,† the inflection being that of the ātm.

The Third Preterite of Passives.

114. In this tense, also, variation from the primitive may occur when the root ends in a vowel. For in that case the insertion of *i* may take place, although forbidden in the primitive, provided the final of the root be changed to Vṛiddhi. Thus, from *chi* may come the base of the 3d pret. pass. *achāyi* (*achāyiṣhi*, &c., form 1. p. 81.) although the base in the ātm. of the primitive is *ache* (*acheṣhi*, &c., form 2.). So also, from *hu* and *kṛi* may come *ahāvi* and *akāri* (*ahāviṣhi*, *akāriṣhi*, form 1.), although the bases in the ātm. of the primitive are *aho* and *akṛi* (*ahoṣhi*, *akṛiṣhi*, form 2.). Again, *i* may be inserted when the root ends in long *ā*, provided that *y* be interposed between final *ā* and inserted *i*. Thus, from *dā* may come *adāyi* (*adāyiṣhi*, &c.), although the base in the ātm. of the primitive is *adi* (*adiṣhi*, &c.).

* This explanation of the passive, although at variance with that of Wilkins and Bopp, rests on the authority of Pāṇini (6. 4. 62.), and the Siddhānta kaumudī.

† The root दृश्, however, in the passive, may be दर्शिताहे, दर्शिष्ये, as well as द्रष्टाहे, द्रक्ष्ये; and हन् may be घानिताहे, घानिष्ये, as well as हन्ताहे, हनिष्ये; and ग्रह् may be ग्राहिताहे, ग्राहिष्ये, as well as ग्रहीताहे, ग्रहीष्ये.

But in all these cases it is permitted to take the base of the primitive for that of the passive (so that the passive of *chi* may be either *achāyiṣhi* or *acheṣhi*), except in the 3d pers. sing. where the terminations *iṣhṭa* and *ṣta* being rejected, the base, as formed by Vṛiddhi and the inserted *i*, must always stand alone; thus, *achāyi*, "it was gathered"; *ahāvi*, "it was sacrificed"; *akāri*, "it was done"; *adāyi*, "it was given."

If the root end in a consonant, the base of the 3d pret. pass. will always be identical with that of the 3d pret. ātm. of the primitive, except in the 3d pers. sing., where *i* (इ) being substituted for the terminations *ishṭa* of the 1st form and *sta* of the 2d form, invariably requires before it the lengthening of a medial *a*, and the *Guna* of any other medial vowel.* Hence, from *tan*, the form of the 1st, 2d, and 3d sing. 3d pret. will be *atuniṣhi, ataniṣhṭhāh, atāni;* from *kship, akshipsi, akshipthāh, akshepi;* from *vid, avediṣhi, avediṣhṭhāh, avedi*. This 3d pers. sing. of the 3d pret. passive is not unfrequently found, even in the simplest writings.

The Benedictive and Conditional of Passives.

In these tenses the same variation is permitted in the case of roots ending in vowels as in the last; that is, the insertion of *i* is allowed, provided that, before it, Vṛiddhi take place in a final vowel capable of such a change, and *y* be interposed after final *ā*. Thus, from *chi* may come the bases *chāyi* and *achāyi* (*chāyiṣhīya, achāyiṣhye*); from *hu, hāvi* and *ahāvi;* from *kri, kāri* and *akāri;* from *dā, dāyi* and *adāyi*. But *cheṣhīya, acheṣhye, hoṣhīya, ahoṣhye, &c.*, the forms belonging to the ātm. of the primitive, are equally admissible in the passive.

Passive Infinitive Mood.

There is no passive infinitive mood in Sanscrit distinct in form from the active. But although the affix *tum* has generally an active, it is capable of a passive sense, when joined with certain verbs, especially with *shak*, "to be able." In the Hitopadesha it is also used passively, in connection with the participles *ārabdha* and *nirūpita*.

Passive Verbs from Causal Bases.

115. In forming a passive verb from a causal base, the affix *ay* is rejected, but the other changes of the root are retained. Thus, from the causal base *pātay* (root *pat*, "to fall") is formed the passive causal base *pāty* (*pātye*, "I am caused to fall"); so also, from *sthāpay* (*sthā*, "to stand"), *sthāpy* (*sthāpye*, "I am made to stand"); from *pāṭhay* (*paṭh*, "to read"), *pāṭhy* (*pāṭhye*, "I am taught to read") from ज्ञपय् (ज्ञा "to know"), ज्ञप्य् (ज्ञप्ये "I am caused to know.")

---

* This rests on the authority of Pāṇini, the Siddhānta kaumudī, and the Bhaṭṭi kāvya (15. 64, 65.).

INFLECTION OF THE BASE OF REGULAR AND IRREGULAR PRIMITIVES, OR VERBS OF THE FIRST NINE CONJUGATIONS.

Before passing to the exhibition in full of the inflection of particular verbs under each conjugation, a synopsis is here given of the inflection, 1st, of the primitive; 2dly, of the causal; 3dly, of the passive forms of the nine roots, बुध् *budh*, "to know," of the 1st conjugation; नृत् *nrit*, "to dance," of the 4th; दिश् *dish*, "to point out," of the 6th; विद् *vid*, "to know," of the 2d; हु *hu*, "to sacrifice," of the 3d; चि *chi*, "to gather," of the 5th; भिद् *bhid*, "to break," of the 7th; तन् *tan*, "to stretch," of the 8th; and पू *pū*, "to purify," of the 9th. In this page is exhibited the inflection in the conjugational tenses of those primitives which we have called *regular*; the base, which is always the same throughout all the persons, being to the left of the terminations. In the two pages which follow this, is exhibited the inflection in the conjugational tenses of those primitives which we have called *irregular*; the base, which varies in different persons, being *above* the terminations. After this, all distinction of conjugation is done away, and in the pages which succeed, the inflection of the nine roots in the non-conjugational tenses of the primitive, and in the causal and passive, is exhibited, one below the other, in regular order.

PRESENT.

ROOT.	BASE.	PAR. S. D. P.	ATM. S. D. P.
		āmi	*e*
		asi	*ase*
		ati	*ate*
1. *Budh*	*bodh*	*āvah*	*āvahe*
4. *Nrit*	*nrity*	*athah*	*ethe*
6. *Dish*	*dish*	*atah*	*ete*
		āmah	*āmahe*
		atha	*adhwe*
		anti	*ante*

1st PRETERITE.

BASE.	PAR. S. D. P.	ATM. S. D. P.
	am	*e*
	ah	*athāh*
	at	*ata*
1. *abodh*	*āva*	*āvahi*
4. *anrity*	*atam*	*ethām*
6. *adish*	*atām*	*etām*
	āma	*āmahi*
	ata	*adhwam*
	an	*anta*

POTENTIAL.

BASE.	PAR. S. D. P.	ATM. S. D. P.
	eyam	*eya*
	eh	*ethāh*
	et	*eta*
1. *bodh*	*eva*	*evahi*
4. *nrity*	*etam*	*eyāthām*
6. *dish*	*etām*	*eyātām*
	ema	*emahi*
	eta	*edhwam*
	eyuh	*eran*

IMPERATIVE.

BASE.	PAR. S. D. P.	ATM. S. D. P.
	āni	*ai*
	a	*aswa*
	atu	*atām*
1. *bodh*	*āva*	*āvahai*
4. *nrity*	*atam*	*ethām*
6. *dish*	*atām*	*etām*
	āma	*āmahai*
	ata	*adhwam*
	antu	*antām*

OBS. The base is to be united with the terminations thus, 1st pers. sing. pres. par. *bodhāmi*, "I know"; 2d sing. *bodhasi*, "thou knowest"; 3d sing. *bodhati*, "he knows"; 1st dual, *bodhāvah*, &c. Atmanepada, *bodhe*, *bodhase*, &c. So also *nrityāmi*, "I dance," *nrityasi*, &c. 1st pret. *abodham*, *abodhah*, *abodhat*, *abodhāva*, &c. So also *anrityam*, &c.

PRESENT.

	PARASMAIPADA. Sing.			Dual			Plur.			ATMANEPADA. Sing.			Dual			Plur.		
2. *Vid*	*ved**	*vet*	*vet*	*vid*	*vit*	*vit*	*vid*	*vit*	*vid*	*vid*	*vit*	*vit*	*vid*	*vid*	*vid*	*vid*	*vid*	*vid*
3. *Hu*	*juho*	*juho*	*juho*	*juhu*	*juhu*	*juhu*	*juhu*	*juhu*	*juhw*	*juhw*	*juhu*	*juhu*	*juhu*	*juhw*	*juhw*	*juhu*	*juhu*	*juhw*
5. *Chi*	*chino*	*chino*	*chino*	*chinu*	*chinu*	*chinu*	*chinu*	*chinu*	*chinw*	*chinw*	*chinu*	*chinu*	*chinu*	*chinw*	*chinw*	*chinu*	*chinu*	*chinw*
7. *Bhid*	*bhinad*	*bhinat*	*bhinat*	*bhind*	*bhint*	*bhint*	*bhind*	*bhint*	*bhind*	*bhind*	*bhint*	*bhint*	*bhind*	*bhind*	*bhind*	*bhind*	*bhind*	*bhind*
8. *Tan*	*tano*	*tano*	*tano*	*tanu*	*tanu*	*tanu*	*tanu*	*tanu*	*tanw*	*tanw*	*tanu*	*tanu*	*tanu*	*tanw*	*tanw*	*tanu*	*tanu*	*tanw*
9. *Pū*	*punā*	*punā*	*punā*	*punī*	*punī*	*punī*	*punī*	*punī*	*pun*	*pun*	*punī*	*punī*	*punī*	*pun*	*pun*	*punī*	*punī*	*pun*
Terminations of the PRESENT	*mi*	*si* in 3.5.8. *ṣhi*	*ti*	*vah*	*thah*	*tah*	*mah*	*tha*	*anti* in 3. *ati*	*e*	*ṣhe* in 2.7. *se*	*te*	*vahe*	*āthe*	*āte*	*mahe*	*dhwe*	*ate*

FIRST PRETERITE.

	PARASMAIPADA. Sing.			Dual			Plur.			ATMANEPADA. Sing.			Dual			Plur.		
2. *Vid*	*aved*	*avet*	*avet*	*avid*	*avit*	*avit*	*avid*	*avit*	*avid*	*avid*	*avit*	*avit*	*avid*	*avid*	*avid*	*avid*	*avid*	*avid*
3. *Hu*	*ajuhav*	*ajuho*	*ajuho*	*ajuhu*	*ajuhu*	*ajuhu*	*ajuhu*	*ajuhu*	*ajuhav*	*ajuhw*	*ajuhu*	*ajuhu*	*ajuhu*	*ajuhw*	*ajuhw*	*ajuhu*	*ajuhu*	*ajuhw*
5. *Chi*	*achinav*	*achino*	*achino*	*achinu*	*achinu*	*achinu*	*achinu*	*achinu*	*achinw*	*achinw*	*achinu*	*achinu*	*achinu*	*achinw*	*achinw*	*achinu*	*achinu*	*achinw*
7. *Bhid*	*abhinad*	*abhinat*	*abhinat*	*abhind*	*abhint*	*abhint*	*abhind*	*abhint*	*abhind*	*abhind*	*abhint*	*abhint*	*abhind*	*abhind*	*abhind*	*abhind*	*abhind*	*abhind*
8. *Tan*	*atanav*	*atano*	*atano*	*atanu*	*atanu*	*atanu*	*atanu*	*atanu*	*atanw*	*atanw*	*atanu*	*atanu*	*atanu*	*atanw*	*atanw*	*atanu*	*atanu*	*atanw*
9. *Pū*	*apunā*	*apunā*	*apunā*	*apunī*	*apunī*	*apunī*	*apunī*	*apunī*	*apun*	*apun*	*apunī*	*apunī*	*apunī*	*apun*	*apun*	*apunī*	*apunī*	*apun*
Terminations of the 1st. PRET.	*am*	*h* omit. in 2.7.	*t* omit. in 2.7.	*va*	*tam*	*tām*	*ma*	*ta*	*an* in 3. *uh*	*i*	*thāh*	*ta*	*vahi*	*āthām*	*ātām*	*mahi*	*dhwam*	*ata*

OBS. The base is to be united with the terminations thus, 1st pers. sing. pres. *vedmi*, "I know"; 2d sing. *vetsi*, 3d sing. *vetti*, 1st dual *vidwah*, &c., 1st pret. *avedam*, *avet*, *avet*, *avidwa*, &c. So also, *chinomi*, "I gather," *chinoshi*, &c.; and *punāmi*, "I purify": 1st pret. *apunām* (*apunā* with *am*).

POTENTIAL.

2. *Vid*	*vid*	*vid*	*vid*	*vid*	*vid*	*vid*	*vid*	*vid*	*vid*	*vid*	*vid*	*vid*	*vid*	*vid*	*vid*	*vid*	*vid*	*vid*
3. *Hu*	*juhu*	*juhu*	*juhu*	*juhu*	*juhu*	*juhu*	*juhu*	*juhu*	*juhu*	*juhw*	*juhw*	*juhw*	*juhw*	*juhw*	*juhw*	*juhw*	*juhw*	*juhw*
5. *Chi*	*chinu*	*chinu*	*chinu*	*chinu*	*chinu*	*chinu*	*chinu*	*chinu*	*chinu*	*chinw*	*chinw*	*chinw*	*chinw*	*chinw*	*chinw*	*chinw*	*chinw*	*chinw*
7. *Bhid*	*bhind*	*bhind*	*bhind*	*bhind*	*bhind*	*bhind*	*bhind*	*bhind*	*bhind*	*bhind*	*bhind*	*bhind*	*bhind*	*bhind*	*bhind*	*bhind*	*bhind*	*bhind*
8. *Tan*	*tanu*	*tanu*	*tanu*	*tanu*	*tanu*	*tanu*	*tanu*	*tanu*	*tanu*	*tanw*	*tanw*	*tanw*	*tanw*	*tanw*	*tanw*	*tanw*	*tanw*	*tanw*
9. *Pū*	*punī*	*punī*	*punī*	*punī*	*punī*	*punī*	*punī*	*punī*	*punī*	*pun*	*pun*	*pun*	*pun*	*pun*	*pun*	*pun*	*pun*	*pun*
Term. of the POTENTIAL	*yām*	*yāh*	*yāt*	*yāva*	*yātam*	*yātām*	*yāma*	*yātu*	*yuh*	*īya*	*īthāh*	*īta*	*īvahi*	*īyāthām*	*īyātām*	*īmahi*	*īdhwam*	*īran*

IMPERATIVE.

2. *Vid*	*ved*	*vid*	*vet*	*ved*	*vit*	*vit*	*ved*	*vit*	*vid*	*ved*	*vit*	*vit*	*ved*	*vid*	*vid*	*ved*	*vid*	*vid*
3. *Hu*	*juhav*	*juhu*	*juho*	*juhav*	*juhu*	*juhu*	*juhav*	*juhu*	*juhw*	*juhav*	*juhu*	*juhu*	*juhav*	*juhw*	*juhw*	*juhav*	*juhu*	*juhw*
5. *Chi*	*chinav*	*chinu*	*chino*	*chinav*	*chinu*	*chinu*	*chinav*	*chinu*	*chinw*	*chinav*	*chinu*	*chinu*	*chinav*	*chinw*	*chinw*	*chinav*	*chinu*	*chinw*
7. *Bhid*	*bhinad*	*bhind*	*bhinat*	*bhinad*	*bhint*	*bhint*	*bhinad*	*bhint*	*bhind*	*bhinad*	*bhint*	*bhint*	*bhinad*	*bhind*	*bhind*	*bhinad*	*bhind*	*bhind*
8. *Tan*	*tanav*	*tanu*	*tano*	*tanav*	*tanu*	*tanu*	*tanav*	*tanu*	*tanw*	*tanav*	*tanu*	*tanu*	*tanav*	*tanw*	*tanw*	*tanav*	*tanu*	*tanw*
9. *Pū*	*punā*	*punī*	*punā*	*punā*	*punī*	*punī*	*punā*	*punī*	*pun*	*pun*	*punī*	*punī*	*punā*	*punā*	*punā*	*punā*	*punī*	*pun*
Terminations of the IMPERATIVE	*āni*	*dhi* in 9. *hi* omit. in 5. 8.	*tu*	*āva*	*tam*	*tām*	*āma*	*ta*	*antu* in 3. *atu*	*ai*	*ṣhwa* in 2. 7. *swa*	*tām*	*āvahai*	*āthām*	*ātām*	*āmahai*	*dhwam*	*atām*

* An anomalous form of the 2d pret. of the root *vid*, "to know," is sometimes used for the present. Thus, sing. *veda, vettha, veda*; dual *vidwa, vidathuh, vidatuh*; plur. *vidma, vida, viduh*. Cf. (as noticed by Bopp, Comp. Gr. Prof. Eastwick's translation) the Greek οἶδα or Fοἶδα from the root Fιδ, also used with a present signification. Cf. also *vidmah* with ἴδμεν, *vittha* with ἴστε, and *viddhi* with ἴσθι.

SECOND PRETERITE.

1st p. sing. PAR.		2d p. sing.		3d p. sing.		DUAL and PL.		ATM.
1. *bubodh*		*bubodh*		*bubodh*		*bubudh*		*e*
2. *vived*	*a*	*vived*	*itha*	*vived*		*vivid*		*iṣhe*
3. *juhāv*		*juhav*		*juhāv*	*a*	*juhuv*		*e*
4. *nanart*		*nanart*		*nanart*		*nanrit*	*iva*	*ivahe*
5. *chichāy*		*chichay*		*chichāy*		*chichy*	*athuh*	*āthe*
6. *didesh*		*didesh*		*didesh*		*didish*	*atuh*	*āte*
7. *bibhed*		*bibhed*		*bibhed*		*bibhid*	*ima*	*imahe*
8. *tatān*		*ten*		*tatān*		*ten*	*a*	*idhwe*
9. *pupāv*		*pupav*		*pupāv*		*pupuv*	*uh*	*ire*

Obs. The base is united with the terminations thus, 1st sing. *bubodha*; 2d, *bubodhitha*; 3d, *bubodha*; 1st dual, *bubudhiva*, &c. Atm. *bubudhe*, *bubudhiṣhe*, &c. When *tha* is the termination of the 2d sing. the bases will vary.

1st FUTURE.

	PAR.	ATM.
1. *bodhi*	*tāsmi*	*tāhe*
2. *vedi*	*tāsi*	*tāse*
3. *ho*	*tā*	*tā*
4. *narti*	*tāswah*	*tāswahe*
5. *che*	*tāsthah*	*tāsāthe*
6. *deṣh*	*tārau*	*tārau*
7. *bhet*	*tāsmah*	*tāsmahe*
8. *tani*	*tāstha*	*tādhwe*
9. *pavi*	*tārah*	*tārah*

Obs. The *ṣh* of *deṣh* changes the initial *t* (त) of the terminations to *ṭ* (ट), r. 91. *d*.

2d FUTURE.

	PAR.	ATM.
1. *bodhi*	*ṣhyāmi*	*ṣhye*
2. *vedi*	*ṣhyasi*	*ṣhyase*
3. *ho*	*ṣhyati*	*ṣhyate*
4. *narti*	*ṣhyāvah*	*ṣhyāvahe*
5. *che*	*ṣhyathah*	*ṣhyethe*
6. *dek*	*ṣhyatah*	*ṣhyete*
7. *bhet*	*ṣhyāmah*	*ṣhyāmahe*
8. *tani*	*ṣhyatha*	*ṣhyadhwe*
9. *pavi*	*ṣhyanti*	*ṣhyante*

Obs. After *bhet* the terminations will be *syāmi*, &c. This applies in all the succeeding tenses.

THIRD PRETERITE.

FORM 1.

	PAR.	ATM.
1. *abodh*	*iṣham*	*iṣhi*
2. *aved*	*īḥ*	*iṣhṭhāḥ*
4. *anart*	*īt*	*iṣhṭa*
8. { *atān*, ātm. *atan* }	*iṣhwa*	*iṣhwahi*
	iṣhṭam	*iṣhāthām*
	iṣhṭām	*iṣhātām*
9. { *apāv*, ātm. *apav* }	*iṣhma*	*iṣhmahi*
	iṣhṭa	*idhwam*
	iṣhuḥ	*iṣhata*

FORM 2.

	PAR.	ATM.
3. { *ahau*, ātm. *aho* }	*ṣham*	*ṣhi*
	ṣhīḥ	*ṣhṭhāḥ*
5. { *achai*, ātm. *ache* }	*ṣhīt*	*ṣhṭa*
Bhid follows	*ṣhwa*	*ṣhwahi*
this form in the	*ṣhṭam*	*ṣhāthām*
ātm.; thus,	*ṣhṭām*	*ṣhātām*
abhitsi, *abhit-*	*ṣhma*	*ṣhmahi*
thāḥ, *abhitta*,	*ṣhṭa*	*dhwam*
abhitswahi, &c., p. 83. *g*.	*ṣhuḥ*	*ṣhata*

FORM 3.

	PAR.	ATM.
	am	*i*
	aḥ	*athāḥ*
6. *adiksh*	*at*	*ata*
7. *abhid*	*āva*	*āvahi*
follows	*atam*	*āthām*
form 2. in	*atām*	*ātām*
the ātm.	*āma*	*āmahi*
	ata	*adhwam*
	an	*anta*

BENEDICTIVE.

	PAR.		ATM.
1. *budh*	*yāsam*	*bodhi*	*ṣhīya*
2. *vid*	*yāḥ*	*vedi*	*ṣhīṣhṭhāḥ*
3. *hu*	*yāt*	*ho*	*ṣhīṣhṭa*
4. *nṛit*	*yāswa*	*narti*	*ṣhīvahi*
5. *chī*	*yāstam*	*che*	*ṣhīyāsthām*
6. *dish*	*yāstām*	*dik*	*ṣhīyāstām*
7. *bhid*	*yāsma*	*bhit*	*ṣhīmahi*
8. *tan*	*yāsta*	*tani*	*ṣhīdhwam*
9. *pū*	*yāsuḥ*	*pavi*	*ṣhīran*

CONDITIONAL.

	PAR.	ATM.
1. *abodhi*	*ṣhyam*	*ṣhye*
2. *avedi*	*ṣhyaḥ*	*ṣhyathāḥ*
3. *aho*	*ṣhyat*	*ṣhyata*
4. *anarti*	*ṣhyāva*	*ṣhyāvahi*
5. *ache*	*ṣhyatam*	*ṣhyethām*
6. *adek*	*ṣhyatām*	*ṣhyetām*
7. *abhet*	*ṣhyāma*	*ṣhyāmahi*
8. *atani*	*ṣhyata*	*ṣhyadhwam*
9. *apavi*	*ṣhyan*	*ṣhyanta*

INFINITIVE.

1. *bodhi*
2. *vedi*
3. *ho*
4. *narti*
5. *che*
6. *deṣh*
7. *bhet*
8. *tani*
9. *pavi*

} *tum* or *ṭum* after *ṣh*, r. 91. *d*.

INFLECTION OF THE BASE OF CAUSALS, OR VERBS OF THE 10th CONJUGATION.

PRESENT.

	PAR.	ATM.
1. bodhay	āmi	e
2. veday	asi	ase
3. hāvay	ati	ate
4. nartay	āvah	āvahe
5. chāpay	athah	ethe
6. deshay	atah	ete
7. bheday	āmah	āmahe
8. tānay	atha	adhwe
9. pāvay	anti	ante

FIRST PRETERITE.

	PAR.	ATM.
1. abodhay	am	e
2. aveday	ah	athāh
3. ahāvay	at	ata
4. anartay	āva	āvahi
5. achāpay	atam	ethām
6. adeshay	atām	etām
7. abheday	āma	āmahi
8. atānay	ata	adhwam
9. apāvay	an	anta

POTENTIAL.

	PAR.	ATM.
1. bodhay	eyam	eya
2. veday	eh	ethāh
3. hāvay	et	eta
4. nartay	eva	evahi
5. chāpay	etam	eyāthām
6. deshay	etām	eyātām
7. bheday	ema	emahi
8. tānay	eta	edhwam
9. pāvay	eyuh	eran

IMPERATIVE.

	PAR.	ATM.
1. bodhay	āni	ai
2. veday	a	aswa
3. hāvay	atu	atām
4. nartay	āva	āvahai
5. chāpay	atam	ethām
6. deshay	atām	etām
7. bheday	āma	āmahai
8. tānay	ata	adhwam
9. pāvay	antu	antām

SECOND PRETERITE.

	PAR.	ATM.
1. bodhayāmās	a	e
2. vedayāmās	itha	iṣhe
3. hāvayāmās	a	e
4. nartayāmās	iva	ivahe
5. chāpayāmās	athuh	āthe
6. deshayāmās	atuh	āte
7. bhedayāmās	ima	imahe
8. tānayāmās	a	iḍhwe
9. pāvayāmās	uh	ire

FIRST FUTURE.

	PAR.	ATM.
1. bodhayi	tāsmi	tāhe
2. vedayi	tāsi	tāse
3. hāvayi	tā	tā
4. nartayi	tāswah	tāswahe
5. chāpayi	tāsthah	tāsāthe
6. deshayi	tārau	tārau
7. bhedayi	tāsmah	tāsmahe
8. tānayi	tāstha	tādhwe
9. pāvayi	tārah	tārah

SECOND FUTURE.

	PAR.	ATM.
1. bodhayi	ṣhyāmi	ṣhye
2. vedayi	ṣhyasi	ṣhyase
3. hāvayi	ṣhyati	ṣhyate
4. nartayi	ṣhyāvah	ṣhyāvahe
5. chāpayi	ṣhyathah	ṣhyethe
6. deshayi	ṣhyatah	ṣhyete
7. bhedayi	ṣhyāmah	ṣhyāmahe
8. tānayi	ṣhyatha	ṣhyadhwe
9. pāvayi	ṣhyanti	ṣhyante

THIRD PRETERITE.

	PAR.	ATM.
1. abūbudh	am	e
2. avīvid	ah	athāh
3. ajūhav	at	ata
4. ananart	āva	āvahi
5. achīchap	atam	ethām
6. adīdish	atām	etām
7. abībhid	āma	āmahi
8. atītan	ata	adhwam
9. apīpav	an	anta

BENEDICTIVE.

PAR.		ATM.	
1. bodh	yāsam	bodhayi	ṣhīya
2. ved	yāh	vedayi	ṣhīṣhṭhāh
3. hāv	yāt	hāvayi	ṣhīṣhṭa
4. nart	yāswa	nartayi	ṣhīvahi
5. chāp	yāstam	chāpayi	ṣhīyāsthām
6. desh	yāstām	deshayi	ṣhīyāstām
7. bhed	yāsma	bhedayi	ṣhīmahi
8. tān	yāsta	tānayi	ṣhīdhwam
9. pāv	yāsuh	pāvayi	ṣhīran

CONDITIONAL.

	PAR.	ATM.
1. abodhayi	ṣhyam	ṣhye
2. avedayi	ṣhyah	ṣhyathāh
3. ahāvayi	ṣhyat	ṣhyata
4. anartayi	ṣhyāva	ṣhyāvahi
5. achāpayi	ṣhyatam	ṣhyethām
6. adeshayi	ṣhyatām	ṣhyetām
7. abhedayi	ṣhyāma	ṣhyāmahi
8. atānayi	ṣhyata	ṣhyadhwam
9. apāvayi	ṣhyan	ṣhyanta

INFINITIVE.

1. bodhayi	tum
2. vedayi	
3. hāvayi	
4. nartayi	
5. chūpayi	
6. deshayi	
7. bhedayi	
8. tānayi	
9. pāvayi	

INFLECTION OF THE BASE OF PASSIVES.

PRESENT.

1. budhy	e
2. vidy	ase
3. hūy	ate
4. nṛity	āvahe
5. chīy	ethe
6. dishy	ete
7. bhidy	āmahe
8. tany	adhwe
9. pūy	ante

FIRST PRETERITE.

1. abudhy	e
2. avidy	athāh
3. ahūy	ata
4. anṛity	āvahi
5. achīy	ethām
6. adishy	etām
7. abhidy	āmahi
8. atany	adhwam
9. apūy	anta

POTENTIAL.

1. budhy	eya
2. vidy	ethāh
3. hūy	eta
4. nṛity	evahi
5. chīy	eyāthām
6. dishy	eyātām
7. bhidy	emahi
8. tany	edhwam
9. pūy	eran

IMPERATIVE.

1. budhy	ai
2. vidy	aswa
3. hūy	atām
4. nṛity	āvahai
5. chīy	ethām
6. dishy	etām
7. bhidy	āmahai
8. tany	adhwam
9. pūy	antām

SECOND PRETERITE.

1. bubudh	e
2. vivid	iṣhe
3. juhuv	e
4. nanṛit	ivahe
5. chichy	āthe
6. didish	āte
7. bibhid	imahe
8. ten	idhwe
9. pupuv	ire

INFLECTION OF THE BASE OF PASSIVES.

FIRST FUTURE.

1. *bodhi*	*tāhe*
2. *vedi*	*tāse*
3. *hāvi* or *ho*	*tā*
4. *narti*	*tāswahe*
5. *chāyi* or *che*	*tāsāthe*
6. *deṣh* (r. 91. *d.*)	*tārau*
7. *bhet*	*tāsmahe*
8. *tani*	*tādhwe*
9. *pāvi* or *pavi*	*tārah*

SECOND FUTURE.

1. *bodhi*	*ṣhye*
2. *vedi*	*ṣhyase*
3. *hāvi* or *ho*	*ṣhyate*
4. *narti*	*ṣhyāvahe*
5. *chāyi* or *che*	*ṣhyethe*
6. *dek*	*ṣhyete*
7. *bhet* *	*ṣhyāmahe*
8. *tani*	*ṣhyadhwe*
9. *pāvi* or *pavi*	*ṣhyante*

THIRD PRETERITE.

		3d pers. sing.	
1. *abodhi*	*ṣhi*	*abodh*	
2. *avedi*	*ṣhṭhāh*	*aved*	
3. *ahāvi* or *aho*		*ahāv*	*i*
4. *anarti*	*ṣhwahi*	*anart*	
5. *achāyi* or *ache*	*ṣhāthām*	*achāy*	
6. *adik* *	*ṣhātām*	*adesh*	
7. *abhit* *	*ṣhmahi*	*abhed*	
8. *atani*	*dhwam*	*atān*	
9. *apāvi* or *apavi*	*ṣhata*	*apāv*	

BENEDICTIVE.

bodhi	*ṣhīya*
vedi	*ṣhīṣhṭhāh*
hāvi or *ho*	*ṣhīṣhṭa*
narti	*ṣhīvahi*
chāyi or *che*	*ṣhīyāsthām*
dik	*ṣhīyāstām*
bhit *	*ṣhīmahi*
tani	*ṣhīdhwam*
pāvi or *pavi*	*ṣhīran*

CONDITIONAL.

abodhi	*ṣhye*
avedi	*ṣhyathāh*
ahāvi or *aho*	*ṣhyata*
anarti	*ṣhyāvahi*
achāyi or *ache*	*ṣhyethām*
adek	*ṣhyetām*
abhet *	*ṣhyāmahi*
atani	*ṣhyadhwam*
apāvi or *apavi*	*ṣhyanta*

* Obs. After *t* the initial *ṣh* of the terminations takes the dental form *s*. In the 3d pret., *adik* and *abhit* reject the sibilant from *ṣhṭhah*, and become *adig* and *abhid* before *dhwam*. Thus, *adikshi*, *adikthāh*, *adeshi*, *adikshwahi*, *adikshāthām*, *adikshātām*, *adikshmahi*, *adigdhwam*, *adikshata*. And *abhitsi*, *abhitthāh*, *abhedi*, *abhitswahi*, *abhitsāthām*, *abhitsātām*, *abhitsmahi* *abhiddhwam*, *abhitsata* (p. 82. *s.*).

AUXILIARY VERBS.

116. There are three auxiliary verbs of constant occurrence: *as*, "to be"; *kṛi*, "to do"; and *bhū*, "to become." The first belongs to the 2d conjugation, the second to the 8th, and the third to the 1st. The first two, however, are too irregular to be placed under any conjugation, and their inflection is therefore exhibited here. The third, *bhū*, will follow in its proper place at the head of the examples under the 1st conjugation.

Root अस् *as*, "to be."

(R. 92. *d.* Cf. the Latin *sum*, *es*, *est*, and the Greek ἐμμί, ἐσσί, ἐστί.)

Present.—"I am." | *First Preterite.*—"I was."

PERS.	SING.	DUAL.	PLURAL.	SING.	DUAL.	PLURAL.
1st,	अस्मि *asmi*,	स्वः *swah*,	स्मः *smah*.	आसं *āsam*,	आस्व *āswa*,	आस्म *āsma*.
2d,	असि *asi*,	स्थः *sthah*,	स्थ *stha*.	आसीः *āsīh*,	आस्तं[a] *āstam*,	आस्त *āsta*.
3d,	अस्ति *asti*,	स्तः *stah*,	सन्ति *santi*.	आसीत् *āsīt*,	आस्तां *āstām*,	आसन् *āsan*.

Potential.—"I may be," &c. | *Imperative.*—"Let me be."

स्यां *syām*,	स्याव *syāva*,	स्याम *syāma*.	असानि *asāni*,	असाव *asāva*,	असाम *asāma*.
स्याः *syāh*,	स्यातं *syātam*,	स्यात *syāta*.	एधि *edhi*,	स्तं *stam*,	स्त *sta*.
स्यात् *syāt*,	स्यातां *syātām*,	स्युः *syuh*.	अस्तु *astu*,	स्तां *stām*,	सन्तु *santu*.

*Second Preterite.**—"I was," &c.

आस *āsa*,	आसिव *āsiva*,	आसिम *āsima*.
आसिथ *āsitha*,	आसथुः *āsathuh*,	आस *āsa*.
आस *āsa*,	आसतुः *āsatuh*,	आसुः *āsuh*.

a) Cf. ἦστον, ἤστην, and pl. ἦσμεν, ἦστε.

* This tense is never found by itself, but is of great use in forming the 2d pret. of causals, &c., see p. 77. *g.* and r. 108.

Root कृ *kṛi*. Infin. कर्तुं *kartum*, "to do" (r. 96.).

PARASMAIPADA.

Present Tense.—"I do."

करोमि *karomi*,	कुर्वः[b] *kurvah*,	कुर्मः *kurmah*.
करोषि[a] *karoṣhi*,	कुरुथः *kuruthah*,	कुरुथ *kurutha*.
करोति *karoti*,	कुरुतः *kurutah*,	कुर्वन्ति[c] *kurvanti*.

First Preterite.—"I was doing," &c.

अकरवं[d] *akaravam,*	अकुर्व *akurva,*	अकुर्म *akurma.*
अकरोः *akaroh,*	अकुरुतं *akurutam,*	अकुरुत *akuruta.*
अकरोत् *akarot,*	अकुरुतां *akurutām,*	अकुर्वन् *akurvan.*

Potential.—"I may do," &c.

कुर्य्यां *kuryām,*	कुर्य्याव *kuryāva,*	कुर्य्याम *kuryāma.*
कुर्य्याः *kuryāh,*	कुर्य्यातं *kuryātam,*	कुर्य्यात *kuryāta.*
कुर्य्यात् *kuryāt,*	कुर्य्यातां *kuryātām,*	कुर्य्युः *kuryuh.*

Imperative.—"Let me do," &c.

करवाणि[e] *karavāṇi,*	करवाव *karavāva,*	करवाम *karavāma.*
कुरु[f] *kuru,*	कुरुतं *kurutam,*	कुरुत *kuruta.*
करोतु *karotu,*	कुरुतां *kurutām,*	कुर्व्वन्तु *kurvantu.*

Second Preterite.—"I did."

चकार[g] *chakāra,*	चकृव[h] *chakṛiva,*	चकृम *chakṛima.*
चकर्थ *chakartha,*	चक्रथुः[i] *chakrathuh,*	चक्र *chakra.*
चकार *chakāra,*	चक्रतुः *chakratuh,*	चक्रुः *chakruh.*

First Future.—"I will do."

कर्त्तास्मि[j] *kartāsmi,*	कर्त्तास्वः *kartāswah,*	कर्त्तास्मः *kartāsmah.*
कर्त्तासि *kartāsi,*	कर्त्तास्थः *kartāsthah,*	कर्त्तास्थ *kartāstha.*
कर्त्ता *kartā,*	कर्त्तारौ *kartārau,*	कर्त्तारः *kartārah.*

Second Future.—"I shall do."

करिष्यामि[k] *karishyāmi,*	करिष्यावः *karishyāvah,*	करिष्यामः *kariṣhyāmah.*
करिष्यसि *kariṣhyasi,*	करिष्यथः *kariṣhyathah,*	करिष्यथ *karishyatha.*
करिष्यति *kariṣhyati,*	करिष्यतः *kariṣhyatah,*	करिष्यन्ति *kariṣhyanti.*

Third Preterite.—"I did."

अकार्षं[l] *akārṣham,*	अकार्ष्व *akārṣhwa,*	अकार्ष्म *akārṣhma.*
अकार्षीः *akārṣhīh,*	अकार्ष्टं *akārṣhṭam,*	अकार्ष्ट *akārṣhṭa.*
अकार्षीत् *akārṣhīt,*	अकार्ष्टां *akārṣhṭām,*	अकार्षुः *akārṣhuh.*

The other tenses are, bened. क्रियासं[m], क्रियाः, क्रियात्, &c., cond. अकरिष्यं[n], अकरिष्यः, अकरिष्यत्, &c.

[a]) r. 30. [b]) See p. 39. note. [c]) r. 7. [d]) r. 10. †. [e]) r. 21. [f]) The eighth conjugation rejects the *hi* of the imperative, in conformity with the fifth conjugation, r. 94. [g]) p. 75. *b.* [h]) See the scheme for the 2d pret. p. 73. [i]) r. 7. [j]) p. 79. *f.* [k]) p. 79. *c.* [l]) p. 82. *f.* [m]) p. 85. *c.* [n]) r. 105.

ATMANEPADA.

Present Tense.

कुर्वे[a] *kurve,*	कुर्वहे *kurvahe,*	कुर्महे *kurmahe.*
कुरुषे[b] *kuruṣhe,*	कुर्वाथे *kurvāthe,*	कुरुध्वे *kurudhwe.*
कुरुते *kurute,*	कुर्वाते *kurvāte,*	कुर्वते *kurvate.*

First Preterite.

अकुर्वि *akurvi,*	अकुर्वहि *akurvahi,*	अकुर्महि *akurmahi.*
अकुरुथाः *akuruthāh,*	अकुर्वाथां *akurvāthām,*	अकुरुध्वं *akurudhwam.*
अकुरुत *akuruta,*	अकुर्वातां *akurvātām,*	अकुर्वत *akurvata.*

Potential.

कुर्वीय *kurvīya,*	कुर्वीवहि *kurvīvahi,*	कुर्वीमहि *kurvīmahi.*
कुर्वीथाः *kurvīthāh,*	कुर्वीयाथां *kurvīyāthām,*	कुर्वीध्वं *kurvīdhwam.*
कुर्वीत *kurvīta,*	कुर्वीयातां *kurvīyātām,*	कुर्वीरन् *kurvīran.*

Imperative.

करवै[c] *karavai,*	करवावहै *karavāvahai,*	करवामहै *karavāmahai.*
कुरुष्व[d] *kuruṣhwa,*	कुर्वाथां *kurvāthām,*	कुरुध्वं *kurudhwam.*
कुरुतां *kurutām,*	कुर्वातां *kurvātām,*	कुर्वतां *kurvatām.*

Second Preterite.

चक्रे[e] *chakre,*	चकृवहे *chakṛivahe,*	चकृमहे *chakṛimahe.*
चकृषे[f] *chakṛiṣhe,*	चक्राथे *chakrāthe,*	चकृध्वे or ढ्वे *chakṛidhwe.*
चक्रे *chakre,*	चक्राते *chakrāte,*	चक्रिरे *chakrire.*

The other tenses are 1st fut. कर्ताहे[g], 2d fut. करिष्ये[h], 3d pret., 1st, 2d, 3d sing. अकृषि[i], अकृथाः, अकृत, bened. कृषीय[j], cond. अकरिष्ये[k].

[a]) r. 7. [b]) r. 30. [c]) r. 10. †. [d]) r. 30. [e]) r. 93. and r. 7. [f]) See the scheme for the 2d pret. p. 73. [g]) p. 79. *f.* [h]) p. 79. *c.* [i]) p. 83. *g.* [j]) p. 85. *c.* [k]) r. 105.

EXAMPLES OF REGULAR PRIMITIVE VERBS OF THE FIRST CONJUGATION (r. 88.)

Root भू *bhū.* Infin. भवितुं *bhavitum,* "to become" or "be."

PARASMAIPADA. *Present Tense.*—"I become" or "I am."

PERS. SING.	DUAL.	PLURAL.
1st, भवामि[a] *bhavāmi,*	भवावः *bhavāvah,*	भवामः *bhavāmah.*
2d, भवसि *bhavasi,*	भवथः *bhavathah,*	भवथ *bhavatha.*
3d, भवति *bhavati,*	भवतः *bhavatah,*	भवन्ति *bhavanti.*

First Preterite.—"I was becoming" or "I was."

अभवं *abhavam,*	अभवाव *abhavāva,*	अभवाम *abhavāma.*
अभवः *abhavah,*	अभवतं *abhavatam,*	अभवत *abhavata.*
अभवत् *abhavat,*	अभवतां *abhavatām,*	अभवन् *abhavan.*

Potential.—"I may become" or "I may be."

भवेयं *bhaveyam,*	भवेव *bhaveva,*	भवेम *bhavema.*
भवेः *bhaveh,*	भवेतं *bhavetam,*	भवेत *bhaveta.*
भवेत् *bhavet,*	भवेतां *bhavetām,*	भवेयुः *bhaveyuh.*

Imperative.—"Let me become" or "let me be."

भवानि *bhavāni,*	भवाव *bhavāva,*	भवाम *bhavāma.*
भव *bhava,*	भवतं *bhavatam,*	भवत *bhavata.*
भवतु *bhavatu,*	भवतां *bhavatām,*	भवन्तु *bhavantu.*

Second Preterite.—"I became," or "I was."

बभूव[b] *babhūva,*	बभूविव *babhūviva,*	बभूविम *babhūvima.*
बभूविथ *babhūvitha,*	बभूवथुः *babhūvathuh,*	बभूव *babhūva.*
बभूव *babhūva,*	बभूवतुः *babhūvatuh,*	बभूवुः *babhūvuh.*

First Future.—"I will become," &c.

भवितास्मि[c] *bhavitāsmi,*	भवितास्वः *bhavitāswah,*	भवितास्मः *bhavitāsmah.*
भवितासि *bhavitāsi,*	भवितास्थः *bhavitāsthah,*	भवितास्थ *bhavitāstha.*
भविता *bhavitā,*	भवितारौ *bhavitārau,*	भवितारः *bhavitārah.*

Second Future.—"I shall become," &c.

भविष्यामि *bhavishyāmi,*	भविष्यावः *bhavishyāvah,*	भविष्यामः *bhavishyāmah.*
भविष्यसि *bhavishyasi,*	भविष्यथः *bhavishyathah,*	भविष्यथ *bhavishyatha.*
भविष्यति *bhavishyati,*	भविष्यतः *bhavishyatah,*	भविष्यन्ति *bhavishyanti.*

The other tenses are, 3d pret. अभूवं, अभूः, अभूत्[d], &c.; bened. भूयासं[e], &c.; cond. अभविष्यं, &c.; pass. part. भूत[f].

a) r. 88. *a*. b) r. 98. c) p. 79. *a*. d) p. 83. *i*. e) p. 85. *b*. f) This is given in anticipation of r. 125. as being the most useful of all the participles.

Root स्मि *smi*. Infin. स्मेतुं *smetum*, "to smile."

ATMANEPADA. *Present Tense.*—"I smile."

स्मये *smaye*[a],	स्मयावहे *smayāvahe*,	स्मयामहे *smayāmahe*.
स्मयसे *smayase*,	स्मयेथे *smayethe*,	स्मयध्वे *smayadhwe*.
स्मयते *smayate*,	स्मयेते *smayete*,	स्मयन्ते *smayante*.

First Preterite.—"I was smiling."

अस्मये *asmaye*,	अस्मयावहि *asmayāvahi*,	अस्मयामहि *asmayāmahi*.
अस्मयथाः *asmayathāh*,	अस्मयेथां *asmayethām*,	अस्मयध्वं *asmayadhwam*.
अस्मयत *asmayata*,	अस्मयेतां *asmayetām*,	अस्मयन्त *asmayanta*.

Potential.—"I may smile."

स्मयेय *smayeya*,	स्मयेवहि *smayevahi*,	स्मयेमहि *smayemahi*.
स्मयेथाः *smayethāh*,	स्मयेयाथां *smayeyāthām*,	स्मयेध्वं *smayedhwam*.
स्मयेत *smayeta*,	स्मयेयातां *smayeyātām*,	स्मयेरन् *smayeran*.

Imperative.—"Let me smile."

स्मयै *smayai*,	स्मयावहै *smayāvahai*,	स्मयामहै *smayāmahai*.
स्मयस्व *smayaswa*,	स्मयेथां *smayethām*,	स्मयध्वं *smayadhwam*.
स्मयतां *smayatām*,	स्मयेतां *smayetām*,	स्मयन्तां *smayantām*.

Second Preterite.—"I smiled."

सिष्मिये[b] *sishmiye*,	सिष्मियिवहे *sishmiyivahe*,	सिष्मियिमहे *sishmiyimahe*.
सिष्मियिषे *sishmiyishe*,	सिष्मियाथे *sishmiyāthe*,	सिष्मियिध्वे *sishmiyidhwe*.
सिष्मिये *sishmiye*,	सिष्मियाते *sishmiyāte*,	सिष्मियिरे *sishmiyire*.

First Future.—"I will smile."

स्मेताहे[c] *smetāhe*,	स्मेतास्वहे *smetāswahe*,	स्मेतास्महे *smetāsmahe*.
स्मेतासे *smetāse*,	स्मेतासाथे *smetāsāthe*,	स्मेताध्वे *smetādhwe*.
स्मेता *smetā*,	स्मेतारौ *smetārau*,	स्मेतारः *smetārah*.

Second Future.—"I shall smile."

स्मेष्ये[c] *smeshye*,	स्मेष्यावहे *smeshyāvahe*,	स्मेष्यामहे *smeshyāmahe*.
स्मेष्यसे *smeshyase*,	स्मेष्येथे *smeshyethe*,	स्मेष्यध्वे *smeshyadhwe*.
स्मेष्यते *smeshyate*.	स्मेष्येते *smeshyete*,	स्मेष्यन्ते *smeshyante*.

P

3d pret. अस्मेषि[d], bened. स्मेषीय[e], cond. अस्मेष्ये, pass. part. स्मित.

a) r. 88. *a*. b) p. 74. note † and r. 30. c) p. 79. *e*. d) p. 83. *g*. e) p. 85. *b*.

Obs. By 2 pr. 1 sin., is meant the 1st person sing. of the 2d preterite; by 2 pr. 1 du., the 1st person dual of the 2d pret; by pass. part., the passive past participle (r. 125.).

Root	*ji*, par. "conquer."	*dru*, par. "run."	*hṛi*, par. "seize."	*tyaj*, par. "quit."	*labh*, ātm. "obtain."	*shubh*, ātm. "shine."
Pres.	जयामि[a]	द्रवामि	हरामि	त्यजामि	लभे	शोभे
1st pret.	अजयं	अद्रवं	अहरं	अत्यजं	अलभे	अशोभे
Pot.	जयेयं	द्रवेयं	हरेयं	त्यजेयं	लभेय	शोभेय
Imp.	जयानि	द्रवाणि	हराणि	त्यजानि	लभै	शोभै
2 pr. 1 sin.	जिगाय[b]	दुद्राव[f]	जहार[i]	तत्याज[l]	लेभे[n]	शुशुभे[r]
2 pr. 1 du.	जिग्यिव[c]	दुद्रुव[g]	जह्रिव	तत्यजिव	लेभिवहे	शुशुभियहे
1st fut.	जेतास्मि[d]	द्रोतास्मि[h]	हर्त्तास्मि[j]	त्यक्तास्मि[m]	लब्धाहे[o]	शोभिताहे
2d fut.	जेष्यामि[d]	द्रोष्यामि[h]	हरिष्यामि[k]	त्यक्ष्यामि[m]	लप्स्ये[o]	शोभिष्ये
Infin.	जेतुं[e]	द्रोतुं	हर्त्तुं	त्यक्तुं	लब्धुं[p]	शोभितुं
Pass. part.	जित	द्रुत	हृत	त्यक्त	लब्ध[q]	शोभित

a) r. 88. *a*. b) p. 77. *f*. p. 75. *c*. c) p. 74. note †. d) p. 79. *e*. e) r. 106.
f) r. 98. g) See the scheme for the 2d pret. p. 73. h) p. 79. *f*. i) r. 98. and 99. *c*.
j) p. 79. *f*. k) p. 79. *c*. l) p. 76. *c*. m) p. 80. n) p. 76. *c*. o) p. 80.
p) r. 106. q) r. 125. *i*. r) p. 74.

Root	*vṛit*, ātm. "be, exist."	*yāch*, par. "ask."	*jīv*, par. "live."	*edh*, ātm. "flourish."	*arh*, par. "deserve."	*nind*, par. "blame."
Pres.	वर्त्ते	याचामि	जीवामि	एधे	अर्हामि	निन्दामि[e]
1st pret.	अवर्त्ते	अयाचं	अजीवं	ऐधे	आर्हं	अनिन्दं
Pot.	वर्त्तेय	याचेयं	जीवेयं	एधेय	अर्हेयं	निन्देयं
Imp.	वर्त्तै	याचानि	जीवानि	एधै	अर्हाणि	निन्दानि
2 pr. 1 sin.	ववृते[a]	ययाच	जिजीव[b]	एधाञ्चक्रे[c]	आनर्ह[d]	निनिन्द[f]
2 pr. 1 du.	ववृतिवहे	ययाचिव	जिजीविव	एधाञ्चकृयहे	आनर्हिव	निनिन्दिव
1st fut.	वर्त्तिताहे	याचितास्मि	जीवितास्मि	एधिताहे	अर्हितास्मि	निन्दितास्मि
2d fut.	वर्त्तिष्ये	याचिष्यामि	जीविष्यामि	एधिष्ये	अर्हिष्यामि	निन्दिष्यामि
Infin.	वर्त्तितुं	याचितुं	जीवितुं	एधितुं	अर्हितुं	निन्दितुं
Pass. part.	वृत्त	याचित	जीवित	एधित	अर्हित	निन्दित

a) r. 98. b) r. 88. *b* with note. c) p. 77. *g*. d) p. 75. *f*. e) r. 88. *b*. f) r. 88. *b*. note.

Root	*sad*, par. "sink."	*gam*, par. "go."	*sthā*, par. "remain."	*drish*, par. "see."	*dah*, par. "burn."	*vah*, par. "bear."
Pres.	सीदामि[a]	गच्छामि[a]	तिष्ठामि[h]	पश्यामि[a]	दहामि	वहामि[q]
1st pret.	असीदं	अगच्छं	अतिष्ठं	अपश्यं	अदहं	अवहं
Pot.	सीदेयं	गच्छेयं	तिष्ठेयं[i]	पश्येयं	दहेयं	वहेयं
Imp.	सीदानि	गच्छानि	तिष्ठानि	पश्यानि	दहानि	वहानि
2 pr. 1 sin.	ससाद	जगाम[d]	तस्थौ[j]	ददर्श	ददाह	उवाह[r]
2 pr. 1 du.	सेदिव[b]	जग्मिव[e]	तस्थिव	ददृशिव	देहिव[o]	ऊहिव[r]
1st fut.	सत्तास्मि	गन्तास्मि[f]	स्थातास्मि[k]	द्रष्टास्मि[f]	दग्धास्मि[p]	वोढास्मि[s]
2d fut.	सत्स्यामि	गमिष्यामि[f]	स्थास्यामि	द्रक्ष्यामि[f]	धक्ष्यामि[p]	वक्ष्यामि[s]
Infin.	सत्तुं	गन्तुं	स्थातुं	द्रष्टुं[m]	दग्धुं[m]	वोढुं[t]
Pass. part.	सन्न[c]	गत[g]	स्थित[l]	दृष्ट[n]	दग्ध[n]	ऊढ[u]

[a]) p. 64. *c.* [b]) p. 76. *c.* [c]) r. 125. *j.* [d]) p. 75. *c.* [e]) p. 77. *e.* [f]) p. 80. [g]) r. 125. *o.* [h]) p. 64. *c.* cf. ἵστημι. [i]) cf. ἱσταίην, and Lat. *stem.* [j]) p. 75. *e.* and 76. *a.* See the 2d pret. of the root *dā*, given at full under the 3d conjugation. [k]) p. 79. *e.* [l]) r. 125. *c.* [m]) r. 106. [n]) r. 125. *i.* [o]) p. 76. *c.* and 68. *h.* [p]) p. 80. and 69. *i.* [q]) Cf. the Lat. *veho.* [r]) p. 76. *d.* [s]) p. 80. Whenever the final ह् blends with the initial of the termination into ढ, the medial *a* of the root, instead of being lengthened by r. 91. *h.*, is changed to *o.* Thus in the 3d pret. par. अवाक्षं, अवाक्षीः, अवाक्षीत्, अवाक्ष्व, अवोढं, अवोढां, अवाक्ष्म, अवोढ, अवाक्षुः; ātm. अवाक्षि, अवोढाः, अवोढ, अवाक्ष्वहि, &c. See p. 82. *f. g.* Similarly *sah*, "to bear." With *avākshīt*, cf. the Lat. *vexit.* [t]) r. 106. [u]) r. 125. *m.*

Root.	*pā*, par. "drink."	*ghrā*, par. "smell."	*dhmā*, par. "blow."	*hwe*, par. "call."	*gai*, par. "sing."	*vas*, par. "dwell."
Pres.	पिबामि[a]	जिघ्रामि[a]	धमामि[d]	ह्वयामि[e]	गायामि[i]	वसामि
1st pret.	अपिबं	अजिघ्रं	अधमं	अह्वयं	अगायं	अवसं
Pot.	पिबेयं	जिघ्रेयं	धमेयं	ह्वयेयं	गायेयं	वसेयं
Imp.	पिबानि	जिघ्राणि	धमानि	ह्वयानि	गायानि	वसानि
2 pr. 1 sin.	पपौ	जघ्रौ[b]	दध्मौ[b]	जुहाव[f]	जगौ[b]	उवास[k]
2 pr. 1 du.	पपिव	जघ्रिव	दध्मिव	जुहुविव	जगिव	ऊषिव[k]
1st fut.	पातास्मि	घ्रातास्मि	ध्मातास्मि	ह्वातास्मि[g]	गातास्मि[g]	वस्तास्मि[l]
2d fut.	पास्यामि	घ्रास्यामि	ध्मास्यामि	ह्वास्यामि[g]	गास्यामि[g]	वत्स्यामि[l]
Infin.	पातुं	घ्रातुं	ध्मातुं	ह्वातुं[g]	गातुं[g]	वस्तुं
Pass. part.	पीत[c]	घ्रात	ध्मात	हूत[h]	गीत[j]	उषित[m]

[a]) p. 64. *c.* Cf. Latin *bibo, bibis, &c.* [b]) p. 76. *a.* See the tense at full under *dā*, 3d conjugation. [c]) r. 125. *c.* [d]) This root substitutes *dham* for *dhmā.*

[e]) r. 10. †. [f]) p. 77. *f.* Other roots in *e* follow the analogy of those in *ā* (p. 76. *a.*); as *dhe, dadhau.* [g]) Roots ending in the diphthongs *e* and *ai* change these letters to *ā* before the *t* and *s* of a termination. Hence, *gai* in the 3d pret. is *agāsam, &c.* *Hwe* may follow Form III. in the 3d pret. rejecting its final; thus, *ahwam, ahwah, &c.* Atm. *ahwe, ahwathāh, &c.*, or Form II. *ahwāsi, &c.* [h]) r. 125. *e.* [i]) r. 8. [j]) r. 125. *f.* [k]) p. 76. *d.* [l]) p. 80. [m]) r. 125. *m.*

EXAMPLES OF REGULAR PRIMITIVE VERBS OF THE FOURTH CONJUGATION (r. 89.).

Root मुह्, *muh.* Infin. मोहितुं, "to be troubled."

PARASMAIPADA. *Present Tense.*—"I am troubled."

मुह्यामि *muhyāmi,*	मुह्यावः *muhyāvah,*	मुह्यामः *muhyāmah.*
मुह्यसि *muhyasi,*	मुह्यथः *muhyathah,*	मुह्यथ *muhyatha.*
मुह्यति *muhyati,*	मुह्यतः *muhyatah,*	मुह्यन्ति *muhyanti.*

First Preterite.—"I was troubled."

अमुह्यं *amuhyam,*	अमुह्याव *amuhyāva,*	अमुह्याम *amuhyāma.*
अमुह्यः *amuhyah,*	अमुह्यतं *amuhyatam,*	अमुह्यत *amuhyata.*
अमुह्यत् *amuhyat,*	अमुह्यतां *amuhyatām,*	अमुह्यन् *amuhyan.*

Potential.—"I may be troubled."

मुह्येयं *muhyeyam,*	मुह्येव *muhyeva,*	मुह्येम *muhyema.*
मुह्येः *muhyeh,*	मुह्येतं *muhyetam,*	मुह्येत *muhyeta.*
मुह्येत् *muhyet,*	मुह्येतां *muhyetām,*	मुह्येयुः *muhyeyuh.*

Imperative.—"Let me be troubled."

मुह्यानि *muhyāni,*	मुह्याव *muhyāva,*	मुह्याम *muhyāma.*
मुह्य *muhya,*	मुह्यतं *muhyatam,*	मुह्यत *muhyata.*
मुह्यतु *muhyatu,*	मुह्यतां *muhyatām,*	मुह्यन्तु *muhyantu.*

Second Preterite.—"I became troubled."

मुमोह *mumoha,*	मुमुहिव *mumuhiva,*	मुमुहिम *mumuhima.*
मुमोहिथ *mumohitha,*	मुमुहथुः *mumuhathuh,*	मुमुह *mumuha.*
मुमोह *mumoha,*	मुमुहतुः *mumuhatuh,*	मुमुहुः *mumuhuh.*

First Future.

मोहितास्मि[a] *mohitāsmi,*	मोहितास्वः *mohitāswah,*	मोहितास्मः *mohitāsmah.*
मोहितासि *mohitāsi,*	मोहितास्थः *mohitāsthah,*	मोहितास्थ *mohitāstha.*
मोहिता *mohitā,*	मोहितारौ *mohitārau,*	मोहितारः *mohitārah.*

Second Future.

मोहिष्यामि *mohiṣhyāmi,*	मोहिष्यावः *mohiṣhyāvah,*	मोहिष्यामः *mohiṣhyāmah.*
मोहिष्यसि *mohiṣhyasi,*	मोहिष्यथः *mohiṣhyathah,*	मोहिष्यथ *mohiṣhyatha.*
मोहिष्यति *mohiṣhyati,*	मोहिष्यतः *mohiṣhyatah,*	मोहिष्यन्ति *mohiṣhyanti.*

3d pret. अमुहं[b], bened. मुह्यासं[c], cond. अमोहिष्यं, p. part. मूढ or मुग्ध[d].

[a]) Or मोढास्मि or मोग्धास्मि, p. 80. [b]) p. 83. *h.* [c]) p. 85. *e.* [d]) r. 125. *i.*

Root	*as,* par. "throw."	*nash,* par. "perish."	*pad,* ātm. "go."	*sham,* par. "be calm."	*sidh,* par. "succeed."	*trip,* par. "be pleased."
Pres.	अस्यामि[a]	नश्यामि[a]	पद्ये[e]	शाम्यामि[h]	सिध्यामि[a]	तृप्यामि[a]
1st pret.	आस्यं	अनश्यं	अपद्ये	अशाम्यं	असिध्यं	अतृप्यं
Pot.	अस्येयं	नश्येयं	पद्येय	शाम्येयं	सिध्येयं	तृप्येयं
Imp.	अस्यानि	नश्यानि	पद्यै	शाम्यानि	सिध्यानि	तृप्याणि
2 pr. 1 sin.	आस[b]	ननाश[c]	पेदे[c]	शशाम[c]	सिषेध	ततर्प[k]
2 pr. 1 du.	आसिव	नेशिव[c]	पेदिवहे	शेमिव	सिषिधिव	ततृपिव
1st fut.	असितास्मि	नशितास्मि[d]	पत्ताहे[f]	शमितास्मि	सेद्धास्मि[f]	तर्प्तास्मि
2d fut.	असिष्यामि	नशिष्यामि	पत्स्ये	शमिष्यामि	सेत्स्यामि	तर्प्स्यामि
Infin.	असितुं	नशितुं	पत्तुं	शमितुं	सेद्धुं	तर्प्तुं
Pass. part.	अस्त	नष्ट	पन्न[g]	शान्त[i]	सिद्ध[j]	तृप्त

[a]) Many of these roots of the 4th conjugation follow the 3d Form for the 3d pret. See p. 83. *k.* [b]) p. 75. *f.* [c]) p. 76. *c.* [d]) This root may optionally reject *i*, and insert a nasal in the futures; thus, नंष्टास्मि, नंक्ष्यामि. [e]) p. 89. note marked *. [f]) p. 80. [g]) r. 125. *j.* [h]) There are seven other useful roots which lengthen the medial *a* after the manner of *sham;* viz. *kram, bhram* (r. 89. *a.*) *dam, klam, ksham, shram, mad.* [i]) r. 125. *p.* [j]) r. 125. *i.* [k]) Cf. τέρπομαι, τεταρπόμην.

Root.	*so,* par. (*vyava*) "strive."	*bhransh,* par. "fall."	*vyadh,* par. "pierce."	*yudh,* ātm. "fight."	*tush,* par. "be content."	*hrish,* par. "rejoice."
Pres.	स्यामि[a]	भ्रश्यामि[e]	विध्यामि[e]	युध्ये	तुष्यामि	हृष्यामि
1st pret.	अस्यं	अभ्रश्यं	अविध्यं	अयुध्ये	अतुष्यं	अहृष्यं
Pot.	स्येयं	भ्रश्येयं	विध्येयं	युध्येय	तुष्येयं	हृष्येयं
Imp.	स्यानि	भ्रश्यानि	विध्यानि	युध्यै	तुष्याणि	हृष्याणि
2 pr. 1 sin.	ससौ[b]	बभ्रंश[f]	विव्याध[i]	युयुधे .	तुतोष	जहर्ष[l]
2 pr. 1 du.	ससिव	बभ्रंशिव	विविधिव	युयुधिवहे	तुतुषिव	जहृषिव
1st fut.	सातास्मि[c]	भ्रंशितास्मि[g]	व्यद्धास्मि[j]	योद्धाहे[j]	तोष्टास्मि[j]	हर्षितास्मि
2d fut.	सास्यामि	भ्रंशिष्यामि	व्यत्स्यामि	योत्स्ये[j]	तोक्ष्यामि[j]	हर्षिष्यामि
Infin.	सातुं	भ्रंशितुं	व्यद्धुं	योद्धुं	तोष्टुं	हर्षितुं
Pass. part.	सित[d]	भ्रष्ट[h]	विद्ध[h]	युद्ध[k]	तुष्ट[k]	हृषित[m]

a) There are three other uncommon roots which follow *so*; viz. *sho*, *chho*, *do*. b) Roots ending in *e* or *o* follow the analogy of those in *ā* and *ai* in the 2d pret., see p. 76. *a*. c) Roots ending in *o* change *o* to *ā* before the *t* and *s* of a termination. d) r. 125. *g*. e) r. 89. *a*. f) p. 75. *a*. and 64. *b*. g) p. 78. note *. h) r. 125. *n*. i) p. 75. *d*. j) p. 80. k) r. 125. *i*. l) p. 75. *c*. m) Or हुर.

EXAMPLES OF REGULAR PRIMITIVE VERBS OF THE SIXTH CONJUGATION (r. 90.).

Root सृज् *sṛij*. Infin. स्रष्टुं *sraṣhṭum*, "to create," or "let go."

PARASMAIPADA only.

Present Tense.—"I create."

सृजामि[a] *sṛijāmi*,	सृजावः *sṛijāvah*,	सृजामः *sṛijāmah*.
सृजसि *sṛijasi*,	सृजथः *sṛijathah*,	सृजथ *sṛijatha*.
सृजति *sṛijati*,	सृजतः *sṛijatah*,	सृजन्ति *sṛijanti*.

First Preterite.—"I was creating."

असृजं *asṛijam*,	असृजाव *asṛijāva*,	असृजाम *asṛijāma*.
असृजः *asṛijah*,	असृजतं *asṛijatam*,	असृजत *asṛijata*.
असृजत् *asṛijat*,	असृजतां *asṛijatām*,	असृजन् *asṛijan*.

Potential.—"I may create."

सृजेयं *sṛijeyam*,	सृजेव *sṛijeva*,	सृजेम *sṛijema*.
सृजेः *sṛijeh*,	सृजेतं *sṛijetam*,	सृजेत *sṛijeta*.
सृजेत् *sṛijet*,	सृजेतां *sṛijetām*,	सृजेयुः *sṛijeyuh*.

Imperative.—"Let me create."

सृजानि *sṛijāni*,	सृजाव *sṛijāva*,	सृजाम *sṛijāma*.
सृज *sṛija*,	सृजतं *sṛijatam*,	सृजत *sṛijata*.
सृजतु *sṛijatu*,	सृजतां *sṛijatām*,	सृजन्तु *sṛijantu*.

Second Preterite.

ससर्ज *sasarja*,	ससृजिव *sasṛijiva*,	ससृजिम *sasṛijima*.
ससर्जिथ[b] *sasarjitha*,	ससृजथुः *sasṛijathuh*,	ससृज *sasṛija*.
ससर्ज *sasarja*,	ससृजतुः *sasṛijatuh*,	ससृजुः *sasṛijuh*.

First Future.

स्रष्टास्मि[c] *srashṭāsmi*,	स्रष्टास्वः *srashṭāswah*,	स्रष्टास्मः *srashṭāsmah*.
स्रष्टासि *srashṭāsi*,	स्रष्टास्थः *srashṭāsthah*,	स्रष्टास्थ *srashṭāstha*.
स्रष्टा *srashṭā*,	स्रष्टारौ *srashṭārau*,	स्रष्टारः *srashṭārah*.

Second Future.

स्रक्ष्यामि[c] *srakshyāmi*,	स्रक्ष्यावः *srakshyāvah*,	स्रक्ष्यामः *srakshyāmah*.
स्रक्ष्यसि *srakshyasi*,	स्रक्ष्यथः *srakshyathah*,	स्रक्ष्यथ *srakshyatha*.
स्रक्ष्यति *srakshyati*,	स्रक्ष्यतः *srakshyatah*,	स्रक्ष्यन्ति *srakshyanti*.

The other tenses are, 3d pret. अस्राक्षं[e], bened. सृज्यासं[d], cond. अस्रक्ष्यं[e] pass. part. सृष्ट[f].

[a]) p. 65. note *. [b]) or ससर्ज. See p. 80. note *, and r. 91. [c]) p. 80. note *. [d]) p. 85. *e*. [e]) r. 105. [f]) r. 125. *i*.

Root	*mṛi*, ātm. "die."	*prachchh*, par. "ask."	*masj*. par. "dive."	*ish*, par. "wish."	*kship*, par. "throw."	*much*, par. "let go."
Pres.	म्रिये[a]	पृच्छामि[a]	मज्जामि[f]	इच्छामि[a]	क्षिपामि[l]	मुञ्चामि[n]
1st pret.	अम्रिये	अपृच्छं	अमज्जं	ऐच्छं[j]	अक्षिपं	अमुञ्चं
Pot.	म्रियेय	पृच्छेयं	मज्जेयं	इच्छेयं	क्षिपेयं	मुञ्चेयं
Imp.	म्रियै	पृच्छानि	मज्जानि	इच्छानि	क्षिपाणि	मुञ्चानि
2 pr. 1 sin.	ममार	पप्रच्छ[c]	ममज्ज[g]	इयेष[k]	चिक्षेप[m]	मुमोच
2 pr. 1 du.	मम्रिव	पपृच्छिव[c]	ममज्जिव	ईषिव[k]	चिक्षिपिव	मुमुचिव
1st fut.	मर्त्तास्मि	प्रष्टास्मि[d]	मंक्तास्मि[h]	एषितास्मि	क्षेप्तास्मि[d]	मोक्तास्मि[d]
2d fut.	मरिष्यामि[b]	प्रक्ष्यामि	मंक्ष्यामि	एषिष्यामि	क्षेप्स्यामि	मोक्ष्यामि
Infin.	मर्त्तुं	प्रष्टुं	मज्जितुं	एषितुं	क्षेप्तुं	मोक्तुं
Pass. part.	मृत	पृष्ट[e]	मग्न[i]	इष्ट	क्षिप्त[e]	मुक्त

[a]) r. 90. *a*. [b]) p. 79. *c*. [c]) p. 77. *f*. With the 2d pers. sing. पप्रच्छिथ, cf. the Latin *poposcisti*. So also with तुतोदिथ (from *tud*), *tutodisti*. [d]) p. 80. [e]) r. 125. *i*. [f]) So *lajjāmi* from *lasj*. But these roots are sometimes written *majj* and *lajj*. [g]) p. 64. *b*. [h]) This root inserts a nasal in the futures. [i]) r. 125. *h*. [j]) r. 88. [k]) p. 75. *f*. [l]) p. 65. note *. [m]) p. 75. *d*. [n]) r. 90. *b*.

EXAMPLES OF IRREGULAR PRIMITIVE VERBS OF THE SECOND CONJUGATION (r. 92.).

Root या. Infin. यातुं, "to go."

PARASMAIPADA only.

Present.—"I go.

यामि *yāmi*,	यावः *yāvah*,	यामः *yāmah*.
यासि *yāsi*,	याथः *yāthah*,	याथ *yātha*.
याति *yāti*,	यातः *yātah*,	यान्ति *yānti*.

First Preterite.

अयां *ayām*,	अयाव *ayāva*,	अयाम *ayāma*.
अयाः *ayāh*,	अयातं *ayātam*,	अयात *ayāta*.
अयात् *ayāt*,	अयातां *ayātām*,	अयान्[b] *ayān*.

Potential.

यायां *yāyām*,	यायाव *yāyāva*,	यायाम *yāyāma*.
यायाः *yāyāh*,	यायातं *yāyātam*,	यायात *yāyāta*.
यायात् *yāyāt*,	यायातां *yāyātām*,	यायुः *yāyuh*.

Imperative.

यानि *yāni*,	याव *yāva*,	याम *yāma*.
याहि *yāhi*,	यातं *yātam*,	यात *yāta*.
यातु *yātu*,	यातां *yātām*,	यान्तु *yāntu*.

2d pret. ययौ[c], &c.; 1st fut. यातास्मि[d], &c.; 2d fut. यास्यामि[d], &c.; 3d pret. अयासिषं[e]; bened. यायासं; cond. अयास्यं; p. part. यात.

Root इ. Infin. एतुं, "to go."

PARASMAIPADA.

Present.—"I go."

एमि[f] *emi*,	इवः *ivah*,	इमः *imah*.
एषि *eṣhi*,	इथः *ithah*,	इथ *itha*.
एति *eti*,	इतः *itah*,	यन्ति[g] *yanti*.

First Preterite.

आयं[h] *āyam*,	ऐव *aiva*,	ऐम *aima*.
ऐः[i] *aih*,	ऐतं *aitam*,	ऐत *aita*.
ऐत् *ait*,	ऐतां *aitām*,	आयन् *āyan*.

Potential.

इयां *iyām*,	इयाव *iyāva*,	इयाम *iyāma*.
इयाः *iyāh*,	इयातं *iyātam*,	इयात *iyāta*.
इयात् *iyāt*,	इयातां *iyātām*,	इयुः *iyuh*.

Imperative.

अयानि[j] *ayāni*,	अयाव *ayāva*,	अयाम *ayāma*.
इहि *ihi*,	इतं *itam*,	इत *ita*.
एतु *etu*,	इतां *itām*,	यन्तु[g] *yantu*.

2d pret. इयाय[k], इययिथ or इयेथ, इयाय, ईयिव, &c.; 1st fut. एतास्मि[d]; 2d fut. एष्यामि; 3d pret. अगाम् (from root गा[e]); bened. ईयासं[l]; cond. ऐष्यं; p. part. इत.

a) p. 70. *b*. b) or अयुः, p. 69. note ‡. c) p. 76. *a*. d) p. 79. *e*. e) p. 82. *d*. f) r. 92. g) r. 7. h) *a* with *e*=*ai*, r. 6., *ai* with *am*=*āyam*, r. 8. i) *a* with *i*=*ai*, r. 88. j) *e* with *āni*=*ayāni*. k) p. 75. *k*. l) p. 85. *b*.

The above root इ *i*, "to go," is constantly compounded with prepositions,* in accordance with the usual rules of combination.

* It is desirable to introduce the inflection of these compound verbs here, although the subject properly belongs to the chapter on compound words.

Thus, with the prep. *ā*, "to;" pres. ऐमि, ऐषि, ऐति; dual एवः, &c.; 1st pret. आयं, ऐः, &c.; pot. इयां, &c.; imp. आयानि, इहि, ऐतु, &c. Again with *apa* prefixed to ऐमि, &c.; pres. अपैमि, &c.; 1st pret. अपायं, &c.; pot. अपेयां, &c.; imp. अपायानि, अपैहि. The preposition *adhi* prefixed to the root इ gives the sense of "to read," and इ *i* then blends with *adhi* into *adhīy* before the vowel, and *adhī* before the consonantal terminations. Hence the pres. (ātm. only) अधीये, अधीषे, अधीते, अधीवहे, &c.; 1st pret. अध्यायि (*adhi + a = adhya*; *adhya + i = adhyai*, r. 88; *adhyai + i = adhyāyi*, r. 8.), अध्यैथाः, अध्यैत; dual अध्यैवहि, अध्यायाथां, &c.; pot. अधीयीय, &c.; imp. अध्ययै (*adhi + e = adhye*; *adhye + ai = adhyayai*), अधीष्व, &c. In the 2d pret. the root is changed to ग्; thus, अधिजगे, अधिजगिषे, अधिजगे, अधिजगिवहे, &c. In the 3d preterite the root becomes गी, and takes Form II.; thus, अध्यगीषि, अध्यगीष्ठाः, अध्यगीष्ट, &c.

Root शी. Inf. शयितुं, "to lie down," "to sleep." ATMANEPADA.

This root takes Guna before *all* the terminations, and inserts *r* in the 3d plur. of the pres. 1st pret. and imp.

Present.			*First Preterite.*		
शये[a]	शेवहे	शेमहे	अशयि	अशेवहि	अशेमहि
शेषे	शयाथे	शेध्वे	अशेथाः	अशयाथां	अशेध्वं
शेते	शयाते	शेरते	अशेत	अशयातां	अशेरत

Potential.			*Imperative.*		
शयीय	शयीवहि	शयीमहि	शयै	शयावहै	शयामहै
शयीथाः	शयीयाथां	शयीध्वं	शेष्व	शयाथां	शेध्वं
शयीत	शयीयातां	शयीरन्	शेतां	शयातां	शेरतां

2d pret. शिश्ये[b], 1st fut. शयिताहे[c], 2d fut. शयिष्ये, 3d pret. अशयिषि, bened. शयिषीय[d], cond. अशयिष्ये, pass. part. शयित[e].

[a]) r. 10. †. Cf. κεῖμαι, κεῖσαι, κεῖται, κείμεθα, &c., and see note, p. 45. [b]) r. 98.
[c]) This is an exception to r. 101. *e*. [d]) p. 85. *b*. [e]) r. 125. *b*. note.

Root स्तु. Inf. स्तोतुं, "to praise." PARASMAIPADA.

Present.			*First Preterite.*		
स्तौमि[a]	स्तुवः	स्तुमः	अस्तुवं	अस्तुव	अस्तुम
स्तौषि	स्तुथः	स्तुथ	अस्तौः	अस्तुतं	अस्तुत
स्तौति	स्तुतः	स्तुवन्ति	अस्तौत्	अस्तुतां	अस्तुवन्

Pot. स्तुयां, &c.; Imp. स्तुवानि (in the Vedas स्तवानि), स्तुहि, स्तौतु, &c.; 2d pret. तुष्टाव[b]; dual तुष्टुव[c]; 1st fut. स्तोतास्मि[d]; 2d fut. स्तोष्यामि; 3d pret. अस्ताविषं[e]; ātm. pres. स्तुवे, &c.

a) p. 70. *c.* स्तु may also make स्तवी before the consonantal P terminations; thus, स्तवीमि, स्तवीषि, &c., after the analogy of ब्रू. It makes *stuv* and rarely *stav* before the vowel P terminations. b) p. 75. *e.* c) See the table, p. 73. d) p. 79. *f.* e) p. 82. *a.*

Root ब्रू (p. 70. *c.*). Inf. वक्तुं[a], "to say."

PARASMAIPADA.			ATMANEPADA.		
		Present.			
ब्रवीमि	ब्रूवः	ब्रूमः	ब्रुवे	ब्रूवहे	ब्रूमहे
ब्रवीषि[b]	ब्रूथः[b]	ब्रूथ	ब्रूषे	ब्रुवाथे	ब्रूध्वे
ब्रवीति[b]	ब्रूतः[b]	ब्रुवन्ति[b]	ब्रूते	ब्रुवाते	ब्रुवते
		First Preterite.			
अब्रुवं	अब्रूव	अब्रूम	अब्रुवि	अब्रूवहि	अब्रूमहि
अब्रवीः	अब्रूतं	अब्रूत	अब्रूथाः	अब्रुवाथां	अब्रूध्वं
अब्रवीत्	अब्रूतां	अब्रुवन्	अब्रूत	अब्रुवातां	अब्रुवत
		Imperative.			
ब्रवाणि[d]	ब्रवाव	ब्रवाम	ब्रुवै[e]	ब्रुवावहै[e]	ब्रुवामहै[e]
ब्रूहि	ब्रूतं	ब्रूत	ब्रूष्व	ब्रुवाथां	ब्रूध्वं
ब्रवीतु	ब्रूतां	ब्रुवन्तु	ब्रूतां	ब्रुवातां	ब्रुवतां

Pot. par. ब्रूयां, ब्रूयाः, ब्रूयात्, &c.; ātm. ब्रुवीय, ब्रुवीथाः, ब्रुवीत, &c. The other tenses are from the root वच्; as, 2d pret. उवाच, du. ऊचिव[c], 1st fut. वक्तास्मि, 2d fut. वक्ष्यामि, 3d pret. अवोचं[f], p. part. उक्त[g].

a) Borrowed from वच्. b) For these are sometimes substituted the termination of the 2d pret. of a defective root अह् with a present signification: thus, 2d sing. आत्थ; 3d sing. आह; 2d dual आहथुः; 3d dual आहतुः; 3d plur. आहुः. c) The radical vowel is here changed to *uv* instead of *av.* *Pāṇini*, 7. 3. 88. In the Vedas *abravam* occurs. d) r. 10. †. e) p. 76. *d.* f) p. 83. *j.* g) r. 125. *m.*

Root हन् (p. 70. *d.*) Inf. हन्तुं, "to kill."

PARASMAIPADA.

Present.			*First Preterite.*		
हन्मि	हन्वः	हन्मः	अहनं[a]	अहन्व	अहन्म
हंसि	हथः	हथ	अहन्[b]	अहतं	अहत
हन्ति	हतः	घ्नन्ति	अहन्[b]	अहतां	अघ्नन्

Imperative.

हनानि	हनाव	हनाम
जहि	हतं	हत
हन्तु	हतां	घ्नन्तु

Pot. हन्यां, &c.; 2d pret. जघान, जघनिथ or जघन्थ, dual जघ्निव[c]; 1st fut. हन्तास्मि[d], &c.; 2d fut. हनिष्यामि, &c.; 3d pret. अवधिषं[e], &c.; p. part. हत[f].

a) Or अघ्नं. b) p. 69. *a.* c) p. 77. *e.* d) p. 80. e) Substituted from वध्, p. 82. *c.* f) r. 125. *o.*

Root शास् (p. 70. *e.*). Infin. शासितुं, "to rule."

Present.

शास्मि	शास्वः	शास्मः
शास्सि	शिष्ठः	शिष्ठ
शास्ति	शिष्टः	शासति[a]

First Preterite.

अशासं	अशास्व	अशास्म
अशात्[b]	अशिष्टं	अशिष्ट
अशात्	अशिष्टां	अशासुः

Imperative.

शासानि	शासाव	शासाम
शाधि[c]	शिष्टं	शिष्ट
शास्तु	शिष्टां	शासतु[a]

Pot. शिष्यां, &c.; 2d pret. शशास; 1st future, शासितास्मि; 2d future, शासिष्यामि; 3d pret. अशिषं[d]; p. part. शिष्ट[e].

a) p. 69. note ‡. b) Or अशाः, the final being changed to Visargah instead of *t.* c) Or शाद्धि, p. 68. *g.* The termination *dhi* (corresponding to the Greek $\theta\iota$) belongs to roots ending in consonants, but was originally applicable to roots ending in vowels. See Prof. Johnson's Mahābhārata Selections, p.107. अपाकृधि. d) p. 83. *j.* e) r. 125. *n.*

Root द्विष् (r. 92.) Infin. द्वेष्टुं, "to hate."

PARASMAIPADA. ATMANEPADA.

Present.

Parasmaipada			Atmanepada		
द्वेष्मि	द्विष्वः	द्विष्मः	द्विषे	द्विष्वहे	द्विष्महे
द्वेक्षि[a]	द्विष्ठः	द्विष्ठ	द्विक्षे[a]	द्विषाथे	द्विड्ढ्वे[e]
द्वेष्टि[b]	द्विष्टः	द्विषन्ति	द्विष्टे[b]	द्विषाते	द्विषते

First Preterite.

Parasmaipada			Atmanepada		
अद्वेषं	अद्विष्व	अद्विष्म	अद्विषि	अद्विष्वहि	अद्विष्महि
अद्वेट्[c]	अद्विष्टं	अद्विष्ट	अद्विष्ठाः	अद्विषाथां	अद्विड्ढ्वं[e]
अद्वेट्	अद्विष्टां	अद्विषन्[d]	अद्विष्ट	अद्विषातां	अद्विषत

Imperative.

द्वेषाणि	द्वेषाव	द्वेषाम	द्वेषै	द्वेषावहै	द्वेषामहै
द्विड्ढि[e]	द्विष्टं	द्विष्ट	द्विक्ष्व[a]	द्विषाथां	द्विड्ढ्वं[c]
द्वेष्टु	द्विष्टां	द्विषन्तु	द्विष्टां	द्विषातां	द्विषतां

Pot. par. द्विष्यां, द्विष्याः, &c.; ātm. द्विषीय, द्विषीथाः, &c.; 2d pret. par. दिद्वेष; ātm. दिद्विषे; 1st fut. द्वेष्टास्मि[f], द्वेष्टाहे; 2d fut. द्वेक्ष्यामि[f], द्वेक्ष्ये; 3d pret. अद्विक्षं[g], अद्विक्षि; bened. द्विष्यासं[h], द्विक्षीय[h]; cond. अद्वेक्ष्यं, अद्वेक्ष्ये; p. part. द्विष्ट[i].

a) p. 68. *e.* b) p. 68. *d.* c) p. 69. *a.* d) Or अद्विषुः, p. 69. note ‡. e) p. 68. *f.* f) p. 80. g) p. 83. *k.* h) p. 85. *e.* i) r. 125. *i.*

Root रुद्. Inf. रोदितुं, "to weep" (p. 70. *d.*).

Present.

रोदिमि	रुदिवः	रुदिमः
रोदिषि	रुदिथः	रुदिथ
रोदिति	रुदितः	रुदन्ति[a]

First Preterite.

अरोदं	अरुदिव	अरुदिम
अरोदः[b]	अरुदितं	अरुदित
अरोदत्[c]	अरुदितां	अरुदन्

Imperative.

रोदानि	रोदाव	रोदाम
रुदिहि	रुदितं	रुदित
रोदितु	रुदितां	रुदन्तु

Pot. रुद्यां, 2d pret. रुरोद, 1st fut. रोदितास्मि, 2d fut. रोदिष्यामि, 3d pret. अरुदं[d], bened. रुद्यासं, cond. अरोदिष्यं, p. part. रुदित.

a) Bopp compares the terminations of this tense to the Latin terminations in *legi*, *legisti*, *legit*, *legimus*, *legitis*, *legunt*. b) Or अरोदीः. c) Or अरोदीत्. d) p. 83. *h.*

Root दुह्. Inf. दोग्धुं, "to milk."

Present.

दोह्मि	दुह्वः	दुह्मः	दुहे	दुह्वहे	दुह्महे
धोक्षि[a]	दुग्धः[b]	दुग्ध[b]	धुक्षे[a]	दुहाथे	धुग्ध्वे[d]
दोग्धि[b]	दुग्धः[b]	दुहन्ति	दुग्धे	दुहाते	दुहते

First Preterite.

अदोहं	अदुह्व	अदुह्म	अदुहि	अदुह्वहि	अदुह्महि
अधोक्[c]	अदुग्धं[b]	अदुग्ध	अदुग्धाः[b]	अदुहाथां	अधुग्ध्वं[d]
अधोक्[c]	अदुग्धां[b]	अदुहन्	अदुग्ध	अदुहातां	अदुहत

Imperative.

दोहानि	दोहाव	दोहाम	दोहै	दोहावहै	दोहामहै
दुग्धि[b]	दुग्धं	दुग्ध	धुक्ष्व[a]	दुहाथां	धुग्ध्वं[d]
दोग्धु	दुग्धां	दुहन्तु	दुग्धां	दुहातां	दुहतां

Pot. par. दुह्यां, ātm. दुहीय; 2d pret. par. दुदोह, ātm. दुदुहे; 1st fut. दोग्धास्मि, ātm. दोग्धाहे[b]; 2d fut. धोक्ष्यामि[a], ātm. धोक्ष्ये; bened. दुह्यासं, ātm. धुक्षीय; 3d pret. अधुक्षं[e], ātm. अधुक्षि[f]; bened. दुह्यासं, ātm. धुक्षीय[a]; cond. अधोक्ष्यं[a], ātm. अधोक्ष्ये; p. part. दुग्ध.

a) p. 69. *i.* b) p. 68. *h.* c) p. 69. *a.* d) ध्वं and ध्वे, like terminations beginning with a sibilant, have the effect of throwing back the aspirate (which has been changed to *g*) on the initial of the root. e) p. 83. *k.* f) p. 84. note.

EXAMPLES OF IRREGULAR PRIMITIVES OF THE THIRD CONJUGATION (r. 93.).

Root भृ. Infin. भर्तुं, "to support," "bear."

PARASMAIPADA.

Present Tense.—"I support" or "bear."

बिभर्मि *bibharmi,*	बिभृवः *bibhṛivah,*	बिभृमः *bibhṛimah.*
बिभर्षि[a] *bibharshi,*	बिभृथः *bibhṛithah,*	बिभृथ *bibhṛitha.*
बिभर्ति[a] *bibharti,*	बिभृतः *bibhṛitah,*	बिभ्रति *bibhrati.*

First Preterite.

अबिभरं *abibharam,*	अबिभृव *abibhṛiva,*	अबिभृम *abibhṛima.*
अबिभर्[b] *abibhar,*	अबिभृतं *abibhṛitam,*	अबिभृत *abibhṛita.*
अबिभर्[b] *abibhar,*	अबिभृतां *abibhṛitām,*	अबिभरुः[c] *abibharuh.*

Imperative.

बिभराणि[d] *bibharāṇi,*	बिभराव *bibharāva,*	बिभराम *bibharāma.*
बिभृहि *bibhṛihi,*	बिभृतं *bibhṛitam,*	बिभृत *bibhṛita.*
बिभर्तु *bibhartu,*	बिभृतां *bibhṛitām,*	बिभ्रतु *bibhratu.*

Pot. बिभृयां *bibhṛiyām,* बिभृयाः, &c.; pres. ātm. बिभ्रे, बिभृषे, &c.; 1st pret. अबिभ्रि[e], अबिभृथाः, &c.; pot. बिभ्रीय; imp. बिभरै, बिभृष्व, &c.; 2d pret. par. बभार[f], dual बभृव, ātm. बभ्रे; 1st fut. भर्तास्मि[g], ātm. भर्ताहे; 2d fut. भरिष्यामि[h], ātm. भरिष्ये; p. part. भृत; 3d pret. अभार्षं[i], ātm. अभृषि[j], अभृथाः, &c.

a) Cf. the Latin *fers*, *fert*, *ferimus*, *fertis*, *ferunt*. b) Or अबिभः. Since the vowel *ṛi* is changed to *ar*, the rule at p. 69. *a.* applies to this verb. c) r. 93. last sentence. d) r. 21. e) r. 7. f) p. 75. *a.* g) p. 79. *f.* h) p. 79. *c.* i) p. 82. *f.* j) p. 83. *g.*

Root दा. Infin. दातुं, "to give." (p. 71. *a.*).

PARASMAIPADA.

Present Tense.—"I give."

ददामि[a] *dadāmi*,	दद्वः *dadwah*,	दद्मः *dadmah*.
ददासि *dadāsi*,	दत्थः *datthah*,	दत्थ *dattha*.
ददाति *dadāti*,	दत्तः *dattah*,	ददति *dadati*.

First Preterite.—"I was giving."

अददां[b] *adadām*,	अदद्व *adadwa*,	अदद्म *adadma*.
अददाः *adadāh*,	अदत्तं *adattam*,	अदत्त *adatta*.
अददात् *adadāt*,	अदत्तां *adattām*,	अददुः *adaduh*.

Imperative.—"Let me give."

ददानि *dadāni*,	ददाव *dadāva*,	ददाम *dadāma*.
देहि[c] *dehi*,	दत्तं *dattam*,	दत्त *datta*.
ददातु *dadātu*,	दत्तां *dattām*,	ददतु *dadatu*.

Pot. दद्यां, &c.; pres. ātm. ददे, दत्से, दत्ते, &c.; 1st pret. अददि; imp. ददै; pot. ददीय.

Second Preterite.—"I gave."

ददौ[d] *dadau*,	ददिव *dadiva*,	ददिम *dadima*.
ददिथ[e] *daditha*,	ददथुः *dadathuh*,	दद *dada*.
ददौ *dadau*,	ददतुः *dadatuh*,	ददुः *daduh*.

2d pret. ātm. ददे, ददिषे[f], ददे, ददिवहे, &c.; 1st fut. par. दातास्मि[g]; 2d fut. दास्यामि[g]; 3d pret. अदां[h]; bened. देयासं[i]; cond. अदास्यं; p. part. दत्त[j].

a) Cf. δίδωμι, p. 69. note *. b) p. 83. note †. c) p. 71. *a.* d) p. 76. *a.* e) Or ददाथ. Cf. the Latin *dedisti*. f) Or ददासे. g) p. 79. *e.* h) p. 83. *i.* i) p. 85. *a.* j) r. 125. *c.*

Root धा. Inf. धातुं, "to place," &c. (p. 71. *a.*)

Present.			*First Preterite.*		
दधामि[a]	दध्वः	दध्मः	अदधां[b]	अदध्व	अदध्म
दधासि	धत्थः	धत्थ	अदधाः	अधत्तं	अधत्त
दधाति	धत्तः	दधति	अदधात्	अधत्तां	अदधुः

Pot. दध्यां, &c.; imp. दधानि, धेहि[c], दधातु, दधाव, धत्तं, धत्तां, दधाम, धत्त, दधतु; pres. ātm. दधे, धत्से, धत्ते, दध्वहे, &c.; 1st pret. अदधि, अधत्थाः, &c.; pot. दधीय; imp. दधै, धत्स्व, &c.; 2d pret. par. दधौ[d]; ātm. दधे; 1st fut. धातास्मि; 2d fut. धास्यामि; 3d pret. अधां[e]; bened. धेयासं[f]; cond. अधास्यं; p. part. हित[g].

a) Cf. τίθημι, τίθης, τίθησι. b) p. 83. note †. c) p. 71. *a.* d) p. 76. *a.* e) p. 83. *i.* f) p. 85. *a.* g) r. 125. *c.*

Root हा. Inf. हातुं, "to quit."

Present.			*First Preterite.*		
जहामि[a]	जहीवः[b]	जहीमः	अजहां	अजहीव[b]	अजहीम
जहासि	जहीथः	जहीथ	अजहाः	अजहीतं	अजहीत
जहाति	जहीतः	जहति[b]	अजहात्	अजहीतां	अजहुः[b]

Pot. जह्यां, &c.; imp. जहानि, जहीहि[c], जहातु, &c.; 2d pret. जहौ[d]; 1st fut. हातास्मि; 2d fut. हास्यामि; 3d pret. अहासिषं[e]; bened. हेयासं[f]; cond. अहास्यं; p. part. हीन[g].

a) r. 93. b) This root changes *ā* to *ī* before the consonantal terminations not marked with P, and drops *ā* altogether before the vowel terminations. c) Or जहिहि. d) p. 76. *a.* e) p. 82. *d.* f) p. 85. *a.* g) r. 125. *c.*

Root भी. Inf. भेतुं, "to fear."

Present.			*First Preterite.*		
बिभेमि	बिभीवः[a]	बिभीमः	अबिभयं	अबिभीव	अबिभीम
बिभेषि	बिभीथः	बिभीथ	अबिभेः	अबिभीतं	अबिभीत
बिभेति	बिभीतः	बिभ्यति	अबिभेत्	अबिभीतां	अबिभयुः[b]

Pot. बिभीयां, &c.; imp. बिभयानि, बिभीहि, बिभेतु, &c.; 2d pret. बिभाय[c]; du. बिभ्यिव; 1st fut. भेतास्मि; 2d fut. भेष्यामि; 3d pret. अभैषं[d]; p. part. भीत.

a) The radical vowel may be optionally shortened (बिभिवः) before a consonant, whenever Guna does not take place. b) r. 93. last sentence. c) r. 98. d) p. 82. *f.*

EXAMPLES OF IRREGULAR PRIMITIVES OF THE FIFTH CONJUGATION (r. 94.).

Root आप्. Infin. आप्तुं, "to obtain."

PARASMAIPADA.

Present Tense.—"I obtain."

आप्नोमि *āpnomi,*	आप्नुवः *āpnuvaḥ,*	आप्नुमः *āpnumaḥ.*
आप्नोषि *āpnoṣhi,*	आप्नुथः *āpnuthaḥ,*	आप्नुथ *āpnutha.*
आप्नोति *āpnoti,*	आप्नुतः *āpnutaḥ,*	आप्नुवन्ति *āpnuvanti.*

First Preterite.—"I was obtaining."

आप्नवं *āpnavam,*	आप्नुव *āpnuva,*	आप्नुम *āpnuma.*
आप्नोः *āpnoḥ,*	आप्नुतं *āpnutam,*	आप्नुत *āpnuta.*
आप्नोत् *āpnot,*	आप्नुतां *āpnutām,*	आप्नुवन् *āpnuvan.*

Imperative.—"Let me obtain."

आप्नवानि *āpnavāni,*	आप्नवाव *āpnavāva,*	आप्नवाम *āpnavāma.*
आप्नुहि *āpnuhi,*	आप्नुतं *āpnutam,*	आप्नुत *āpnuta.*
आप्नोतु *āpnotu,*	आप्नुतां *āpnutām,*	आप्नुवन्तु *āpnuvantu.*

Pot. आप्नुयां *āpnuyām,* आप्नुयाः *āpnuyāḥ,* आप्नुयात् *āpnuyāt,* &c.; 2d pret. आप[a]; dual आपिव; 1st fut. आप्तास्मि[b]; 2d fut. आप्स्यामि[b]; 3d pret. आपं[c]; bened. आप्यासं; cond. आप्स्यं; p. part. आप्त.

a) p. 75. *f.* b) p. 80. c) p. 83. *h.*

Root अश्. Infin. अशितुं, "to pervade," "obtain," "enjoy."

ATMANEPADA.

Present.			*First Preterite.*		
अश्नुवे	अश्नुवहे	अश्नुमहे	आश्नुवि	आश्नुवहि	आश्नुमहि
अश्नुषे	अश्नुवाथे	अश्नुध्वे	आश्नुथाः	आश्नुवाथां	आश्नुध्वं
अश्नुते	अश्नुवाते	अश्नुवते	आश्नुत	आश्नुवातां	आश्नुवत

Pot. अश्नुवीय; imp. अश्नवै, अश्नुष्व, अश्नुतां, अश्नवावहै, &c.; 2d pret. आनशे[a], आनशिषे, &c.; 1st fut. अशिताहे[b]; 2d fut. अशिष्ये[c]; 3d pret. आशिषि[d], आशिष्ठाः, &c.; bened. अशिषीय; cond. आशिष्ये; p. part. अष्ट.

a) This root, although not ending in a double consonant, requires that the reduplicated syllable be *ān,* see p. 75. *f.* b) Or अष्टाहे. c) Or अक्ष्ये. d) p. 82. *a.*

Root शक्. Infin. शक्तुं, "to be able."

Present.			*First Preterite.*		
शक्नोमि	शक्नुवः	शक्नुमः	अशक्नवं	अशक्नुव	अशक्नुम
शक्नोषि	शक्नुथः	शक्नुथ	अशक्नोः	अशक्नुतं	अशक्नुत
शक्नोति	शक्नुतः	शक्नुवन्ति	अशक्नोत्	अशक्नुतां	अशक्नुवन्

Pot. शक्नुयां, &c.; imp. शक्नवानि, &c.; 2d pret. शशाक[a]; dual, शेकिव[a], &c.; 1st fut. शक्तास्मि[b]; 2d fut. शक्ष्यामि[b]; 3d pret. अशकं[c]; p. part. शक्त.

a) p. 76. *c.* b) p. 80. c) p. 83. *h.*

Root श्रु. Infin. श्रोतुं, "to hear."

Present.			*First Preterite.*		
शृणोमि[a]	शृणुवः[b]	शृणुमः[c]	अशृणवं	अशृणुव	अशृणुम
शृणोषि	शृणुथः	शृणुथ	अशृणोः	अशृणुतं	अशृणुत
शृणोति	शृणुतः	शृण्वन्ति	अशृणोत्	अशृणुतां	अशृण्वन्

Pot. शृणुयां; imp. शृणवानि, शृणु, शृणोतु, शृणवाव, &c.; 2d pret. शुश्राव, dual शुश्रुव[d]; 1st fut. श्रोतास्मि[e]; 2d fut. श्रोष्यामि[e]; 3d pret. अश्रौषं[f]; pass. part. श्रुत.

a) r. 21. b) Or शृण्वः. c) Or शृण्मः. d) See the scheme of terminations, p. 73. e) p. 79. *f.* f) p. 82. *f.*

EXAMPLES OF IRREGULAR PRIMITIVES OF THE SEVENTH CONJUGATION (r. 95.).

Root छिद्. Infin. छेत्तुं, "to cut."

Present.—"I cut."

छिनद्मि *chhinadmi,*	छिन्द्वः *chhindwah,*	छिन्द्मः *chhindmah.*
छिनत्सि *chhinatsi,*	छिन्थः[a] *chhinthah,*	छिन्थ[a] *chhintha.*
छिनत्ति *chhinatti,*	छिन्तः[a] *chintah,*	छिन्दन्ति *chhindanti.*

First Preterite.—"I was cutting."

अच्छिनदं[b] *achhinadam,*	अच्छिन्द्व *achhindwa,*	अच्छिन्द्म *achhindma.*
अच्छिनत्[c] *achhinat,*	अच्छिन्तं *achhintam,*	अच्छिन्त *achhinta.*
अच्छिनत् *achhinat,*	अच्छिन्तां *achhintām,*	अच्छिन्दन् *achhindan.*

Pot. छिन्द्यां, &c.; imp. छिनदानि, छिन्द्धि[d], छिनत्तु, &c.; ātm. pres.

छिन्दे, छिन्त्से, छिन्ते, &c.; 1st pret. अच्छिन्दि; pot. छिन्दीय; imp. छिनदै, छिन्त्स्व, &c.; 2d pret. par. चिच्छेद; ātm. चिच्छिदे; 1st fut. छेत्तास्मि[e]; 2d fut. छेत्स्यामि[e]; 3d pret. par. अच्छैत्सं[f]; ātm. अच्छित्सि[g], अच्छित्थाः, अच्छित्त, &c.; pass. part. छिन्न[h].

a) Roots ending in *t* or *d* may reject these letters before *th* and *t*, when *n* immediately precedes. b) Or अच्छिनदं, &c. c) p. 69. *a.* or अच्छिनः. d) Or छिन्धि. e) p. 80. f) p. 82. *f.* g) p. 83. *g.* h) r. 125. *j.*

Root रुध्. Infin. रोद्धुं, "to hinder."

Present.			*First Preterite.*		
रुणध्मि[a]	रुन्ध्वः	रुन्ध्मः	अरुणधं	अरुन्ध्व	अरुन्ध्म
रुणत्सि[b]	रुन्द्धः[c]	रुन्द्ध[c]	अरुणत्[d]	अरुन्द्धं	अरुन्द्ध
रुणद्धि[c]	रुन्द्धः[c]	रुन्धन्ति	अरुणत्[d]	अरुन्द्धां	अरुन्धन्

Pot. रुन्ध्यां; imp. रुणधानि, रुन्द्धि[d], रुणद्धु, &c.; ātm. pres. रुन्धे, &c.; 1st pret. अरुन्धि, अरुन्द्धाः, &c.; pot. रुन्धीय; imp. रुणधै; 2d pret. par. रुरोध; ātm. रुरुधे; 1st fut. रोद्धास्मि[e]; 2d fut. रोत्स्यामि[e]; 3d pret. par. अरौत्सं[f]; ātm. अरुत्सि[g]; p. part. रुद्ध.

a) R. 95. b) p. 68. *b.* c) p. 67. *a.* d) p. 69. *a.*, or अरुणः. e) p. 80. f) p. 82. *f.* g) p. 83. *g.*

Root युज्. Infin. योक्तुं, "to join."

PARASMAIPADA.	*Present.*		ATMANEPADA.	*Present.*	
युनज्मि	युंज्वः	युंज्मः[b]	युञ्जे	युंज्वहे	युंज्महे
युनक्षि[a]	युंक्थः	युंक्थ	युंक्षे[a]	युञ्जाथे	युंग्ध्वे
युनक्ति	युंक्तः	युञ्जन्ति[b]	युंक्ते	युंजाते	युञ्जते

First Preterite.			*First Preterite.*		
अयुनजं	अयुंज्व	अयुंज्म	अयुञ्जि	अयुंज्वहि	अयुंज्महि
अयुनक्[c]	अयुंक्तं	अयुंक्त	अयुंक्थाः	अयुञ्जाथां	अयुंग्ध्वं
अयुनक्[c]	अयुंक्तां	अयुञ्जन्	अयुंक्त	अयुञ्जातां	अयुञ्जत

Pot. par. युंज्यां, &c.; ātm. युञ्जीय, &c.; imp. par. युनजानि, युंग्धि[c], युनक्तु, युनजाव, &c; ātm. युनजै, युंक्ष्व, युंक्तां, युनजावहै, &c.; 2d pret. par. युयोज; ātm. युयुजे; 1st fut. योक्तास्मि; 2d fut. योक्ष्यामि; 3d pret. par. अयौक्षं[d]; ātm. अयुक्षि[e], अयुक्थाः, अयुक्त, &c.; pass. part. युक्त.

a) R. 91. b) Cf. the Latin *jungimus, jungunt.* c) p. 69. *a.* d) p. 82. *f.* (e p. 83. *g.*

Root हिंस्. Infin. हिंसितुं, "to injure."

Present.			*First Preterite.*		
हिनस्मि	हिंस्वः	हिंस्मः	अहिनसं	अहिंस्व	अहिंस्म
हिनस्सि[a]	हिंस्थः	हिंस्थ	अहिनत्[b]	अहिंस्तं	अहिंस्त
हिनस्ति	हिंस्तः	हिंसन्ति	अहिनत्	अहिंस्तां	अहिंसन्

Pot. हिंस्यां, &c.; imp. हिनसानि, &c.; 2d pret. जिहिंस[c]; 1st fut. हिंसितास्मि[d]; 2d fut. हिंसिष्यामि; 3d pret. अहिंसिषं[d]; pass. part. हिंसित.

a) According to Carey हिनश्चि. b) Or अहिनः. c) p. 75.c. d) p. 64., note †.

For examples of verbs of the 8th conjugation the student is referred to the auxiliary verb कृ *kṛi*, at p. 101, and the verb तन् in the tables, pp. 94—97. These are the only two roots in this conjugation that are ever likely to occur.

EXAMPLES OF IRREGULAR PRIMITIVES OF THE NINTH CONJUGATION (r. 97.)

Root ज्ञा. Infin. ज्ञातुं, "to know."

PARASMAIPADA. *Present Tense.*—"I know."

जानामि *jānāmi*,	जानीवः *jānīvah*,	जानीमः *jānīmah*.
जानासि *jānāsi*,	जानीथः *jānīthah*,	जानीथ *jānītha*.
जानाति *jānāti*,	जानीतः *jānītah*,	जानन्ति *jānanti*.

First Preterite.—"I was knowing."

अजानां *ajānām*,	अजानीव *ajānīva*,	अजानीम *ajānīma*.
अजानाः *ajānāh*,	अजानीतं *ajānītam*,	अजानीत *ajānīta*.
अजानात् *ajānāt*,	अजानीतां *ajānītām*,	अजानन् *ajānan*.

Imperative.—"Let me know."

जानानि *jānāni*,	जानाव *jānāva*,	जानाम *jānāma*.
जानीहि *jānīhi*,	जानीतं *jānītam*,	जानीत *jānīta*.
जानातु *jānātu*,	जानीतां *jānītām*,	जानन्तु *jānantu*.

ATMANEPADA. *Present.*—"I know."

जाने *jāne*,	जानीवहे *jānīvahe*,	जानीमहे *jānīmahe*.
जानीषे *jānīshe*,	जानाथे *jānāthe*,	जानीध्वे *jānīdhwe*.
जानीते *jānīte*,	जानाते *jānāte*,	जानते *jānate*.

First Preterite.—" I was knowing."

अजानि *ajāni*,	अजानीवहि *ajānīvahi*,	अजानीमहि *ajānīmahi*.
अजानीथाः *ajānīthāḥ*,	अजानाथां *ajānāthām*,	अजानीध्वं *ajānīdhwam*.
अजानीत *ajānīta*,	अजानातां *ajānātām*,	अजानत *ajānata*.

Imperative.—" Let me know."

जानै *jānai*,	जानावहै *jānāvahai*,	जानामहै *jānāmahai*.
जानीष्व *jānīshwa*,	जानाथां *jānāthām*,	जानीध्वं *jānīdhwam*.
जानीतां *jānītām*,	जानातां *jānātām*,	जानतां *jānatām*.

Pot. par. जानीयां, जानीयाः, जानीयात्, &c.; ātm. जानीय, जानीथाः, &c.; 2d pret. par. जज्ञौ[a]; dual जज्ञिव, &c.; ātm. जज्ञे; 1st. fut. ज्ञातास्मि[b]; 2d fut. ज्ञास्यामि[b]; 3d pret. अज्ञासिषं[c]; ātm. अज्ञासि; p. part. ज्ञात.

a) p. 76. *a*. b) p. 79. *e*. c) p. 82. *d*.

Root ग्रह्. Infin. ग्रहीतुं, "to take."

Present.

गृह्णामि	गृह्णीवः	गृह्णीमः
गृह्णासि	गृह्णीथः	गृह्णीथ
गृह्णाति	गृह्णीतः	गृह्णन्ति

First Preterite.

अगृह्णां	अगृह्णीव	अगृह्णीम
अगृह्णाः	अगृह्णीतं	अगृह्णीत
अगृह्णात्	अगृह्णीतां	अगृह्णन्

Imperative.

गृह्णानि	गृह्णाव	गृह्णाम
गृहाण	गृह्णीतं	गृह्णीत
गृह्णातु	गृह्णीतां	गृह्णन्तु

Pot. गृह्णीयां, &c.; 2d pret. जग्राह[a], जग्रहिथ; dual जगृहिव[a], &c.; 1st fut. ग्रहीतास्मि[b]; 2d fut. ग्रहीष्यामि; 3d pret. अग्रहीषं[c]; p. part. गृहीत.

a) p. 77. *f*. b) This root lengthens the inserted *i*. c) This is on the authority of the Siddhānta Kaumudī, but Carey and Wilkins give अग्रहिषं. All agree in making the ātm. अग्रहीषि.

Root अश्. Infin. अशितुं, "to eat."

Present.

अश्नामि	अश्नीवः	अश्नीमः
अश्नासि	अश्नीथः	अश्नीथ
अश्नाति	अश्नीतः	अश्नन्ति

First Preterite.

आश्नां	आश्नीव	आश्नीम
आश्नाः	आश्नीतं	आश्नीत
आश्नात्	आश्नीतां	आश्नन्

Pot. अश्नीयां, &c.; imp. अश्नानि, अशान[a], &c.; 2d pret. आश[b]; 1st fut. अशितास्मि; 2d fut. अशिष्यामि; 3d pret. आशिषं[c]; pass. part. अशित.

a) R. 97. last paragraph. b) p. 75. *f*. c) p. 82. *e*.

Root क्री. Infin. क्रेतुं, "to buy."

Present.			*First Preterite.*		
क्रीणामि[a]	क्रीणीवः	क्रीणीमः	अक्रीणां[b]	अक्रीणीव	अक्रीणीम
क्रीणासि	क्रीणीथः	क्रीणीथ	अक्रीणाः	अक्रीणीतं	अक्रीणीत
क्रीणाति	क्रीणीतः	क्रीणन्ति	अक्रीणात्	अक्रीणीतां	अक्रीणन्

Pot. क्रीणीयां, &c.; imp. क्रीणानि, क्रीणीहि, &c.; 2d pret. चिक्राय[c], चिक्रयिथ or चिक्रेथ; dual चिक्रियिव[d]; 1st fut. क्रेतास्मि; 2d fut. क्रेष्यामि; 3d pret. अक्रैषं[e]; pass. part. क्रीत.

a) Cf. περνᾶμαι. b) Cf. ἐπερνᾶν. c) p. 75. *b*. d) p. 74. †. e) p. 82. *f*.

Root स्तॄ or स्तृ. Infin. स्तरितुं, "to spread."

Present.			*First Preterite.*		
स्तृणामि[a]	स्तृणीवः	स्तृणीमः	अस्तृणां	अस्तृणीव	अस्तृणीम
स्तृणासि	स्तृणीथः	स्तृणीथ	अस्तृणाः	अस्तृणीतं	अस्तृणीत
स्तृणाति	स्तृणीतः	स्तृणन्ति	अस्तृणात्	अस्तृणीतां	अस्तृणन्

Pot. स्तृणीयां; imp. स्तृणानि; ātm. pres. स्तृणे; 1st pret. अस्तृणि; pot. स्तृणीय; imp. स्तृणै; 2d pret. par. तस्तार[b], तस्तरिथ, &c.; dual तस्तरिव[c]; ātm. तस्तरे[c], &c.; 1st fut. स्तरितास्मि[d] or स्तरीतास्मि; 2d fut. स्तरिष्यामि[d] or स्तरीष्यामि; 3d pret. अस्तारिषं[e]; pass. part. स्तीर्ण[f].

a) This verb is also of the 5th conjugation स्तृणोमि, स्तृणोषि, स्तृणोति, स्तृणुथः, &c., when there is a striking resemblance to the Greek στορνύμι, στόρνυς, &c.; and imperf. ἐστόρνυν, ἐστόρνυς, &c. b) p. 75. *c*. c) p. 76. *b*. d) p. 79. *b*. e) p. 82. *a*. f) r. 125. *d*.

EXAMPLE OF CAUSALS, OR VERBS OF THE TENTH CONJUGATION (p. 86. r. 107.).

Root दृश् *drish*. Inf. दर्शयितुं, "to cause to see," "show."

PARASMAIPADA. *Present.*—"I cause to see."

दर्शयामि *darshayāmi*,	दर्शयावः *darshayāvah*,	दर्शयामः *darshayāmah*.
दर्शयसि *darshayasi*,	दर्शयथः *darshayathah*,	दर्शयथ *darshayatha*.
दर्शयति *darshayati*,	दर्शयतः *darshayatah*,	दर्शयन्ति *darshayanti*.

Imperfect. "I was causing to see."

अदर्शयं *adarshayam*,	अदर्शयाव *adarshayāva*,	अदर्शयाम *adarshayāma*.
अदर्शयः *adarshayah*,	अदर्शयतं *adarshayatam*,	अदर्शयत *adarshayata*.
अदर्शयत् *adarshayat*,	अदर्शयतां *adarshayatām*,	अदर्शयन् *adarshayan*.

Potential.—"I may cause to see."

दर्शयेयं *darshayeyam*,	दर्शयेव *darshayeva*,	दर्शयेम *darshayema*.
दर्शयेः *darshayeh*,	दर्शयेतं *darshayetam*,	दर्शयेत *darshayeta*.
दर्शयेत् *darshayet*,	दर्शयेतां *darshayetām*,	दर्शयेयुः *darshayeyuh*.

Imperative.—"Let me cause to see."

दर्शयानि *darshayāni*,	दर्शयाव *darshayāva*,	दर्शयाम *darshayāma*.
दर्शय *darshaya*,	दर्शयतं *darshayatam*,	दर्शयत *darshayata*.
दर्शयतु *darshayatu*,	दर्शयतां *darshayatām*,	दर्शयन्तु *darshayantu*.

Second Preterite.—"I caused to see."

दर्शयामास[a] *darshayāmāsa*,	दर्शयामासिव *darshayāmāsiva*,	दर्शयामासिम *darshayāmāsima*.
दर्शयामासिथ *darshayāmāsitha*,	दर्शयामासथुः *darshayāmāsathuh*,	दर्शयामास *darshayāmāsa*.
दर्शयामास *darshayāmāsa*,	दर्शयामासतुः *darshayāmāsatuh*,	दर्शयामासुः *darshayāmāsuh*.

First Future.—"I will cause to see."

दर्शयितास्मि *darshayitāsmi*,	दर्शयितास्वः *darshayitāswah*,	दर्शयितास्मः *darshayitāsmah*.
दर्शयितासि *darshayitāsi*,	दर्शयितास्थः *darshayitāsthah*,	दर्शयितास्थ *darshayitāstha*.
दर्शयिता *darshayitā*,	दर्शयितारौ *darshayitārau*,	दर्शयितारः *darshayitārah*.

Second Future.—"I will cause to see."

दर्शयिष्यामि *darshayishyāmi*,	दर्शयिष्यावः *darshayishyāvah*,	दर्शयिष्यामः *darshayishyāmah*.
दर्शयिष्यसि *darshayishyasi*,	दर्शयिष्यथः *darshayishyathah*,	दर्शयिष्यथ *darshayishyatha*.
दर्शयिष्यति *darshayishyati*,	दर्शयिष्यतः *darshayishyatah*,	दर्शयिष्यन्ति *darshayishyanti*.

3d pret. अदीदृशं[b] or अददर्शं; bened. दर्श्यासं[c]; cond. अदर्शयिष्यं; Atm. pres. दर्शये, दर्शयसे, दर्शयते, &c.; 1st pret. अदर्शये; pot. दर्शयेय; imp. दर्शयै, दर्शयस्व, &c.; 2d pret. दर्शयाञ्चक्रे; 1st fut. दर्शयिताहे; 2d fut. दर्शयिष्ये; 3d pret. अदीदृशे, अदीदृशथाः, &c.; bened. दर्शयिषीय; cond. अदर्शयिष्ये; p. part. दर्शित[d].

[a]) or दर्शयाञ्चकार *darshayānchakāra*, p. 87. r. 108. [b]) r. 109. [c]) r. 110. [d]) r. 125. r.

After this model may be conjugated all causal verbs.

128. EXAMPLES OF PASSIVE VERBS. (p. 89. r. 111.).

Root दा. Infin. दातुं, "to be given." (p. 90. r. 112.).

Present.—"I am given."

दीये *dīye,*	दीयावहे *dīyāvahe,*	दीयामहे *dīyāmahe.*
दीयसे *dīyase,*	दीयेथे *dīyethe,*	दीयध्वे *dīyadhwe.*
दीयते *dīyate,*	दीयेते *dīyete,*	दीयन्ते *dīyante,*

First Preterite.—"I was given."

अदीये *adīye,*	अदीयावहि *adīyāvahi,*	अदीयामहि *adīyāmahi.*
अदीयथाः *adīyathāh,*	अदीयेथां *adīyethām,*	अदीयध्वं *adīyadhwam.*
अदीयत *adīyata,*	अदीयेतां *adīyetām,*	अदीयन्त *adīyanta.*

Potential.—"I may be given."

दीयेय *dīyeya,*	दीयेवहि *dīyevahi,*	दीयेमहि *dīyemahi.*
दीयेथाः *dīyethāh,*	दीयेयाथां *dīyeyāthām,*	दीयेध्वं *dīyedhwam.*
दीयेत *dīyeta,*	दीयेयातां *dīyeyātām,*	दीयेरन् *dīyeran.*

Imperative.—"Let me be given."

दीयै *dīyai,*	दीयावहै *dīyāvahai,*	दीयामहै *dīyāmahai.*
दीयस्व *dīyaswa,*	दीयेथां *dīyethām,*	दीयध्वं *dīyadhwam.*
दीयतां *dīyatām,*	दीयेतां *dīyetām,*	दीयन्तां *dīyantām.*

Second Preterite.—"I have been given."

ददे *dade,*	ददिवहे *dadivahe,*	ददिमहे *dadimahe.*
ददिषे *dadiṣhe,*	ददाथे *dadāthe,*	ददिध्वे *dadidhwe* (or ढ्वे).
ददे *dade,*	ददाते *dadāte,*	ददिरे *dadire.*

First Future.—"I shall be given."

दाताहे *dātāhe,* or दायिताहे *dāyitāhe,*	दातास्वहे *dātāswahe,* दायितास्वहे *dāyitāswahe,*	दातास्महे *dātāsmahe, &c.* दायितास्महे *dāyitāsmahe, &c.*

Second Future.—"I shall be given."

दास्ये *dāsye,* or दायिष्ये *dāyiṣhye,*	दास्यावहे *dāsyāvahe,* दायिष्यावहे *dāyiṣhyāvahe,*	दास्यामहे *dāsyāmahe, &c.* दायिष्यामहे *dāyiṣhyāmahe, &c.*

Third Preterite.—"I was given."

अदिषि *adiṣhi,* or अदायिषि *adāyiṣhi,*	अदिष्वहि *adiṣhwahi,* अदायिष्वहि *adāyiṣhwahi,*	अदिष्महि *adiṣhmahi.* अदायिष्महि *adāyiṣhmahi.*
अदिथाः *adithāh,* or अदायिष्ठाः *adāyiṣhṭhāh,*	अदिषाथां *adiṣhāthām,* अदायिषाथां *adāyiṣhāthām,*	अदिढ्वं *adiḍhwam.* अदायिढ्वं *adāyidhwam.*
अदायि *adāyi,* "it was given,"	अदिषातां *adiṣhātām,* अदायिषातां *adāyiṣhātām,*	अदिषत *adiṣhata.* अदायिषत *adāyiṣhata.*

Bened. दासीय or दायिषीय, &c.; cond. अदास्ये or अदायिष्ये.

Root कृ. Inf. कर्त्तुं, "to be made" or "done" (p. 90. *b.*).

Present.—"I am made."

क्रिये	क्रियावहे	क्रियामहे
क्रियसे	क्रियेथे	क्रियध्वे
क्रियते	क्रियेते	क्रियन्ते

First Preterite.—"I was made."

अक्रिये	अक्रियावहि	अक्रियामहि
अक्रियथाः	अक्रियेथां	अक्रियध्वं
अक्रियत	अक्रियेतां	अक्रियन्त

Potential.—"I may be made."

क्रियेय	क्रियेवहि	क्रियेमहि
क्रियेथाः	क्रियेयाथां	क्रियेध्वं
क्रियेत	क्रियेयातां	क्रियेरन्

Imperative.—"Let me be made."

क्रियै	क्रियावहै	क्रियामहै
क्रियस्व	क्रियेथां	क्रियध्वं
क्रियतां	क्रियेतां	क्रियन्तां

Second Preterite.

चक्रे	चकृवहे	चकृमहे
चकृषे	चक्राथे	चकृढ्वे
चक्रे	चक्राते	चक्रिरे

First Future.

{ कर्त्ताहे कर्त्तास्वहे कर्त्तास्महे, &c.
{ or कारिताहे कारितास्वहे कारितास्महे, &c.

Second fut. करिष्ये or कारिष्ये, &c.

Third Preterite.

SING.	DUAL.	PLURAL.
अकृषि or अकारिषि	अकृष्वहि or अकारिष्वहि	अकृष्महि or अकारिष्महि
अकृथाः or अकारिषाः	अकृषाथां or अकारिषाथां	अकृढ्वं or अकारिढ्वं
अकारि, "it was done,"	अकृषातां or अकारिषातां	अकृषत or अकारिषत

Bened. कृषीय or कारिषीय; cond. अकरिष्ये or अकारिष्ये.

The following is an example of a passive verb from a root ending in a consonant.

Root युज्. Infin. योक्तुं, "to be fitting."

Pres. युज्ये, "I am fitting," युज्यसे, युज्यते, &c.; 1st pret. अयुज्ये, अयुज्यथाः, अयुज्यत, &c.; pot. युज्येय, &c.; imp. युज्यै, युज्यस्व, युज्यतां, &c.; 2d pret. युयुजे, युयुजिषे, युयुजे, &c; 1st fut. योक्ताहे, योक्तासे, योक्ता, &c.; 2d fut. योक्ष्ये, योक्ष्यसे, योक्ष्यते, &c.; 3d pret. अयुक्षि, अयुक्थाः, अयोजि, अयुक्ष्वहि, अयुक्षाथां, &c.; bened. युक्षीय, &c.; cond. अयोक्ष्ये, &c.

DESIDERATIVE VERBS.

119. Although this form of the root rarely appears in its character of a verb, yet nouns and participles derived from the desiderative base are not uncommon (see p. 23. xiii. r. 40., and p. 141. *s.*). Some explanation, therefore, of its structure is indispensable. Moreover, there are certain roots which take a desiderative form, without exactly yielding a volitive signification; and these, as being equivalent to primitive verbs (amongst which they are sometimes classed), may occur in the best writers. For example, *jugups*, "to blame," from the root *gup*; *chikits*, "to cure," from *kit*; *titiksh*, "to bear," from *tij*; *mīmāns*, "to reason," from *man*; *bībhats*, "to abhor," from *bādh*.

The Terminations.

a. Desideratives take the terminations of the regular scheme at p. 63., and their inflection either in the par. or ātm. is determined by the practice of the primitive verb. Thus, the root *budh*, taking both inflections in the primitive, may take both in the desiderative (*bubodhiṣhāmi*, &c., or *bubodhiṣhe*, &c.); and *labh*, taking only the ātm. in the primitives, may take only the ātm. in the desiderative (*lipse*, &c.).

FORMATION OF THE BASE.

Conjugational Tenses.

b. The initial consonant and vowel of the root are reduplicated, and if the root inserts *i* in the primitive (see p. 79.), then *iṣh* is affixed: if the root rejects *i*, then simply *s*, changeable to ष् *ṣh*, is affixed. Thus, from *kship*, "to throw," the base *chikships* (चिक्षिप्सामि *chikshipsāmi*, &c.); but from *vid*, "to know," taking inserted *i* in the primitive, *vividiṣh* (विविदिषामि *vividiṣhāmi*, &c.). The reduplication of the consonant is strictly in conformity with the rules laid down at p. 75., and that of the vowel of the initial consonant follows the analogy of causal third preterites (p. 88.); that is, the vowel *i* (generally, however, short) is reduplicated for *a*, *ā*, *i*, *ī*, *ṛi*, *ṛī*, *e*, or *ai*; but the vowel *u* for *u*, *ū*, and *o*.* Thus,

* And if the root begin with a vowel the reduplication still follows the analogy of the same tense; thus, from *ash*, *ashish*, and with *iṣh* added, *ashishiṣh*. See p. 89.

from *pach, pipaksh*; from *yāch, yiyāchiṣh*; from *jīv, jijīviṣh*; from *dṛish, didṛiksh*; from *sev, siseviṣh*; from *gai, jigās*; but from *yuj, yuyuksh*; from *pū, pupūṣh*.

c. It has been said that the annexation of *iṣh* or *s* to the reduplicated root is generally determined by the assumption or rejection of inserted *i* in the primitive. When *iṣh* is affixed, the radical vowel may in general be optionally changed to Guna. Thus, from *mud*, either *mumodiṣh* or *mumudiṣh*.

d. When *s* is affixed to roots ending in vowels it has the effect of lengthening a final *i* or *u*, and changing *ṛi* or *ṛī* to *īr*; thus, from *chi, chichīṣh*; from *shru, shushrūṣh*; from *kṛi, chikīrṣh*; from *tṛī, titīrṣh*.* When to roots ending in consonants, the radical vowel remains unchanged, but the final consonant combines with the initial sibilant, in accordance with the rules laid down in pp. 67. 68.; as, from *yudh, yuyuts* (p. 68. *b.*); from *dah, didhaksh* (p. 69. *i.*).

e. The following roots form their desiderative bases anomalously. From *dā*, "to give," *dits* (*ditsāmi*, "I wish to give"); from *āp*, "to obtain," *īps*; from *dhā, dhits*; from *ji*, "to conquer," *jigīṣh*; from *chi, chikīṣh*, as well as *chichīṣh*; from *han*, "to kill," *jighāns*; from ग्रह्, जिघृक्ष्; from प्रच्छ्, पिपृच्छिष्; from स्वप्, सुषुप्स्; from शक्, "to be able," शिक्ष्; from लभ्, "to obtain," लिप्स्; from रभ्, रिप्स्; पत्, पित्स्.

Non-Conjugational Tenses.

The second preterite is formed by affixing *ām* to the desiderative base, as already formed, and adding the second preterite of either one of the auxiliaries *kṛi* or *bhū* (see p. 77. *g.*). Thus from *pach*, the 2d pret. *pipakshāñchakāra*, "I wished to cook." In all the remaining tenses it is an universal rule that inserted *i* be assumed after the desiderative base, whether formed by *s* or *iṣh*, except in the bened. par. Thus, 1st fut. of *pipaksh*, 1st pers. sing. *pipakshitāsmi*, &c.; 2d fut. *pipakshishyāmi*, &c.; 3d pret. *apipakshiṣham*, &c. (form 1. p. 81.); bened. par. *pipakshyāsam*, &c.; ātm. *pipakshiṣhīya*, &c.; condit. *apipakshishyam*, &c. So, also, taking *vividiṣh* (formed with *iṣh* from *vid*), the 1st fut. is *vividiṣhitāsmi*; 2d fut. *vividiṣhiṣhyāmi*; 3d pret. *avividiṣhiṣham*, &c.

---

* But the root पॄ may make पुपूर्ष्; भॄ, बुभूर्ष्; and वॄ, वुवूर्ष्.

INTENSIVE OR FREQUENTATIVE VERBS.

120. This form of the root is even less used than the desiderative. In the present participle, however, and in a few nouns, it may sometimes appear (r. 38. xiii. and 124.). It gives intensity to the radical idea, especially in the case of roots signifying "to shine," "to be beautiful," or "to lament." Thus, from *dīp*, "to shine," comes the intensive form *dedīpy*, "to shine brightly," and the present participle *dedīpyamāna* (see r. 124.); so also from *shubh*, *shoshubhy* and *shoshubyamāna*; from *rud*, *rorudy* and *rorudyamāna*. There are two kinds of intensive verb, the one a reduplicated ātmanepada verb, conforming, like neuter and passive verbs, to the 4th conjugation, and usually found in a neuter or passive signification; the other a reduplicated parasmaipada verb, formed analogously to the 3d conjugation. The first of these is the only form ever likely to occur.

The Terminations.

The terminations may be either those of the ātm. of the regular scheme at p. 63., or the par. of the irregular scheme at p. 66.; the former being adapted to that form of intensive which results from a reduplication of the passive; the latter to that form which bears analogy to the 3d conjugation.

FORMATION OF THE BASE OF THE ATMANEPADA FORM OF INTENSIVES.

Conjugational Tenses.

The general rule is, that the initial consonant and vowel of the passive base be reduplicated. The consonant being reduplicated according to the usual rules (p. 75.), with the Guna substitute of the radical vowel, whether it be long or short. Thus, from the passive base *dīy* (of *dā*, "to give") comes the intensive base *dedīy* (*dedīye*, *dedīyase*, &c., see p. 127.); from *hīy* (passive of *hā*), *jehīy* (*jehīye*, &c.); from *stīry*, *testīry*; from *pūy*, *popūy*; from *vidy*, *vevidy*; from *budhy*, *bobudhy*.

If the passive base contain a medial *a*, long *ā* is substituted in the reduplication, as *pāpachy* from *pach*; *sāsmary* from *smary*: if a medial *ā*, *e*, or *o*, the same are reduplicated; as *yāyāchy* from *yāch*, *seshevy* from *sev*, *lolochy* from *lochy*: if a medial *ṛi*, then *arī* is substituted in the reduplication, as *darīdṛishy* from *dṛishy*, *parīspṛishy* from *spṛishy*.

If a passive base contain रि *ri*, this becomes री in the intensive base; as चेक्रीय् from क्रिय् (pass. of कृ, "to do"). If the base begin with *a*, as in *aṭy* (from अट्, "to wander"), the initial *aṭ* is repeated, and the radical *ā* lengthened, thus *aṭāṭy*.

If the passive base contain a nasal after short *a*, this nasal is often repeated; as from *gam*, *jan·gamy* (जङ्गम्ये, &c.), "to walk crookedly"; from *bhram*, *bambhramy*. The passive bases *japy*, *jalpy*, *dashy*, *bhajy*, and some others, may insert nasals, instead of lengthening the vowel in the reduplication. Thus *jañjapy*, &c. *Pady* inserts *nī*; as *panīpady*; and from *chary* is formed *chañchūry*; from *hany*, *jeghnīy*; from *ghrāy*, *jeghrīy*; from *dhmāy*, *dedhmīy*.

Non-Conjugational Tenses.

In these tenses intensives follow the analogy of passives and reject the affix *y*. Since, however, the base of the second pret. is formed by affixing *ām* (as usual in all polysyllabic forms, p. 77. *g*.), and since, in all the other tenses, inserted *i* is assumed, a coalition of vowels might arise were it not allowed to retain the *y* in all cases in which a vowel immediately precedes that affix.* Thus, from *dedīpy* is formed the 2d pret. (1st pers. sing.) *dedīpāñchakre*, &c. rejecting *y*; but from *dedīy*, *dedīyāñchakre*, &c. retaining it. Similarly in the other tenses: 1st fut. *dedīpitāhe*, &c.; *dedīyitāhe*, &c.: 2d fut. *dedīpishye*, &c., *dedīyishye*, &c.; 3d pret. *adedīpishi*, &c., *adedīyishi*, &c.; bened. *dedīpishīya*, &c., *dedīyishīya*, &c.; cond. *adedīpishye*, &c., *adedīyishye*, &c.

FORMATION OF THE BASE OF THE PARASMAIPADA FORM OF INTENSIVES.

Conjugational Tenses.

121. The base is here also formed by a reduplication similar to that of ātmanepada intensives; not, however, from the passive, but from the root. Thus from the root *pach*, *pāpach*; from *vid*, *vevid*; from *drish*, *darīdrish*; from *kri*, *charīkri*.† Moreover, in accordance with the rules for the 2d and 3d conjugation (pp. 69. 70.) the radical vowel requires Guna before the P terminations of the scheme (p. 66.). Hence the two bases *veved* and *vevid* (pres. *vevedmi*, *vevetsi*, *vevetti*; dual, *vevidwah*, &c.; 1st pret. *avevedam*, *avevet*, *avevet*, *avevidwa*, &c.; pot. *vevidyām*, &c.; imp.

---

* In passives this coalition of vowels is avoided by the change of a final vowel to Vriddhi, as of *chi* to *chāy*, of *hu* to *hāv*, and of *kri* to *kār*; and by the change of final *ā* to *āy*, as of *dā* to *dāy*, see r. 113.

† In the par. form of intensive, the reduplication may also be *darīdrish*, *charikri*, or, according to the general rule *dardrish*, *charkri*.

vevedāni, veviddhi, vevettu, vevedāva, vevittam, &c.). Again, the base will vary in accordance with the rules of combination at p. 67., as in *budh* (pres. *bobodhmi, bobhotsi, boboddhi, bobudhwah, &c.*). And in further analogy to the 2d conjugation (r. 92. *c.*) long *ī* is often optionally inserted before the consonantal P terminations (pres. *vevedīmi, vevedīshi, vevedīti;* dual, *vevidwah, &c.;* 1st pret. *avevedam, avevedīh, avevedīt, avevidwa, &c.;* imp. *vevedāni, veviddhi, vevedītu.*).

Lastly, when the root ends in a vowel, the usual changes take place of *i* and *ī* to *y* or *iy;* of *u* and *ū* to *uv;* and of *ṛi* to *r:* as in the roots *bhī, bhū, kṛi* (pres. 1st sing. *bebhemi, bobhomi, charkarmi;* 3d plur. *bebhyati, bobhuvati, charkrati*).

Non-Conjugational Tenses.

The second preterite follows the usual rule for polysyllabic bases (p. 77. *g.*), and affixes *ām* with the auxiliaries. Thus from *vid* (1st pers. sing.), *vevidāmāsa;* from *bhī, bebhyāmāsa.* In the other tenses, excepting the bened., inserted *i* is invariably assumed, and before this inserted *i* a root ending in a vowel forbids the usual Guna change in the futures, but admits Vṛiddhi in the 3d pret. Thus, 1st fut. (1st sing.) *veveditāsmi, &c., bebhyitāsmi, &c.;* 2d fut. *vevedishyāmi, &c., bebhyishyāmi, &c.;* 3d pret. *avévedisham, &c., abebhāyisham, &c.;* bened. *vevidyāsam, &c., bebhiyāsam;* cond. *avevedishyam, abebhyishyam.* This rejection of Guna is taken from Forster, but admits of question, especially in the case of roots in *u* or *ū*.

NOMINALS, OR VERBS DERIVED FROM NOUNS.

122. These are formed by adding certain affixes to the crude of nouns. They are not in very common use, but, theoretically, there is no limit to their formation. They may be classed under three heads: 1st, transitive nominals, yielding the sense of performing, practising, making or using the thing or quality expressed by the noun; 2d, intransitive nominals, giving a sense of behaving like, becoming like, acting like the person or thing expressed by the noun; 3d, desiderative nominals, yielding the sense of wishing for the thing expressed by the noun. The latter are rarely found.

The Terminations.

a. All the nominal verbs make use of the regular scheme at p. 63.; but it should be observed that they are rarely found conjugated in any other tense than the present.

Formation of the Base of Transitive Nominals.

b. These are formed from nouns in the way that causals are formed from roots, by the addition of *ay* to the crude. But the final vowel or final consonant, and preceding vowel of the crude, must be rejected before this affix is annexed. Thus, from *vastra*, "cloth," is formed *vastray*, "to clothe" (3d sing. वस्त्रयति *vastrayati*, "he clothes"); from *varman*, "armour," *varmay*, "to put on armour" (वर्म्मयति *varmayati*); from प्रमाण, "authority," प्रमाणय्, "to propose as authority." Whatever modifications adjectives may undergo before the affixes *īyas* and *ishṭha* (p. 47. †.), the same are required before this nominal affix: thus, from *dirgha*, "long," *drūghay*, "to lengthen"; from *antika*, "near," *neday*, "to make near," &c.

In the Mitralabha (Prof. Johnson's edition, p. 97.) there is an instance of a nominal verb formed by adding the terminations directly to the noun; thus, चञ्च्वामि, "I peck," from चञ्चु, "a beak."

Formation of the Base of Intransitive Nominals.

c. The final of the crude of the noun is rejected, as in the last case, and *āy* affixed. Thus, from *paṇḍita*, "wise," *paṇḍitāy*, "to act the part of a wise man" (3d sing. पण्डितायते); from *druma*, "a tree," *drumāy*, "to be like a tree" (द्रुमायते); from *rājan*, "a king," *rājāy*, "to act the king" (राजायते). This nominal usually has a neuter or passive signification, and is generally restricted to the ātm. It is found, however, in an active sense, especially when derived from nouns expressive of colour; as, from कृष्ण, "black," कृष्णाय्, "to blacken" (कृष्णायते).

Formation of the Base of Desiderative Nominals.

d. These are formed by affixing *y* to the final vowel of a crude noun. The effect, however, of this affix is to change a final *a* or *ā* to *ī*, to lengthen a final *i* or *u*, and to change ऋ *ṛi* to री. Thus from *putra*, "a son," *putrīy*, "to desire a son" (3d sing. पुत्रीयति); from *pati*, "a husband," *patīy*, "to desire a husband" (पतीयति). So also from मातृ, मात्रीय्; from *rājan*, *rājīy* (r. 20. †.).

A desiderative nominal verb may also be formed by adding *kāmy* (derived from *kam*, "to desire") to the crude of nouns: thus from *putra*, *putrakāmy*, "to desire a son" (3d sing. पुत्रकाम्यति); or by affixing *sy*; as from *dhana*, *dhanasy*, "to desire wealth" (धनस्यति).

CHAPTER VII.

PARTICIPLES.

THIS is a subject in some respects perhaps the most important that has hitherto engaged our attention. We have endeavoured in the last chapter to show, that however complex the structure of the Sanscrit verb, and however repulsive to the student at the commencement of his studies, this complexity is one rather of theory than practice, and one that hardly extends beyond the pages of the grammar, and is little felt, provided the attention be confined to the earlier and purer specimens of Hindu literature. The cause of this has been shown to be, that the difficulty of the verb expends itself on tenses that are rarely if ever used by the best writers. We are now to show that the necessity for these tenses is superseded by participles, the use of which prevails to an extent wholly unparalleled in any other language, even in the Greek. These participles often discharge the functions of the verb itself, and are constantly found occupying the place of past and future tenses, and more especially those of passive verbs; insomuch that an instance of a passive in any other tense than the present or imperative rarely occurs. The consideration, therefore, of this portion of our subject bears most closely upon the idiomatic structure of the language; and so prominent a position do these verbal derivatives hold in the construction of sentences and collocation of words, that an accurate knowledge of the mode of their formation and the nature of their duties affords the best insight into the peculiarities of Sanscrit syntax, and elucidates many of the difficulties of idiom in the cognate dialects of India.

It may be desirable to premise that the *most important* of these participles are not derived immediately from the verb, but from a common source with the verb, viz. the root. The subject, therefore, has not been mixed up with that of verbal inflection, although in the very first instance, and in others which follow, the participle is deducible directly from a tense.

PRESENT PARTICIPLES. PARASMAIPADA.

Formation of the Crude.

123. These are the only participles that have any affinity with the conjugational structure of the verb. The crude is formed by substituting *at* for *anti*, the termination of the 3d person plural of the present tense, so that the peculiarities of conjugation necessarily appear in the participle. Thus, from *pachanti*, "they cook" (3d plur. pres. of पच्, 1st conj.), comes पचत् *pachat*, "cooking"; from *ghnanti* (3d plur. of *han*, 2d conj.), *ghnat*; from यन्ति, "they go," यत्, "going"; from यान्ति, यात्; from *juhwati* (3d plur. of *hu*, 3d conj.), जुह्वत् *juhwat*; from *nrityanti* (4th conj.), *nrityat*; from *chinwanti* (5th conj.), चिन्वत् *chinwat*; from *āpnuvanti* (5th conj.), *āpnuvat*; from *rundhanti* (*rudh*, 7th conj.), *rundhat*; from *kurvanti* (कृ, 8th conj.), *kurvat*; from *punanti* (*pū*, 9th conj.), *punat*. So again from *santi* (3d plur. of *as*, "to be"), *sat*; from the causal *darshayanti* (p. 125.), *darshayat*; from the desiderative *ditsanti* (p. 130. *e*.), *ditsat*.

a. It has been remarked (p. 62. and p. 89., note †.) that the passive verb may sometimes assume a parasmaipada inflection; and that all the neuter verbs placed under the 4th conjugation may be considered as so many examples of this form of the passive. This theory is corroborated by the fact of the existence of a parasmaipada present participle derivable from a passive base. Thus from दृश्य्, दृश्यत्, "being seen"; from चीय्, चीयत्, "being gathered."

Declension.

b. This in general conforms to r. 63. Thus, पचत्, nom. sing. du. pl. masc. पचन् *pachan*, पचन्तौ *pachantau*, पचन्तः *pachantah*; fem. पचन्ती, पचन्त्यौ, पचन्त्यः; neut. पचत्, पचन्ती, पचन्ति.

c. But in irregular primitives of the 3d conj., and all verbs from polysyllabic roots, and all other verbs which reject the nasal from the plural of the parasmaipada (see p. 69. note), the nom. sing. masc. is identical with the crude, and ends in *at* instead of *an*; and the nasal is, moreover, rejected from the du. and pl.

masc., and from the fem. Thus, *bibhrat* (from भृ, "to bear," 3d conj.), nom. sing. du. pl. masc. *bibhrat, bibhratau, bibhratah;* fem. *bibhratī, bibhratyau, bibhratyah.* So also *jāgrat* (from जागृ) and *shāsat* (from शास्). They also drop the nasal in the dual neut.

d. It must also be taken as a general rule, that all other irregular primitives of the 2d, 5th, 7th, 8th, and 9th conjugations reject the nasal in the feminine, although they retain it in the masculine. Thus, *adat* (from *ad,* 2d conj.), nom. masc. *adan, adantau, adantah;* fem. *adatī,* &c.; and *rundhat* (from *rudh,* 7th conj.), nom. masc. *rundhan, rundhantau,* &c., fem. *rundhatī,* &c. But this rule is not universal, for *kurvat* (from कृ, 8th conj.) is *kurvantī* in the nom. fem.

PRESENT PARTICIPLES. ATMANEPADA.

Formation of the Crude.

124. The crude is formed by substituting *amāna* for *ante,* the termination of the 3d plur. pres. of regular primitive and passive verbs; and by substituting *āna* for *ate,* the termination of the 3d plur. pres. of irregular primitives. Causal verbs take either *amāna* or *āna,* but more frequently the latter. Thus, from पचन्ते *pachante,* पचमान *pachamāna;* from तिष्ठन्ते (*sthā,* 1st conj.), तिष्ठमान; from नृत्यन्ते (4th conj.), नृत्यमान; from लिम्पन्ते (*lip,* 6th conj.), लिम्पमान; from the causal *darshayante* (p. 126.), either *darshayamāna,* or, more frequently, *darshayāna;* from *vedayante, vedayāna;* from the desiderative *ditsante, ditsamāna.*

a. But from ब्रुवते *bruvate* (ब्रू, 2d conj.), ब्रुवाण *bruvāṇa;* from दधते (*dhā,* 3d conj.), दधान; from *chinvate* (5th conj.), *chinvāna;* from युञ्जते (7th conj.), युञ्जान; from कुर्वते (8th conj.), कुर्वाण; from पुनते (9th conj.), पुनान. The root आस्, "to sit" (2d conj.), makes आसीन for आसान.

Declension.

b. These participles are declined like nouns of the first class, p. 31. Thus, *pachamāna,* nom. masc. *pachamānah,* fem. *pachamānā,* neut. *pachamānam.*

PAST PARTICIPLES.

Passive Past Participle.—Formation of the Crude.

125. This is the most useful derivative in the language, and is

of constant occurrence. It corresponds to the Latin participle in *tus*, and, like it, often supplies the place of the past tense. In neuter roots, especially those which imply motion of any kind, it is used actively, and often stands for the perfect tense active; as, विवरं प्रविष्टः, "he entered his hole"; ग्रामं गतः, "he went to the village." And in all cases this participle may be used to supply the place of the past tenses of the passive verb, the agent being placed in the instrumental case, and the participle agreeing with the object: as, तेन बन्धनानि छिन्नानि, "by him the bonds were cut."* Moreover, it may be used with the auxiliary verbs अस् and भू, "to be," to form a compound past or future tense, as the Latin participle is used with the auxiliary *sum*. Thus, प्राप्तोऽस्ति, "he has obtained"; प्राप्तो भविष्यति, "he will have obtained"; गतोऽस्मि, "I am gone"; कृतमस्ति, "it is done." Lastly, it is sometimes used in the neuter gender for a substantive; as, दत्तं, "a gift"; खातं, "an excavation."†

This participle may be regarded as falling under four heads: 1st, as derived from roots; 2dly, as derived from causal bases; 3dly, as derived from desiderative bases; 4thly, as derived from nominal bases.

1. *Derived from Roots.*

a. In general the crude is formed by adding *ta* (त) directly to the root; as, from क्षिप् *kship*, "to throw," *kshipta*, "thrown"; or if the root end in ॠ *ṝ*, by adding *na* (न); as, from कॄ *kṝ*, "to scatter," कीर्ण *kīrṇa*, "scattered." Some roots in *ā*, *ī*, and *ū*, some in *ai* preceded by two consonants, with some of those in *d*, *r*, and *j*, rejecting inserted *i*, also take *na* instead of *ta*.

b. Roots ending in vowels do not admit inserted *i* in this

* This kind of construction is exceedingly common in Sanscrit, and has been transferred from it to Hindūstanī. The particle *ne* in this latter language corresponds most clearly to the Sanscrit *na*, which is the usual sign of the instrumental case, and can never occasion any difficulty if it be regarded in this light.

† In a few instances this participle has a present signification; as, भीत, "fearing," स्थित, "standing."

participle, although they may admit it in the futures* (p. 79. *a. b. c.*), but attach *ta* or *na* directly to the root: as, from *yā*, *yāta*; from *ji*, *jita*; from *nī*, *nīta*; from *shru*, *shruta*; from *bhū*, *bhūta*; from कृ, कृत; from घ्रा, घ्राण (r. 21.); from *lī*, *līna*; from ह्री, ह्रीण; from *lū*, *lūna*.

c. But in certain cases the final vowel of the root is changed; thus, some roots in *ā* change *ā* to *i* before *ta*: as, from *sthā*, *sthita*; from *mā*, *mita*; from *daridrā*, *daridrita*. *Dhā*, "to place," becomes *hita*; *dā*, "to give," *datta*;† *pā*, "to drink," *pīta*. *Hā*, "to quit," becomes *hī* before *na* (हीन). Some roots in *ā* take both *na* and *ta*; as, from घ्रा, घ्राण and घ्रात; from वा with the preposition निर्, निर्वाण and निर्वात.

d. Roots in ॠ *ṛī* change *ṛī* to *īr* before *na*, which passes into *ṇa* (ण) by r. 21.; as, from तॄ, "to pass," तीर्ण, "passed." But from पॄ, पूर्ण, "full."

e. The root *dhe*, "to suck," becomes *dhī* before *ta*; *hve*, "to call," *hū* (हूत); *ve*, "to weave," *u* (उत).

f. Roots in ऐ *ai* generally change *ai* to *ā*, before *na* or *ta*; as, from म्लै *mlai*, "to fade," म्लान *mlāna*; from ध्यै, "to meditate," ध्यात; from दै, "to purify," दात; from त्रै, "to rescue," त्राण or त्रात. But from गै, "to sing," गीत; from क्षै, "to waste," क्षाम.

g. Roots in ओ *o* change *o* to *i*; as, from *so*, *sita*; from शो, शित.

h. Those roots ending in consonants which take the inserted *i* (p. 79. *d.*) generally take this vowel also in the past participle. In such cases *ta* is affixed, and never *na*; as, from *pat*, "to fall," *patita*, "fallen"; and if *u* or *ṛi* precede the final consonant of the root, these vowels may take Guna; as, from *dyut*, *dyotita*; from मृष्, मर्षित. *Grah*, lengthens the inserted *i* (गृहीत, "taken").

i. Roots ending in consonants which forbid the inserted *i* must be combined with *ta*, agreeably to the rules at pp. 67, 68. Whatever form, therefore, the final consonant assumes before the termination *tā* of the 1st future (p. 80.), the same form will gene-

---

* शी, however, makes शयित, and पू may be पवित as well as पूत.

† When prepositions are prefixed to *datta*, the initial *da* may be rejected; thus, *ātta* for *ādatta*, "taken"; *pratta* for *pradatta*, "bestowed"; *vyātta* for *vyādatta*, "expanded"; *parītta* for *paridatta*; *sūtta* for *sudatta*, the *i* and *u* being lengthened.

rally be preserved before the *ta* of the past participle; so that, in many cases, this participle may be derived from the 3d sing. of the 1st future by shortening the final *ā*, and, if necessary, restoring the radical vowel to its original state. Thus, taking some of the examples at p. 80; *shaktā*, "he will be able," gives *shakta*, "able"; *sektā*, "he will sprinkle," *sikta*, "sprinkled"; *moktā*, *mukta*; प्रष्टा, पृष्ट; *tyaktā*, *tyakta*; *yoktā*, *yukta*; स्रष्टा, सृष्ट; मार्ष्टा, मृष्ट; *seddhā*, *siddha*; *boddhā*, *buddha*; *yoddhā*, *yuddha*; *ksheptā*, *kshipta*; *loptā*, *lupta*; *sarptā*, *sṛipta*; *kalptā*, *klṛipta*; *labdhā*, *labdha*; *lobdhā*, *lubdha*; वेष्टा, विष्ट; द्रष्टा, दृष्ट; क्रोष्टा, क्रुष्ट; तष्टा, तष्ट; एष्टा, इष्ट; द्वेष्टा, द्विष्ट; दोष्टा, दुष्ट; क्रष्टा, कृष्ट; दग्धा, दग्ध; सोढा, सोढ; नद्धा, नद्ध; गाढा, गाढ; लेढा, लीढ (p. 68. *h.*); देग्धा, दिग्ध; स्नेग्धा, स्निग्ध; रोढा, रूढ (p. 68. *h.*); मोढा, मूढ; or मोग्धा, मुग्ध; दोग्धा, दुग्ध; गोढा, गूढ.

j. Most roots ending in *d*, forbidding the inserted *i*, take *na* instead of *ta*, and are combined with *na*, agreeably to r. 15; as, from *pad*, *panna*; from *ad*, *anna*; from *bhid*, *bhinna*; from सद्, with the preposition वि, विषण्ण (r. 30. and 21.)

k. Those roots ending in *j*, which take *na*, change *j* to *g* before *na*; as, from *vij*, *vigna*; from *ruj*, *rugna*. So from *masj*, rejecting the *s*, *magna*; from *lasj*, *lagna*.

l. Some roots which admit *i* in the futures, forbid it in this participle; as, धृष्, in 1st fut. धर्षिता, in part. धृष्ट; so अर्द्, अर्दिता, but अर्ण (with *ā* prefixed, आर्त्त, "pained"); दृह्, दर्हिता, but दृढ; मद्, मदिता, but मत्त. See also p. 109.

m. If in forming the passive base (p. 90. *f.*), or in the 2d pret. (p. 76. *d.*), the *v* or *y* contained in a root are changed to their semi-vowels *u* or *i*, the same change takes place in the pass. participle; thus, from *vach*, "to say," *ukta*; from *vap*, *upta*; from वह्, ऊढ; from स्वप्, सुप्त; from यज्, इष्ट. Similarly, from दिव्, द्यून or द्यूत; from त्वर्, तूर्ण.

n. Some other changes which take place in forming the passive base (see p. 90. *d. f.*) are preserved before *ta*; thus, from शास्, शिष्ट; from व्यध्, विद्ध. And when the root ends in two conjunct consonants, of which the first is a nasal, this nasal is rejected; as, from बन्ध्, बद्ध; from भ्रंश्, भ्रष्ट; from स्रञ्ज्, स्रक्त; from सञ्ज्, सक्त; from भञ्ज्, भग्न: but not if *i* is inserted; as, from खण्ड्, खण्डित; from क्रन्द्, क्रन्दित (except मन्थ्, making मथित).

o. Roots ending in *m* or *n* reject these nasals before *ta*; as, from *gam*, "to go," *gata;* from *yam*, *yata;* from *ram*, *rata;* from *tan*, *tata;* from *han*, *hata:* but retain them if *i* is inserted; as, from *swan*, *swanita*. From *jan*, "to be born," is formed *jāta;* from *khan*, *khāta;* the *a* being lengthened.

p. Those roots ending in *m*, of the 4th conjugation, which lengthen a medial *a* before the conjugational affix *y*, also lengthen it before *ta*, and change *m* to *n* as in the futures; thus, from *kram* (r. 89. *a*.), *krānta;* from *bhram*, *bhrānta;* from *sham*, *shānta;* from *dam*, *dānta;* from *ksham*, *kshānta;* from *klam*, *klānta*. Similarly, from *vam*, *vānta;* from *kam*, *kānta*.

q. From स्फाय्, "to swell," is formed स्फीत; from प्याय्, पीन or प्यान.

r. The following are quite anomalous; from *pach*, "to cook," *pakwa;* from शुष्, "to dry," शुष्क; from क्षीव्, "to be drunk," क्षीब.

2. *Derived from Causal Bases.*

r. In forming the passive past participles from these, the causal affix *ay* is rejected, but the inserted *i* is always assumed. Thus, from *kāray*, *kārita;* from *sthāpay*, *sthāpita;* from *veday*, *vedita*.

3. *Derived from Desiderative Bases.*

s. In adding *ta* to a desiderative base, the only rule to be observed is the invariable insertion of *i*; as, from *pipās*, *pipāsita;* from *chikīrsh*, *chikīrshita;* from *īps*, *īpsita*.

4. *Derived from Nominal Bases.*

t. There are in Sanscrit certain participles, which are said to be formed by adding *ita* to nouns. Thus, from शिथिल, "loose," शिथिलित, "loosened"; from जिह्म, "crooked," जिह्मित, "curved." These may be regarded as the passive participles of the transitive nominal verbs शिथिलयति, जिह्मयति (r. 122. *b*.); and whenever this kind of adjective is found, it may indicate that a nominal verb is in use, whence the participle is derived.

Declension of Passive Past Participles.

They all follow the declension of the first class of nouns (r. 48. 49. 50.), and in this exhibit a perfect similarity to the declension of the Latin participle in *tus*. Thus, *kṛita*, nom. masc. fem. neut. *kṛitah*, *kṛitā*, *kṛitam*.*

* Since *h* is equivalent to *s* and *a* to *u*, the nom. might be written *-tus*, *-tā*, *-tum*.

ACTIVE PAST PARTICIPLES.

126. These are of two kinds; 1st, those derived from the passive past participle; 2dly, those derived from the second preterite. These latter rarely occur. The former are much used (especially in modern Sanscrit, and in the writings of commentators), to supply the place of a perfect tense active. Thus, *tat kṛitavān*, "he did that"; *tat kṛitavatī*, "she did that." They may also be used with the auxiliaries *as* and *bhū*, to form a compound perfect tense; thus, *tat kṛitavān asti*, "he has done that"; *tat kṛitavān bhavishyati*, "he will have done that."

Formation of the Crude.

a. In the case of those derived from the passive past participle, the crude is easily formed by adding *vat* to that participle. Thus, from *kṛita, kṛitavat* (कृतवत्); from *dagdha, dagdhavat;* from *ukta, uktavat;* from *bhinna, bhinnavat;* from *sthāpita, sthāpitavat*, &c.

b. In the case of those derived from the 2d pret., either *vas* or *ivas* is added to the base of that tense, as formed in the dual and plur. *Vas*, when the base in the dual and plur. consists of more than one syllable; as, from *vivid* (p. 96.), *vividwas;* from *chichi* (p. 96.), *chichivas*. But *ivas*, when the base in the dual and plur. consists of one syllable only; as from *ten* (p. 96.) *tenivas;* from *jagm* (p. 77. *c.*), *jagmivas*. There is an ātmanepada participle of the 2d pret. formed by adding *āna* to the base; thus, *vividāna, chichyāna, tenāna, jagmāna*.

Declension.

127. Those formed from the passive past participle are declined r. 62.; thus, *kṛitavat*, nom. masc. fem. neut. *kṛitavān, kṛitavatī*, r. 49., *kṛitavat*.

Those formed from the 2d pret. are declined in the last paragraph of p. 44.; thus, *vividwas*, nom. masc. fem. neut. *vividwān, vividushī, vividwah;* and *chichivas*, nom. *chichivān, chichyushī, chichivah*. Those formed with *ivas* do not retain *i* in the fem.; thus, *tenivas*, nom. masc. fem. neut. *tenivān, tenushī*,* *tenivah;* and *jagmivas*, nom. *jagmivān, jagmushi, jagmivah*. The ātmanepada participles are declined like nouns of the first class, p. 31.

---

* Similarly the instr. case masc. is *tenushā*. There seems, however, much difference of opinion as to the rejection of *i*, and some Grammarians make the fem. *tenyushī*, and the inst. masc. *tenyushā*.

INDECLINABLE PAST PARTICIPLES.

128. These may be classed under two heads: 1st, as formed by affixing त्वा *twā* to uncompounded roots; as, from *bhū*, "to be," *bhūtwā*, "having been"; 2dly, as formed by affixing य *ya* to roots compounded with prepositions or other adverbial prefixes; as, from *anubhū*, *anubhūya*, "having perceived"; from *sajjībhū*, *sajjībhūya*, "having become ready." These indeclinable participles are of the utmost importance, and some of the chief peculiarities of the syntax of the language are to be traced to the frequency of their occurrence.

The sparing use made in Sanscrit composition of relative pronouns, conjunctions, and connective particles, is partly to be attributed to the continual appearance of these indeclinable participles, by means of which the sense of a whole clause may be suspended, and sentence after sentence strung together without the aid of a single copulative. The sense involved in them is generally expressed by the English "when," "after," "having," or "by"; thus, *tat kritwā* (तत् कृत्वा), "when he had done that," "after he had done that," "having done that," "by doing that." See syntax.

Formation of the Indeclinable Participle from Uncompounded Roots.

a. When the root stands alone and uncompounded, the indeclinable participle is formed with त्वा *twā*.*

This affix is closely allied to the *ta* of the passive past participle, r. 125., insomuch that the rules for the annexation of *ta* to the root apply equally to the indeclinable affix *twā*. The formation, therefore, of one participle generally involves that of the other; thus, *kshipta*, "thrown," *kshiptwā*, "having thrown"; कृत, "done," कृत्वा, "having done"; so स्थित, स्थित्वा; दृष्ट, दृष्ट्वा; दत्त, दत्त्वा; पीत, पीत्वा; क्रान्त, क्रान्त्वा; गृहीत, गृहीत्वा; उषित, उषित्वा; उक्त, उक्त्वा; युद्ध, युद्ध्वा; ऊढ, ऊढ्वा; हित (from धा), हित्वा. And where *i* is inserted there is often an optional change of the radical vowel to Guna, as

* There are one or two instances in which an uncompounded root takes य; as, सच्यै, "having reverenced."—Manu, 7th Book, 145. I. 4. Mahābh. 3. 8017.

in the passive participle (r. 125. *h.*); thus, *dyutitwā* or *dyotitwā* from *dyut*; and मृष् *always* takes Guna (मर्षित्वा). There are a few instances in which the inserted *i* is admitted before *twā*, although rejected before *ta*; as, *lagna*, *lajjitwā*; and, *vice versâ*, as उषित, उष्ट्वा.

b. A penultimate nasal is not always rejected before *twā*; thus, from रञ्ज्, रक्त, but रंक्त्वा or रक्त्वा, the rejection in the indeclinable participle being generally optional.

c. The causal verb, which rejects its characteristic *ay* before the *ita* of the passive participle, retains it before *itwā*. Thus, *sthāpita*, "made to stand" (from the causal base *sthāpay*), but *sthāpayitwā*, "having made to stand."

d. The only important variation from the passive participle occurs in those roots which take *na* for *ta* (r. 125. *a.*). In such roots no corresponding change takes place of *twā* to *nwā*. Thus, from जॄ, जीर्ण, but जरित्वा (or जरीत्वा); from तॄ, तीर्ण, but तीर्त्वा; from छिद्, छिन्न, but छित्त्वा; from भञ्ज्, भग्न, but भंक्त्वा or भक्त्वा; from रुज्, रुग्ण, but रुक्त्वा; from हा, हीन, but हित्वा, "having quitted" (not distinguishable from हित्वा, "having placed," from धा).

Formation of the Indeclinable Participle from Compounded Roots.

When a root is compounded with a preposition or indeclinable word, the indeclinable participle cannot be formed with *twā*.* The affix य *ya* is then used, and the rules which regulate its annexation to the root are some of them analogous to those which prevail in other cases in which *y* is affixed; see the rules for the formation of neuters (r. 89.), passives (p. 90.), and the benedictive mood (p. 85.).

a. But if a root end in a short vowel, instead of any lengthening of this vowel, *t* is interposed; as, from *āshri*, "to take refuge" (root श्रि), *āshritya*, "having taken refuge"; from निश्रि, निश्रित्य; from उत्प्लु, उत्प्लुत्य; from संस्कृ, संस्कृत्य; from निःसृ, निःसृत्य. The lengthening of the radical vowel by coalition does not prevent this rule; as, from *atī* (*ati* with *i*), *atītya*.

b. If a root end in long *ā*, *ī*, or *ū*, no change takes place: as, from *vihā*, *vihāya*; from *upakrī*, *upakrīya*; from *vidhū*, *vihhūya*.

c. If in long ॠ *rī*, this vowel becomes *īr*; as, from अवकॄ, अवकीर्य. But from आपॄ, आपूर्य.

d. Final diphthongs pass into *ā*: as, from परिव्ये, परिव्याय (also परिवीय); from अभिध्ये, अभिध्याय; from अवसो, अवसाय. But from सो with व्यव, व्यवस्य; from आह्वे, आहूय.

e. A penultimate nasal is generally rejected; as, from *samāsanj*, *samāsajya;* from *pramanth*, *pramathya* (used adverbially, "violently"); but from आशङ्क्, आशङ्क्य; from आलिङ्ग्, आलिङ्ग्य.

f. If a root end in a consonant the general rule is, that no change takes place; as, from *nikship*, *nikshipya;* from *prāp* (*pra* and *āp*), *prāpya;* from *vīksh* (*vi* and *īksh*), *vīkshya.*

g. But some roots ending in *am* and *an* may optionally reject the nasal, and interpose *t* between short *a* and *ya.;* as, from *nirgam*, *nirgatya* or *nirgamya;* from *nihan*, *nihatya.* *Jan* and *khan* instead of interposing *t*, lengthen the *a;* as, from *utkhan*, *utkhāya.*

h. The changes which take place in certain roots before the *y* of the passive (p. 90. *f.*) are preserved before *ya;* as, from विग्रह्, विगृह्य; from आप्रछ्, आपृच्छ्य; from *āvyadh*, *āvidhya;* from *vivas*, *vyushya.* स्फुर् lengthens its vowel before *ya*; as, विस्फूर्य.

i. In affixing *ya* to causal bases the characteristic *ay* is generally rejected:* as, from *prabodhay*, *prabodhya* (प्रबोध्य); from प्रसादय्, प्रसाद्य; from सन्दर्शय्, सन्दर्श्य.†

Adverbial Indeclinable Participle.

There is another indeclinable participle yielding the same sense as those formed with *twā* and *ya*, but of very rare occurrence except in the Bhaṭṭi kāvya. It is equivalent to the accusative case of a noun derived from a root, used adverbially; and is formed by adding *am* to the root, before which affix changes of the radical vowel take place, similar to those required before the causal affix *ay* (p. 86. *c.*). Thus, from *nī*, "to lead," *nāyam*, "having led"; from *pā*, "to drink," *pāyam*, "having drunk"; from *hwe*, *hwāyam;* from *pach*, *pācham;* from *kship*, *kshepam;* from *han*, "to kill," *ghātam.* It often occupies the last place in a compound; as in

* It is retained in some few instances; as, विगणय्य, "having calculated"; आकलय्य, "having imagined"; सङ्कथय्य, "having narrated."

† There are one or two instances of compounded roots formed with *twā;* as, अनुध्यात्वा (from ध्यै), Rām. 1. 2. 20. Especially in the case of causals, as निवर्त्तयित्वा.

the expression समूलघातं, "having totally exterminated"; and in the following passage from Bhaṭṭi:

लतानुपातं कुसुमान्यगृह्णात् स नद्यवस्कन्दमुपास्पृशच्च
कुतूहलाच्चारुशिलोपवेशं काकुत्स्थ ईषत्स्मयमान आस्त

"The descendant of Kakutstha, smiling softly, repeatedly bending down the creepers, would pluck the blossoms; descending to the streams, would sip (the waters); seating himself on some variegated rock, would recline in admiration (of the scene)."

These participles generally imply repetition of the action, as in the passage above, and in this sense are themselves often repeated; as, *dāyam, dāyam*, "having repeatedly given."

FUTURE PASSIVE PARTICIPLES.

129. These are amongst the most common and useful of all participles, and may be classed under three heads: 1st, as formed with the affix तव्य *tavya;* 2dly, as formed with अनीय *anīya;* 3dly, as formed with य *ya.* These affixes yield a sense corresponding to the Latin *dus* and the English *able* and *ible,* and most commonly denote obligation or propriety and fitness. Thus, from *bhuj,* "to eat," *bhoktavya,* or *bhojanīya,* or *bhojya,* "edible," "eatable," "that ought to be eaten"; from *vach,* "to speak," *vaktavya,* or *vachanīya,* or *vāchya,* "to be spoken," "*dicendus.*" They sometimes denote simple futurity; as, भोक्तव्य, "about to be eaten": and as the passive past participle supplies the place of a past tense, so the future passive participle may supply the place of a future tense passive; as in the following sentence, यदि पक्षी पतति तदा मया खादितव्यः, "If the bird falls, then it shall be eaten by me."

Formation of Future Passive Participles with the affix तव्य tavya.

a. These are formed by substituting *tavya* for *tā,* the termination of the 3d pers. sing. of the 1st future. Thus, from क्षेप्ता *kṣheptā,* "he will throw," क्षेप्तव्य *kṣheptavya,* "to be thrown"; *kartā,* "he will do," *kartavya,* "to be done"; from *bhavitā,* "he will be," *bhavitavya,* "about to be." And in the case of roots ending in consonants rejecting *i,* whatever changes take place before *tā,* the same take place before *tavya* (see p. 80.); thus, *tyaktā, tyaktavya* (*relinquendus*); प्रष्टा, प्रष्टव्य; द्रष्टा, द्रष्टव्य; *boddhā, boddhavya; dagdhā, dagdhavya,* &c.

Formation of Future Passive Participles with the affix अनीय anīya.

b. This affix is added directly to the root, without any other change than the Guna of the radical vowel. Thus, from चि *chi*, "to gather," चयनीय *chayanīya*, "to be gathered"; from *bhū*, *bhavanīya*; from कृ, करणीय (r. 21.); from लिख्, लेखनीय; from शुष्, शोषणीय; from स्पृश्, स्पर्शनीय; from कृष्, कर्षणीय (r. 21.). A final diphthong is changed to *ā*; as, from ध्यै, ध्यानीय; from गै, गानीय.

Formation of Future Passive Participles with the affix य ya.

c. Before this affix, as before all others beginning with *y*, certain changes of final vowels become necessary. If a root end in *ā*, or in *e*, *ai*, *o*, changeable to *ā*, this vowel becomes *e* (cf. p. 85. *a.*); as, from *mā*, "to measure," *meya*, "to be measured," "measurable"; from *hā*, *heya*; from *dhyai*, *dhyeya*, &c.

d. If in *i*, *ī*, *u*, or *ū*, these vowels take Guna; as, from *chi*, *cheya*. But the Guna *o* is changed to *av*, and sometimes *e* to *ay*, before *ya* (as if before a vowel): thus, from *bhū*, *bhavya*; from *ji*, "to conquer," *jayya*. The Guna *o*, however, oftener passes into *āv* before *y*; as, from श्रु, श्राव्य; from *plu*, *plāvya*.

e. If in *ṛi* or *ṛī* these vowels take Vṛiddhi; as, from कृ, कार्य.

f. Sometimes if a root end in a short vowel no change takes place, but *t* is interposed, after the analogy of the indeclinable participle formed with *ya* (p. 144. *a.*), so that the crude of the future participle is not distinguishable from the indeclinable, except by the absence of a preposition. Thus, from *ji*, *jitya*, "conquerable"; from *stu*, *stutya*, "laudable"; from *kṛi*, *kṛitya*, "practicable."

g. If a root end in a single consonant with a medial *a*, Vṛiddhi sometimes takes place; as, from *grah*, *grāhya*: but not always; as, from *shak*, *shakya*; from *sah*, *sahya*; from *badh*, *badhya*; and rarely if the final is a labial; as, from *gam*, *gamya*; from *labh*, *labhya*.

h. If with a medial *i* or *u*, Guna generally takes place; as, from *bhuj*, *bhojya*; from *lih*, *lehya*.

i. If with a medial *ṛi*, no change takes place; as, from स्पृश्, स्पृश्य.

j. A final *ch* may be changed to *k*, and *j* to *g*; and other changes may take place, some of which are similar to those before the *y* of passives; as, from *pach*, *pākya*; from *vach*, *vākya*; from *bhuj*, *bhogya;* from *grah, gṛihya,* as well as *grāhya;* from *vad, ūdya;* from *yaj, ijya;* from *shās, shishya* (p. 90. *d. f.*); from *khan, kheya.*

k. Many of these latter are used as substantives, and there are other examples of substantives formed with this affix; as, भार्या (fem.), "a wife," from भृ, "to support," &c.

Declension of Future Passive Participles.

They are all declined like nouns of the first class, pp. 31, 32. Thus, *kartavya;* nom. m. f. n. *kartavyah, kartavyā, kartavyam.* Similarly, *karaṇīya* and *kārya.*

PARTICIPLES OF THE SECOND FUTURE.

Formation of the Crude.

130. These are not very common. They are of two kinds, either as belonging to the parasmaipada, or to the ātmanepada; the former being formed by changing *anti,* the termination of the 3d plur. of the 2d fut., into *at;* the latter by changing *ante* into *amāna.* Thus, from *karishyanti* and *karishyante,* "they will do," *karishyat* and *karishyamāṇa* (करिष्यत् करिष्यमाण), "about to do"; from the passive 2d fut. *vakshyante,* "they will be said," *vakshyamāṇa,* "about to be said."

These participles, in the mode of their formation from the 3d pers. plur., by the affixes *at* and *amāna,* resemble present participles, r. 123.

Declension of Participles of the Second Future.

a. Their declension also conforms to that of present participles. Those of the parasmaipada are declined according to p. 136. *b.*, and those of the ātmanepada according to p. 137. *b.*

PARTICIPIAL NOUNS OF AGENCY.

131. These have been already incidentally noticed in Chap. III. As, however, they partake of the nature of participles, and are of great practical utility, some further mention of them is necessary in the present chapter. They may be classed under three heads; 1st, as formed from the root; 2dly, as formed from the 1st future; 3dly, as formed from the causal base.

1. The crude of the first class is formed from the root by affixing *a*, before which Guna, and rarely Vṛiddhi, of a final vowel is required; as, from *ji*, "to conquer," *jaya* (जय), "conquering." Medial vowels are generally unchanged; as, from *vad*, "to say," *vada*, "saying"; from *tud*, "to vex," *tuda*, "vexing": and final *ā*, *am*, or *an*, are dropped; as, from *dā*, "to give," *da* (द), "giving"; from *gam*, "to go," *ga* (ग), "going"; from *jan*, "to be born," *ja*, "being born" (see their declension, r. 38. 1. and p. 31.). These nouns of agency are constantly used in poetry as a substitute for the present participle,* sometimes governing the same case as this participle, but always united with the word which they govern in one compound; thus, *purañjaya* (पुरञ्जय), "city-conquering"; *priyamvada* (प्रियंवद), "speaking kind words"; *jalechara* (जलेचर) "going in the water"; *sarasija*, "lake-born." The word which they govern often remains in the crude form; as, from *tejas* and *kṛi*, *tejaskara*, "light-making" (*s* remaining unchanged, in violation of r. 29.); from *manas* and *hṛi*, *manohara*, "mind-captivating" (r. 29.); from *bahu* and *dā*, *bahuda*, "giving much"; from आत्मन् and ज्ञा, आत्मज्ञ, "self-knowing."

2. The crude of the second class is formed from the 3d pers. sing. of the 1st future of primitive verbs, by substituting the vowel ऋ *ṛi* for the final vowel *ā*, the nominative case being therefore *identical* with the 3d pers. sing. of that tense (see p. 77. r. 100. p. 37. and r. 41.). Thus, from *bhoktā*, "he will eat," *bhoktṛi*, "an eater" (nom. *bhoktā*); from योद्धा, "he will fight," योद्धृ, "a fighter"; from *yāchitā*, *yāchitṛi*; from सोढा, सोढृ, &c. This noun of agency is sometimes, but rarely, found as a participle governing the case of the verb; as, वक्ता वाक्यं, "speaking a speech" (Draupadīharaṇam, 32.); वोढा वहुमागंगां, "bearing the Ganges" (Ratnāvali, p. 1.).

3. The crude of the third class is formed in three ways.

a. By adding *in* to the root, before which affix changes take place similar to those required before the causal affix *ay* (r. 107. *c*. *d*.); as, from *kṛi*, *kārin* (कारिन्), "a doer"; from *han*, *ghātin*, "a killer"; from *shī*, *shāyin*, "a sleeper": *y* being inserted after roots

* Implying, however, *habitual* action, and therefore something more than present time.

in *ā*, as, from *pā*, *pāyin*, "a drinker"; from *dā*, *dāyin*, "a giver" (see their declension, r. 43. iii. and p. 43.). This noun of agency has often, like the first class, the sense of a present participle, and is then always united with the crude of the word which it governs in one compound: thus, from *manas* and *hṛi*, *manohārin*, "mind-captivating" (r. 29.). It sometimes, also, governs the case of the verb, being still united with the word which it governs in one compound; as, *grāmevāsin*, "dwelling in the village."

b. By adding *aka* to the root before which affix changes take place analogous to those before the causal *ay* (r. 107. *c. d. e. f.*); as, from *kṛi*, *kāraka* (कारक), "a doer," "doing"; from *nī*, *nāyaka*, "a leader," "leading"; from *grah*, *grāhaka*; from *sidh*, *sādhaka*; from *han*, *ghātaka*; from दुष्, दूषक; from *kram*, *kramaka*; from *nand*, *nandaka*; from *sthā*, *sthāpaka* (see their declension, r. 38. ii. and p. 31.). This participial noun is also often joined with the crude of the noun which it governs in one compound word; as, कार्य्यसाधक, "effecting the business." It is very rarely found governing the case of the verb; as, मुकुलानि चुम्बकः, "kissing the buds" (Ratnāvali, p. 7.).

c. By adding *ana* to some few roots ending in consonants, after changes similar to those required before the causal affix; as, from *nand*, *nandana*, "rejoicing"; from दुष्, दूषण, "vitiating"; from शुध्, शोधन, "cleansing" (see their declension, r. 38. iii. and p. 31.)

CHAPTER VIII.

INDECLINABLE WORDS.

Adverbs.

132. Adverbs, like nouns and verbs, may be divided into simple and compound. The latter are treated of in the next Chapter on Compound Words.

Simple adverbs may be classed under four heads; 1st, as

formed from the cases of nouns; 2dly, as formed with affixes; 3dly, as of uncertain derivation; 4thly, as prefixes to other words.

Adverbs formed from the Cases of Nouns.

The following cases of nouns are used adverbially:

a. The nominative or accusative neuter of any adjective; as, सत्यं, "truly"; बहु, "much"; शीघ्रं, क्षिप्रं, "quickly"; युक्तं, "fitly"; समीपं, "near"; लघु, "lightly"; निर्भरं, अत्यन्तं, गाढं, भृशं, "exceedingly"; अवश्यं, "certainly"; नित्यं, "constantly"; बलवत्, "strongly." The nom. or acc. neuter of certain pronouns; as, तत्, "therefore"; यत्, "wherefore," "when"; तावत्, "so long as"; यावत्, "as long as"; किम्, "why?" The nom. or acc. neut. of certain substantives and obsolete words; as रहः, "secretly"; कामं, "willingly"; नाम, "by name," "that is to say"; वारं वारं, "repeatedly"; चिरं, "long ago"; सुखं, "pleasantly"; साम्प्रतं, "now"; नक्तं, "by night" (*noctu*).

b. The instrumental case of nouns and pronouns; as, धर्म्मेण, "virtuously"; दक्षिणेन, "southwards"; उत्तरेण, "northwards"; उच्चैः, "above"; नीचैः, "below"; शनैः, "slowly"; तेन, "therefore"; येन, "wherefore." The instr. case of certain obsolete nouns; as, चिरेण, "for a long time"; अचिरेण, "in a short time"; दिवा, "by day"; दिष्ट्या, "fortunately"; सहसा, अञ्जसा, "quickly"; अधुना, "now."

c. The ablative case of a few nouns and pronouns; as, बलात्, "forcibly"; दूरात्, "at a distance"; तस्मात्, "therefore"; कस्मात्, "wherefore"? अकस्मात्, "without cause," "unexpectedly"; उत्तरात्, "from the north": and of a few obsolete nouns; as, चिरात्, "for a long time"; पश्चात्, "afterwards."

d. The locative case of a few nouns and obsolete words; as, रात्रौ, "at night"; दूरे, "far off"; प्राह्णे, "in the forenoon"; स्थाने, "suitably"; अग्रे, "in front"; एकपदे, "at once"; सपदि, "instantly"; अन्तरे, "within."

Adverbs formed with Affixes.

133. चित् *chit*, अपि *api*, and चन *chana*, may form *Indefinite* adverbs of time and place, when affixed to interrogative adverbs; as, from कदा, "when?" कदाचित्, कदापि, and कदाचन, "sometimes"; from कुत्र and क्व, "where?" कुत्रचित्, कुत्रापि, क्वचित्, क्वापि, "somewhere"; from कुतस्, "whence?" कुतश्चित् and कुतश्चन, "from somewhere"; from

कर्हि, "when?" कर्हिचित्, "at some time"; from कथं, "how?" कथञ्चन, "somehow or other" (cf. r. 85.).

a. तस् *tas* (changeable to तः or तो, r. 29.) may be added to any noun, and to some pronouns, to form adverbs; as, from यत्न, यत्नतः, "with effort"; from आदि, आदितः, "from the beginning"; from त (the proper crude of the pronoun तद्), ततः, "thence"; similarly, अतः, इतः, "hence." This affix usually gives the sense of the prepositions *with* and *from*, and is often equivalent to the ablative case; as, in मत्तः, "from me"; त्वत्तः, "from thee":* but it is sometimes vaguely employed to express other relations; as, पृष्ठतः, "behind the back"; प्रथमतः, "in the first place"; समन्ततः, "on all sides"; अग्रतः, "in front"; अभितः, "near to."

b. त्र *tra*, forming adverbs of *Place*; as, अत्र, "here"; तत्र, "there"; कुत्र, "where?" यत्र, "where"; सर्व्वत्र, "everywhere"; अन्यत्र, "in another place"; एकत्र, "in one place"; बहुत्र, "in many places"; अमुत्र, "there," "in the next world."

c. था *thā* and थं *tham*, forming adverbs of *Manner*; as, तथा, "so"; यथा, "as"; सर्व्वथा, "in every way"; अन्यथा, "otherwise"; कथं, "how?" इत्थं, "thus."

d. दा *dā*, forming adverbs of *Time* from pronouns, &c.; as, तदा, "then"; यदा, "when"; कदा, "when?" एकदा, "once"; नित्यदा, "constantly"; सर्व्वदा, सदा, "always."

e. धा, *dhā*, forming adverbs of *Distribution* from numeral adjectives; as, एकधा, "in one way"; द्विधा, "in two ways"; षोधा, "in six ways"; शतधा, "in a hundred ways"; सहस्रधा, "in a thousand ways"; बहुधा, "in many ways."

f. वत् *vat* may be added to any noun to form adverbs of *Similitude*; as, from सूर्य्य, सूर्य्यवत्, "like the sun"; from पूर्व्व, पूर्व्ववत्, "as before."

g. शस् *shas*, forming adverbs of *Quantity*; as, बहुशः, "abundantly"; अल्पशः, "in small quantities"; एकशः, "singly"; शतसहस्रशः, "by hundreds and thousands"; क्रमशः, "by degrees."

* These are the forms generally used for the ablative case of the personal pronouns, the proper ablative cases मत्, त्वत् being never used except as substitutes for the crude, in compound words.

Adverbs of Uncertain Derivation.

134. Of *Affirmation*:—नूनं, खलु, किल, एव, "indeed"; अपि, "even."

a. Of *Negation.*—न, नो, नहि, "not." मा, मास्म are prohibitive; as, मा कुरु, "do not." मा is often used with the 3d preterite, the augment being rejected, as मा कार्षीः, "do not" (p. 102.).

b. Of *Interrogation.*—किन्नु, कच्चित्, नु, ननु, किमुत, "whether?"

c. Of *Comparison.*—इव, "like"; एव, एवं, "so"; किम्पुनर्, "how much rather."

d. Of *Quantity.*—अतीव, "exceedingly"; ईषत्, "a little"; सकृत्, "once"; असकृत्, पुनः पुनर्, मुहुस्, भूयस्, "repeatedly."

e. Of *Manner.*—इति, एवं, "so," "thus"; पुनर्, "again"; प्रायस्, "for the most part"; नाना, "variously"; पृथक्, "separately"; मिथ्या, "falsely"; वृथा, मुधा, "in vain"; अलं, "enough"; झटिति, आशु (cf. ὠκύς), "quickly"; तूष्णीं, "silently."

f. Of *Time.*—अद्य, "to day," "now"; इदानीं, सम्प्रति, "now"; तदानीं, "then"; पुरा, "formerly"; पुरस्, पुरस्तात्, प्राक्,* "before"; युगपत्, "at once"; सद्यस्, "instantly"; प्रेत्य,* "after death"; परं,* "afterwards"; जातु, "ever"; न जातु, "never."

g. Of *Place.*—इह, "here"; क्व, "where?" बहिस्, "without."

h. Of *Doubt.*—किंस्वित्, अपिनाम, "perhaps."

Adverbial Prefixes.

135. अ *a* prefixed to nouns and even to participles with a privative or negative force, corresponding to the Greek *α*, the Latin *in*, and the English *in, im, un*; as, from शक्य, "possible," अशक्य, "impossible"; from स्पृशत्, "touching" (pres. part.), अस्पृशत्, "not touching." When a word begins with a vowel, अन् is euphonically substituted; as, अन्त, "end"; अनन्त, "endless."

a. अति *ati*, "excessively," "very"; as, अतिमहत्, "very great."

b. आ *ā*, prefixed to imply "diminution"; as, आपाण्डु, "somewhat pale." ईषत् is prefixed with the same sense.

c. का *kā* or कु *ku*, prefixed to words to imply "disparagement"; as, कापुरुष, "a coward"; कुरूप, "deformed."

d. दुर् *dur*, prefixed to imply "badly," or "with difficulty"; as, दुष्कृत, "badly done" (cf. p. 15. note); दुर्भेद्य, "not easily broken." It is opposed to सु, and corresponds to the Greek δυσ.

* These, however, admit of derivation, and a few others less obviously.

e. निर् *nir* and वि *vi* are prefixed to nouns like अ *a* with a privative or negative sense; as, निर्बल, "powerless"; विशस्त्र, "unarmed"; but not to participles.

f. सु *su*, prefixed to imply "well," "easily"; as, सुकृत, "well done"; सुभेद्य, "easily broken." In this sense it is opposed to दुर्, and corresponds to the Greek εὖ. It is also used for अति, to imply "very," "excessively"; as, सुमहत्, "very great."

CONJUNCTIONS.

Copulative.

136. च *cha*, "and," "also," corresponding to the Latin *que* and not *et*. It can never, therefore, stand as the *first word* in a sentence. It is not, however, like *que*, necessarily interposed between the first and second words, but may be admitted to any part of the sentence, being only excluded from the first place.

a. हि, "for," like च is always placed after its word, and never admitted to the first place in a sentence.

b. यदि, चेत्, "if"; अथ, "then," "now," used very commonly as an inceptive particle. ततस्, "upon that," "then" (r. 133. *a.*). अन्यच्च, किञ्च, अपरञ्च, परञ्च, अपिच, "again," "moreover," used very commonly before quotations. चैव, "also."

Disjunctive.

137. वा *vā*, "or," corresponds to the Latin *ve*, and is always placed after its word, being never admitted to the first place in a sentence. तु, किन्तु, "but"; the former is placed after its word; यद्यपि, "although"; तथापि, "nevertheless," "yet," sometimes used as a correlative to the last; अथवा, किम्वा, "or else"; नवा, "or not"; यदिवा, "whether," "whether or no." स्म, ह, तु, वै, are expletives, often used in poetry with no other object than to fill up the verse.

PREPOSITIONS.

138. Of all the internal evidences of the antiquity of Sanscrit, there is none more decisive than the sparing use which this language makes of prepositions, in expressing the dependence of one word upon another. These aids to syntactical combination are always to be regarded as a result of modern refinement, incom-

patible with the sternness and simplicity of the most ancient languages. Thus, even the Greek, which of all others is the most copiously provided with these auxiliaries, made comparatively small use of them in the days of Homer, and imitated the Sanscrit in expressing a variety of different relations by some of the cases of its nouns. It cannot be doubted that much ambiguity may result from this rigid rejection of any other aid to the construction of sentences than nominal inflection; but when, as in Sanscrit, even this inflection is but sparingly used, and long compounds are formed, consisting of words joined together in their crude state, the last only taking any case; and when even the assistance of a verb is often denied to guide the reader to the nature of the dependence of these words upon each other; we are forced to admit that this language would gain much in ease and perspicuity, if it were more abundantly supplied with such important elements of syntactical arrangement.

But let not the reader imagine that no prepositions exist in Sanscrit. It will be found by a reference to r. 165. that they exist in great abundance, but only as inseparable prefixes, qualifying the sense of roots, and the nouns and verbs derived from roots. There are only three, out of all this list of prepositions, that are ever used in government with nouns; viz. आ *ā*, प्रति *prati*, and अनु *anu*; and of these the two last are never so used, except as *postpositions*.

a. आ *ā*, generally signifying "as far as," "up to," governs the ablative case; as, आसमुद्रात्, "as far as the ocean"; आमनोः, "up to Manu"; and rarely the accusative, as शतम् आजातीः, "for a hundred births." But instances are not common of words in regimen with this preposition.

b. प्रति *prati*, generally signifying "at," "with regard to," "against," governs the accusative; as, गङ्गां प्रति, "at the Ganges"; धर्मं प्रति, "with regard to justice"; शत्रुं प्रति, "against an enemy." It sometimes has the force of *apud;* as, मां प्रति, "*apud me,*" "as far as regards me."

c. अनु is occasionally found governing the accusative; as, तदनु, "after that."

The preposition आ, however, is not separated from the word

which it governs, and may be regarded as forming with it a kind of adverbial compound, especially as instances are not uncommon of other prepositions united in composition with the neuter form or accusative case of nouns; as, प्रतिस्कन्धं, "upon the shoulders"; प्रतिमुखं, "face to face"; अधिवृक्षं, "upon the tree"; अनुगङ्गं, "along the Ganges" (see r. 171. 6.).

ADVERBS USED FOR PREPOSITIONS.

139. There are certain adverbs used for prepositions in government with nouns, but generally placed after the nouns which they govern.

a. ऋते, "besides," governing the accusative and sometimes ablative case. यावत्, "up to," "as far as," sometimes found with the accusative.

b. सह, सार्द्धं, "with," "along with," governing the instrumental.

c. विना, "without," with the instrumental or accusative, or sometimes the ablative.

d. वहिर्, "out" and प्रभृति, "*inde a*," "from a particular time," with the ablative.

e. अर्थं, अर्थे, हेतोः, हेतौ, कृते, निमित्ते, "on account of," "for the sake of," with the genitive, or more usually with the crude form. उपरि, "above" (cf. *ὑπερ*, *super*), with the genitive. So अधस् or अधस्तात्, "below"; समीपं, सकाशं, "near"; सकाशात् "from"; अग्रे, समक्षं, &c., "in the presence of"; पश्चात्, "after"; प्राक्, "before"; अन्तरेण, "without," "except"; अन्तर्, "within"; all governing the genitive. उपरि and अधस् are sometimes doubled; thus, उपर्युपरि, अधोऽधः.

INTERJECTIONS.

140. भोः, भो, हे, are vocative; रे, अरे, less respectfully vocative, or sometimes expressive of contempt. धिक् expresses "abhorrence"; आः, अहो, अहह, "surprise"; हा, हाहा, अहो, अहोवत्, "grief"; साधु, सुष्ठु, "approbation"; स्वस्ति, "salutation."

CHAPTER IX.

COMPOUND WORDS.

COMPOUNDS abound in Sanscrit to a degree wholly unequalled in any other language, and it becomes necessary to study the principles on which they are constructed, before the learner can hope to understand the simplest sentence in the most elementary book. In the foregoing chapters we have treated of simple nouns, simple verbs, and simple adverbs. We have now to treat of compound nouns, compound verbs, and compound adverbs.

Observe, that in this chapter a dot placed underneath marks the division of the words in a compound.

SECT. I.—COMPOUND NOUNS.

141. The student has now arrived at that portion of the subject in which the use of the crude state of the noun becomes most strikingly apparent. This use has been already noticed at r. 36., pp. 19, 20; and its formation explained, pp. 21—27. In all compound nouns (with some few exceptions) the last word alone admits of declension, and the preceding word or words require to be placed in the crude form, this crude form admitting of a plural as well as singular signification.

Native grammarians class compound nouns under five heads: the 1st they call TATPURUṢHA, or those composed of two nouns, the first of which (being in the crude) would be, if uncompounded, in a case different from, or dependent on, the last; as, चन्द्रप्रभा, "moon-light" (for चन्द्रस्य प्रभा, "the light of the moon"); शस्त्रकुशलः, -ला, -लं,* "skilled in arms" (for शस्त्रेषु कुशलः); मणिभूषितः, -ता, -तं,

* Observe, that in this chapter the nom. case, and not the crude, of a substantive terminating a compound will be given, and in the instance of an adjective forming the last member of a compound, the nom. case masc., fem., and neut. The examples are chiefly taken from the Hitopadesha, and sometimes the oblique cases in which they are there found have been retained.

"adorned with gems" (for मणिभिर् भूषितः). The 2d, DWANDWA, or those formed by the aggregation into one compound of two or more nouns (the last word being, according to circumstances, either in the dual, plural, or neuter singular, and the preceding word or words being in the crude), when, if uncompounded, they would all be in the same case, connected by a copulative conjunction; as, गुरुशिष्यौ, "master and pupil" (for गुरुः शिष्यश्च); मरणव्याधिशोकाः, "death, sickness, and sorrow" (for मरणं व्याधिः शोकश्च); पाणिपादं, "hand and foot" (for पाणिः पादश्च). The 3d, KARMADHÁRAYA, or those composed of an adjective and substantive, the adjective being placed first in its crude state, when, if uncompounded, it would be in grammatical concord with the substantive; as, साधुशीलः, "a good disposition" (for साधुः शीलः); सर्व्वद्रव्याणि, "all things" (for सर्व्वाणि द्रव्याणि). The 4th, DWIGU, or those in which a numeral in its crude state is compounded with a noun, either so as to form a singular collective noun, or an adjective; as, त्रिगुणं, "three qualities" (for त्रयो गुणाः); त्रिगुणः, -णा, -णं, "possessing the three qualities." The 5th, BAHUVRÍHI,* or those formed of any number of words associated to form an epithet to a noun; as, चन्द्रप्रभः, -भा, -भं, "brilliant as the moon"; मरणव्याधिशोकः, -का, -कं, "liable to death, sickness, and sorrow"; साधुशीलः, -ला, -लं, "well-disposed."

Such then, in brief, is the native division of compound words, a division leading to some confusion, from the incompleteness and want of sufficient comprehensiveness in the definitions, and the absence of sufficient distinctness and opposition between the seve-

---

* These names either furnish examples of the several kinds of compounds, or give some sort of definition of them. Thus, तत्पुरुषः, "his servant," is an example of the 1st kind (for तस्य पुरुषः); द्वन्द्वः is a definition of the 2d kind, meaning "conjunction"; कर्म्मधारयः is a definition of the 3d kind, *i.e.* "containing the object," (कर्म्म); द्विगुः is an example of the 4th kind, meaning "any thing to the value of two cows"; बहुव्रीहिः is an example of the 5th kind, meaning "possessed of much rice." There is a 6th class of compounds called अव्ययीभावः *avyayībhāvah*, *i.e.* "the indeclinable state"; but these will be noticed under the head of compound adverbs.

ral parts or members of the division. For it is plain, from the examples given, that the 5th class of compounds may often be regarded as another name for the first three, when they take the form of adjectives declinable in three genders; and that the second species of the 4th class is for this reason referrible to the 5th. The student, moreover, finds it difficult to understand why, if the definition of the 5th class of compounds be, that they are epithets of other nouns; such compounds as शस्त्रकुशल and मणिभूषित should not be comprehended under it. And further, he is often at a loss to refer a compound to its proper head,* from the inadequacy of the definitions to express all the cases included under each class.

In the following pages the subject is discussed according to a different method, although it has been thought desirable to keep the native arrangement in view.

Compound nouns may be regarded either as *simply* or *complexly* compounded. The latter have reference to a class of compounds within compounds, very prevalent in poetry, involving two or three species of simple compounds under one head.

SIMPLY COMPOUNDED NOUNS.

142. These will be divided into, 1st, Dependent in case (corresponding to *Tatpurusha*); 2d, Aggregative (*Dwandwa*); 3d, Descriptive † (corresponding to *Karmadhāraya*); 4th, Collective (corresponding to *Dwigu*); 5th, Relative (corresponding to *Bahuvrīhi*). This last includes, *a.* Relative form of absolute Dependent compounds, terminated by substantives; *b.* Relative form of Aggregative compounds; *c.* Relative form of Descriptive compounds; *d.* Relative form of Collective compounds; *e.* Relative form of substantives in composition with certain adverbial prefixes.

---

* As, for instance, such a compound as कृष्णशुक्लः, -क्ला, -क्लं, "any thing black and white."

† As being composed of an adjective or participle preceding a substantive, and always descriptive of the substantive. Prof. Bopp calls them "Determinativa," a word of similar import. The names "Dependent" and "Collective" were suggested by Prof. Bopp's "Dependentia" and "Collectiva."

DEPENDENT COMPOUNDS, OR COMPOUNDS DEPENDENT IN CASE (TATPURUṢHA).

Accusatively Dependent.

143. These comprehend all those compounds in which the relation of the first word (being in the crude) to the last is equivalent to that of an accusative case. They are generally composed of a noun in the first member, and a participle or noun of agency in the last; as, स्वर्गप्राप्तः, -प्ता, -प्तं, "one who has obtained heaven" (equivalent to स्वर्गं प्राप्तः); प्रियवादी, "one who speaks kind words"; बहुदः, "one who gives much"; शस्त्रभृत्, "one who bears arms."

a. Before the nouns of agency the accusative case is often retained, especially in poetry; as, अरिंदमः, -मा, -मं, "enemy-subduing"; हृदयङ्गमः, -मा, -मं, "heart-touching"; भयङ्करः, -रा, -रं, "fear-inspiring" (see r. 131. 1.).

Instrumentally Dependent.

144. Or those in which the relation of the first word (being in the crude) to the last is equivalent to that of an instrumental case. These are very common, and are, for the most part, composed of a substantive in the first member, and a passive participle in the last; as, लोभमोहितः, -ता, -तं, "beguiled by avarice" (for लोभेन मोहित); वस्त्रवेष्टितः, -ता, -तं, "covered with clothes"; राजपूजितः, -ता, -तं, "honoured by kings"; विद्याहीनः, -ना, -नं, "deserted by (*i.e.* destitute of) learning"; दुःखार्त्तः, -र्त्ता, -र्त्तं, "pained with grief"; आत्मकृतः, -ता, -तं, "done by one's self"; आदित्यसदृशः, -शी, -शं, "like the sun" (for आदित्येन, सदृशः).

a. Sometimes, but rarely, this kind of compound contains a substantive or noun of agency in the last member; as, विद्याधनं, "money acquired by science"; शस्त्रोपजीवी, "one who lives by arms."

Datively Dependent.

145. Or those in which the relation of the first word to the last is equivalent to that of a dative; as, परिधानवल्कलं, "bark for clothing"; शरणागतः, -ता, -तं, "come for protection" (for शरणाय आगत). This kind of compound is very rare, and is generally supplied by the use of अर्थं (r. 139. *e.*); as, शरणार्थम् आगतः.

Ablatively Dependent,

146. Or those in which the relation of the first word to the last is equivalent to that of an ablative; as, राज्यभ्रष्टः, -ष्टा, -ष्टं, "fallen from the kingdom" (for राज्याद् भ्रष्टः); भवदन्यः, "other than you" (for भवतोऽन्यः); भवद्भयं, "fear of you."

Genitively Dependent,

147. Or those in which the relation of the first word to the last is equivalent to that of a genitive. These are the most common of all dependent compounds, and may generally be expressed by a similar compound in English. They are for the most part composed of two substantives; as, समुद्रतीरं, "sea-shore" (for समुद्रस्य तीरं, "shore of the sea"); अश्वपृष्ठं, "horse-back"; धनुर्गुणः, "bow-string"; इष्टिकागृहं, "brick-house"; गिरिनदी, "mountain-torrent"; अर्थागमः, "acquisition of wealth"; विपद्दशा, "state of misfortune"; सुहृद्भेदः, "separation of friends"; यन्मूर्द्धि, "on whose brow" (loc. c.); तद्वचः, "his words"; किमर्थं, "on what account?" धर्म्मार्थं, "on account of virtue"; मूर्खशतैः, "with hundreds of fools" (inst. c.); श्लोकद्वयं, "a couple of shlokas"; भूतलं, "the surface of the earth"; पृथिवीपतिः, "lord of the earth"; तज्जीवनाय, "for his support" (dat. c.); अस्मत्पुत्राः, "our sons"; त्वत्कर्म्म, "thy deed"; पितृवचनं, "a father's speech"; मृत्युद्वारं, "the gate of death"; इच्छासम्पत्, "fulfilment of wishes"; मात्रानन्दः, "a mother's joy."

a. Sometimes an adjective in the superlative degree, used substantively, occupies the last place in the compound; as, नरश्रेष्ठः or पुरुषोत्तमः, "the best of men."

b. In a few instances the genitive case is retained; as, विशाम्पतिः, "lord of men"; दिवस्पतिः, "lord of day."

Locatively Dependent,

148. Or those in which the relation of the first word to the last is equivalent to that of a locative case; as, पङ्कमग्नः, -ग्ना, -ग्नं, "sunk in the mud" (for पङ्के मग्न); गगनविहारी, "sporting in the sky; जलक्रीडा, "sport in the water"; ग्रामवासी, "a dweller in a village"; जलजः, "born in the water."

a. It is very usual to retain the locative case, especially before nouns of agency; as, ग्रामेवासी, "a villager"; जलेचरः, "going in the water"; उरसिभूषितः, -ता, -तं, "ornamented on the breast" (see r. 131. 1.).

Dependent in more than one Case.

149. Dependent compounds do not always consist of two words. They may be composed of almost any number of nouns, all depending upon each other, in the manner that one case depends upon another in a sentence; thus, चक्षुर्विषयातिक्रान्तः, -न्ता, -न्तं, "passed beyond the range of the eye" (for चक्षुषो विषयम् अतिक्रान्तः); रथमध्यस्थः, "standing in the middle of the chariot"; भीतपरित्राणवस्तूपालम्भपण्डितः, "skilful in censuring the means of rescuing those in danger."

AGGREGATIVE COMPOUNDS (DWANDWA).

150. This class of compounds has no parallel in other languages. When two or more persons or things are enumerated together, it is usual in Sanscrit, instead of connecting them by a copulative, to aggregate them into one compound word. No syntactical dependence of one case upon another subsists between the members of Dwandwa compounds, since they must always consist of words which, if uncompounded, would be in the *same* case; and no other grammatical connection exists than that which would ordinarily be expressed by the use of the copulative conjunction *and* in English, or च in Sanscrit. And it should be observed, that the chief difference between this class and the last turns upon this dependence *in case* of the words compounded on each other; insomuch that the existence or absence of such dependence, as deducible from the context, is, in some cases, the only guide by which the student is enabled to refer the compound to the one head or to the other. Thus, गुरुशिष्यसेवकाः may either be a Dependent compound, and mean "the servants of the pupils of the Guru," or an Aggregative, "the Guru, and the pupil, and the servant." And मांसशोणितं may either be Dependent, "the blood of the flesh," or Aggregative, "flesh and blood." This ambiguity, however, can never occur in aggregatives inflected in the dual, and very rarely occasions any practical difficulty.

There are three kinds of Aggregative compounds: 1st, inflected in the plural; 2d, inflected in the dual; 3d, inflected in the singular. In the first two cases the final letter of the crude of the word terminating the compound determines the declension, and its gender the particular form of declension; in the third case it seems to be a law that this kind of compound cannot be formed unless the last word ends in *a*, or in a vowel changeable to *a*, or in a consonant to which *a* may be subjoined; and the gender is invariably neuter, whatever may be the gender of the final word.

Inflected in the Plural.

151. When *more than two* animate objects are enumerated, the last is inflected in the plural; as, इन्द्रानिलयमार्काः, "Indra, Anila, Yama, and Arka" (for इन्द्रः अनिलः यमः अर्कः); रामलक्ष्मणभरताः, "Rāma, Lakshmaṇa, and Bharata"; मृगव्याधसर्पशूकराः, "the deer, the hunter, the serpent, and the hog." The learner will observe, that although the last member of the compound is inflected in the plural, each of the members has here a singular acceptation. But a plural signification may often be inherent in some or all of the words constituting the compound; thus, मित्रोदासीनशत्रवः, "friends, neutrals, and foes" (for मित्राणि, उदासीनाः, शत्रवः); सिंहव्याघ्रमहोरगाः, "lions, tigers, and serpents"; श्वगृध्रकङ्ककाकोलभासगोमायुवायसाः, "dogs, vultures, herons, ravens, kites, jackals, and crows."

a. So also when *more than two* inanimate objects are enumerated, the last may be inflected in the plural; as, धर्म्मार्थकाममोक्षाः, "virtue, wealth, enjoyment, and beatitude" (for धर्म्मः, अर्थः, कामः, मोक्षः); इज्याध्ययनदानानि, "sacrifice, study, and liberality" (for इज्या, अध्ययनं, दानं). In some of the following a plural signification is inherent; as, पुष्पमूलफलानि, "flowers, roots, and fruits"; अजातमृतमूर्खाणां, "of the unborn, the dead, and the foolish" (for अजातानां, मृतानां, मूर्खाणां); नेत्रमनःस्वभावाः, "eyes, mind, and disposition"; रोगशोकपरितापबन्धनव्यसनानि, "sickness, sorrow, anguish, bonds, and afflictions."

b. So also when *only two* animate or inanimate objects are enumerated, in which a *plural* signification is inherent, the last is inflected in the plural; as, देवमनुष्याः, "gods and men"; पुत्रपौत्राः, "sons and grandsons"; पातोत्पाताः, "falls and rises"; प्राकारपरिखाः, "ramparts and trenches"; सुखदुःखेषु, "in pleasures and pains" (for सुखेषु, दुःखेषु); पापपुण्यानि, "sins and virtues."

Inflected in the Dual.

152. When *only two* animate objects are enumerated, in each of which a *singular* signification is inherent, the last is inflected in the dual; as, राम.लक्ष्मणौ, "Rāma and Lakshmaṇa" (for रामः लक्ष्मणः); चन्द्र.सूर्यौ, "the moon and sun"; मृग.काकौ, "a deer and a crow."

a. So also when *only two* inanimate objects are enumerated, in each of which a *singular* signification is inherent, the last is inflected in the dual; as, अनुरागापरागौ, "affection and enmity" (for अनुरागः, अपरागः); क्षुत्पिपासे, "hunger and thirst" (for क्षुत् पिपासा); क्षुद्व्याधी, "hunger and sickness"; स्थानासनाभ्यां, "by standing and sitting" (for स्थानेन, आसनेन); मधु.सर्पिषी, "honey and ghee"; सुख.दुःखे, "pleasure and pain."

b. In aggregating two nouns of relationship, formed with the affix तृ (r. 41.), the first is placed in the nominative case instead of the crude; as, मातापितरौ, "mother and father."

Inflected in the Singular Neuter.

153. When two or more *inanimate* objects are enumerated, whether singular or plural in their signification, the last may either be inflected as above, r. 151. *a.* *b.* r. 152., or in the singular number, neut. gender; as, पुष्पमूलफलं, "flowers, roots and fruits" (for पुष्पाणि, मूलानि, फलानि); यवसान्नोदकेन्धनं, "grass, food, water, and fuel" (for यवसः, अन्नं, उदकं, इन्धनं); अहोरात्रं, "a day and night" (for अहः, रात्रिः); दिग्देशं, "quarters and countries" (for दिशः, देशाः).

a. Sometimes two or more animate objects are thus compounded; as, पुत्र.पौत्रं, "sons and grandsons"; हस्त्यश्वं, "elephants and horses"; especially inferior objects, as श्व.चाण्डालं, "a dog and an outcast."

b. In enumerating two qualities the opposite of each other, it is common to form a Dwandwa compound of this kind, by doubling an adjective or participle, and interposing the negative *a*; as, चराचरं, "moveable and immoveable" (for चरम् अचरं च); शुभाशुभं, "good and evil"; प्रियाप्रिये, "in agreeable and disagreeable" (for प्रिये अप्रिये च); दृष्टादृष्टं, "seen and not seen"; कृताकृतं, "done and not done."

DESCRIPTIVE COMPOUNDS (KARMADHĀRAYA).

154. In describing, qualifying, or defining a substantive by

means of an adjective or participle, it is common in Sanscrit to compound the two words together, placing the adjective or participle in the first member of the compound in its crude state; as, साधुजनः, "a good man" (for साधुर् जनः); चिरमित्रं, "an old friend" (for चिरं मित्रं); प्रियभार्य्या*, "a dear wife" (for प्रिया भार्य्या); रूपवद्भार्य्या*, "a beautiful wife" (for रूपवती भार्य्या); क्षुब्धार्णवः, "a troubled ocean"; पुण्यकर्म्म, "a holy act"; अनन्तात्मा, "the infinite soul"; संस्कृतोक्तिः, "polished speech"; पुण्यकर्म्माणि, "holy acts" (for पुण्यानि कर्म्माणि); उत्तमनराणां, "of the best men" (for उत्तमानां नराणां).

a. महा is substituted for the crude महत्, "great," in the first member of a Descriptive compound†; as, महापुरुषः, not महत्पुरुषः, "a great man" (for महान् पुरुषः); महापातकं, "a great crime" (for महत्पातकं); महाकुलं, "a great family."

b. When the substantive राजन्, "a king," is taken to form the last member of a Descriptive compound, it loses its proper form of declension as a noun of the 6th class (p. 41.), and is declined like a noun of the 1st class (see p. 42. note *.). सखि, "a friend"; पथिन्, "a road"; अक्षि, "the eye"; रात्रि, "the night," and some other words undergo a similar change in inflection, and become nouns of the 1st class; as, प्रियसखः, "a dear friend"; दीर्घरात्रं, "a long night." When these latter words form the last member of Dependent or Collective compounds the same holds good; as in धर्म्मराजः, अग्निसखः, गवाक्षः.

c. Numerals in their crude state are sometimes found occupying the place of adjectives in the first member of a compound of this class; as, चतुर्वर्णाः, "the four castes"; पञ्चबाणाः, "five arrows."

d. Adjectives, used substantively, sometimes occupy the last place in Descriptive compounds; as, परमधार्म्मिकः, "a very just man"; परमाद्भुतं, "a very wonderful thing."

e. Compounds expressing comparison fall under this class, and are composed of two substantives, the last being generally the name of an animal denoting superiority; as, पुरुषपुङ्गवः, पुरुषसिंहः, पुरुषर्षभः, equivalent to "an illustrious man."

---

* Feminine nouns are rarely compounded in this way; and there can be no question that प्रिया and रूपवती are the proper crudes of the feminine form of the adjective. When the feminine of an adjective is used substantively, it does not give place to the crude; as, कामिनीजनः, "a wanton woman."

† But महत् is retained in a Dependent; as, महदाश्रयः, "recourse to the great."

COLLECTIVE COMPOUNDS (DWIGU).

155. A numeral is often compounded with a substantive to form a collective noun of the neuter gender; thus, चतुर्युगं, "the four ages" (for चत्वारि युगानि); चतुर्दिशं, "the four quarters"; त्रिदिनं, "three days" (cf. the Latin *triduum*); त्रिरात्रं, "three nights" (रात्र being substituted for रात्रि); त्र्यब्दं, "three years" (cf. *triennium*).

a. Sometimes the final vowel of the substantive is changed to ई; as, त्रिलोकी, "the three worlds."

RELATIVE COMPOUNDS (BAHUVRĪHI).

156. The greater number of compounds in the preceding four divisions are terminated by substantives, the sense of each being in that case absolute and complete in itself. All such compounds may be used *relatively*, that is, as epithets of other words, the final substantive becoming susceptible of three genders, like an adjective (p. 32. †. p. 34. †.): and it cannot be too forcibly impressed upon the student that the terms *Relative* and *Bahuvrīhi* have reference to the adjective use of those compounds only which have a substantive in the last member. This is not to be regarded, therefore, as a distinct division of the subject of compound words, so much as a distinct view of the *same* subject, the object of which is to show that all compounds, which are in themselves absolute and complete in sense, and are terminated by substantives, may be used adjectively, and in the relation of an epithet to some other word in the sentence. We have given the name *relative* to compounds when thus used, not only for the obvious reason of their being relatively and not absolutely employed, but also because they usually involve a relative pronoun, and are sometimes translated into English by the aid of this pronoun, and are, moreover, resolved by native commentators into their equivalent uncompounded words by the aid of the genitive case of the relative (यस्य). Thus, महाधनं is a Descriptive compound, meaning, "great wealth": and may be used adjectively in relation to पुरुषः; as, महाधनः पुरुषः, "a man *who* has great wealth": or to स्त्री; as, महाधना स्त्री, "a woman *who* has great wealth," and would be resolved by commentators into यस्य or यस्याः महद् धनं. In English we have similar compounds; as, "high-minded," "left-handed," and the like, where

the substantive terminating the compound is converted into an adjective.

Relative Form of Dependent Compounds.

157. Many Dependent compounds (especially those that are instrumentally dependent) are already ***in their own nature*** relative, and cannot be used except in connection with some other word in the sentence. But, on the other hand, many others, and especially those which are genitively dependent, constituting by far the largest number of this class of compounds, are in their nature absolute, and yield a sense complete in itself. These may be made relative by declining the final substantive after the manner of an adjective. The following are instances: चन्द्राकृतिः, -तिः, -ति, "moon-shaped" (p. 34. †.), from the absolute compound चन्द्राकृतिः, "the shape of the moon"; देवरूपः, -पी, -पं,* "whose form is god-like"; सूर्य्यप्रभावः, -वा, -वं,* "splendid as the sun"; हस्तिपादः, -दा, -दं,* "elephant-footed"; सागरान्तः, -न्ताः, -न्तं,* "ending at the sea"; मरणान्तः, -न्ता, -न्तं, "terminated by death"; कर्णपुरोगमः, -मा, -मं, or कर्णमुखः, -खा, -खं,* "headed by Karṇa"; विष्णुशर्म्मनामा, -मा, -म, "named Vishṇu-sharma" (p. 42. note †.); पुण्डरीकाक्षः, -क्षी, -क्षं, "lotus-eyed" (r. 154. *b.*); नारायणाख्यः, -ख्या, -ख्यं, "called Nārāyaṇa"; धनमूलः, -ला, -लं, "founded on wealth": लक्षसंख्यानि (agreeing with धनानि), "money to the amount of a lac"; गदाहस्तः, -स्ता, -स्तं, "having a club in the hand"; शस्त्रपाणिः, -णिः, -णि, "having arms in the hand"; पुष्पविषयः, -या, -यं, "on the subject of flowers," "relating to flowers." These examples are not distinguishable from absolute dependent compounds, except by declension in three genders.

a. Many of them, however, are not found, except as relatives; and if used absolutely would yield a different sense; thus, कर्णमुखं means "the face of Karṇa," but when used relatively to राजानः, "the kings headed by Karṇa." So also चारचक्षुः signifies "the eye of the spy," but when used relatively to राजा, "a king who sees by means of his spies," the nom. case masc. being then चारचक्षुः.

b. The substantive आदि, "a beginning," when it occurs in

---

* See p. 32. †. पाद् may be substituted for पाद in compounds like हस्तिपाद.

the last member of a compound of this nature, is always used relatively to some word expressed or understood; and yields a sense equivalent to *et cetera*. It is necessarily found either in the plural or neuter singular; as, इन्द्रादयः, "Indra and the others" (agreeing with the nom. case सुराः expressed or understood, "the gods commencing with Indra"); अग्न्यादीनां, "of Agni and the others" (agreeing with पूर्वोक्तानां understood, "of those above-named things of which Agni was the first"); चक्षुरादीनि, "the eyes, &c." (agreeing with इन्द्रियाणि, "the senses commencing with the eyes"). When used in the neut. sing. it either agrees with पूर्वोक्तं, "the aforesaid," understood, or with a number of things taken collectively, and the adverb *iti** may be prefixed; as, देवानित्यादि, "the word *devān*, &c." (agreeing with पूर्वोक्तं understood, "the aforesaid sentence of which *devān* is the first word"); दानादिना, "by liberality, &c." (agreeing with some class of things understood, "by that class of things of which liberality is the first"). Sometimes आदिक is used for आदि; as, दानादिकं, "gifts, &c.": and sometimes आद्य; as, इन्द्राद्याः सुराः, "the gods of whom Indra is the first"; or sometimes the substantive प्रभृति; as, इन्द्रप्रभृतयः सुराः.

Relative Form of Aggregative Compounds.

158. Aggregative compounds are sometimes used relatively; as, मरणव्याधिशोकः, -का, -कं, "that which is liable to sorrow, sickness, and death"; especially in the case of adjectives or participles; as, कृष्णशुक्लः, -क्ला, -क्लं, "black and white"; स्नातानुलिप्तः, -प्ता, -प्तं, "bathed and anointed"; पौरजानपदः, -दा, -दं, "city and country"; कृतापकृतः, -ता, -तं, "done and done badly"; शुभाशुभः, -भा, -भं, "good and evil" (r. 153. *b.*). Examples are still more common under the head of complex compounds.

Relative Form of Descriptive Compounds.

159. A greater number of compound words may be referred to this head than to any other. Every style of writing abounds

---

* Sometimes *evam* is prefixed; as, एवमादीनि प्रलापानि, "lamentations beginning thus."

with them. The following may serve as examples: अल्पशक्तिः, -क्तिः, -क्ति, "whose strength is small" (p. 34. †.); महाबलः, -ला, -लं, "whose strength is great" (r. 154. *a.* p. 32. †.); महातेजाः, -जाः, -जः, "whose glory is great" (r. 68. 69.); महात्मा, -त्मा, -त्म, "high-minded" (p. 41, 42.); उदारचरितः, -ता, -तं, "of noble demeanour"; परिणतबुद्धिः, -द्धिः, -द्धि, "of wise intellect" (p. 34. †.); प्रियभार्य्यः, -र्य्या, -र्य्यं, "having a dear wife";* अशक्यसन्धानः, -ना, -नं, "not to be reconciled."

a. Although a passive participle is not often prefixed to a noun in an absolute sense, this kind of combination prevails most extensively in the formation of relative compounds; as, प्राप्तकालः, -ला, -लं, "whose time has arrived"; जितेन्द्रियः, -या, -यं, "whose passions are subdued"; शान्तचेताः, -ताः, -तः, "whose mind is composed"; भग्नाशः, -शा, -शं, "whose hopes are broken"; हृतराज्यः, -ज्या, -ज्यं, "whose kingdom is taken away"; अमिततेजाः, -जाः, -जः, "whose glory is boundless"; कृतकामः, -मा, -मं, "whose desire is accomplished," *i.e.* "successful"; अनधिगतशास्त्रः, -स्त्रा, -स्त्रं, "by whom the shāstras have not been read"; भिन्नहृदयः, -या, -यं, "whose heart is pierced."

Relative form of Collective Compounds.

160. The following are examples of Collective or Dwigu compounds used relatively: द्विपर्णः, -र्णा, -र्णं, "two-leaved"; त्रिलोचनः, -नी, -नं, "tri-ocular"; त्रिमूर्द्धः, -र्द्धा, -र्द्धं, "three-headed" (मूर्द्ध being substituted for मूर्द्धन्); चतुर्मुखः, -खी, -खं, "four-faced"; चतुष्कोणः, -णा, -णं, "quadrangular"; शतद्वारः, -रा, -रं, "hundred-gated"; चतुर्विद्यः, -द्या, -द्यं, "possessed of the four sciences"; सहस्राक्षः, -क्षी, -क्षं, "thousand-eyed."

Relative form of Substantives compounded with certain Adverbial Prefixes.

161. This includes a class of compounds possessing no corresponding absolute form,† and composed of an adverb prefixed to a substantive. By far the greater number of these are formed with

* Occasionally the feminine of the adjective appears in the compound; as, षष्ठीभार्य्यः, "having a sixth wife."

† Unless they be regarded as the relative form of Avyayibhāva compounds.

the adverbial preposition सह, "with," contracted into स; as, सक्रोधः, -धा, -धं, "angry"; सफलः, -ला, -लं, "fruitful" (p. 32. †.); सबन्धुः, -न्धुः, -न्धु, "possessed of kindred" (r. 54, 55, 56.); सयत्नः, -त्ना, -त्नं, "energetic"; सानन्दः, -न्दा, -न्दं, "joyful"; ससचिवः, -वा, -वं, "accompanied by ministers"; सज्यः, -ज्या, -ज्यं, "strung" (as a bow). The following are examples of other adverbial prefixes: उद्यतायुधः, -धा, -धं, "with uplifted weapon"; नानाप्रकारः, -रा, -रं, "of various forms"; क्वनिवासः, -सा, -सं, "where dwelling"? क्वजन्मा, -न्मा, -न्म, "where born"? अपभीः, -भीः, -भि, "fearless" (p. 33. †.); तथाविधः, -धा, -धं, "of that kind."

COMPLEX COMPOUND NOUNS.

162. We have now to speak of those complex compound words, or compounds within compounds, which form the most remarkable feature in Sanscrit poetical composition. Instances might be given of twenty or thirty words thus compounded together, but these are the productions of the vitiated taste of more modern times, and are only curious as showing that the power of compounding words may often be perverted to the formation of a style the most extravagant and ridiculous. But even in the best specimens of Sanscrit composition, and in the simplest prose writings, four, five, or even six words are commonly compounded together, involving two or three forms under one head. It will be easy, however, to determine the character of the forms involved, by the rules propounded in the preceding pages; in proof of which the student has only to study attentively the examples we are about to give.

a. Instances of absolute complex compounds, whose sense is complete and unconnected, are not very abundant. The following may be taken as examples: कालान्तरावृत्तिशुभाशुभानि, "good and evil (occurring) in the revolutions of the interval of time," the whole being a dependent, involving a dependent and an aggregative; सेनापतिबलाध्यक्षौ, "the general and the overseer of the forces," the whole being an aggregative, involving two dependents; शोकारातिभयत्राणं, "the protection from sorrow, enemies, and perils," the whole being a dependent, involving an aggregative; अवधीरितसुहृद्वाक्यं, "the disregarded words of a friend," the whole being a descriptive, involving a dependent.

b. But the greater number of complex compounds are used relatively, as epithets of some other word in the sentence; as, गलित-नख-नयनः, -नी, -नं, "whose teeth and eyes were decayed," the whole being the relative form of descriptive, involving an aggregative; शुक्ल-माल्यानुलेपनः, -ना, -नं, "having a white garland and unguents," the whole being the relative form of aggregative, involving a descriptive; पूर्व-जन्म-कृतः, -ता, -तं, "done in a former birth," the whole being the relative form of dependent, involving a descriptive; विद्या-वयो-वृद्धः, -द्धा, -द्धं, "advanced in learning and age," the whole being the relative form of dependent, involving an aggregative; हृषित-स्रग्-रजो-हीनः, -ना, -नं, "having fresh garlands, and being free from dust," the whole being the relative form of aggregative, involving a descriptive and dependent; अभिषेकार्द्र-शिराः, -राः, -रः, "whose head was moist with unction."

c. The substantive आदि, "a beginning," often occurs in complex relative compounds, as in simple relatives (r. 157. *b.*); thus, शुक-सारिकादयः, "parrots, starlings, &c." (agreeing with पक्षिणः, "birds beginning with parrots and starlings"), the whole being the relative form of dependent, involving an aggregative; सन्धि-विग्रहादि, "peace, war, &c." (agreeing with पूर्वोक्तं understood); गृह-देवागारादि-युक्तः, -क्ता, -क्तं, "possessed of houses, temples, &c." Similarly, आद्य in the example उत्तम-गन्धाद्याः (agreeing with स्रजः, "garlands possessing the best odour and other qualities").

d. Long complex compounds may be generally translated by beginning at the last word and proceeding regularly backwards; as in the following मत्त-मधुकर-निकर-मुक्त-झङ्कार-मिलित-कोकिलालाप-सङ्गीतक-सुखावहः, -हा, -हं, "causing pleasure by the music of the voice of the cuckoo, blended with the hum emitted by the swarms of joyous bees."

e. आत्मक or रूप, as occupying the last place in a complex relative, denote "composed of"; thus, हस्त्यश्व-रथ-पदाति-कर्मकरात्मकं बलं, "a force consisting of elephants, horses, chariots, infantry, and servants"; प्राग्-जन्म-सुकृत-दुष्कृत-रूपे कर्मणी, "the two actions consisting of the good and evil done in a former birth."

Certain Anomalous Compounds.

f. There are certain compounds which are too anomalous in their formation to admit of ready classification under any one of the preceding heads. Amongst these may be placed those compounds expressive of comparison or likeness, usually included under the Karmadhāraya or Descriptive class. In these the adjective is placed last; as, छायाचञ्चलः, -ला, -लं, "fickle as a shadow"; फेनोपमः, -मा, -मं, "like foam"; अम्बुदश्यामः, -मा, -मं, "dark as a cloud"; भूधरविस्तीर्णः, -र्णा, -र्णं, "spread out like a mountain"; जलविन्दुलोलचपलः, -ला, -लं, "unsteady as a trembling drop of water"; नलिनीदलतोयतरलः, -ला, -लं, "tremulous as water on the leaf of a lotus"; the last two examples are complex.

g. There is a common anomalous compound formed by placing अन्तर after another word, to express "another," "other"; as, स्थानान्तरं, "another place"; राजान्तरेण सह, "along with another king"; जन्मान्तराणि, "other births." The following examples, also, are not readily assignable to any class: त्यक्तजीवितयोधी, "a fighter who abandons all idea of life"; सारसद्वितीयः, -या, -यं, "accompanied by the Sārasa";* अदृष्टपूर्व, "never before seen."

Compound Nouns formed from Roots combined with Prepositions.

163. In the next section it will be shewn that the combination of roots with prepositions prevails most extensively in Sanscrit. From roots thus combined nouns of the most various significations may be formed; thus, from हृ, "to seize," with वि and अव, is formed व्यवहारः, "practice," from कृ, "to do," with अनु, अनुकार, "imitation." Hardly a line can occur in any book that does not afford an example of this kind of compound.

SECT. II.—COMPOUND VERBS.

164. The learner might look over the list of 1900 simple roots, and very well imagine that in some of these would be contained every possible variety of idea, and that the aid of prepositions and adverbial prefixes to expand and modify the sense of each root would be unnecessary. But the real fact is, that there are comparatively very few Sanscrit roots in common use; and that whilst those that are so appear in a multitude of different forms by the prefixing of one or two or even three prepositions, the remainder

---

* So छायाद्वितीयः in Nala, translated by Bopp, *umbra geminatus*.

are quite useless for any practical purposes, except the formation of nouns.

Hence it is that compound verbs are of more frequent occurrence than simple ones. They are formed in two ways: 1st, by combining roots with prepositions; 2dly, by combining the auxiliaries कृ, "to do," and भू, "to be," with adverbs, or nouns converted into adverbs.

Compound Verbs formed by combining Prepositions with Roots.

165. The following list exhibits the prepositions chiefly used in combination with roots:

अति *ati*, "across," "beyond"; as, अतिया (p. 112.); अती, "to pass by," "transgress" (pres. अत्येमि, &c. p. 112.).

अधि *adhi*, "above," "upon," "over"; as, अधिष्ठा, "to stand over," "preside" (p. 107. pres. अधितिष्ठामि); अधिरुह्, "to climb upon"; अधिशी, "to lie upon" (p. 113.); अधिगम्, "to go over towards" (p. 107.); अधी, "to go over" in the sense of "reading" (p. 113.).

अनु *anu*, "after"; as, अनुचर्, "to follow"; अनुष्ठा, "to follow," in the sense of "performing"; अनुकृ, "to imitate" (p. 102.); अनुमन्, "to assent."

अन्तर् *antar*, "within" (cf. *inter*); as, अन्तर्धा, "to place within," "conceal" (p. 119.), in pass. "to vanish"; अन्तर्भू, "to be within" (p. 104.); अन्तश्चर्, "to walk in the midst" (r. 31.).

अप *apa*, "off," "away" (cf. ἀπὸ); as, अपगम्, अपसृ, अपे (from अप and इ, p. 112.), "to go away"; अपनी, "to lead away"; अपकृष्, "to abstract"; अपवह्, "to bear away." It also implies detraction; as, अपवद्, "to defame."

अपि *api*, "on," "over," only used with धा and नह्; as, अपिधा, "to shut up"; अपिनह्, "to bind on." The initial *a* is generally rejected, leaving पिधा, पिनह्.

अभि *abhi*, "to," "towards" (cf. ἐπὶ); as, अभिया, अभी, "to go towards"; अभिधाव्, "to run towards"; अभिदृश्, "to behold" (p. 107.); अभिवद्, "to address," "salute."

अव *ava*, "down," "off"; as, अवरुह्, अवतॄ, "to descend"; अवेक्ष्, "to look down"; अवकॄ, "to throw down," "scatter"; अवकृत्, "to cut off." It also implies disparagement; as, अवज्ञा, "to despise" (p. 123.); अवक्षिप्, "to insult" (p. 111.).

आ *ā*, "to," "towards," "up" (Latin *ad*); as, आविश्, "to enter"; आक्रम्, "to go towards"; आरुह्, "to mount up." When prefixed to गम् and या, "to go," and दा, "to give," it reverses the action; as, आगम्, आया, "to come"; आदा, "to take." With चर्, "to practise."

उत् *ut*, "up," "upwards" (opposed to नि); as, उच्चर् (r. 16.), उदि, "to go up," "rise" (pres. उदयामि, 1st conj.); उड्डी, "to fly up"; उद्धृ (उत् and हृ, r. 18.), "to extract"; उन्मिष् and उन्मील् (r. 15.), "to open the eyes"; उत्कृत्, उच्छिद्, "to cut up"; उन्मूल्, "to root up"; उच्छ्रि, "to lift up" (उत् and श्रि, r. 17.). When prefixed to स्था it causes the elision of *s*; as, उत्था, "to stand up." In some cases it reverses the action; as, from पत्, "to fall," उत्पत्, "to leap up"; from नम्, "to bend down," उन्नम् (r. 15.), "to raise up"; from यम्, "to keep down," उद्यम्, "to lift up."

उप *upa*, "to," "towards" (cf. ὑπὸ), joined like आ and अभि to roots of motion; as, उपया, "to approach"; उपचर्, "to wait upon," with विश्, "to sit down."

नि *ni*, "down," "downwards," "under" (opposed to उत्); as, निपत् "to fall down"; नियम्, "to suppress"; निमिष् and निमील्, "to close the eyes"; निक्षिप्, निधा, न्यस्, "to lay down," "deposit"; निविश्, "to go within," "encamp." With वृत् it signifies "to return," "desist"; with शम्, "to hear." In some cases it does not alter the sense; as, निहन्, "to kill."

निर् *nir*, "out"; as, निष्क्रम् (cf. note, p. 15.), निर्गम्, निःसृ (r. 31.), "to go out"; निष्कृत्, "to cut up"; निर्वृत्, "to come to an end," "cease." With चि, "to determine."

परा *parā*, "back," "backwards" (cf. παρα), combined with जि and भू in the sense of "defeat"; as, पराजि, "to overcome" (cf. παρανικάω, Æsch. Chöe.); पराभू, "to be defeated." When joined with इ, 2d conj., it signifies "to retire towards" (pres. परैमि); when with इ, 1st conj. ātm., "to run away," "to retreat," *r* being changed to *l* (pres. पलाये).

परि *pari*, "around" (cf. περί, *per*); as, परिवेष्ट्, परिवृ, "to surround"; परिचर्, परिगम्, "to go round"; परीक्ष्, "to look round," "examine"; परिवृत्, "to turn round"; परिधाव्, "to run round." When prefixed to कृ it signifies "to adorn," and स् is inserted, परिष्कृ. With भू, "to despise," and with हृ, "to avoid." It sometimes merely gives intensity to the action; as, परित्यज्, "to abandon altogether."

प्र *pra*, "before," "forward" (cf. προ, *pro*, *pra*); as, प्रगम्, प्रसृप्, "to proceed"; प्रयम्, "to set before," "present"; प्रक्रम्, "to begin"; प्रधाव्, "to run forward"; प्रस्था, "to set out," "advance"; प्रभू, "to be superior," "prevail"; प्रदृश्, "to foresee." With लभ्, "to deceive." In combination with the causal of इष्, it drops its final *a*; as, प्रेषयामि, "I send." The *r* influences a following nasal by r. 21.; as, प्रणम्, "to bend before," "salute."

प्रति* *prati*, "against," "towards," "back again"; as, प्रतियुध्, "to fight against"; प्रती, "to go towards" (pres. प्रत्येमि); प्रतिगम्, "to return"; प्रतिकृ, "to counteract"; प्रतिहन्, "to beat back," "repel"; प्रतिवच्, "to answer"; प्रतिलभ् "to recover"; प्रतिनी, "to lead back"; प्रतिनमस्कृ, "to re-salute." With श्रु, "to promise"; with पद्, "to arrive at," "obtain."

वि *vi*, "apart," implying "*separation*," "*distinction*," "*distribution*," "*dispersion*" (Latin *dis*, *se*); as, विचर्, "to wander about"; विचल्, "to vacillate"; विहृ, "to roam for pleasure"; विकॄ, "to dissipate"; विदॄ, "to tear asunder"; विभज्, "to divide"; विविच्, "to distinguish." Sometimes it gives a privative signification; as, वियुज्, "to disunite"; विस्मृ, "to forget"; विक्री, "to sell." With कृ, "to change for the worse." Sometimes it has no apparent influence on the root; as, विनश्, "to perish."

सम् *sam*, "with," "together with" (συν, *con*); as, सञ्चि, सङ्ग्रह्, "to collect"; संयुज्, "to join together"; सङ्गम्, "to meet together"; सम्पद्, "to happen"; सङ्क्षिप्, "to contract." With कृ it signifies "to perfect," and स् is inserted, संस्कृ. It is often prefixed without altering the sense; as, सञ्जन्, "to be produced."

166. Two prepositions are often combined with a root; as, व्यादा, "to open" (वि, आ); समे, "to assemble" (सम्, आ, with root इ); प्रणिपत्, "to prostrate one's self" (प्र, नि, r. 21.); प्रोद्धृ, "to raise up" (प्र, उत्, with root हृ).

Occasionally three prepositions are combined; as, प्रव्याहृ, "to predict" (प्र, वि, आ); प्रत्युदाहृ, "to answer" (प्रति, उत्, आ).

---

* The final *i* of the prepositions, प्रति, परि, नि, is optionally lengthened in forming certain nouns; as, प्रतीकार, परीहास, नीकार.

167. In conjugating compound verbs formed with prepositions, the augment and reduplication do not change their position, but are inserted between the preposition and the root;* as, पर्यणयं, 1st pret. of नी, with परि; उपाविशं, 1st pret. of विश्, with उप; अन्वतिष्ठं, 1st pret. of स्था, with अनु; प्रतिजघान, 2d pret. of हन्, with प्रति; प्रोज्जहार, 2d pret. of हृ, with प्र and उत्.

168. Grammarians restrict certain roots to particular voices, when in combination with particular prepositions; as, for example, the root जि, "to conquer," with वि, and the root विश्, "to enter," with नि, are restricted to the ātmanepada; but no certain rules can be propounded on this subject: and in the two epic poems especially, the choice of voice seems so entirely arbitrary and subservient to the purposes of metre, that many ātmanepada primitive, and even passive verbs, are occasionally permitted to take a parasmaipada inflection.†

Compound Verbs formed by combining Adverbs with the Roots कृ *and* भू.

169. These are of two kinds; 1st, those formed by combining adverbs with कृ and भू; 2dly, those formed by combining nouns used adverbially with these roots. Examples of the first kind are, अलङ्कृ, "to adorn"; आविष्कृ, "to make manifest" (cf. note, p. 15.); बहिष्कृ, "to eject"; पुरस्कृ, "to place in front" "follow"; विनाकृ, "to deprive"; सत्कृ, "to entertain as a guest"; नमस्कृ, "to revere"; साक्षाद्भू, प्रादुर्भू, "to become manifest," &c.

170. In forming the second kind, the final of a crude word being *a* or *ā*, is changed to *ī*; as, from सज्ज, सज्जीकृ, "to make ready;" from कृष्ण, कृष्णीकृ, "to blacken"; or, in a few cases, to *ā*, as प्रियाकृ from प्रिय. A final *i* or *u* are lengthened; as, from शुचि, शुचीभू, "to become pure"; from लघु, लघूकृ, "to lighten." A final *ṛi* is

* There are a few exceptions to this rule in the Mahābhārata; as in अन्वसञ्चरत् (Prof. Johnson's Ed. p. 33.).

† Thus, यत्, "to strive," and प्रार्थ्, "to beg for," which are properly ātmanepada verbs, are found in the paras. Instances of passive verbs have been given at p. 89. note †. On the other hand, नन्द्, "to rejoice," which is properly a parasmaipada verb, is found in the ātm.

changed to री *rī;* as, from मातृ, मात्रीभू, "to become a mother." A final *as* becomes either *ī*, as, from सुमनस्, सुमनीभू, "to be of good mind"; or *asī*, as, from शिरस्, शिरसोधा, "to place on the head."

a. But the greater number of compounds of this kind are formed from crude nouns in *a*. The following are other examples: तृणीकृ, "to esteem as a straw"; स्तब्धीकृ, "to stiffen"; एकचित्तीभू, "to fix the mind on one object."

b. Sometimes सात्, placed after a crude noun, is used to form a compound verb of this kind; as, from जल, "water," जलसात्कृ, "to reduce to liquid"; from भस्मन्, "ashes," भस्मसात्कृ, "to reduce to ashes."

SECT. III.—COMPOUND ADVERBS (CORRESPONDING TO AVYAYĪBHĀVA COMPOUNDS).

171. Compound adverbs are formed by combining adverbs, prepositions, or adverbial prefixes with nouns in the singular number neuter gender.

a. The greater number are formed with the adverbial preposition सह *saha*, contracted into स *sa;* as, from कोप, "anger," सकोपं, "angrily"; from आदर, "respect," सादरं, "respectfully"; from अष्टाङ्गपात, "prostration of the limbs," साष्टाङ्गपातं, "reverentially." As, however, the neuter of all adjectives may be used adverbially, these compound adverbs may be regarded as the neuter of the fifth form of relative compounds (r. 161.).

b. The following may be taken as examples of compound adverbs formed with other prefixes: अनुज्येष्ठं, "according to seniority"; प्रत्यङ्गं, "over every limb"; प्रतिमासं, "every month"; यथाविधि, "according to rule"; यथाशक्ति, or यावच्छक्यं, "according to one's power"; यथासुखं, "happily"; समक्षं, "before the eyes" (अक्ष being substituted for अक्षि, cf. p. 165. *b.*); असंशयं, "undoubtedly"; निर्विशेषं, "without distinction."

c. Some of the adverbs at r. 139. may be placed after crude nouns; thus, बालकसमीपं, "near the child"; रक्षार्थं, "for the sake of protection."

d. A kind of compound adverb is formed by doubling a noun, lengthening the final of the first word, and changing the final of the last to *i*; as, from दण्ड, "a stick," दण्डादण्डि, "mutual striking."

e. Complex compound adverbs, involving other compounds, are sometimes found; as, स्वगृहनिर्विशेषेण, "not differently from one's own house"; स्तनभरविनमन्मध्यभङ्गानपेक्षं, "regardlessly of the curving of her waist bending under the weight of her bosom."

f. The indec. part. आरभ्य, "having begun," is joined with अद्य, "to day" (अद्यारभ्य), in the sense of "from this time forward." प्रभृति is placed adverbially after words, in the same sense; as, जन्मप्रभृति, "from birth upwards."

CHAPTER X.

SYNTAX.

STRIVE as we may, it is impossible to free the orthographical and etymological part of Sanscrit Grammar from a certain degree of intricacy and complexity. But admitting, as we do, this complexity in the early part of the subject to be greater than is ordinarily found, we at the same time affirm, that, in the aggregate calculation, the preponderance of difficulty is on the side of the classical languages. When the student has once thoroughly mastered the rules relating to the combination of letters and the inflection of nouns and verbs, the path, in Sanscrit, becomes easy to him, and he passes with the utmost certainty to a complete acquaintance with the subject in all its bearings. Not so in Greek or Latin. At the point in Sanscrit where our labours end, at that point in the others do our real labours begin; and the young scholar, however versed in the declension of nouns and conjugation of verbs, finds, when he enters upon the syntax of these two languages, that he has hardly passed the threshold of his studies. It is in the syntax of Greek and Latin that the true test of scholarship lies. It is here that an almost interminable field of inquiry opens before the grammarian, and difficulties assail the student, demanding, for their complete mastery, a more than ordinary degree of mental application and capacity. In Sanscrit, on the other hand, the subject of syntax is reducible to a few plain rules, and might almost be merged in that of compound words. The almost entire absence of prepositions in government with nouns removes one fertile source of difficulty; and such is the extraordinary prevalence of compounds, that the student who has acquired a thorough insight into their formation has little else to learn, and the writer who has properly expounded this portion of the grammar has already more than half completed his investigation into the laws which regulate syntactical combinations. We shall endeavour, in the present chapter, to collect together all the most useful rules for the connection and collocation of uncompounded words, presupposing, as we have done throughout, that the student is acquainted with the general principles of the subject before us. Much vagueness and uncertainty, however, may be expected to attach to the rules propounded, when it is remembered that Sanscrit literature consists almost entirely of poetry, and that the laws of syntax are ever prone to yield to the necessities of metrical composition.

Observe, in the present chapter on Syntax, that the subject may be made as clear as possible, each word will be separated from the next, and vowels will not be allowed to coalesce, although such coalition be required by the laws of combination. Whenever compounds are introduced into the examples, a dot, placed underneath, will mark the division of the words. The examples have been, in general, selected from the Hitopadesha, or the Mahābhārata, with the view of serving as an easy delectus, in which the beginner may exercise himself before passing to continuous translation.

CONCORD OF THE VERB WITH THE NOMINATIVE CASE.

172. The verb must agree with the nominative case in number and person, as in the following examples: अहं करवाणि, "I must perform;" त्वम् अवधेहि, "do thou attend"; स ददाति, "he gives"; आवां ब्रूवः, "we two say"; कपोता ऊचुः, "the pigeons said"; राजा मन्त्री च जग्मतुः, "the king and minister went": यावत् चन्द्रार्कौ तिष्ठतः, "as long as the moon and sun remain"; युवां चिन्तयतं, "do you two reflect"; यूयम् आयात, "do ye come"; सज्जनाः पूज्यन्ते, "good men are honoured"; वाति पवनः, "the wind blows"; उदयति शशाङ्कः, "the moon rises"; स्फुटति पुष्पं, "the flower blossoms."

a. When a participle takes the place of the verb, it must agree with the nominative in number and *gender*; as, स गतः, "he went"; सा गता, "she went"; नार्य्याव् उक्तवत्यौ, "the two women spoke"; राजा हतः, "the king was killed"; बन्धनानि छिन्नानि, "the bonds were cut."

b. Sometimes, when it is placed between two or more nominative cases, it agrees with one only; as, स्ववधूः प्रबोधिता पुत्रश्च, "his wife and son were awakened."

c. Very often the copula, or verb which connects the subject with the predicate, is omitted; when, if an adjective stand in the place of the verb, it will follow the rules of concord in gender and number; as, धनं दुर्लभं, "wealth is difficult of attainment"; आवां कृताहारौ, "we two have finished eating." But if a substantive stand in the place of the verb, no concord of gender or number need take place; as, सम्पदः पदम् आपदां, "successes are the road to misfortunes."

CONCORD OF THE ADJECTIVE WITH THE SUBSTANTIVE.

173. An adjective, participle, or adjective pronoun, qualifying a substantive, when not compounded with it, must agree with the substantive in gender, number, and case; as, साधुः पुरुषः, "a good man"; महद् दुःखं, "great pain"; एतेषु पूर्व्वोक्तेषु राष्ट्रेषु, "in these before-mentioned countries"; त्रीणि मित्राणि, "three friends."

CONCORD OF THE RELATIVE WITH THE ANTECEDENT.

174 The Relative must agree with the antecedent noun in gender, number, and person; but, in Sanscrit, the relative pronoun almost invariably precedes the noun to which it refers, and this noun is then put in the same case with the relative, and the pronoun सः generally follows in the latter clause of the sentence; as, यस्य नरस्य बुद्धिः स बलवान्, "of whatever man there is intellect, he is strong." The noun referred to by the relative may also be joined with सः, as, यस्य बुद्धिः स नरो बलवान्; or may be omitted altogether, as, यत् प्रतिज्ञातं तत् पालय, "What you have promised, that abide by"; येषाम् अपत्यानि खादितानि तैः (पक्षिभिः, understood) जिज्ञासा समारब्धा, "By those (birds) whose young ones were devoured, an inquiry was set on foot."

a. The Relative sometimes stands alone, an antecedent noun or pronoun being understood, from which it takes its gender and number; as, नास्ति पुण्यवान् (तस्मात् understood) यस्य मित्रेण सम्भाषः, "there is not a happier (than that man) of whom there is conversation with a friend"; धनेन किं यो न ददाति, "What is the use of wealth (to him) who does not give?"

b. Sometimes, though rarely, the antecedent noun precedes the relative in the natural order; as, न सा भार्य्या यस्यां भर्त्ता न तुष्यति, "She is not a wife in whom the husband does not take pleasure."

c. तावत् and यावत् stand to each other in the relation of demonstrative and relative; as, यावन्ति तस्य द्वीपस्य वस्तूनि तावन्ति अस्माकम् उपनेतव्यानि, "As many products as belong to that island, so many are to be brought to us."

d. Similarly, तादृश and यादृश; as, यादृशं वृत्तं तादृशं तस्मै कथितवन्तः, "As the event occurred, so they related it to him."

SYNTAX OF SUBSTANTIVES.

Under this head it is proposed to explain the construction of substantives, without reference to their connection with particular adjectives, verbs, or participles; and for this purpose it will be desirable to exhibit examples under each case.

Nominative Case.

A substantive simply and absolutely expressed must be placed in the nominative case; as, हितोपदेशः, "the Hitopadesha"; भट्टिकाव्यं, "the poem of Bhatti."

a. Two nominative cases in different numbers may be placed in apposition to each other; as, तृणानि शय्या, "grass as a bed."

Accusative Case.

b. Substantives are not found in the accusative, unconnected with verbs or participles, except as expressing duration of time or space. See r. 180. 181.

Instrumental Case.

175. This case yields a variety of senses. The most usual is that of the instrument or means by which any thing is done; as, मया (उक्तं), "by me it was said"; व्याधेन (पाशो योजितः), "by the fowler a snare was laid"; वेदाध्ययनेन, "by the study of the Vedas"; स्वचक्षुषा, "with one's own eye."

a. It also has the force of "with" in expressing other collateral ideas; as, बलीयसा स्पर्द्धा, "vying with the strong"; मित्रेण सम्भाषः, "conversation with a friend"; पशुभिः सामान्यं, "equality with beasts"; पितुर् गोचरेण, "with the knowledge of (his) father"; especially when accompaniment is intended; as, शिष्येण गुरुः, "the master with his pupil."

b. The other senses yielded by this case are "through," "by reason of"; as, कृपया, "through compassion"; तेन अपराधेन, "on account of that transgression."

c. "According to," "by"; as, विधिना, "according to rule"; मम सम्मतेन, "according to my opinion"; जात्या, "by birth."

d. The "manner" in which any thing is done, as denoted in English by the adverbial affix *ly*, or by the prepositions *in*, *at*; as, बाहुल्येन, "in abundance"; धर्म्मेण, "virtuously"; स्वेच्छया, "at pleasure"; सुखेन, "at ease"; अनेन विधिना, "in this way"; महता स्नेहेन (निवसतः), "they both dwell together in great intimacy"; (नृपः सर्व्वभूतानि अभिभवति) तेजसा, "a king surpasses all beings in glory"; मनसा (न कर्त्तव्यं), "such a deed must not even be imagined in the mind"; मानुषरूपेण, "in human form."

e. Substantives expressive of "want," "need," may be joined with the instrumental of the thing wanted; as, चर्च्चया न प्रयोजनं, "there is no occasion for inquiry"; मया सेवकेन न प्रयोजनं, "there is no need of me as a servant"; तृणेन कार्य्यं, "there is use for a straw."

f. The price for which any thing is done may be in the instrumental; as, पञ्चभिः पुराणैर् (याति दासत्वं), "for five purāṇas he becomes a slave"; बहुभिर् दत्तैर् (युध्यन्ते), "they fight for great rewards." Similarly, प्राणपरित्यागमूल्येन (श्रीर् न लभ्यते), "fortune is not obtained at the price of the sacrifice of life."

g. So, also, difference between two things; as, त्वया समुद्रेण च महद् अन्तरं, "there is great difference between you and the ocean."

h. The English expression "under the idea that" is expressed by the inst. case of the substantive बुद्धि; as, व्याघ्रबुद्ध्या, "under the idea that he was a tiger."

Double Instrumental.

i. Sometimes when two substantives come together, expressing parts of a common idea, they are both placed in the instrumental, instead of one in the genitive; as, बकुलैः पुष्पैर् वास्यते, "an odour is emitted by the bakul-plants by their flowers" (for बकुलानां पुष्पैः). Similarly, ताम् आश्वासयामास प्रेष्याभिश् चन्दनोदकैः, "he caused her to revive by her attendants by sandal-water."

Dative Case.

176. This case is of very limited applicability, and its functions, irrespectively of the influence of verbs, are restricted to the expression of the object, motive, or cause for which any thing is done, or the result to which any act tends; as, आत्मविवृद्धये, "for self-aggrandizement"; आपत्प्रतीकाराय, "for the counteraction of calamity"; शस्त्रं च शास्त्रं च प्रतिपत्तये, "arms and books (lead) to renown." When, as in the last example, the result or end to which any thing leads is denoted by this case, the verb is seldom expressed, but appears to be involved in the case itself. The following are other examples, यत्र आस्ते विषसंसर्गो ऽमृतं तदपि मृत्यवे, "where there is admixture of poison, then even nectar (leads) to death"; उपदेशो मूर्खाणां प्रकोपाय न शान्तये, "advice to fools (leads) to irritation, not to conciliation; स वृद्धपतिस् तस्याः सन्तोषाय न अभवत्, "that old husband was not to her liking."

a. It will be seen hereafter that certain verbs of "giving" and "relating," govern the dative. Substantives derived from such verbs exercise a similar influence; as, अन्यस्मै दानं, "the giving to another"; अन्यस्मै कथनं, "the telling to another."

b. Words expressive of salutation or reverence are joined with the dative; as, गणेशाय नमः, "reverence to Gaṇesha"; कुशलं ते, "health to thee."

Ablative Case.

177. The proper force of the ablative case is expressed by "from"; as, लोभात् (क्रोधः प्रभवति), "from avarice anger arises"; गिरेः पतनं, "falling from a mountain"; चाराणां मुखात्, "from the mouth of the spies."

a. Hence this case passes to the expression of various correlative ideas; as, आहारात् किञ्चित्, "a portion of (from) their food"; and like the instrumental it very commonly signifies "by reason of," "in consequence of"; as, गोमनुष्याणां वधात्, "on account of the slaughter of cows and men": अनवसरप्रवेशात् (पुत्रं निन्दति), "he blames his son for entering inopportunely"; दण्डभयात्, "through fear of punishment"; अस्मत्पुण्योदयात्, "by reason of my good fortune."

b. "According to"; as, मन्त्रिवचनात्, "according to the advice of the minister." Abstract nouns in त्व are often found in this case to express some of these ideas; as, अनवस्थितचित्तत्वात्, "by reason of the unsteadiness of his mind." Especially in the writings of commentators; as, वक्ष्यमाणत्वात्, "according to what will be said hereafter."

c. It also expresses "through the means" or "instrumentality of"; as, शृगालात् पाशबद्धः, "caught in the toils through the instrumentality of the jackall"; न औषधपरिज्ञानाद् (व्याधेः शान्तिर् भवेत्), "the alleviation of disease is not effected by the mere knowledge of the medicine."

d. The "manner" in which any thing is done, is occasionally expressed by the ablative; as, यत्नात्, "with diligence"; बलात्, "forcibly"; कुतूहलात्, "with wonder"; मूलाद् उद्धरणं, "tearing up by the roots"; or by the ablative affix तस्; as, स्वेच्छातः, "at one's own pleasure" (cf. p. 152. *a.*).

e. This case also denotes "after"; as, शरीरविगमात्, "after separation from the body"; मुख्यप्रतिबन्धनात्, "after the imprisonment of the Chief"; तस्य आगमनात्, "since his arrival."

f. In reference to time, "within"; as, त्रिपक्षात्, "within three fortnights."

g. Nouns expressive of fear are joined with the ablative of the thing feared; as, मृत्योर् भयं, "fear of death"; चौरतो भयं, "fear of robbers."

Genitive Case.

178. This and the locative case are of the most extensive application, and are often employed, in a vague and indeterminate manner, to express relations properly belonging to the other cases.

The true force of the genitive is equivalent to "of," and this case appears most frequently when two substantives are to be connected, so as to present one idea; as, मित्रस्य वचनं, "the speech of a friend"; भर्त्ता नार्य्याः परमं भूषणं, "the best ornament of a woman is her husband"; न नरस्य नरो दासो दासस् तु अर्थस्य, "man is not the slave of man, but the slave of wealth."

a. Possession is frequently expressed by the genitive case alone, without a verb; as, सर्व्वाः सम्पत्तयस् तस्य सन्तुष्टं यस्य मानसं, "all riches belong to him who has a contented mind"; धन्योऽहं यस्य ईदृशी भार्य्या, "happy am I in possessing such a wife."

b. It often, however, has the force of "to," and is very generally used to supply the place of the dative; as, प्राणा आत्मनो ऽभीष्टाः, "one's own life is dear to one's self"; न योजनशतं दूरं वाह्यमानस्य तृष्णया, "a hundred yojanas is not far to one borne away by thirst (of gain)"; किं प्रज्ञावताम् अविदितं, "what is unknown to the wise"? किम्

अन्धस्य प्रकाशयति प्रदीपः, "what does a lamp show to a blind man"? किं मया अपकृतं राज्ञः, "what offence have I committed towards the king"? किम् अयम् अस्माकं कर्तुं समर्थः, "what can this man do to us?"

c. And not unfrequently of "in" or "on"; as, स्त्रीणां विश्वासः, "confidence in women"; मम आयत्तत्वं, "dependence on me."

d. It is even equivalent occasionally to "from" or "by," as usually expressed by the ablative or instrumental; as, न कस्यापि (उपायनं गृह्णीयात्), "one ought not to accept a present from any one"; अस्माकं (वनं त्याज्यं), "the wood is to be abandoned by us"; स धन्यो यस्य अर्थिनो न प्रयान्ति विमुखाः, "he is blessed from whom suppliants do not depart in disappointment."

e. Difference between two things is expressed by this case; as, सेव्य-सेवकयोर् महद् अन्तरं, "there is great difference between the master and the servant." Cf. p. 182. *g.*

Locative Case.

179. The locative, like the genitive, expresses the most diversified relations, and frequently usurps the functions of the other cases. Properly, it has the force of "in," "on," or "at," as expressive of many collateral and analogous ideas; thus, रात्रौ, "in the night"; ग्रामे, "in the village"; पृष्ठे, "on the back"; त्वयि विश्वासः, "confidence in you"; मरु-स्थल्यां वृष्टिः, "rain on desert ground"; प्रथम-बुभुक्षायां, "at the first desire of eating"; पृथिव्यां रोपितो वृक्षः, "a tree planted in the earth."

a. Hence it passes into the sense "towards"; as, क्षमा शत्रौ च मित्रे च, "leniency towards an enemy as well as a friend"; सर्व-भूतेषु दया, "compassion towards all creatures"; सुहृत्सु अजिह्मः, "upright towards friends"; सुकृत-शतम् असत्सु नष्टं, "a hundred good offices are thrown away upon the wicked."

b. Words signifying "cause," "motive," or "need," are joined with the locative; as, सत्रपत्वे हेतुः, "the cause of his modesty"; भूपालयोर् विग्रहे भवद्वचनं निदानं, "your speech was the cause of the war between the two princes"; प्रार्थकाभावः सतीत्वे कारणं स्त्रियाः, "the absence of a suitor is the cause of a woman's chastity"; नौकायां किं प्रयोजनं, "what need of a boat." Also, words signifying employment or occupation; as, अर्थार्जने प्रवृत्तिः, "engaging in the acquisition of wealth." Words derived from the root *yuj* usually require the locative; as, मम राज्य-रक्षायाम् उपयोगः, "I am of service in preserving the kingdom."

c. This case may yield other senses equivalent to "by reason of," "for," &c.; as, मे छिद्रेषु, "through my faults"; चारः पर-राष्ट्राणाम् अवलोकने, "a spy is for the sake of examining the territory of one's enemies"; युद्धे कालोऽयं, "this is the time for battle"; तस्याम् अनुरागः, "affection for her"; उपदेशे अनादरः, "disregard for advice"; का चिन्ता मरणे रणे, "what anxiety about dying in battle?"

d. It is also used in giving the meaning of a root; as, ग्रह् उपादाने, "the root *grah* is in *taking*," *i.e.* conveys the idea of "*taking*."

SYNTAX OF NOUNS OF TIME.

180. When reference is made to any particular division of time, the instrumental case is usually required; as, त्रिभिर् वर्षैः, "in three years"; द्वादशभिर् मासैः, "in twelve months"; क्षणेन, "in an instant"; कियता कालेन, "in how long time"? वर्षशतैः, "in hundreds of years"; कालपर्यायेण, "in process of time."

a. When, to duration of time, the accusative case is generally used; as, अनेककालं, "for a long time"; एकं मासं, "for one month"; द्वौ मासौ, "for two months"; वर्षशतं, "for a hundred years"; शाश्वतीः समाः, "to all eternity." The instrumental, however, is sometimes used in this sense also; as, द्वादशभिर् वर्षैर् वाणिज्यं कृत्वा, "having traded for twelve years"; कतिपयदिवसैः, "for a few days."

b. When any particular period or epoch is referred to, the locative may be employed; as, कस्मिंश्चिद् दिवसे, "on a certain day"; तृतीये दिवसे, "on the third day;" or sometimes the accusative; as, यां रात्रिं ते दूताः प्रविशन्ति स्म पुरीं तां रात्रिं भरतेन स्वप्नो दृष्टः, "on the night when the ambassadors entered the city, on that night a dream was seen by Bharata."

NOUNS OF PLACE AND DISTANCE.

181. Nouns expressive of distance between two places (according to Carey) may be in the nominative; as, कृष्णः शतं क्रोशाः सोमनाथात्, "Krishṇa is a hundred Kos from Somanāth." Space may also be expressed by the accusative; as, क्रोशं गिरिः, "a hill for a Kos"; or by the instrumental; as, क्रोशेन गत्वा, "having gone for a Kos." The place in which any thing is done may be in the locative; as, विदर्भेषु, "in Vidarbha."

SYNTAX OF ADJECTIVES.

Accusative after the Adjective.

182. The only adjectives governing an accusative are those formed from desiderative bases; as, स्वगृहं जिगमिषुः, "desirous of

going home"; पुत्रम् अभीप्सुः, "desirous of obtaining a son"; राजानं दिदृक्षुः, "desirous of seeing the king."

Instrumental after the Adjective.

a. Adjectives or participles used adjectively, expressive of want or possession, require this case; as, अर्थेन हीनः, "destitute of wealth"; अर्थैः समायुक्तः, "possessed of riches"; वारिणा पूर्णो घटः, "a jar full of water."

b. So also of "likeness" or "equality"; as, अनेन सदृशो लोके न भूतो न भविष्यति, "there has never been, nor will there ever be, any one like him in this world"; ब्रह्महत्या समं पापं, "a crime equal to that of killing a Brahman"; प्राणैः समा पत्नी, "a wife as dear as life"; आदित्येन तुल्यः, "equal to the sun." These are also joined with a genitive.

Genitive after the Adjective.

183. Adjectives signifying "dear to," or the reverse, are joined with the genitive; as, राज्ञां प्रियः, "dear to kings"; भर्तारः स्त्रीणां प्रियाः, "husbands are dear to women"; न कश्चित् स्त्रीणाम् अप्रियः, "women dislike nobody"; द्वेष्यो भवति मन्त्रिणां, "he is detestable to his ministers."

a. Adjectives expressive of equality often require this case as well as the instrumental; thus, सर्वस्य समः, "equal to all"; तस्य अनुरूपः, "like him"; चन्द्रस्य कल्पः, "like the moon"; न तस्य तुल्यः कश्चन, "nobody is equal to him."

b. So also other adjectives; as, परोपदेशः सर्वेषां सुकरः नृणां, "giving advice to others is *easy* to all men"; सुखानाम् उचितः, "*worthy* of happiness"; उचितः क्लेशानां, "*capable* of toil."

Locative after the Adjective.

184. Adjectives or participles used adjectively, expressive of "power" or "ability," are joined with this case; as, अध्वनि क्षमा अश्वाः, "horses able for the journey"; महति शत्रौ क्षमो राजा, "a king who is a match for a great enemy"; अशक्ता गृहकरणे शक्ता गृहभञ्जने, "unable to build a house, but able to demolish one."

a. So also other adjectives; as, शस्त्रेषु कुशलः, "*skilled* in arms"; अल्पेषु प्राज्ञः, "*wise* in trifles"; त्वयि अनुरक्तो विरक्तो वा स्वामी, "is your master *attached* or *adverse* to you?" अनुजीविषु मन्दादरः, "*neglectful* of his dependants."

SYNTAX OF THE COMPARATIVE AND SUPERLATIVE DEGREE.

185. Adjectives in the comparative degree require the ablative case; as, पत्नी प्राणेभ्योऽपि गरीयसी, "a wife dearer even than one's life"; पुत्रस्पर्शात् सुखतरः स्पर्शो लोके न विद्यते, "there is no pleasanter touch in this world than the touch of a son"; वर्द्धनात् प्रजारक्षणं श्रेयः, "the protection of one's subjects is better than aggrandizement"; न मत्तो दुःखिततरः पुमान् अस्ति, "there is not a more wretched man than I"; मतिर् बलाद् बलीयसी, "mind is more powerful than strength."

a. Sometimes they govern the instrumental; as, प्राणैः प्रियतरः, "dearer than life"; न अस्ति मया कश्चिद् अल्पभाग्यतरो भुवि, "there is nobody upon earth more unfortunate than I."

b. When it is intended to express "the better of two things" the genitive may be used; as, अनयोर् देशयोः को देशो भद्रतरः, "of these two countries which is the better?"

c. The comparative, in Sanscrit, is often resolved into the expression "better and not"; as, वरं प्राणपरित्यागो न पुनर् ईदृशे कर्म्मणि प्रवृत्तिः, "better abandon life than (literally, and not) engage in such an action"; वरं मौनं कार्य्यं न च वचनम् उक्तं यद् अनृतं, "it is better that silence should be kept than a speech uttered which is untrue."

d. The superlative degree is usually joined with the genitive; as, ब्राह्मणो द्विपदां श्रेष्ठो गौर् वरिष्ठा चतुष्पदां । गुरुर् गरीयसां श्रेष्ठः पुत्रः स्पर्शवतां वरः, "a Brahman is the best of all bipeds, a cow of quadrupeds, a Guru of venerable things, a son of things possessed of touch"; but sometimes with the locative; as, नरेषु बलवत्तमः, "the most powerful of men"; and even with an ablative; as, धान्यानां सङ्ग्रह उत्तमः सर्व्वसङ्ग्रहात्, "a store of grain is the best of all stores."

e. Comparison is often expressed by an adjective in the *positive* degree, joined with a noun in the ablative case; as, नास्ति तस्मात् पुण्यवान्, "there is not a happier than he."

f. Many words are in their nature comparative and require an ablative case, especially वरं, अवरं, अन्य, अन्यदा, अन्यत्र, इतर, पर, अधिक, ऊन; as, प्रक्षालनात् पङ्कस्य अस्पर्शनं वरं, "it is better not to touch mud than to wash it off"; दारिद्र्यम् अवरं मरणात्, "poverty is less desirable than death"; को मां मित्राद् अन्यस् त्रातुं समर्थः, "who is able to rescue me, other than a friend?" किन्नु दुःखम् अतः परं, "what grief is greater than this?" न श्रुताद् अन्यद् विब्रूयात्, "one ought not to speak differently from what one has heard"; तत्कालाद् अन्यदा, "at another time than the present"; नरस्य न अन्यत्र मरणाद् भयं, "there is no cause of fear to man from any other quarter than from death"; योजनशताद् अधिकं, "more than a hundred yojanas"; कान्तोदन्तः सङ्गमात् किञ्चिद् ऊनः, "intelligence of a lover is something less than a meeting."

g. Numerals if used partitively may take the genitive; as, अश्वानां शतसहस्राणि, "a hundred thousand of the horses"; and, if comparatively, the ablative; as, विवादात् द्विगुणं दमं, "a fine the double of that which is in dispute."

SYNTAX OF PRONOUNS.

186. The chief peculiarities in the syntax of pronouns have already been noticed in Chapter V., pp. 50—55. It remains to offer one or two remarks with reference more especially to the relative and interrogative.

a. In the use of these pronouns a very peculiar *attraction* is often to be observed; that is, when either a relative or interrogative pronoun has been used, and an indefinite pronoun would naturally be expected to follow, the relative or interrogative are repeated, as in the following examples: यो यस्य (for कस्यचित्) भावः स्यात्, "whatever may be the disposition of whom (*i.e.* any one)"; यद् रोचते यस्मै, "whatever is pleasing to any one"; यस्य ये गुणाः सन्ति, "whatever excellencies belong to any one"; यद् येन युज्यते, "whatever corresponds with any thing"; केषां किं शास्त्रम् अध्ययनीयं, "what book is to be read by whom? (*i.e.* by any one)."*

187. The relative and interrogative are sometimes used together in an indefinite distributive sense; as, यानि कानि मित्राणि, "any friends whatever"; or more usually with चित् affixed to the interrogative; as, यस्मै कस्मैचित्, "to any one whatever."

a. The neuter of the interrogative is often joined with the instrumental to signify "what is the use of?" "there is no need of"; as, श्रुतेन किं यो न धर्मम् आचरेत् किम् आत्मना यो न जितेन्द्रियो भवेत्, "of what use is scriptural knowledge (to one) who does not practice virtue, of what use is a soul (to one) whose passions are not kept in subjection?" किं ते अनेन प्रश्नेन, "what business have you to make this inquiry?"

---

* See, on this subject, Bopp's Comp. Gram. (Prof. Eastwick's Translation), vol. ii. p. 537.

b. As already shewn (p. 166.), a relative pronoun is sometimes rendered unnecessary by the use of the relative compound; thus, नगरी चन्द्रिकाधौतहर्म्या is equivalent to नगरी यस्याश् चन्द्रिकाधौतानि हर्म्याणि, "a city whose palaces were silvered by the moon-beams." The relative, when followed by a pluperfect tense, may sometimes be expressed by the indeclinable participle; thus, सिंहो व्याधं हत्वा, "a lion having killed a hunter," or "a lion who had killed a hunter."

SYNTAX OF VERBS.

188. Nothing is more common in Sanscrit syntax than for the verb to be omitted altogether, or supplied from the context. This is more especially the case with the copula, or substantive verb; thus, यावन् मेरुस्थिता देवा यावद् गङ्गा महीतले । चन्द्रार्कौ गगने यावत् तावद् विप्रकुले वयं, "as long as the gods have existed in Meru, as long as the Ganges upon earth, as long as the sun and moon in the sky, so long have we (existed) in the family of Brahmans";* परिच्छेदः पाण्डित्यं, "discrimination (is) wisdom."

Nominative, Genitive, and Locative Absolute.

189. These cases are used absolutely with participles. The nominative is very rarely thus used; as, सुहृन् मे समायातः पुण्यवान् अस्मि, "my friend having arrived, I am happy." The genitive more frequently; as, आपदाम् आपतन्तीनां, "calamities impending"; पश्यतां नराणां, "the men looking on." The locative very commonly; as, तस्मिन् जीवति जीवामि मृते तस्मिन् म्रिये पुनः, "he living I live, he dying I die"; अवसन्नायां रात्रौ, "the night being ended"; असति उपायान्तरे, "there being no other expedient." Sometimes the verb is omitted; as, दूरे भये, "the danger (being) distant." When the passive participle is thus used absolutely with a noun in the locative case, the present participle of अस्, "to be," is often redundantly added; as, तथा कृते सति, "it being so done."

Hence it is evident that the genitive or locative absolute often takes the place of the particles, "when," "while," "since," "although."

Nominative Case after the Verb.

190. Verbs signifying "to be," "to become," "to appear," "to

---

* The writer of these pages is indebted for this couplet to Mr. Seton Karr, of the Bengal Civil Service. It is in the mouth of all the *Kulīn* Brahmans of Bengal, and is that on which they found their claim to precedence.

be called," or "to be esteemed," and other passive verbs used denominatively, may take a nominative after them; as, राजा प्रजापालकः स्यात्, "let a king be the protector of his subjects"; सा निरानन्दा प्रतिभाति, "she appears sorrowful"; ग्रामोऽरण्यं प्रतिभाति, "the village appears like a desert"; राजा धर्म्म अभिधीयते, "a king is called Justice"; श्रुतो हितोपदेशोऽयं, "this (book) is called Hitopadesha."

Accusative Case after the Verb.

191. Transitive verbs generally govern this case; as, विश्वंससर्ज वेधाः, "Brahmā *created* the universe"; पुष्पाणि चिनोति नारी, "the woman *gathers* flowers"; प्राणान् जहौ मुमूर्षुः, "the dying man *gave up* the ghost"; मधु वर्जयेत्, "one should *avoid* wine"; तत्त्वं ब्रूहि, "*speak* the truth."

a. So also verbs of "motion"; as, सरति तीर्थं मुनिः, "the holy man *goes* to the place of pilgrimage"; नद्यः समुद्रं द्रवन्ति, "rivers *run* into the ocean"; भ्रमति महीं, "he wanders over the earth."

b. Verbs of motion are not unfrequently used with substantives to supply the place of other verbs; as, ख्यातिं याति, "he goes to fame" for "he becomes famous"; समताम् एति, "he goes to equality" for "he becomes equal."

c. The following are other examples: अप्राप्यम् इच्छति, "he *desires* what is unattainable"; विद्यां चिन्तयेत्, "he should *think on* wisdom"; अश्वम् आरोहति, "he *mounts* his horse"; कर्म्माणि आरेभिरे, "they *began* the business"; गतान् मा शुचः, "*grieve not for* the departed"; सर्व्वलोकाधिपत्यम् अर्हति, "he *deserves* the sovereignty of the universe"; पर्व्वतकन्दरं शेते, "he *lies down* in a cave of the mountain."

d. There are certain verbs which take a redundant accusative case after them of a substantive derived from the same root; as, शपथं शेपे, "he swore an oath"; वसति वासं, "he dwells"; वर्त्तते वृत्तिं, "he conducts himself"; वाक्यं वदति, "he speaks a speech"; नदति नादं, "he raises a cry" (cf. the Greek expressions λέγω λόγον, χαίρω χαράν, &c.).

Double Accusative after the Verb.

192. Verbs of "*asking*" govern a double accusative; as, देवं वरं याचते, "he seeks a boon of the god"; धनं राजानं प्रार्थयते, "he begs money from the king." Of "*speaking*"; as, राजानं वचनम् अब्रवीत्, "he addressed a speech to the king."

a. Causal verbs; as, अतिथिं भोजयति अन्नं, "he causes the guest to eat food"; त्वां बोधयामि यत् ते हितं, "I cause you to know what is for your interest"; शिष्यं वेदान् अध्यापयति गुरुः, "the Guru teaches his pupil the Vedas"; तां गृहं

प्रवेशयति, "he causes her to enter the house"; फलपुष्पोदकं माहयामास नृपात्मजं, "he presented the king's son with fruits, flowers, and water"; पुत्रम् अङ्कम् आरोपयति, "she causes her son to sit on her lap" (literally "her hip"); विद्या नरं नृपं सङ्गमयति, "learning leads a man into the presence of a king."

b. The following are other examples: तं सेनापतिम् अभिषिषिचुः, "they *inaugurated* him general," more usually joined with an acc. and loc.; देवं पतिं वरयति, "she *chooses* a god for her husband"; अवचिनोति कुसुमानि वृक्षान्, "she *gathers* blossoms from the trees"; तान् प्राहिणोद् यमसादनं, "he *sent* them to the abode of Yama" (Hades); स्वचेष्टितानि नरं गुरुत्वं विपरीततां वा नयन्ति, "his own acts *lead* a man to eminence or the reverse."

Instrumental Case after the Verb.

193. Any verb may be joined with the instrumental, to express the instrument, or cause, or manner of the action; as, पुष्पं वातेन म्लायति, "the flower fades by reason of the wind"; अक्षैः क्रीडति, "he plays with dice"; मेघोऽग्निं वर्षैर् निर्वापयति, "the cloud puts out the fire with its rain"; सुखेन जीवति, "he lives happily."

a. In this sense many causals take an instrumental; as, तां मिष्टान्नैर् भोजयामास, "he caused her to eat sweet-meats."

b. After verbs of "*motion*" this case is used in reference either to the *vehicle by which*, or the *place on which*, the motion takes place; as, रथेन प्रयाति, "he goes *in a chariot*"; अश्वेन सञ्चरति, "he goes *on horse-back*"; मार्गेण गच्छति, "he goes *on the road*"; पुप्लुवे सागरं नौकया, "he navigated the ocean *in a boat*." Similarly, सुस्राव नयनैः सलिलं, "tears flowed through the eyes."

c. After verbs of "*carrying*," "*placing*," *&c.*, it is used in reference to the place on which any thing is carried or placed: as, वहति मूर्ध्ना इन्धनं, "he bears faggots *on his head*"; कुक्कुरः स्कन्धेन उह्यते, "the dog is borne *on the shoulders*." कृ is found with this case in the sense of placing; as, शिरसा पुत्रम् अकरोत्, "he placed his son on his head." The following are other examples: शिष्येण गच्छति गुरुः, "the master *goes in company with* the pupil"; मन्त्रयामास मन्त्रिभिः, "he *consulted with* his ministers." But in this sense सह is usually placed after it. भर्त्ता भार्य्यया सङ्गच्छति, "the husband *meets* the wife"; संयोजयति रथं हयैः, "he *harnesses* the horses to the chariot; देहेन वियुज्यते, "he *is separated from* the body," more usually with the ablative. युध्यते शत्रुभिः, "he *fights* his enemies," or शत्रुभिः सह.

d. Verbs of "*boasting*"; as, विद्यया विकत्थसे, "you *boast* of your learning"; परेषां यशसा श्लाघसे, "you *glory in* the fame of others." Of "*swearing*"; as, धनुषा शेपे, "he *swore* by his bow."

c. Verbs of "*buying*" and "*selling*" take the instrumental of the price; as, सहस्रैर् अपि मूर्खाणाम् एकं क्रीणीष्व पण्डितं, "*buy* one wise man even for thousands of fools"; गवां सहस्रेण गृहं विक्रीणीते, "he *sells* his house for a thousand cows."

Dative after the Verb.

194. All verbs in which a sense of *imparting* or *communicating* any thing to any object is inherent, may take an accusative of the thing imparted, and a dative of the object to which it is imparted. (Frequently, however, they take a genitive or even a locative of the object). पुत्राय मोदकान् ददाति, "he *gives* sweetmeats to his son"; विप्राय गां प्रतिशृणोति, "he *promises* a cow to the Brahman"; देवदत्ताय धनं धारयति, "he *owes* money to Devadatta"; कन्यां तस्मै प्रतिपादय, "*consign* the maiden to him," more usually with the locative. The following are other examples of the dative; तेषां विनाशाय प्रकुरुते मनः, "he *sets his mind on* their destruction"; गमनाय मतिं दधौ, "he set his mind on departure," or with the locative. तन् मह्यं रोचते, "that *is pleasing to* me"; शिष्येभ्यः प्रवक्ष्यामि तत्, "I will *declare* this to my pupils"; सर्वं राज्ञे विज्ञापयति, "he *makes known* all to the king," these are also joined with the genitive of the person. अमृतत्वाय कल्पते, "he is *rendered fit for* immortality"; प्रभवति मम वधाय, "he *has the power* to kill me"; तान् मातुर् वधाय अचोदयत्, "he *incited* them to the murder of their mother"; पुत्राय क्रुध्यति, "he is *angry* with his son."

Ablative after the Verb.

195. All verbs may take an ablative of the object from which any thing proceeds, or arises, or is produced; as, भ्रश्यति वृक्षात् पत्रं, "the leaf falls from the tree"; रुधिरं स्रवति गात्रात्, "blood flows from the body"; आसनाद् उत्तिष्ठति, "he rises from his seat"; मृत्पिण्डतः कर्ता कुरुते यद्यद् इच्छति, "from the lump of clay the artist makes whatever he wishes" (p. 152. *a.*); विनयाद् याति पात्रतां, "from education a person attains capacity"; निर्जगाम नगरात्, "he went out from the city."

a. Verbs of "*fearing*" may be joined with the ablative; as, साधुर् न तथा मृत्योर् बिभेति यथा अनृतात्, "a good man does not fear death so much as falsehood"; दण्डाद् उद्विजते जगत्, "the whole world stands in awe of punishment."

b. The following are other examples: प्रासादाद् अवरोहति, "he *descends from* the palace"; विष्णुः स्वर्गाद् अवततार, "Vishṇu *descended from* heaven"; कनकसूत्रम् अङ्गाद् अवतारयति, "he *takes off* (causes to descend) the golden bracelet from his body"; निवर्त्तते पापात्, "he *ceases from* wickedness"; वचनाद् विरराम, "he *left off* speaking"; नरकात् पितरं त्रायते पुत्रो धार्म्मिकः, "a virtuous son *saves* his father from hell"; अश्वमेधसहस्रात् सत्यम् अतिरिच्यते, "truth *is superior to* a thousand sacrifices"; स्वहितात् प्रमाद्यति, "he *neglects* his own interest."

Genitive after the Verb.

196. The genitive, in Sanscrit, is constantly interchangeable with the dative, locative, or even accusative.* It is more especially, however, used to supply the place of the first of these cases, so that almost all verbs may take a genitive as well as dative of the object to which any thing is imparted. For example, दरिद्रस्य धनं ददाति, "he *gives* money to the poor." It may be used for the locative after verbs of "consigning"; as, निक्षेपं मम समर्पयति, "he deposits a pledge with me": or, of "trusting"; as, न कश्चित् स्त्रीणां श्रद्दधाति, "nobody puts trust in women"; and for the accusative, in examples such as, अचिन्तितानि दुःखानि आयान्ति देहिनां, "unexpected ills come upon corporeal beings."

a. Other examples are: अजानताम् अस्माकं ख्यापय कस्य असि भार्य्या, "*tell* us who are ignorant of it, whose wife you are?" कस्य (for कस्मात्) बिभ्यति धार्म्मिकाः, 'of whom are the righteous *afraid*?" यद् अन्यस्य प्रतिजानीते न तद् अन्यस्य दद्यात्, "one should not *give* to one what one *promises* to another,"; मम न शृणोति, "he does not *hear* me" (cf. the Greek usage); मम स्मरेः, "*remember* me," or with the accusative. अस्माकं मृत्युः प्रभवति, "death *overcomes* us"; अग्निर् न तृप्यति काष्ठानां, "fire is not *satisfied with* fuel"; तेषां क्षमेथाः, "*forgive* them."

Locative after the Verb.

197. This case is very widely applicable, but, as elsewhere remarked, is frequently interchangeable with the dative and genitive. The first sense of the locative requires that it should be united with verbs, in reference only to the place or time in which any thing is done; as, पङ्के मज्जति, "he sinks in the mud"; पुरे वसति, "he dwells in the city"; रणमूर्द्धि तिष्ठति, "he stands in the front of the fight"; सूर्य्योदये प्रबुध्यते, "at sun-rise he awakes." But the transition from the place to the object, or recipient of any action, is

---

* This vague use of the genitive to express various relations prevails also in early Greek."

natural, and hence it is that verbs are found with the locative of the object to which any thing is imparted or communicated, as in the following examples: मा प्रयच्छ ईश्वरे धनं, "*bestow* not money on the mighty"; तस्मिन् कार्य्याणि निक्षिपामि, "I *intrust* my affairs to him"; पुत्रे अङ्गुरीयकं समर्पयति, "he *consigns* a ring to his son"; योग्ये सचिवे न्यस्यति राज्यभारं, "he *intrusts* the burthen of the kingdom to a capable minister"; प्रेतं भूमौ निदध्यात्, "one should *place* (bury) a dead man in the ground"; धर्म्मे मनो दधाति, "he *applies* his mind to virtue." In this sense कृ is used; as, पृष्ठे इन्धनम् अकरोत्, "he *placed* the wood on his back"; मतिं पापे करोति, "he *applies* his mind to sin."

a. When दा, "to give," is used for "to put," it follows the same analogy; as, तस्य पुच्छाग्रे हस्तं देहि, "*put* your hand on the end of its tail;" भस्मचये पदं ददौ, "he *placed* his foot on a heap of ashes." Similarly, वस्त्राञ्चले धृतोऽस्ति, "he was *held* by the skirt of his garment." So also verbs of "seizing," "striking," केशेषु गृह्णाति or आकृषति, "he *seizes* or *drags* him by the hair"; सुप्ते प्रहरति, "he *strikes* a sleeping man."

b. Other examples are, उग्रे तपसि वर्त्तते, "he is *engaged in* a very severe penance"; परकार्य्येषु मा व्यापृतो भूः, "do not *busy yourself* about other people's affairs"; विषयेषु सज्यते, "he is *addicted to* objects of sense"; सर्व्वलोकहिते रमते, "he *delights in* the good of all the world"; दुर्गाधिकारे नियुज्यते, "he is *appointed to* the command of the fort"; द्वौ वृषभौ धुरि नियोजयति, "he *yokes* two bulls to the pole"; सैनापत्ये अभिषिञ्च मां, "*anoint* me to the generalship"; यतते पापनिग्रहे, "he *strives* to suppress evil-doers."

c. न मद्विधे युज्यते वाक्यम् ईदृशं, "such language is not *suited* to a person like me"; प्रभुत्वं त्वयि प्रयुज्यते, "sovereignty is *suited* to you"; आसने उपाविशत्, "he *reclined* on a seat"; वृष्याम् आसस्व, "*sit* thou on a cushion"; शत्रुषु विश्वसिति, "he *confides* in his enemies"; चरणयोः पतति, "it *falls* at his feet"; लुठति पादेषु, "it *rolls* at the feet."

Change of Case after the same Verb.

198. This sometimes occurs; as, विधुरो धृतराष्ट्राय कुन्ती च गान्धार्य्याः सर्व्वं न्यवेदयेतां, "Vidhura and Kuntī announced every thing, the one to Dhṛitarāshṭra, the other to Gāndhārī" (Astrashikshā 34. Ed. Prof. Johnson), where the same verb governs a dative and genitive. Similarly, in the Mitralābha (p. 10.), शृङ्गिणां विश्वासो न कर्त्तव्यः स्त्रीषु च, "confidence is not to be placed in horned animals or women."

SYNTAX OF PASSIVE VERBS.

199. The prevalence of a passive construction is the most remarkable feature in the syntax of this language. Passive verbs are joined with the agent, instrument, or cause, in the instrumental case,* and agree with the object in number and person; as, वातेन रज उद्धूयते, "the dust is raised by the wind"; तेन सर्व्वद्रव्याणि सज्जीक्रियन्तां, "let all things be prepared by him"; इषुभिर् आदित्यो ऽन्तरधीयत, "the sun was concealed by arrows." But the passive participle, as elsewhere observed, usually takes the place of the *past tenses* of the passive verb, and agrees with the object in *gender* as well as number; as, नेत्राणि समाप्लुतानि वारिणा, "(their) eyes were suffused with tears"; तेन उक्तं (इदं being understood), "it was said by him." This is the favourite construction of Sanscrit prose composition, and the love for this idiom is very remarkably displayed in such phrases as the following: दुःखेन गम्यते, "he is gone to by misery," for दुःखं गच्छति; and आगम्यतां देवेन, "let it be come by your majesty," for आगच्छतु देवः; and again, अस्माभिर् एकत्र स्थीयतां, "let it be remained by us in one spot," for "let us remain in one spot"; येन मार्गेण इष्टं तेन गम्यतां, "by whatever road it is desired, by that let it be gone."

a. Active or causal verbs, which take a double accusative, will retain one accusative when constructed passively; but the other accusative passes into a nominative case: thus, instead of स मां परुषाणि उवाच, "he addressed me in harsh words," may be written तेन अहं परुषाणि उक्तः, "by him I was addressed in harsh words."

SYNTAX OF THE INFINITIVE.

200. The student must guard against supposing that the infinitive, in Sanscrit, may be used with the same latitude as in other languages. Its use is very limited, corresponding rather to that of the Latin *supines*, as, indeed, its termination *um* may be supposed to indicate. And this restriction in the employment of a part of speech so important, might be expected to cripple very seriously the syntactical capabilities of the language, were it not that the power of compounding words abundantly compensates for any such deficiency. Let the student, therefore, accurately distin-

* There are a few instances of the agent in the genitive case; as, मम कृतं पापं, "a crime committed by me," for मया.

guish between the infinitive of Sanscrit, and the infinitive of the classical languages. In these latter we have this part of speech constantly made the subject of a proposition; or, in other words, standing in the place of a nominative, and an accusative case often admissible before it. We have it also assuming different forms, to express present, past, or future time, and completeness or incompleteness in the progress of the action. The Sanscrit infinitive, on the other hand, can never be made the subject or nominative case to a verb, admits of no accusative before it, and can only express indeterminate time and incomplete action. Wherever it occurs it must always be considered as the object, and never the subject, of some verb expressed or understood. And as the object of the verb, it may be regarded as equivalent to an indeclinable substantive, in which the force of two cases, an accusative and dative,* is inherent, and which differs from other substantives in its power of governing a case. Its use as a substantive with the force of the *accusative* case corresponds to one use of the Latin infinitive; thus, तत् सर्वं श्रोतुम् इच्छामि, "I desire to hear all that," "*id audire cupio,*" where श्रोतुं and *audire* are both equivalent to accusative cases, themselves also governing an accusative. Similarly, रोदितुं प्रवृत्ता, "she began to weep"; and महीं जेतुम् आरेभे, "he began to conquer the earth," where महीजयम् आरेभे, "he began the conquest of the earth," would be equally correct. But the Sanscrit infinitive appears most commonly in the character of a substantive with the force of a *dative* case; or, in other words, will be found in most instances to involve a sense which belongs especially to the Sanscrit dative, viz. that of the end or purpose for which any thing is done, and which it would often be equally idiomatic to express by that case; thus, शावकान् भक्षितुम् आगच्छति, "he comes to devour the young ones"; शत्रून् योद्धुं सैन्यं प्राहिणोत्, "he sent an army to fight the enemy." In these cases it would be equally correct in Sanscrit to substitute for the infinitive the dative case of the verbal noun formed with the affix *ana*; thus, भक्षणाय.

* Bopp considers the termination of the infinitive to be the accusative of the affix तु, and it is certain that in the Vedas an irregular infinitive in तवे and तवै is found, which would seem to be the dative of the same affix. See Pāṇini 3. 4. 9.

"for the eating"; योधनाय, "for the fighting"; and in Latin the infinitive could not be used at all, but either the supine, *devoratum, pugnatum,* or still more properly, the conjunction with the subjunctive mood, "*ut devoret,*" "*ut pugnarent.*" The following are other examples in which the infinitive has a dative force in expressing the purpose of the action: पानीयं पातुं नदीम् अगमत्, "he went to the river to drink water"; मम बन्धनं छेत्तुम् उपसर्पति, "he comes to cut asunder my bonds"; मां त्रातुं समर्थः (अस्ति being understood), "he is able to rescue me"; पाशान् संवरितुं सयत्नो बभूव, "he busied himself about collecting together the snares."

a. The Sanscrit infinitive, therefore, rather deserves the name of a supine than an infinitive, and in its character of supine is susceptible of either an active or passive signification. In its passive character, however, like the Latin supine in *u*, it is joined with certain words only, the most usual being the passive verb शक्, "to be able," and its derivatives; thus, पाशो न छेत्तुं शक्यते, "the snare cannot be cut"; न शक्याः समाधातुं ते दोषाः, "those evils cannot be remedied." The following are other instances: मण्डपः कारयितुम् आरब्धः, "the shed was begun to be built"; राज्ये अभिषेक्तुं भवान् निरूपितः, "your honour has been selected to be inaugurated to the kingdom"; अर्हति कर्तुं, "it deserves to be done" (Naishadiya, 5. 112.); कर्तुम् अनुचितं, "improper to be done" (cf. *factu indignum* and *ποιεῖν αἰσχρόν*).

b. The root अर्ह्, "to deserve," when used in combination with an infinitive, is usually equivalent to an entreaty or respectful imperative; as, धर्मान् नो वक्तुम् अर्हसि, "deign (or simply 'be pleased') to tell us our duties." It sometimes has the force of the Latin *debet;* as, न मादृशी त्वाम् अभिभाषितुम् अर्हति, "such a person as I ought not to address you"; न एनं शोचितुम् अर्हसि, "you ought not to bewail him."

c. The infinitive is sometimes joined with the noun काम, "desire," to form a kind of compound adjective, expressive of the "wish to do any thing," and the final *m* of the infinitive is then rejected; thus, द्रष्टुकामः, -मा, -मं, "desirous of seeing"; जेतुकामः, -मा, -मं, "wishing to conquer."

USE AND CONNEXION OF THE TENSES.

201. **PRESENT TENSE.**—This tense, besides its proper use, is frequently used for the future; as, क्व गच्छामि, "whither shall I go?" कदा त्वां पश्यामि, "when shall I see thee?"

a. In narration it is commonly used for the past tense; as, स भूमिं स्पृष्ट्वा कर्णौ स्पृशति ब्रूते च, "he, having touched the ground, touches his ears and says."

b. It may denote habitual or repeated action; as, मृगः प्रत्यहं तत्र गत्वा शस्यं खादति, "the deer going there every day was in the habit of eating the corn"; यदा स मूषिकशब्दं शृणोति तदा बिडालं संवर्द्धयति, "whenever he heard the noise of the mouse then he would feed the cat."

c. It is usually found after यावत्; as, यावन् मे दन्ता न त्रुट्यन्ति तावत् तव पाशं छिनद्मि, "as long as my teeth do not break, so long will I gnaw asunder your fetters." (Cf. the use of *dum*).

d. The present tense of the root आस्, "to sit," "remain," is used with the present participle of another verb to denote continuous or simultaneous action; as, पशूनां वधं कुर्वन् आस्ते, "he keeps making a slaughter of the beasts"; मम पश्चाद् आगच्छन् आस्ते, "he is in the act of coming after me."

e. The particle स्म, when used with the present, gives it the force of a perfect; as, प्रविशन्ति स्म पुरीं, "they entered the city."

202. FIRST PRETERITE.—Although this tense properly has reference to past incomplete action, and has been so rendered in the examples given at pp. 101—123., yet the student must guard against supposing that this is its usual force. It is most commonly used to denote indefinite past time, without any necessary connexion with another action; as, अर्थं महीतुं यत्नम् अकरवं, "I made an effort to collect wealth," not necessarily, "I was making."

203. POTENTIAL.—The name of this tense is no guide to its numerous uses. Perhaps its most common force is that of fitness in phrases, where in Latin we should expect to find *oportet* with the infinitive; as, आगतं भयं वीक्ष्य नरः कुर्याद् यथोचितं, "having beheld danger actually present, a man should act in a becoming manner."

a. It is also employed, as might be expected, in indefinite general expressions; as, यस्य यो भावः स्यात्, "whatever may be the disposition of any one"; यदा राजा स्वयं न कुर्यात् कार्यदर्शनं, "when the king may not himself make investigation of the case"; अप्राप्तकालवचनं ब्रुवन् प्राप्नुयाद् अपमानं, "by uttering unseasonable words one may meet with dishonour."

b. Especially in conditional sentences; as, यदि राजा दण्डं न प्रणयेत् स्वाम्यं कस्मिंश्चिन् न स्यात् सर्वसेतवश्च भिद्येरन्, "if the king were not to inflict punishment, ownership would remain with nobody, and all barriers would be broken down." Sometimes the conjunction is omitted; as, न भवेत्, "should it not be so"; न स्यात् पराधीनः, "were he not subject to another."

c. The potential often occurs as a softened imperative, this language, in common with others in the East, being averse to the more abrupt form; thus, गच्छेः, "do thou go," for गच्छ; and खादेत् फलानि, "let him eat fruits," for खादतु.

204. IMPERATIVE.—This tense yields the usual force of "command" or "entreaty"; as, आश्वसिहि, "take courage"; माम् अनुस्मर, "remember me." मा and not न must be used in prohibition; as, अनृतं मा ब्रूहि, "do not tell a falsehood." The first person is used to express necessity, see example, r. 172.

a. It is sometimes employed in conditional phrases to express contingency; as, अनुजानीहि मां गच्छामि, "permit me (and) I will go," *i.e.* "if you will permit me, I will go"; आज्ञापय हन्मि दुष्टजनं, "if you command me I will kill the villain"; अभयवाचं मे यच्छ गच्छामि, "if you give me a promise of security I will go."

205. SECOND PRETERITE.—As observed at p. 57., this tense is properly used to express an action done at some definite period of past time; as, कौशल्यादयो नृपतिं दशरथं चक्रन्दुः, "Kaushalyā and the others bewailed king Dasharatha." It is frequently, however, employed indeterminately.

206. FIRST FUTURE.—This tense expresses definite futurity; as, तासु दिक्षु कामस्य फलं लब्धासि, "in those regions thou shalt obtain the fruit of thy desire"; but is rarely found.

207. SECOND FUTURE.—This tense, although properly indefinite, is employed to express all degrees and kinds of futurity, immediate or remote, definite or indefinite; as, स्वादु पयः पास्यसि, "thou shalt drink sweet water"; तत्र अवश्यं पत्नीं द्रक्ष्यति, "there certainly he will see his wife."

a. It is sometimes used for the imperative; as, यद् देयं तद् दास्यसि, "whatever is to be given that you will give" (do thou give).

208. THIRD PRETERITE.—This tense properly expresses time indefinitely past; as, अभून् नृपः, "there lived (in former times) a king." It is not, however, often used as a past tense by earlier writers, but is frequently employed to supply the place of the imperative, after the prohibitive particle मा or मास्म, the augment being omitted; as, मा कृथाः, "do not make"; मा त्याक्षीः समयं, "do not lose the opportunity"; मास्म अनृतं वादीः, "do not tell an untruth"; मा क्रुधः, "do not be angry"; मा शुचः, "do not grieve"; मा हिंसीः, "do not injure."

209. BENEDICTIVE.—Only one example of this tense occurs in the Hitopadesha: नित्यं भूयात् सकलसुखवसतिः, "may he constantly be the abode of all happiness." It is only used in pronouncing benedictions.

210. CONDITIONAL.—This tense is even less frequent than the last. It is used in conditional propositions, as illustrated by the following example from Manu: यदि राजा दण्डं न प्रणयेत् तदा शूले मत्स्यान् इव अपक्ष्यन् दुर्बलान् बलवत्तराः, "if the king were not to inflict punishment, then the stronger would roast the weak like fish on a spit"; or, according to the Scholiast, हिंसाम् अकरिष्यन्, "would cause injury."

SYNTAX OF PARTICIPLES.

211. Participles govern the cases of the verbs whence they are derived; as, व्याधं पश्यन्, "seeing the fowler"; अरण्ये चरन्, "walking in the forest"; शब्दम् आकर्ण्य, "having heard a noise"; पानीयम् अपीत्वा गतः, "he went away without drinking water."

Passive Past Participle.

212. The syntax of this most useful participle has been explained at p. 137. r. 125. and r. 199. When used actively it may often govern the accusative case; as, वृक्षम् आरूढः, "he ascended the tree"; वर्त्म तीर्णः, "having crossed the road"; अहं नगरीम् अनुप्राप्तः, "I reached the city." But its active use is restricted to neuter verbs. The following are other examples; पक्षिण उत्पतिताः, "the birds flew away"; व्याधो निवृत्तः, "the fowler returned"; स प्रसुप्तः, "he fell asleep."

Active Past Participle.

213. This participle is commonly used for a perfect tense active, and may govern the case of the verb; as, सर्वं श्रुतवान्, "he heard everything"; पत्नी पतिम् आलिङ्गितवती, "the wife embraced her husband"; राज्ञो हस्ते फलं दत्तवान्, "he gave the fruit into the hand of the king."

Indeclinable Past Participles.

214. The importance of these participles has been noticed, p. 143. They occur, in narration, more commonly than any other, and are almost invariably used for the past tense, as united with a copulative conjunction; thus, तद् आकर्ण्य निश्चितम् एष अयं कुक्कुर इति मत्वा छागं

त्यक्त्वा स्नात्वा स्वगृहं ययौ, "having heard this, having thought to himself 'this is certainly a dog,' having abandoned the goat, having bathed, he went to his own house." In all these cases we should use in English the past tense with a conjunction; thus, "When he had heard this, he thought to himself that it must certainly be a dog. He then abandoned the goat, and when he had bathed, went to his own house." It is evident from this example that the indeclinable participles often stand in the place of a pluperfect tense, a tense which does not really exist in Sanscrit.

a. But although they always refer to something past, it should be observed that they may frequently be rendered in English by the present participle, as in the fifth sentence of the story at r. 220.

b. Another though less frequent use of them is as gerunds in *do;* thus, नराः शास्त्राण्य् अधीत्य* भवन्ति पण्डिताः, "men become wise *by* reading the Shāstras"; भार्य्या अप्य् अकार्य्यशतं कृत्वा भर्त्तव्या, "a wife is to be supported even by doing a hundred wrong things"; किं पौरुषं हत्वा सुप्तं, "what bravery is there *in* killing a sleeping man?"

c. Prof. Bopp considers the termination of this participle (त्वा) to be the instrumental case of the same affix of which the infinitive termination (*um*) is the accusative. Whether this be so or not, there can be little doubt that the indeclinable participle bears about it much of the character of an instrumental case. And the proof ot this is, that it is constantly found in grammatical connexion with the agent in this case; thus, सर्व्वैः पशुभिर् मिलित्वा सिंहो विज्ञप्तः, "by all the beasts having met together the lion was informed"; सर्व्वैर् जालम् आदाय उड्डीयतां, "by all having taken up the net let it be flown away."

Future Passive Participles.

215. The usual sense yielded by this participle is that of "fitness" or "necessity"; and the usual construction required is, that the agent on whom the duty or necessity rests, be in the instrumental case, and the participle agree with the object; as, त्वया प्रवृत्तिर् न विधेया, "by you the attempt is not to be made." Sometimes, however, the agent is the genitive case. Cf. p. 196. note.

---

* As the Latin gerund is connected with the future participle in *dus*, so the Sanscrit indeclinable participle in *ya* is connected with the future passive participle in *ya*. This is noticed by Bopp.

a. If the verb govern two accusatives, one may be retained after the participle; as, नयनसलिलं त्वया शान्तिं नेयं, "the tear of the eye is to be brought to assuagement by thee."

b. Occasionally the neuter of this participle is used impersonally, in which case it does not agree with the object, but may govern it in the manner of the verb; thus, मया ग्रामं गन्तव्यं, "it is to be gone by me to the village," for मया ग्रामो गन्तव्यः. So also त्वया सभां प्रवेष्टव्यं, "by you it is to be entered into the assembly."

c. The neuter भवितव्यं (from भू) is thus impersonally used, and in accordance with r. 190. requires the instrumental after it, as well as before; thus, केनापि कारणेन भवितव्यं, "by something it is to be become the cause," *i.e.* "there must be some cause"; स्वामिना सविशेषेण भवितव्यं, "a ruler ought to be possessed of discrimination"; मया तव अनुचरेण भवितव्यं, "I must become your companion."

d. It is not uncommon to find this participle standing merely in the place of a future tense, no propriety or obligation being implied; as, नूनम् अनेन लुब्धकेन मृगमांसार्थिना गन्तव्यं, "in all probability this hunter will go in quest of the deer's flesh"; where गन्तव्यं is used impersonally. त्वां दृष्ट्वा लोकैः किञ्चिद् वक्तव्यं, "when the people see you they will utter some exclamation." See also the eleventh sentence of the story, r. 220.

e. It would appear that the neuter of this participle is sometimes used infinitively, as expressive merely of the indeterminate action of the verb, in the manner of a future infinitive, without implying necessity or fitness. In such cases इति is added; thus, वञ्चयितव्यम् इति, "the being about to deceive"; मर्तव्यम् इति, "the being about to die."

SYNTAX OF ADVERBS, CONJUNCTIONS, AND INTERJECTIONS.

216. The following examples illustrate the construction of the adverbs enumerated at p. 156., or elsewhere in Chapter VIII. न दण्डाद् ऋते शक्यः कर्तुं पापविनिग्रहः, "the restraint of crime cannot be made without punishment"; शतं जन्मानि यावत्, "for a hundred births"; सर्पविवरं यावत्, "up to the serpent's hole"; पुत्रेण सह, "along with his son"; हेतुं विना, "without cause"; अपराधेन विना, "without fault"; विवराद् बहिर् निःसृत्य, "creeping out of the hole"; अवलोकनक्षणात् प्रभृति, "from the moment of seeing (him)"; ततः प्रभृति, "from that time forward"; धनस्य अर्थे, "for the sake of wealth" (cf. r. 171. *c.*); तस्याः कृते, "for her sake." उपरि, with the genitive, occurs rather frequently, and with some latitude of meaning; thus, सिंहस् तस्य उपरि पपात, "the lion fell upon him"; मम उपरि

विकारिताः, "changed in his feelings towards me"; तव उपरि असदृशव्यवहारी, "not behaving properly towards thee"; पुत्रस्य उपरि क्रुद्धः, "angry with his son." वृक्षस्य अधस्तात्, "beneath the tree"; राज्ञः समीपं, "near the king"; पितुः सकाशाद् धनम् आददाति, "he receives money from his father"; मांसं शुनोऽग्रे निक्षिप्तं, "flesh thrown before the dog"; मम समक्षं, "in my presence"; अस्माकं पश्चात्, "after us." साक्षात् may take an instrumental; as, अन्यैः साक्षात्, "before others." प्राक् may govern an ablative; as, प्राग् उपनयनाद् वेदं नोच्चारयेत्, "before investiture let him not utter the Veda": or an accusative; as, प्राग् द्वादश समाः, "before twelve years are over."

a. अलं, "enough," is used with the instrumental, with the force of a prohibitive particle; as, अलं शङ्कया, "away with fear," "do not fear."

b. मात्रं, "even," "merely," when compounded with another word is declinable; as, उत्तरमात्रं न ददाति, "he does not even give an answer"; न शब्दमात्राद् भेतव्यं, "one ought not to be afraid of mere noise."

c. तथा and यथा, when used as correlatives, are equivalent to the English *so that*, and the Latin *ita ut;* thus, यथा स्वामी जागर्त्ति तथा मया कर्त्तव्यं, "I must so act that my master awake," *i.e.* "I must do something to make my master awake." So also त्वं न जानासि यथा गृहरक्षां करोमि, "do not you know that I keep watch in the house?"

d. यत् is also used for "*that*"; as, अयं नूतनो न्यायो यद् अरातिं हत्वा सन्तापः क्रियते, "this is a new doctrine, that having killed an enemy remorse should be felt."

e. किं, "why?" may often be regarded as a note of interrogation which is not to be translated, but affects only the tone of voice in which a sentence is uttered; as, जातिमात्रेण किं कश्चित् पूज्यते, "is any one honoured for mere birth?"

It sometimes has the force of "whether?" as, ज्ञायतां किम् उपयुक्त एतावद् वर्त्तनं गृह्णाति अनुपयुक्तो वा, "let it be ascertained whether he is worthy to receive so large a salary, or whether he is unworthy"; मन्त्री वेत्ति किं गुणयुक्तो राजा न वा, "the minister knows whether the king is meritorious or not."

217. The conjunctions यदि and चेत्, "if," are commonly used with the indicative; as, यदि जीवति भद्राणि पश्यति, "if he live he will behold prosperity"; यदि मया प्रयोजनम् अस्ति, "if there is need of me"; तृष्णा चेत् परित्यक्ता को दरिद्रः, "if avarice were abandoned who would be poor?"

218. The interjections धिक् and हा require the accusative; as, धिक् पापिष्ठं, "woe to the wretch!" and the vocative interjections the vocative case; as, भोः पान्थ, "O traveller!"

ON THE USE OF इति WITH THE *RECTA ORATIO.*

219. All the languages of the East are averse to the use of the *obliqua oratio.* In Sanscrit it is never admitted, and when any one relates the words or describes the sentiments or thoughts of another, the relator invariably represents him as speaking the actual words in his own person. In such cases the particle इति (properly meaning "so," "thus,") is often placed after the words quoted, and may be regarded as serving the purpose of inverted commas; thus, शिष्या ऊचुः कृत.कृत्या वयम् इति, the pupils said, "we have accomplished our object," not according to the English or Latin idiom, "the pupils said *that they had* accomplished their object." So also कलहकारी इति ब्रूते भर्त्ता, your husband calls you "quarrelsome," where कलहकारी is in the nominative case, as being the actual word supposed to be spoken by the husband himself in his own person. So again युष्मान् विश्वास.भूमय इति सर्व्वे पक्षिणो मम अग्रे प्रस्तुवन्ति, all the birds praise you in my presence, saying, "he is an object of confidence," where the particle इति is equivalent to "saying," and the word विश्वास.भूमयः is not. in the accusative, to agree with युष्मान्, as might be expected, but in the nominative, as being the actual word supposed to be uttered by the birds in their own persons. In some cases, however, the accusative is retained before इति; as, in the following example from Manu: अज्ञं बालम् इत्य् आहुः, they call an ignorant man "child." But in the latter part of the same line it passes into a nominative; as, पितेत्य् एव तु मन्त्रदं, but (they call) a teacher of scripture "father." II. 153.

a. The use of इति is by no means restricted to the quotation of the words spoken by another. It often has reference merely to what is passing in the mind either of another person or of one's self. When so employed, it is usually joined with the indeclinable participle, or of some other part of a verb, signifying, "to think," "suppose," &c., and may be translated by the English conjunction *that,* to which, in fact, it may be regarded as equivalent; thus, मर्कटो घण्टां वादयति इति परिज्ञाय, "having ascertained *that* it is a monkey who rings the bell"; पुनर् अर्थ.वृद्धिः करणीया इति मतिर् बभूव, "his idea was *that* an increase of wealth ought again to be made"; धन्यो ऽहं यस्य एतादृशी भार्य्या इति मनसि निधाय, "reflecting in his mind *that* I am happy in possessing such a wife." The accusative is also retained before इति in this sense; as, मृतम् इति मत्वा, "thinking that he was dead." In all these examples the use of इति indicates that a quotation is made of the thoughts of the person at the time when the event took place.

b. Not unfrequently the participle "thinking," "supposing," &c. is omitted altogether, and इति itself involves the sense of such a participle; as, बालोऽपि न अवमन्तव्यो मनुष्य इति भूमिपः, "a king even though a child is not to be despised, *saying to one's self* he is a mortal"; सौहार्दाद् वा विधुर इति वा मय्य् अनुक्रोशात्, "either through affection or through compassion towards me, *saying to yourself* what a wretched man he is."

EXERCISES IN TRANSLATION AND PARSING.

220. The following two stories, taken from the 4th Book of the Hitopadesha, will conclude the chapter on Syntax. A literal translation is given to both stories, and to the first a grammatical analysis is subjoined. All the rules of combination are observed, but the words are separated from each other, contrary to the usual practice of the Hindūs. In the two cases where such separation is impossible, viz. where a final and initial vowel blend together into one sound, and where crude words are joined with others to form compounds, a dot placed underneath marks the division:

1. अस्ति गौतमस्य मुनेस् तपो.वने महा.तपा नाम मुनिः, "There is in the sacred grove of the sage Gautama a holy-sage named Mahātapāh (Great-devotion)."

2. तेना.श्रम.सन्निधाने मूषिक.शावकः काकमुखाद् भ्रष्टो दृष्टः, "By him, in the neighbourhood of his hermitage, a young mouse, fallen from the beak of a crow, was seen."

3. ततो दया.युक्तेन तेन मुनिना नीवार.कणैः संवर्द्धितः, "Then by that sage, touched with compassion, with grains of wild rice it was reared."

4. तदनन्तरं मूषिकं खादितुम् अनुधावन् विडालो मुनिना दृष्टः, "Soon after this, a cat was observed by the sage running after the mouse to devour it."

5. तं मूषिकं भीतम् आलोक्य तपःप्रभावात् तेन मुनिना मूषिको बलिष्ठो विडालः कृतः, "Perceiving the mouse terrified, by that sage, through the efficacy of his devotion, the mouse was changed into a very strong cat."

6. स विडालः कुक्कुराद् विभेति । ततः कुक्कुरः कृतः । कुक्कुरस्य व्याघ्रान् महद् भयं । तदनन्तरं स व्याघ्रः कृतः, "The cat fears the dog. Upon that it was changed into a dog. Great is the dread of the dog for a tiger; then it was transformed into a tiger."

7. अथ व्याघ्रम् अपि मूषिकनिर्विशेषं पश्यति मुनिः, "Now the sage regards even the tiger as not differing at all from the mouse."

8. अतः सर्वे तत्रस्था जनास् तं व्याघ्रं दृष्ट्वा वदन्ति, "Then all the persons residing in the neighbourhood, seeing the tiger, say."

9. अनेन मुनिना मूषिकोऽयं व्याघ्रतां नीतः, 'By this holy-sage this mouse has been brought to the condition of a tiger,'

10. एतच् छ्रुत्वा स व्याघ्रः सव्यथोऽचिन्तयत्, "The tiger overhearing this, being uneasy, reflected."

11. यावद् अनेन मुनिना जीवितव्यं तावद् इदं मम स्वरूपाख्यानम् अकीर्त्तिकरं न पलायिष्यते, "As long as it shall be lived by this sage, so long this disgraceful story of my original condition will not die away."

12. इति समालोच्य मुनिं हन्तुं समुद्यतः, "Thus reflecting he prepared (was about) to kill the sage."

13. मुनिस् तस्य चिकीर्षितं ज्ञात्वा पुनर् मूषिको भव इत्य् उक्त्वा मूषिक एव कृतः, "The sage discovering his intention, saying, 'again become a mouse,' he was reduced to (his former state of) a mouse."

The student will observe in this story four peculiarities: 1st, the simplicity of the style; 2dly, the prevalence of compound words; 3dly, the scarcity of verbs; 4thly, the prevalence of participles in lieu of verbs.

First sentence.—*Asti*, "there is," 3d sing. pres. of the root *as*, 2d conj., p. 101. *Gautamasya*, "of Gautama," noun of the first class, masc. gend. gen. case (p. 31.). *Munes*, "of the sage," noun of the second class, masc. gend. gen. case (p. 33.). Visargah changed to *s* by r. 25. *a*. p. 14. *Tapovane*, "in the sacred grove," or "grove of penance," genitively dependent compound, p. 161., the first member of the compound formed by the crude noun *tapas*, "penance," *as* being changed to *o* by r. 29.; the last member, by the loc. case of *vana*, "grove," noun of the first class, neut. (p. 32.). *Mahātapā*, "great devotion," relative form of descriptive compound, p. 168., the first member formed by the crude adjective *mahā* (substituted for *mahat*), "great"; the last member, by the nom. case of *tapas*, "devotion," noun of the seventh class, neut. (pp. 43. 44.), Visargah being dropped by r. 28. *b*. p. 14. *Nāma*, "by name," an adverb, p. 151. *a*. *Munih*, "a sage," noun of the second class, masc., nom. case. Vis. remains by r. 24. *b*.

Second sentence.—*Tena*, "by him," instr. case of the pronoun *tat*, p. 51. r. 77. *Āshramasannidhāne*, "in the neighbourhood of his hermitage," genitively dependent compound, p. 161., the first member formed by the crude noun *āshrama*, "hermitage"; the last member by the loc. case of *sannidhāna*, "neighbourhood," noun of the first class, neut. (p. 32.). The initial *ā* of this word blends with the final of *tena* into *ā*, by r. 4. p. 7. *Mūṣhikashāvakah*, "a young mouse," or "the young of a mouse," genitively dependent compound, p. 161., the first member formed by the crude noun *mūṣhika*, "a mouse"; the last, by the nom. case of *shāvaka*, "the young of any animal," noun of the first class (p. 31.). Vis. remains by r. 24. *a*. *Kākamukhād*, "from the beak (or mouth) of a crow," genitively dependent compound, p. 161.; the first member, formed by the crude noun *kāka*, "a crow"; the last, by the abl. case of *mukha*, "mouth," noun of the first class, neut. (p. 32.), *t* being changed to *d* by r. 14. p. 11. *Braṣhṭo*, "fallen," nom. case, sing. masc. of the pass. past part. of the root *bhransh*, p. 140. *n.*; *ah* changed to *o* by r. 26. *a*. *Dṛiṣhṭah*, "seen," nom. case, sing. masc. of the pass. past part. of the root *dṛish* (दृश्), p. 130. *i*. Vis. remains by r. 24. *b*.

Third sentence.—*Tato*, "then," adv. p. 152. *a.*; *as* changed to *o* by r. 29. and 26. *a*. *Dayāyuktena*, "touched with compassion," instrumentally dependent compound, p. 160.; the first member formed by the crude noun *dayā*, "compassion"; the last, by the instr. case of *yukta*, "endowed with," pass. past part. of the root *yuj*, p. 139. *i*. *Tena*, see second sentence. *Muninā*, "by the sage," noun of the second class, masc. gend. instr. case (p. 33.). *Nīvārakaṇaih*, "with grains of wild rice," genitively dependent compound, p. 161.; the first member formed by the crude noun *nīvāra*, "wild rice"; the second, by the instr. plur. of *kaṇa*, noun of the first class, masc. Vis. remains by r. 24. *a*. *Sanvarddhitah*, "reared," nom. case, sing. of the pass. past part. of the causal form of the root *vṛidh*, p. 141. Vis. remains by r. 24. *b*.

Fourth sentence.—*Tadanantaram*, "soon after this," compound adverb, the first member formed with the pronoun *tat*, "this"; the second by the adverb *anantaram*, "after." *Mūṣhikam*, noun of the first class, masc. gend., acc. case (p. 31.). *Khāditum*, "to eat," infinitive mood of the root *khād*, p. 85. r. 106. and r. 200. *Anudhāvan*, "pursuing after," "running after," nom. case, sing. masc. of the pres. part. paras. of the root *dhāv*, "to run," with the preposition *anu*, "after," p. 136. *b*. *Viḍālo*, "a cat," noun of the first class, masc. (p. 31.), nom. case; *ah* changed to *o* by r. 26. *a*. *Muninā*, see third sentence. *Dṛiṣhṭah*, see second sentence.

Fifth sentence.—*Tam*, acc. case of the pronoun *tat* (p. 51.), used as a definite article, p. 28. r. 46. *Mūṣhikam*, see fourth sentence. *Bhītam*, "terrified," acc. case, sing. masc. of the pass. past part. of the root *bhī*, p. 138. *b*. *Ālokya*, "perceiving," indeclinable part. of the root *lok*, with the prep. *ā*, p. 145. *f.* *Tapahprabhāvāt*, "through the efficacy of his devotion" (p. 184. *c.*), genitively dependent compound, p. 161.; the first member formed by the crude noun *tapas*, "devotion," *s* being changed to Visargah, by r. 29. and 24. *a.*; the second, by the abl. case of *prabhāva*, noun of the first class, masc. (p. 31.). *Tena*, see second sentence. *Muninā*, see third sentence. *Mūshiko*, nom. case, *ah* changed to *o* by r. 26. *a.* *Balishṭho*, "very strong," nom. case, masc. of the superlative form of the adj. *balin*, "strong" (see p. 47.), *ah* changed to *o* by r. 26. *a.* *Vidālah*, see fourth sentence. Vis. remains by r. 24. *a.* *Kṛitah*, "changed," "made," nom. case, sing. of the pass. past part. of the root *kṛi*, p. 138. *b.* Vis. remains by r. 24. *b.*

Sixth sentence.—*Sa*, nom. case of the pronoun *tat* (p. 51.), used as a definite article, p. 28. r. 46. Vis. dropped, by note †, p. 14. *Vidālah*, see fourth sentence. *Kukkurād*, "the dog," noun of the first class, masc. (p. 31.), abl. case after a verb of fearing (p. 193. *a.*), *t* changed to *d* by r. 14. *Bibheti*, "fears," 3d sing. pres. tense of the root *bhī*, 3d conj. p. 119. *Tatah*, "upon that," adv. p. 152. *a.*; *as* changed to *ah*, by r. 29. and 24. *a.* *Kukkurah*, "the dog," nom. case (p. 31.). Vis. remains by r. 24. *a.* *Kṛitah*, see fifth sentence. *Kukkurasya*, "of the dog," gen. case (p. 31.). *Vyāghrān*, "for the tiger," noun of the first class, masc. (p. 31.), abl. case, after a noun of "fear" (p. 184. *g.*), *t* changed to *n* by r. 15. *Mahad*, "great," noun adj. of the fifth class, r. 63. nom. case, sing. neut. *t* changed to *d* by r. 14. *Bhayam*, "fear," noun of the first class, neut. (p. 32.), nom. case. *Tadanantaram*, see fourth sentence. *Vyāghrah*, nom. case. Vis. remains by r. 24. *a.* *Kṛitah*, see fifth sentence.

Seventh sentence.—*Atha*, "now," inceptive particle, p. 154. *b.* *Vyāghram*, acc. case. *Api*, "even," adv. *Mūshikanirvisheṣham*, "as not differing at all from the mouse," compound adverb; the first member formed by the crude noun *mūshika*; the second by the neut. form of the substantive *visheṣha*, "difference," with *nir* prefixed, see p. 177. *b.* *Pashyati*, 3d sing. pres. tense of the root *drish*, 1st conj. p. 107. *Munih*, see first sentence.

Eighth sentence.—*Atah*, "then," adv. p. 152. *a.* *Sarve*, "all," pronominal adj. nom. case, plur. masc. p. 54. r. 87. *Tatrasthā*, "residing in the neighbourhood," anomalous compound, in its character resembling a locatively dependent; the first member being formed by the adverb *tatra* (p. 152. *b.*), "there," or "in that place"; the second by the nom. plur. masc. of the participial noun of agency of the root *sthā*, "to remain," p. 149. 1. Vis. dropped by r. 28. *b.* *Janās*, "persons," noun of the first class, masc. gend. (p. 31.) nom. case, plur. Vis. changed to *s* by r. 25. *a.* *Tam*, acc. case of the pronoun *tat* (p. 51.), used as a definite article. *Vyāghram*, "tiger," noun of the first class, masc. gend. (p. 31.) acc. case. *Drishṭwā*, "having seen," indeclinable past participle of the root *drish* (दृश्), p. 143. *a.* *Vadanti*, "they say," 3d plur. pres. of the root *vad*, 1st conj.

Ninth sentence.—*Anena*, "by this," instr. case of the demonstrative pronoun *ayam*, p. 52. *Muninā*, see third sentence. *Mūshiko*, nom. case, *ah* changed to *o* by r. 26. *b.* *Ayam*, "this," nom. case of the demonstrative pron., p. 52. The initial *a* cut off by r. 26. *b.* *Vyāghratām*, "the condition of a tiger," fem. abstract noun of the first class (p. 31.), acc. case, formed from the substantive *vyāghra*, "a tiger," by the affix *tā*, p. 24. xiv. *Nītah*, "brought," nom. case, sing. masc. of the pass. part. of the root *nī*, p. 138. *b.*

Tenth sentence.—*Etach*, "this," acc. case, neut. of the demonstrative pron. *etat*, p. 52. r. 79., *t* being changed to *ch* by r. 17. *Chhrutwā*, "overhearing," indeclinable participle of the root *shru* (श्रु), p. 143. *a.* श्रुत्वा becomes छ्रुत्वा by r. 17. *Vyāghrah*, nom. case. Vis. remains by r. 24. *a.* *Savyatho*, "uneasy," relative compound, formed by prefixing the preposition *saha* to the fem. substantive *vyathā*, p. 169. r. 161. See also p. 32. †, *ah* changed to *o* by r. 26. *b.* *Achintayat*, "reflected," 3d sing. 1st pret. of the root *chint*, 10th conj. p. 87. *e;* the initial *a* cut off by r. 26. *b.*

Eleventh Sentence.—*Yāvad*, "as long as," adv. p. 151. *a.*, *t* changed to *d* by r. 14. *Anena*, see ninth sentence. *Jīvitavyam*, "to be lived," nom. case, neut. of the fut. pass. part. of the root *jīv*, p. 146. *a.* See also r. 215. *c. d.* *Tāvat*, "so long," adv. correlative to *yāvat*, p. 151. *a.* *Idam*, "this," nom. case, neut. of the demonstrative pron. *ayam*, p. 52. *Mama*, "of me," gen. case of the pronoun *aham*, "I," p. 50. *Swarūpākhyānam*, "story of my original condition," genitively dependent compound, p. 161.; the first member formed by the crude noun *swarūpa*, "natural form" (cf. r. 83.); the second by the nom. case of *ākhyāna*, noun of the first class, neuter, *m* retained by r. 23. *Akīrtikaram*, "disgraceful," accusatively dependent compound; the first member formed by the crude noun *akīrti*, "disgrace"; the second by the nom. case, neut. of the participial noun of agency *kara*, p. 149. 1. *Na*, "not," adv. p. 153. *a.* *Palāyishyate*, "will die away," 3d sing. 2d fut. ātm. of the compound verb *palāy*, formed by combining the root *i* with the prep. *parā*, p. 174.

Twelfth Sentence.—*Iti*, "thus," adv. p. 153. *e.* See also r. 219. *a.* *Samālochya*, "reflecting," indeclinable part. of the compound verb *samāloch* (p. 145. *f.*), formed by combining the root *loch* with the prepositions *sam* and *ā*, pp. 174. 175.

Munim, acc. case. *Hantum*, "to kill," infinitive mood of the root *han*, pp. 85. and 115. and r. 200. *Samudyatah*, "prepared," nom. case, sing. masc. of the pass. past part. of the compound verb *samudyam* (p. 140. *o.*), formed by combining the root *yam* with the prepositions *sam* and *ut*.

Thirteenth sentence.—*Munis*, nom. case. Vis. changed to *s* by r. 25. *a.* *Tasya*, "of him," gen. case of the pron. *tat*, p. 51. *Chikīrshitam*, "intention," acc. case, neut. of the pass. past part. of the desiderative base of the root *kri*, "to do" (p. 141. *s.*), used as a substantive. *Gyātwā*, or *Jnātwā*, "discovering," indecl. part. of the root *jnā*, p. 143. *a.* *Punar*, "again," adv. p. 153. *e.*, *r* remains by r. 32. *Mūshiko*, nom. case, *ah* changed to *o* by r. 26. *a.* *Bhava*, "become," 2d sing. imperat. of the root *bhū*, p. 104. *Ity* answers to inverted commas, see r. 219., the final *i* changed to *y* by r. 7. *Uktwā*, "saying," indecl. part. of the root *vach*, p. 143. *a.* *Mūshika*, nom. case. Vis. dropped by r. 28. *a.* *Eva*, "indeed," adv. r. 134.

STORY OF THE BRAHMAN AND HIS WEASEL.

अस्त्य्[1] उज्जयिन्यां[2] माधवो[3] नाम ब्राह्मणः । तस्य ब्राह्मणी[4] प्रसूता[5] । सा[6] बालापत्यस्य[7] रक्षार्थं[8] ब्राह्मणम् अवस्थाप्य[9] स्नातुं[10] गता[11] । अथ ब्राह्मणस्य कृते[12] राज्ञः[13] पार्वणश्राद्धं[14] दातुम्[15] आह्वानम् आगतं । तच्[16] छ्रुत्वा[17] ब्राह्मणः सहजदारिद्राद्[18] अचिन्तयत्[19] । यदि सत्वरं[20] न गच्छामि[21] तदाऽन्यः[22] कश्चिच्[23] छ्राद्धं ग्रहीष्यति[24] । किन्तु शिशोर्[25] अत्र रक्षकः कोऽपि[26] नास्ति[27] तत्[28] किं करोमि[29] । यातु[30] । चिरकालपालितम्[31] इमं[32] पुत्रनिर्विशेषं[33] नकुलं बालकरक्षार्थं[34] व्यवस्थाप्य[35] गच्छामि । तथा कृत्वा[36] गतः । ततस्[37] तत्र नकुलेन बालकसमीपं[38] तूष्णीम् आगच्छन्[39] कृष्णसर्पो[40] व्यापादितः[41] खण्डितश्च[42] । ततोऽसौ[43] नकुलो ब्राह्मणम् आयान्तम्[44] अवलोक्य[45] रक्तविलिप्तमुखपादः[46] सत्वरम् उपागम्य[47] ब्राह्मणस्य चरणयोर्[49] लुलोठ[49] । ततोऽसौ ब्राह्मणस्[50] तं तथाविधं[51] दृष्ट्वा[52] मम पुत्रोऽनेन[53] भक्षित[54] इत्य्[55] अविचार्य्य[56] व्यापादितवान्[57] । अनन्तरं यावद् असाव्[58] उपसृत्य[59] पश्यति[60] तावद् बालकः सुस्थः स्वपिति[61] सर्पस्[62] तु व्यापादितस् तिष्ठति[63] । तत[64] उपकारकं[65] नकुलं निरूप्य[66] सन्तप्तचेताः[67] स परं विषादम् उपगतः

[1]) p. 101. the final changed to *y* by r. 7. [2]) loc. c. of *ujjayinī*, p. 31. [3]) *ah* changed to *o* by r. 26. *a.* [4]) p. 24. xv. [5]) pass. past part. of the root *sū*, with the preposition *pra*, p. 138. *b.* [6]) p. 51. [7]) r. 154. [8]) p. 177. *c.* [9]) p. 145. *i.* [10]) r. 106. and r. 200. [11]) r. 125. p. 140. *o.* and p. 180. *a.* [12]) p. 156. *e.* [13]) p. 41. [14]) p. 161. r. 147. [15]) p. 118. r. 200. [16]) p. 11. r. 17. [17]) p. 143. [18]) r. 154., *dāridra* is an abstract noun, formed according to p. 23. viii. [19]) 1st pret. of the root *chint*, 10th conj. p. 126. [20]) r. 171. *a.* [21]) p. 107. [22]) or तदान्यः, r. 4. [23]) r. 85. r. 17. [24]) p. 124. [25]) gen. case of *shishu*, p. 35. [26]) r. 85. [27]) r. 4. [28]) p. 151. *a.* [29]) p. 101. and r. 201. [30]) p. 112. [31]) anomalous dependent compound. According to r. 180. *a.* it may be regarded as accusatively dependent. [32]) p. 52. [33]) anomalous dependent compound. [34]) r. 171. *c.* [35]) indecl. part. of the causal form of the root *sthā*, with the prepositions *vi* and *ava*, p. 145. *i.* [36]) p. 143. *a.* [37]) Visargah changed to *s* by r. 25. *a.* [38]) p. 177. *c.* [39]) pres. part. of the root *gam*, p. 107. p. 136. with *ā* prefixed, p. 174. [40]) r. 154. [41]) p. 141. 2. root *pad*, with *vi* and *ā*. [42]) Vis. changed to *sh* by r. 25. *a.* [43]) The initial *a* cut off by r. 9. [44]) pres. part. of *yā*, with *ā*, r. 123. [45]) p. 145. *f.*

[46]) complex relative compound (p. 171. *b.*), the whole being the relative form of descriptive, involving a dependent and an aggregative. [47]) p. 145. *g.* root *gam*, with prep. *upa* and *ā*. [48]) loc. case, dual of *charaṇa*, p. 31., see p. 105. *c.* [49]) 2d pret. of root लुट्, p. 74. [50]) Vis. to *s* by r. 25. *a.* [51]) r. 171. *b.* [52]) p. 143. *a.* [53]) p. 52. [54]) p. 139. *h.* [55]) r. 210. *a.* the final changed to *y* by r. 7. [56]) p. 145. *i.* root *char*, with prep. *vi* and negative prefix *a.* [57]) p. 142. root *pad*, with *vi* and *ā*. [58]) r. 8. [59]) p. 144. *a.* [60]) p. 107. and p. 199. *c.* [61]) p. 70. *d.* [62]) Vis. to *s* by r. 25. *a.* [63]) p. 107. [64]) Vis. dropped by r. 28. *a.* [65]) r. 143. [66]) p. 145. *f.* root *rūp*, with *ni.* [67]) r. 159. *a.*

Translation.

There lives in Oujein,* a Brahman, named Mādhava. His wife bore him (a son). She having stationed the Brahman (her husband) to take charge of the young child, went to perform ablution. Meanwhile a message came from the king for the Brahman to perform the Pārvaṇa Shrāddha.† On hearing which the Brahman, from his natural neediness, thought to himself, "if I do not go quickly some other Brahman will take the Shrāddha. But there is none here (that I may leave) as a guardian to the child,—what then can I do? Come, having stationed this long-cherished weasel, dear to me as a son, in charge of the infant, I will go." Having so done, he went. Presently a black serpent silently approaching the child was killed by the weasel and torn in pieces. By and by the weasel seeing the Brahman returning, quickly running to meet him, his mouth and feet smeared with blood, rolled himself at the Brahman's feet. Then that Brahman seeing him in such a condition, hastily concluding that he had eaten the child, killed him. Afterwards no sooner did he come up than he beheld the infant slumbering safely and the black serpent lying dead. Then looking at his benefactor the weasel, and bitterly repenting (of his precipitation), he experienced exceeding grief.

---

* The oldest city in India.

† The Shrāddha is a funeral ceremony, consisting of oblations of water and fire to the gods and manes, and gifts to the officiating Brahmans, performed at various fixed periods, in behalf of a deceased parent or ancestor, to secure the happy condition of his soul. The Pārvaṇa is a particular form of Shrāddha, in behalf of *three* ancestors.

SELECTIONS

IN PROSE AND VERSE.

OBSERVE, that the greater number of the words in the following Selections will be found in the Vocabulary to Professor Johnson's edition of the Hitopadesha. And whenever a word does not occur in that Vocabulary, it is given at the foot of the page.

The words of the text have been printed separately from each other, as it is imagined that the permutation of final and initial letters is of itself a difficulty, unknown in other languages, sufficient to retard the progress of the beginner in his first effort at translation. It seems, therefore, wholly unreasonable and unnecessary to increase this difficulty by an useless conformity to the practice of the natives, in joining together all the words in a sentence, until the student has attained a certain degree of proficiency. When, however, a final and initial vowel blend into one sound, and when crude nouns are associated to form compounds, separation is impossible, and in such cases a dot placed underneath marks the division.

The substance of the following simple story of the Brahman Vedagarbha and his pupils, is taken from a little book, printed in Calcutta, called the Sanskṛitamālā.

॥ अथ वेदगर्भोपाख्यानं ॥

गङ्गा.तटे[1] पूर्व्वं[2] वेदगर्भ.नामा[3] ब्राह्मण[4] आसीत्[5] ॥ स[6] च वेद.वेदान्त.वेदाङ्गादीनां[7] सर्व्वेषां[8] शास्त्राणां पार.दृश्वा[9] ॥ ततः[10] स[6] पाठ.शालां[11] कृत्वा[12] बहून्[13] विद्यार्थिनः[14] शास्त्राण्य्[15] अध्यापयत्[16]॥ अथ[17] समीप.ग्राम.वासिनो[18] विंशतिर्[19] विद्यार्थिनः[20] पाठशालां समागताः[21] ॥ तदा[22] वेदगर्भ उत्थाय[23] तेषां[24] जाति.वसति.नामानि[25] पृष्ट्वागमन.[26]प्रयोजनं[27] पृष्टवान्[28] ॥ ततस्[29] ते[24] प्रत्यूचुः[30] । भवान्[31] वेदाचार्य्यः[32] सर्व्व.विद्या.विशारद[33] इति[34] भवतः[31] पाण्डित्य.ख्यातिं[35] वयम्[36] अतिदूरे[37] श्रुत्वाऽन्य.[38]पाठशालात[39] इहायाताः[40][41] ॥

1) P. 161. r. 147. 2) p. 151. *a.* 3) r. 157. p. 42. note †. 4) Vis. dropped by r. 28. *a.* 5) p. 101. 6) p. 14. note †. 7) p. 167. *b.* p. 171. *c.* The Vedānta is the theological part of the Vedas contained in those chapters called Upanishads; the Vedāngas are the sciences subordinate to the Vedas; such as Grammar, Prosody, Astronomy, &c., see Manu II. 105. 8) p. 54. r. 87. 9) lit. "seeing to the opposite bank," *i.e.* "thoroughly acquainted with," r. 43. 1. 10) p. 152. *a.* Vis. remains by r. 29. and 24. *a.* 11) acc. case of पाठशाला, "a school," lit. "a reading-room," r. 147. 12) p. 143. *a.* 13) p. 35. r. 54. 14) acc. case pl. of विद्यार्थिन्, "a seeker of knowledge," "student," p. 43. r. 147. 15) acc. plur. neut. p. 32. *i* changed to *y* by r. 7. 16) p. 87. note *, and r. 192. *a.* 17) p. 154. *b.* 18) p. 149. *a.* p. 171. *b.* 19) p. 49. 20) nom. case pl. Vis. remains by r. 24. *a.* 21) p. 140. *o.* root *gam* with prep. *ā* (p. 174.) and *sam* (175). 22) p. 152. *d.* 23) p. 144. p. 174. 24) p. 51. 25) p. 163. *a.* 26) पृष्ट्वा, "having asked," p. 143. *a.* The final *ā* of this word blends with the initial *ā* of the next by r. 4. 27) आगमन, "arrival," प्रयोजन, "cause," r. 147. 28) "he asked," p. 142. *a.* 29) Vis. to *s* by r. 25. *a.* 30) p. 76. *d.* p. 175. 31) p. 54. r. 84. 32) "a teacher of the Vedas," r. 147. See Manu II. 140. 141. for the difference between an *āchārya* and an *upādhyāya.* 33) p. 171. *b.* Vis. dropped by r. 28. *a.* 34) r. 219. 35) पाण्डित्य, "learning" (p. 23. vii.), ख्याति, "fame" (p. 24. ii.) r. 147. 36) p. 50. 37) p. 152. *a.* 151. *d.* 38) p. 143. *a.* 39) "from another school," affix *tas*, p. 152. *a.* Vis. dropped by r. 28. *a.* 40) p. 153. *g.*, the final *a* blends with the initial *ā* of *āyātāh.* 41) p. 138. *b.* p. 174.

तदाचार्य्येणोक्तं[42] । भद्रं कृतं[43] भवद्भिर्[31] यद्[44] अहं[26] जानामि[45] तद् अहं युष्मान्[24] अध्यापयिष्यामि[46] । इति कथयित्वा[47] स तेषाम् उपवेशनार्थम्[48] आसनानि[49] दापितवान्[50] ॥ तेषु विद्यार्थिषु[51] सुखम्[52] उपविष्टेषु[53] वेदगर्भो विद्यागर्भं स्वपुत्रम्[54] अवदत्[55] । विद्यागर्भ त्वम्[56] एतेषां सर्व्वेषां[57] विद्यार्थिनां निवासार्थं[58] प्रत्येकम्[59] मठं[60] दर्शयित्वा[61] देहि[62] ॥ ततो विद्यागर्भो गुरोर्[63] यथानिदेशं[64] तथानुष्ठितवान्[65] ॥

अथ परेद्युः प्रातः[66] स्नात्वा कृताह्निकः[67] स आचार्य्यः स पुत्रः[68] पाठशालां समेत्योपविष्टः[69] ॥ तदा पुत्रेण समाहूताः[70] सर्व्वे छात्राः[71] पाठशालाम् आगताः ॥ तत आचर्य्यस् तान् अपृच्छत्[72] । केषां[73] किं शास्त्रम् अध्ययनीयं[74] ? ॥ केचित् प्रत्यूचुः । अस्माकं[75] वेदाः पठनीयाः[77] ॥ केचिद् ऊचुः । अस्माभिः[76] स्मृतयो[78]ऽध्येत[79]-व्याः ॥ केचिद् ऊचुः । वयं तर्कान्[80] अध्येष्यामहे[1] ॥ आचा-

42) for तदा आचार्य्येण उक्तं, r. 4. r. 5. r. 199. 43) p. 138. *b.* 44) r. 174. 45) p. 123. 46) 2d future, p. 88. 47) p. 144. *c.* 48) उपवेशन, "sitting down," p. 177. *c.* 49) acc. pl. neut. p. 32. 50) "He gave," p. 142. *a.* 51) locative absolute, r. 189. 52) p. 151. *a.* 53) p. 139. *i.* p. 174. 54) p. 53. r. 83. 55) 1st pret. of root *vad.* 56) p. 51. 57) r. 79. 58) p. 177. *c.* 59) "to each one," r. 171. *b.* 60) मठ, "a cell or student's apartment." 61) p. 144. *c.* p. 126. 62) p. 118. 63) gen. c. p. 35. Vis. changed to *r* by r. 27. *a.* 64) "according to the order," r. 171. *b.* 65) "he performed," root *sthā*, with prep. *anu* (p. 173.), see also p. 142. *a.* 66) प्रातर्, "in the morning," r. 31. 67) कृताह्निक, "having performed his daily prayers, or religious observances," r. 159. 68) r. 161. 69) "having arrived at," root *i*, with *sam* and *ā*, r. 166. p. 144. *a.* 70) p. 139. *e.* 71) छात्र, "a scholar." 72) r. 90. *a.* p. 111. 73) r. 186. *a.* 74) p. 113. p. 147. *b.* 75) p. 54. r. 85. 76) r. 215. and p. 50. 77) "are to be read," nom. pl. m. root पठ्. 78) nom. pl. of स्मृति, "law," as delivered by Manu and other legislators, p. 34. 79) p. 146. *a.* 80) acc. pl. of तर्क, "logical treatise." 1) 2d fut. ātm. of *i*, with *adhi*, p. 79. *e.*

र्य्येणोक्तं । भवंतु[2] तावद् भवताम् अभिमतं ॥ पुनर्[3] आह[4] । प्रथमं वेद.पाठिन[5] उपविशन्तु ॥ ततो यथाविधि[6] तान् वेद.पाठान्[7] अपाठयत्[8] ॥ तदनन्तरं गुरुर्[9] आह । इदानीं[10] तर्काध्यायिन[11] आगच्छन्तु[12] ॥ तेष्व् आगतेषु तांस्[13] तर्कान् अध्यापितवान्[14] ॥ इत्थं[15] स्मार्त्तान्[16] स्मृतीर् अध्याप्य[17] गुरुर् गृहं गतः ॥ एवं क्रमेण[18] प्रत्यहं[19] वेदादीनि[20] शास्त्राणि पाठयति स्म[21] ॥

अथैकदा[22] विद्यागर्भः स्व.गृहे पितरं[23] विज्ञापयामास[24] । पितस्[25] तावद् अस्माकं पाठशालाया[26] मठाश्[27] चत्वारिंशत्[28]संख्यकाः सन्ति[29] । शिष्यास्[30] तु शतं[31] निवसन्ति[32] । अत[33] एकैकस्मिन्[34] मठे द्वौ[35] द्वौ त्रयस्[35] त्रयश्च विद्यार्थिनो वसन्ति । तत्र तेषां भोजन.शयनादिषु[36] क्रियासु महत्[37] कष्टं जायते[38] । किं तावत् कर्त्तव्यं[39] ॥ इति श्रुत्वा[40] सोऽध्यापकः[41] किमपि[42] प्रत्युत्तरम्[43]

2) p. 104. 3) p. 153. *e.* 4) See root ब्रू, p. 114. note *b.* 5) "readers of the Vedas," nom. pl. m. (p. 149. *a.*) 6) p. 177. *b.* 7) पाठ, "a lesson," "lecture," r. 192. *a.* 8) p. 87. *e.* 9) r. 27. *a.* 10) p. 153. *f.* 11) nom. pl. of अध्यायिन्, "a reader," p. 149. *a.* 12) p. 174. 13) r. 20. 14) p. 142. *a.* 15) p. 152. *c.* 16) स्मार्त्त, "a student of स्मृति or law," p. 23. viii. 17) p. 145. *i.* 18) p. 151. *b.* 19) "every day," प्रति is often prefixed in this sense, p. 177. *b.* 20) p. 167. *b.* 21) p. 199. *e.* 22) for अथ एकदा, r. 6. See also p. 152. *d.* 23) p. 37. 24) 2d pret. of the causal of ज्ञा, "to know," with prep. वि, p. 87. *d.* and r. 108. 25) voc. case, p. 37. and r. 31. 26) gen. case, p. 31. and r. 28. *b.* 27) r. 25. *a.* 28) p. 48. संख्याः is the proper form (r. 157.), but क may be redundantly added to any word. 29) p. 101. 30) r. 25. *a.* 31) p. 49. 32) root *vas*, with prep. *ni*, p. 107. 33) p. 152. *a.* r. 28. *a.* 34) loc. c. (r. 72.) of *ekaika*, "each single," *eka* being doubled, r. 6. The doubling of a word in a distributive sense is very usual. 35) p. 48. 36) p. 171. *c.* 37) r. 63. 38) r. 89. *a.* 39) p. 146. *a.* 40) r. 26. *b.* 41) p. 150. *b.* 42) "any," p. 54. r. 85. 43) "answer," acc. c.

अदत्त्वा[44] क्षणं[45] चिन्तापरो[46] भूत्वा[47] मनसा[48] बहु[49] विचार्य्य[50] बुद्ध्या[51]
तद् उपायं निश्चितवान्[52] । पश्चात्[53] पुत्रम् उवाच[54] । शृणु[55] पुत्र
प्रवक्ष्यामि[56] । अस्माकं पाठशालाया ये ये[57] मठाः सन्ति ते सर्व्वे
पाषाण[58].निर्म्मिताः । अधुना[59] तादृशानां[60] मठानां निर्म्माणं[61]
बहु.धन.व्यय[62].साध्यं । तावन्ति[63] धनानि च मम गृहे नेदानीं[64]
सन्ति । किन्तु[65] धनं विना[66] ते कथं[67] भविष्यन्ति[68] । यतः ।

विना वित्त[69].व्ययं क्वापि[70] कार्य्य.सिद्धिर् न जायते
धन[71].मूलाः क्रियाः सर्व्वा यत्नस् तस्यार्ज्जने[72] मतः[73]

अतोऽत्र मया निश्चितम् एतत् । त्वं गृहे तिष्ठ[74] । अहं
श्वो[75] ग्रामान्तरं[76] गन्तास्मि[77] । बहवो[78] धनिनः[79] सन्ति दातारः[80] ।
किन्तु सर्व्वेषां मध्ये बहु[81].धनो धर्म्मिष्ठो[82] वदान्यश्च[83] वीरजिन्नामा[84]
राजास्ति[85] । तस्यैव गृहं गमिष्यामि[86] । इत्य् उक्त्वा स आचार्य्यः
सर्व्वाञ्[87] छिष्यान् समाहूय[88] तैः सह काशी.राज.गृहं[89] ययौ[90] ॥

44) "without giving," p. 143. *a.* r. 135. 45) r. 180. *a.* 46) "lost in thought," nom. c. 47) p. 143. *a.* 48) p. 43. p. 182. *d.* 49) p. 151. *a.* 50) "having deliberated," root *char* in caus. with prep. *vi*, p. 145. *i.* 51) inst. c. of बुद्धि, "mind." 52) "he fixed upon," p. 142. 53) p. 151. *c.* 54) p. 76. *d.* 55) r. 94. 56) "I will declare," 2d fut. of *vach* (p. 80.), with prep. प्र. 57) r. 86. 58) "built with stone," r. 141. 59) p. 151. *b.* 60) "of such like," gen. pl. दृश is added to the crude pronouns त, एत, य, to express similarity, the final *a* being lengthened. 61) "the building," nom. c. n. 62) "to be effected by the outlay of much money," p. 171. *b.* 63) r. 61. 64) for न इदानीं, r. 5. 65) r. 137. 66) p. 150. *c.* 67) p. 152. *c.* 68) p. 104. 69) r. 147. 70) r. 85. 71) r. 157. 72) loc. case of अर्ज्जन, "acquisition," p. 185. *c.* 73) "is recommended," p. 140. *o.* 74) p. 107. 75) श्वस्, "tomorrow," r. 26. *a.* 76) p. 172. *g.* 77) 1st fut. of *gam*, "to go," p. 80. 78) p. 35. 79) p. 43. 80) p. 37. 81) r. 150. 82) p. 47. 83) "munificent," r. 25. *a.* 84) वीरजित्, proper name, "Hero-conqueror," r. 42., *t* changed to *n* by r. 15. (see p. 107.). 85) p. 41. r. 64. 86) 2d fut. p. 80. 87) for सर्व्वान् शिष्यान्, r. 20. †. 88) p. 145. *d.* 89) "to the palace of the king of Benares." 90) p. 70. *a.* p. 112. and r. 191. *a.*

अथ वेदगर्भः सर्वैः शिष्यैः सह नाना.शास्त्रालापैर्[1] बहु.दूरं गत्वा गङ्गा.तीरे माध्याह्निकीं[2] क्रियां चकार[3] । ततस् तत्र दण्डम्[4] एकं विश्रम्य[5] पुनर् जगाम[6] । तदनन्तरं गत्वा गत्वा[7] बहून्य्[8] अदृष्ट.पूर्वाणि[9] राजकीयैश्वर्य्याणि[10] पश्यन्तस्[11] ते ब्राह्मणा[12] बहु.जनाकुलं[13] राज.द्वारं[14] प्रापुः[15] । तत्र द्वौ दौवारिकौ[16] दण्ड.हस्तौ[17] तान् ब्राह्मणान् दृष्ट्वा प्रणेमतुः[18] पप्रच्छतुश्च[19] । भवन्तः[20] कुत्र[21] यास्यन्तीति[22] । वेदगर्भः प्रत्याह[23] । राज.सन्निधिं[24] गन्तु.कामा[25] वयं तत्रास्मान् नयतं[26] । ततस् तयोर्[27] एकः शीघ्रं[28] गत्वा तेषाम् आगमन.वार्त्तां मन्त्रिणे[29]ऽकथयत् । मन्त्री राजानं विज्ञापि-

[1]) "with conversations on various books of science," or "with various conversations on literary topics." [2]) "belonging to mid-day," acc. case, fem. p. 23. viii. [3]) p. 102. [4]) acc. case of दण्ड, "a space of twenty-four minutes," r. 180. *a.* [5]) "having rested" (p. 145. *f.*), from श्रम्, "to be weary," see the force of वि, p. 175. [6]) p. 107. [7]) The repetition of the word gives continuity to the action, "as they kept on advancing." [8]) acc. case, plur. neut. p. 36. r. 7. [9]) p. 172. *g.* [10]) राजकीय, "regal" (p. 23. xi.); ऐश्वर्य, "supremacy" (p. 23. vii.), "signs of regal supremacy," r. 154. [11]) p. 107. r. 123. [12]) r. 28. *b.* [13]) "thronged with many people," p. 171. *b.* [14]) r. 147. [15]) 3d plur. 2d pret. of *āp* (p. 120.) with प्र. [16]) nom. case, dual of दौवारिक, "a porter." In forming a noun according to p. 23. ix., when the initial is a double consonant, consisting of two letters of which the last is *v* or *y*, this double consonant is resolved into a syllable by the insertion of *u* for *v*, or *i* for *y*, and this *u* or *i* take the Vṛiddhi change required by the rule. [17]) दण्ड, "a mace," "staff," r. 157. [18]) 3d dual, 2d pret. of नम्, "to bow" (p. 76. *c.*), with prep. प्र, see p. 175. [19]) 3d dual, 2d pret. of प्रच्छ्, "to ask." According to Wilkins and Bopp (whose authority was followed at p. 77. *f.* and p. 111.) this should be पपृच्छतुः, but the form पप्रच्छतुः is correct according to the Ṣiddhānta Kaumudī 142, and on the same authority the base पप्रच्छ् will be retained throughout this tense. [20]) r. 84. [21]) p. 152. *b.* [22]) p. 112. and r. 4. [23]) see ब्रू, note *b.* p. 114. and p. 175. [24]) "the king's presence," r. 147. [25]) p. 198. *c.* [26]) 2d dual, imperat. of नी, "to lead." [27]) p. 51. [28]) p. 151. [29]) dat. case, p. 43.

तवान्। ततो राजाज्ञया[30] सोऽमात्यः समेत्य बहु.मान.पुरःसरं[31] तान् राज.सभां समानयत्[32]। तदा राजा सिंहासनाद् उत्थाय तम् आचार्य्यं प्रणनाम। तदानीं वेदगर्भो राजानं वर्णयितुम्[33] आरब्धवान्[34]।

भवन्तो धार्म्मिका[35] धीरा धनिनो दान.शीलिनः[36]।
दया.दाक्षिण्य[37].सम्पन्नाः सत्य.व्रत.परायणाः[38] ॥
सौन्दर्य्य.भूमयः[39] शूरा यायजूका[40] जितेन्द्रियाः[41]।
जित.रोष.रयाः[42] सौम्याः[43] सु.शीलाः सत्त्व.शालिनः[44] ॥
श्रुतस्य पार.दृश्वानो राज.नीति.विचक्षणाः।
सदोद्यमाः[45] सदाचाराः[46] प्रजा.पालन.तत्पराः[47] ॥
नाना.देश.विशेष.ज्ञा[48] नाना.भाषासु[49] पण्डिताः।
नाना.गुणि.गणैः[50] सेव्याः[51] सु.सञ्चित.यशो.धनाः[52] ॥

राज्ञोक्तं। साधु[53] पाण्डित्यं साधु कवित्वं[54]। पाण्डित्यं

30) आज्ञा, "an order," p. 182. *c.* 31) "with great respect," lit. "preceded by great respect." 32) 1st pret. of नी with *sam* and *ā*. 33) inf. mood of root वर्ण्, "to eulogize," 10 conj. 34) "began," root रभ् with prep. आ, r. 126. See also p. 197. 35) nom. plur. (r. 28. *b.*) p. 23. ix. See also r. 188. 36) nom. plur. "of a generous disposition." 37) p. 171. *b.* 38) "devoted to the sincere (discharge of) religious observances." 39) सौन्दर्य्य, "beauty" (p. 23. vii.); भूमि, "site" (p. 34.). 40) nom. plur. of यायजूक, "the performer of frequent sacrifices." 41) p. 169. *a.* 42) रोष, "passion"; रय, "current," "the current of whose passion is restrained." 43) सौम्य, "handsome as the moon." 44) सत्त्व, "excellence"; शालिन्, "possessing." 45) सदा, "always"; उद्यम, "exertion," r. 5. r. 161. 46) सत्, "good"; आचार, "practice," r. 14. r. 159. 47) "devoted to the protection of your subjects." 48) "knowing the peculiarities of various countries"; ज्ञ, "knowing," p. 149. 1. 49) loc. case of भाषा, "a dialect." 50) गुणिन्, "a gifted person" (r. 20. last paragraph); गण, "a multitude." 51) "to be honoured," root *sev*, p. 147. *c.* 52) "possessing a large accumulation of fame and riches," r. 171. *b.* 53) r. 140. 54) p. 33. p. 22. vi.

राज्यतो[55] वरं। सु.कविता चेद्[56] अस्ति राज्येन किं[57]? यतः।

चारैः पश्यन्ति[58] राजानः शास्त्रैः पश्यन्ति पण्डिताः॥

चार.चक्षुषो[59]ऽपि राजानो न सर्व्व.ज्ञाः। शास्त्र.चक्षुषः पण्डिता एव सर्व्व.ज्ञा अतो राजत्वात् पाण्डित्यस्य विशिष्टतास्ति[60]। वेदगर्भ[61] उवाच। भद्रम् उक्तं भवता किन्तु सर्व्व.प्राणिनां[62] पालकत्वाद्[63] राज्ञः प्रधानत्वं। अपरञ्च[64]।

इन्द्रियाणि विनिर्जित्य[65] तप[66] उग्रं चकार यः।

दत्त.दानः[67] स्व.धर्म्म.स्थः[68] स राजा जायते क्षितौ[69]॥

इत्य् आकर्ण्य राजा हृष्ट.चित्तस्[70] तं विप्रं बहु प्रशंस्य[71] तस्मै[72] सहस्रं[73] रूप्य.मुद्रा[74] ददौ[75]। तदनन्तरं सिंहासनाद् उत्थाय स्वान्तःपुरं[76] प्रविष्टवान्। मन्त्री स.शिष्यं वेदगर्भम् आह। भवद्भिर्[77] अद्य[78] स्थातव्यं। नृपतिर् भवतां वेद.पाठान् श्रोतुम्[79] इच्छति। श्वः प्रातः पाठं श्रावयित्वा[80] गन्तव्यं[1]॥

अथ कार्य्याधीश[2] आगत्य[3] तान् विप्रान् वास.गृहं नीत्वा[4]

55) "than royalty," p. 152. *a*. p. 188. *f*. 56) r. 217. 57) r. 187. *a*. 58) p. 107. 59) p. 167. *a*. 60) विशिष्टता, "superiority," p. 24. xiv. p. 188. *f*. 61) r. 28. *a*. 62) r. 154. प्राणिन्, "a living creature," p. 27. iv. 63) "from his being the पालक (p. 150. *b*.) or protector," see r. 177. *b*. 64) p. 154. *b*. 65) root जि, "to conquer," with prep. वि and निर्, p. 144. *a*. 66) acc. case, neut. p. 43. r. 28. *a*. 67) "one by whom gifts are given," "liberal," p. 169. *a*. 68) p. 149. 1. 69) loc. case of क्षिति, "the earth," p. 34. 70) p. 169. *a*. 71) root शंस्, "to praise," p. 145. *e*. 72) r. 194. 73) p. 49. 74) "silver coins," acc. case, plur. fem. (p. 31.), r. 28. *b*. 75) p. 118. 76) acc. case of अन्तःपुर, "the inner or private apartments." 77) p. 153. *f*. 78) p. 146. *a*. 79) p. 197. 80) causal of श्रु, "to hear," p. 144. *c*. 1) p. 203. *b*. 2) lit. "the superintendant of affairs" (r. 147.), "the steward," r. 28. *a*. 3) p. 145. *g*. 4) नी, "to lead," r. 192. *b*.

लेह्यं[5] पेयं[5] चर्व्व्यं[5] चोष्यम्[5] इति चतुर्व्विधैर् अन्नैर् भोजयाञ्चकार[6]॥

अथ राजा माध्याह्निकं कृत्यं समाप्य[7] मन्त्रिणम् आहूतवान्। तदामात्यः समेत्योपविवेश[8]। राजा मन्त्रिणा सह राजकीयं कार्य्यं मन्त्रयित्वा[9] पश्चाद् आह। मन्त्रिन्[10] वेदगर्भस्यागमन-प्रयोजनं जानासि[11]?। मन्त्री ब्रूते[12]। प्रभो[13] विप्रोऽसौ महाविज्ञान्[14]। सर्व्वदा[15] शास्त्राध्यापनेन कालं यापयति[16]। विद्यार्थिभ्यो[17] विद्यादानात्[18] तस्य कार्य्यं नान्यत्। तस्मात्[19] तत्साहाय्यसंसाधनम्[20] एव तस्य गमनप्रयोजनम् इत्य् अनुमीयते[21]। राजाह। भद्रं तावद् अस्माभिस् तत्साहाय्यं कर्त्तव्यं। इत्य् उक्त्वा भूपतिः क्षणं विचार्य्य पुनर् अब्रवीत्[12]। एवं भवतु वयं पाठशालां कारयित्वा दास्यामः[22]। अध्यापकाय विद्यार्थिभ्यश्च वृत्तिं दास्यामः। इत्य् उक्त्वा परिचारकान्[23] प्राह। कार्य्याधीशम् आह्वयत[24]। ततः कार्य्याधीशेनागत्य[25] प्रणामे[26] कृते। राजा तम् आज्ञापयति। वेदगर्भस्य प्राचीनायाः[27] पाठशाला-

5) लिह्, "to lick" (p. 147. *h.*); पा, "to drink" (*c.*); चर्व्, "to chew" (*g.*); चूष्, "to suck" (*h.*). This division of food into four kinds, *lickables*, *drinkables*, *chewables*, and *suckables*, is not unusual in Indian writings. 6) caus. of *bhuj*, "to eat," r. 108. r. 193. *a.* 7) "having finished," caus. of root आप् with सम्, p. 145. *i.* 8) समेत्य उपविवेश (r. 5.), "having arrived, sat down," 2d pret. of विश्. 9) मन्त्र्, "to consult," 10th conj. p. 102. *c.* 10) voc. case, p. 43. 11) p. 123. 12) p. 114. 13) voc. case of प्रभु, "master," p. 35. 14) p. 165. *a.* विद्वान् is here used as a substantive, "a learned man" (p. 44.). 15) p. 152. *d.* 16) "causes to go," "passes," caus. of *yā*, p. 87. *d.* 17) r. 176. *a.* 18) p. 188. *f*, see r. 108. 19) p. 151. *c.* 20) साहाय्य, "assistance"; संसाधन, "effecting," "the effecting some assistance in this matter." 21) "is inferred," pass. of *mā* with *anu*, r. 112. 22) root *dā*, "to give," p. 79. *e.* 23) acc. case plur. of परिचारक, "an attendant." 24) root *hwe* (p. 107.) with prep. *ā*. 25) p. 202. *c.* 26) "on an obeisance being made," r. 189. 27) gen. case, fem. of प्राचीन, "old."

याः समीपे वेदगर्भेण निर्दिशिते[28] स्थाने चतुर्दिक्षु[29] बहून् मठान् मध्ये महतीं पाठशालां च शीघ्रं निर्म्मापय[30] । मास.त्रय.मध्ये गृहाणां पाषाण.चूर्णैः[31] सु.निर्म्माणं[32] सम्पूर्णं[33] कर्त्तव्यं ॥

तम् इत्य् आदिश्य[34] नृपतिः पुनः पार्श्व.स्थान् परिचारकान् प्रोवाच । कोषाधीशम्[35] आह्वयत । ततो भृत्याह्वानात्[36] समुपागत्य[37] कोषाधीशे कृत.प्रणामे[38] सति[39] नृपतिस् तम् आज्ञापयत् । द्वे[40] सहस्रे[41] मुद्राः[42] कोषाद् देहि[43] । भृति.दानार्थं[44] सहस्रम् एकं । पाषाण.चूर्णादि.क्रयणार्थं[45] सहस्रम् एकं । पश्चात् प्रयोजनानुरूपं[46] यद् यद् देयं तद् दास्यसि[47] ॥

अथ मन्त्री स.शिष्यं वेदगर्भं समेत्य सर्व्वं राज्ञोक्तं[48] श्रावयामास[49] । सर्व्वैः शिष्यैर् उक्तं । भद्रं भद्रं कृत.कृत्या[50] वयम् इति । आचार्य्यश्चावदत् । अस्माकं स.जातीयो[51] भवान् स.पक्षो[52] महा.बुद्धिः[53] सु.धार्म्मिकः परोपकारी महा.कार्य्य.साधन.हेतुः[54] ।

28) loc. case, "pointed out." 29) "on all four sides," p. 165. *c.*; दिश्, "a quarter," loc. case plur. p. 45. 30) "cause to be built," caus. of मा (p. 87. *d.*) with prep. *nir.* 31) पाषाण, "stone"; चूर्ण, "mortar," "lime," p. 163. *b.* 32) निर्म्माण, "construction." 33) "completed." 34) root दिश् with prep. आ, "to command," p. 145. *f.* 35) acc. case, "the superintendant of the कोष or treasury," "the treasurer." 36) आह्वान, "summons," r. 177. *b.* 37) root गम् with *sam*, *upa*, and *ā*, p. 145. *g.* 38) p. 169. *a.* loc. case. 39) r. 189. 40) acc. neut. (p. 48.). 41) acc. dual neut. 42) acc. plur. fem. p. 31. 43) p. 118. 44) "for the payment of wages," r. 171. *c.* 45) p. 171. *c.* 46) "according to need," r. 171. *c.* 47) r. 207. *a.* 48) for राज्ञा उक्तं, "that which had been said by the king." 49) caus. of श्रु, "to hear," r. 108. 50) p. 205. 51) "of the same class or caste" (p. 23. xi.), the prep. स when compounded with जाति and पक्ष has the force of समान, "same." 52) "of the same party." 53) r. 159. 54) "the instrument of the accomplishment of great affairs.

ब्राह्मणस्य ब्राह्मणो गतिः। विद्वान् हि विद्वांसं[55] वेत्ति[56]। का चिन्ता नः कार्य्य.सिद्धये[57]?॥

अथ प्रातर् वेदगर्भः समुत्थाय सर्व्वैः शिष्यैः सह जलाशये नित्य.कृत्यं कृत्वा राज.द्वारं समागतः। तदा मन्त्री तत्रागत्य तान् ब्राह्मणान् नीत्वा शुचौ[58] स्थाने उपवेशयामास[59]। तस्मिन्नेव[60] समये राजा तत्रागत्य विप्रान् प्रणनाम। तदा वेदगर्भः पंक्ति.क्रमेण[61] शिष्यान् उपवेश्य[62] तैः सह साम.वेद[63].गानं समारेभे। राजा सु.श्राव्यं[64] सु.ललितम्[65] अश्रुत.पूर्व्वं[66] साम.गानं श्रुत्वा चमत्कृत्य[67] पुलकित.तनुः[68] प्रेमाश्रु.गलित.नेत्रो[69] जात.श्रद्धा.भक्तिर्[70] गद्गदया[71] वाचा साधु साध्व् इत्य् अब्रवीत्। सर्व्वे विप्रा राजन्[72] जय[73] जयेत्य्[74] ऊचुः। अथ वेदगर्भो ऽपृच्छत्[75]। भो[76] भूपते[77] भवतो विभूत्या वयं सर्व्वे सिद्ध.मनोरथा[78] इदानीं स्व.गृहं जिगमिषवः[79]। राजावदत्। यथाभिमतं भवतां तथा भवतु। तदा स आचार्य्य उत्थाय शिष्यैः सह प्रतस्थे[80]। ततो मन्त्री किञ्चिद्

55) acc. case, p. 44. 56) p. 94. 57) dat. case of सिद्धि (p. 34.), "why need we be anxious about the success of our affairs?" 58) r. 39. 59) r. 108. 60) r. 10. 61) "in a line." 62) p. 145. *i*. 63) सामवेद, the Sāma Veda is the third of the four Vedas, composed in metre, and therefore always chaunted; गान, "a chaunt," r. 147. 64) "delightful to be heard," p. 147. *d*. 65) "very charming." 66) p. 172. *g*. 67) "being astonished," चमत् is a sound of surprise prefixed to कृ. 68) "having the hair of his body erect with delight," p. 169. *a*. 69) "his eyes shedding tears of (religious) sympathy," p. 171. *b*. 70) "his faith and devotion being excited." 71) गद्गद, "indistinct," or "convulsive," from emotion. 72) voc. case, p. 41. 73) 2d sing. imperat. of root *ji*, p. 106., a word used in acclamation. 74) p. 205. 75) p. 111. 76) r. 140. 77) p. 35. †. 78) p. 160. *a*. 79) r. 182. and p. 35. 80) 3d sing. 2d pret. ātm. of स्था (p. 76. *a*.) with प्र, p. 175.

दूरं विप्रान् अनुव्रज्य[1] परावर्वृते[2]। कार्य्याधीशेन प्रेरिताः कार्य्यकारादयो[3] विप्राणां पश्चाच्[4] चलिताः। ते सर्व्वे शीघ्रम् आगत्य गङ्गा.तटं प्राप्ताः[5]। ततः कार्य्यकाराज्ञया नाविकैर्[6] नौका[7] समानीता[8]। ते सर्व्वे नौकाम् आरुह्य[9] पारं[10] गताः। ततस् ते सन्ध्या.काले पाठशालां प्रापुः[11]॥

अथ वेदगर्भो गृहं प्राप्य रात्रौ तेषां कार्य्यकारादीनाम्[12] आतिथ्यं[13] चकार। प्रभाते कृत.प्रातः.कृत्यस्[14] तान् पाठशालां[15] नीत्वा छात्रैः सह बहु विचार्य्य नवीनायाः[16] पाठशालाया[17] निर्म्माणार्थं[18] स्थानं दर्शयामास[19]। तदा कार्य्यकार आचार्य्या-ज्ञां प्राप्य स्थपतीन्[20] भृतकांश्च[21] कार्य्ये[22] नियोजयामास[23]। मास.-त्रय.मध्ये मठाश्च पाठशाला च सुनिर्म्मिता जाताः[24]॥

अथ चारैर्[25] आगत्य सर्व्वो वृत्तान्तो राज्ञे[26] विज्ञापितः। राजा कार्य्याधीशम् आज्ञापयत्। पत्र.लेखकम्[27] आह्वय[28]। वेदगर्भाय पत्रं लेखय। ततः कार्य्याधीशो राज.लेखकम्[29] आहूयाकथयत्[30]।

1) व्रज् to go with अनु, p. 173. 2) 2d pret. of वृत्, "to turn" (p. 106.), with परा, p. 174. 3) कार्य्यकार, "the managing workman," p. 167. *b*. 4) p. 156. *e*. and r. 16. 5) r. 212. 6) inst. case, plur. of नाविक, "a boat-man." 7) नौका, "a boat." 8) "was brought," root नी, p. 138. *b*. 9) p. 174. 10) पार, "the opposite bank." 11) 2d pret. p. 120. 12) p. 167. *b*. 13) "hospitality," p. 23. vii. 14) "after he had performed his morning exercises (of religion)," p. 169. *a*. 15) r. 192. *b*. 16) gen. case, fem. of नवीन, "new." 17) r. 28. *b*. 18) p. 177. *c*. 19) p. 126. 20) acc. case, plur. masc. of स्थपति, "an architect," "master-builder." 21) acc. case, plur. masc. of भृतिक, "a hired labourer," *sh* inserted before च by r. 20. 22) p. 105. *b*. 23) caus. of *yuj* with *ni*, r. 108. 24) p. 140. *o*. 25) p. 202. *c*. 26) r. 194. 27) acc. case, पत्र, "a letter"; लेखक, "a writer" (p. 150. *b*.). 28) 2d sing. imp. p. 107. 29) r. 20. †. 30) p. 145. *d*.

आचार्य्याय पत्रं लेखनीयं[31]। तस्यात्रागमनार्थं[32] गद्य.पद्यादि.युक्तं[33] पत्रं लिख। ततस् तेन पत्रे[34] लिखिते कार्य्याधीशो राजानं श्रावयित्वा राज.मुद्राङ्कितं[35] कृत्वा पत्र.वाहकम्[36] आहूय प्रेषया-[37]मास। राज.पत्रं प्राप्य वेदगर्भो द्वाभ्यां[38] शिष्याभ्यां सह शीघ्रं राज.सन्निधिम् आगमत्[39] ॥

अथ राजा वेदगर्भम् आगतं दृष्ट्वा[40] प्रणनाम। आचार्य्यस् तु[41] वेदं पठित्वाशिषं[42][43] ददौ[44]। राजा पृच्छति[45]। भो विद्वन्[46] पाठ-शाला कीदृशी[47] जाता मठाश्च कीदृशाः कति[48] जाताः? । आचार्य्येणोक्तं। भूपते द्वे शते मठा निर्म्मिताः। मध्ये महती पाठशाला सुनिर्म्मिताभवत्[49]। भूपतिनोक्तं[50]। तत्र छात्राः प्रवेशनीया[51] भवता। वेदगर्भः प्रत्याह। स्वयं गत्वा नव.गृह.-प्रवेशो राज्ञा कारयितव्यः[52]। ततो भूपतिर् भद्रं भद्रम् इत्य् उक्त्वा भृत्यान् अवदत्। मौहूर्त्तिक[53] आहूयतां[54]। ततस् तैर् आहूतो गणक[55] आगत्योपविष्टः[56] ॥

अथ नृपतिस् तम् आज्ञापयति। भो ज्योतिषिक[57] नव.-

[31]) p. 147. *b*. [32]) "for his coming hither," "containing an invitation for him to come hither." [33]) गद्य, "prose"; पद्य, "verse," p. 171. *c*. [34]) r. 189. [35]) मुद्रा, "a seal"; अङ्कित, "stamped." [36]) "letter-carrier," root वह्, p. 150. *b*. [37]) 2d pret. (r. 108.) of caus. of इष् with प्र, p. 175. [38]) p. 48. [39]) 3d pret. of *gam*, "to go," with prep. *ā*, p. 83. *h*. [40]) p. 143. *a*. [41]) r. 137. [42]) "having recited," p. 143. *a*. [43]) acc. case of *āshis*, p. 44. †. [44]) p. 118. [45]) r. 140. [46]) voc. case of *vidwas*, p. 44. [47]) nom. fem. of कीदृश, "what kind?" [48]) p. 54. †. [49]) p. 104. [50]) p. 35. †. [51]) "are to be made to enter" (p. 147. *b*.) caus. of root विश् with प्र, see also r. 215. [52]) caus. of कृ, p. 146. *a*. [53]) "the astrologer," formed by p. 23. ix., from मुहूर्त्त, "an hour." [54]) 3d sing. imp. pass. p. 90. *f*. [55]) गणक, "an astrologer," from गण्, "to calculate," p. 150. *b*. [56]) r. 5. [57]) ज्योतिषिक, "an astrologer," from ज्योतिस्, "a star."

गृह.प्रवेशाय[57] दिनं निरूपणीयं[58]। ततः स विचार्य्य नव.गृह.-प्रवेश.योग्यं लग्नं[59] कथयामास[60]। राजोवाच। तत्पूर्व्व.दिने[61] तत्रा-स्माभिर् गन्तव्यं[62] भवान् यद्[63] यत् कर्म्म[64] तत्र करणीयं[65] तत् सर्व्वं स्वयं विधास्यति[66]। अथ वेदगर्भो राजानुज्ञां[67] गृहीत्वा[68] गृहं गतः ॥

परेऽहनि[69] प्रातः स राजा मन्त्रिणम् आज्ञापितवान्[70]। पाठशालां प्रति[1] लोकान् प्रेषय[2]। ते तत्र द्रव्याण्य्[3] आसादयन्तु[4] स्थानानि परिष्कुर्व्वन्तु[5]। ततः स धनं दत्त्वा बहून् कार्य्य.कारिणो[6] जनान् प्राहिणोत्[7]। तदनन्तरं स राजा भृत्य.मन्त्रि.-पुरोहितैः[8] सहितः शुभे मुहूर्त्ते[9] तत्र जगाम। नृपतिर् गज.-वाहनेन[10] पुरोहितश्च मन्त्रि.प्रभृतयस्[11] तुरग.वाहनैश्[12] चलिताः। भृत्याः पदैर् वव्रजुः[13] ॥

अथ तत्र गत्वा राजा निरूपित.दिवसे ब्राह्मणैर्[14] वास्तुया-[15]

57) r. 176. 58) "is to be chosen," "fixed upon," root रूप् with नि. 59) "auspicious moment," "favourable season." 60) r. 108. 61) "on the day before that (fixed upon for the ceremony)." 62) p. 203. b. 63) r. 86. 64) p. 42. 65) p. 147. b. 66) "will arrange," root धा with prep. वि, p. 119. 67) acc. case of अनुज्ञा, "permission to depart," r. 147. 68) p. 143. a. 69) loc. case of अहन्, "a day." 70) r. 126. 1) p. 155. b. 2) p. 175. 3) r. 7. 4) 3d plur. imp. of caus. of सद् with आ, "let them procure." 5) "let them decorate," p. 102. p. 174. 6) acc. case, p. 43. 7) 1st pret. of हि, "to send," with prep. प्र, 5th conj. r. 94. 8) पुरोहित, "the family priest," "with the servants, the minister, and the priest," r. 151. 9) "at an auspicious moment," a *muhūrta* is two *dandas* or forty-eight minutes. 10) r. 193. b. वाहन is applied to any thing which carries, p. 150. c. 11) "the minister and the others," r. 157. 12) तुरग, "a horse," r. 25. a. 13) 2d pret. of व्रज्, "to go," r. 98. 14) r. 193. a. "having caused the ceremony to be performed by the Brahmans." 15) वास्तुयाग, "a ceremony or sacrifice performed on entering a new habitation," r. 157.

गादिकं कारयित्वा बहु.ब्राह्मणान् भोजयित्वा नृत्य.गीत.वा[16]-
दित्रैर् महोत्सवं कारयित्वा छात्रान् नवं वेश्म[17] प्रावेशयत्[18]।
तदनन्तरं नरपतिः कार्य्यकारादिभ्यः[19] पारितोषिकं[20] प्रादात्[21]।
तत्परदिने स्व.पुरं प्रति जिगमिषुं[22] राजानं वेदगर्भः परितुष्ट[23]-
मना अब्रवीत्। स.परिवारस्य[24] राज्ञः शुभं भूयात्[25]। भूयात्
पुनर्दर्शनं।

रिपुञ्जयो[26] भवान् भूयात् प्रजानां च प्रपालकः[27]।
निरामयो[28] निरातङ्कः[29] सदा.भक्तिः[30] परेश्वरे[32]॥

इत्य् आशिषं समाकर्ण्य स राजा जात.भक्तिस् तैर् ब्राह्मणैर् अनुज्ञातः[33] सहामात्य.भृत्य.पुरोहितैः स्व.पुरं प्रति प्रतस्थे।

अथ वेदगर्भस्य पाठशालायाः सु.ख्यातिर् बहु.दूरं व्याप्नोत्[34]। विद्यार्थिनश्च नाना.दिग्देशेभ्यः क्रमश आगत्य त्रीणि शतानि बभूवुः[35]। स च तान् सर्वान् अन्तेवासिनः[36] प्रति.दिनं[37] त्रि.कालम्[38] अध्यापयति स्म[39]॥

16) नृत्य, "dancing"; गीत, "singing"; वादित्र, "musical instrument," r. 151. *a.* 17) r. 43. i. 18) 1st pret. r. 102. *a.* 19) r. 194. and r. 157. 20) acc. case, "a gratuity," that which causes परितोष, "satisfaction" (p. 23. ix.). 21) 3d pret. of *dā* with prep. *pra*, p. 83. *i.* 22) r. 182. 23) p. 169. *a.* 24) "together with his retinue," r. 161. 25) r. 200. 26) "the conqueror of your enemies," p. 140. 1. 27) "the guardian." 28) "free from आमय or sickness," p. 154. *e.* r. 161. 29) "free from all आतङ्क, apprehension." 30) "always devoted to," r. 161. 32) loc. case, "the Supreme Lord," "the Deity," r. 184. *a.* 33) "permitted to depart." 34) "spread abroad," root *āp* with *vi*, p. 120. 35) p. 104. 36) acc. case, plur. of अन्तेवासिन्, "a pupil," p. 43. 37) प्रति give the sense of "every," r. 171. *b.* 38) "at the three seasons," *i.e.* "morning, noon, and evening." 39) p. 199. *e.*

॥ मनुसंहितासारः ॥

SELECTIONS FROM THE INSTITUTES OF MANU.

ORIGIN OF THE FOUR CLASSES, AND GENERAL VIEW OF THEIR DUTIES.

सर्व्वस्यास्य तु सर्गस्य[1] गुप्त्यर्थं[2] स महा.द्युतिः[3] ।
मुख.बाहू[4]रु.पज्ज्ञानां[5] पृथक् कर्म्माण्य्[6] अकल्पयत्[7] ॥ १ ॥
अध्यापनम् अध्ययनं यजनं[8] याजनं[9] तथा ।
दानं प्रतिग्रहं[10] चैव ब्राह्मणानाम्[11] अकल्पयत् ॥ २ ॥
प्रजानां रक्षणं दानम् इज्याध्ययनम् एव च ।
विषयेष्व् अप्रसक्तिश्च क्षत्त्रियस्य समासतः[12] ॥ ३ ॥
पशूनां रक्षणं दानम् इज्याध्ययनम् एव च ।
वणिक्पथं[13] कुसीदं[14] च वैश्यस्य कृषिम् एव च ॥ ४ ॥
एकम् एव तु शूद्रस्य प्रभुः कर्म्म समादिशत् ।
एतेषाम् एव वर्णानां शुश्रूषाम्[15] अनसूयया[16] ॥ ५ ॥
भूतानां[17] प्राणिनः श्रेष्ठाः प्राणिनां बुद्धि[18].जीविनः ।
बुद्धिमत्सु[19] नराः श्रेष्ठा नरेषु ब्राह्मणाः स्मृताः ॥ ६ ॥

1) Gen. case, sing. of सर्ग, "creation." 2) r. 171. *c.* 3) r. 159. 4) ऊरु, masc. "the thigh." 5) पद्, masc. "the foot," r. 16. This is a complex compound, the whole being a dependent involving an aggregative, p. 171. *b.* 6) r. 7. 7) 1st pret. of क्लृप्, "to enjoin," 10th conj. p. 87. *e* 8) acc. case of यजन, n. "the performance of a sacrifice." 9) the lengthening of the *a* shows that this word is from the causal, p. 87. *e.* 10) acc. case of प्रतिग्रह, "acceptance." 11) r. 196. 12) "summarily," p. 152. *a.* 13) acc. case of वणिक्पथ, n. "traffic," lit. "way of merchants." 14) acc. case of कुसीद, n. "usury." 15) acc. case of शुश्रूषा, fem. "service," lit. "desire to hear," p. 23. xiii. 16) instr. case of अनसूया, fem. "absence of envy or grudge," p. 182. *d.* 17) p. 188. *d.* 18) r. 144. *a.* 19) r. 42. ii. and p. 188. *d.*

ब्राह्मणेषु च विद्वांसो[18] विद्वत्सु कृत.बुद्धयः ।
कृत.बुद्धिषु कर्त्तारः[19] कर्तृषु ब्रह्म[20].वेदिनः ॥ ७ ॥
विप्राणां ज्ञानतो[21] ज्यैष्ठ्यं[22] क्षत्रियाणां तु वीर्य्यतः[21] ।
वैश्यानां धान्य.धनतः[21] शूद्राणाम् एव जन्मतः[21] ॥ ८ ॥
ब्राह्मणः क्षत्रियो वैश्यस् त्रयो[23] वर्णा द्विजातयः ।
चतुर्थ एक.जातिस् तु शूद्रो ना्स्ति तु पञ्चमः ॥ ९ ॥

THE FIRST OR SACERDOTAL CLASS (OR BRAHMANS).

Duties of the Brahman in the first Order (Āshrama) or Quarter of his Life, as a Brahmachārī, or Student of Religion, subject to his Guru or Preceptor.

विद्या ब्राह्मणम् एत्या्ह[24] सेवधिस्[25] ते ऽस्मि[1] रक्ष[2] मां ।
असूयकाय[3] मां मा ऽदास्[4] तथा स्यां वीर्य्यवत्तमा[5] ॥ १० ॥
यम्[6] एव तु शुचिं विद्या[7] नियत.ब्रह्मचारिणं ।
तस्मै[8] मां ब्रूहि[9] विप्राय निधिपाया[10]ऽप्रमादिने[11] ॥ ११ ॥
धर्म्मा्र्थौ[12] यत्र न स्यातां शुश्रूषा वा्पि तद्विधा ।
तत्र विद्या न वप्तव्या[13] शुभं वीजम् इवो्षरे[14] ॥ १२ ॥

18) p. 44. 19) p. 37. 20) ब्रह्म, "the divine spirit, from which all things are supposed to emanate, and to which they return." 21) p. 152. *a.* 22) p. 23. viii. 23) p. 48. 24) indec. part. of root *i*, "to go," with prep. *ā*, p. 144. *a.* 25) nom. case (r. 25. *a.*) of सेवधि, "a divine treasure."
1) r. 9. 2) p. 101. 3) dat. case of असूयक, "a detracter." 4) r. 208. and p. 83. *i.* 5) nom. fem. of the superl. degree of वीर्य्यवत्, "possessed of vigour," r. 42. i. r. 71. 6) r. 174. 7) 2d sing. pot. of *vid*, "to know," p. 95. and r. 28. *b.* 8) r. 194. 9) p. 114. 10) dat. case of निधिप, "the protector of a treasure"; प, "a protector," from पा, "to protect," by r. 131. 1. 11) dat. case of अप्रमादिन्, "not negligent," p. 43. 12) r. 152. *a.* 13) nom. fem. of fut. pass. part. of *vap*, "to sow," p. 146. *a.* 14) ऊषर, n. "a barren salt soil."

[15]विद्ययैव समं [16]कामं मर्त्तव्यं [17]ब्रह्म.वादिना ।
आपद्य् अपि हि घोरायां न त्व् [18]एनाम् [19]इरिणे वपेत् ॥ १३ ॥
[20]ब्राह्मस्य [21]जन्मनः कर्त्ता [22]स्व.धर्म्मस्य च [23]शासिता ।
बालोऽपि विप्रो वृद्धस्य पिता भवति [24]धर्म्मतः ॥ १४ ॥
न तेन वृद्धो भवति येनास्य [25]पलितं शिरः ।
यो वै युवाप्य् [26]अधीयानस् तं देवाः स्थविरं [27]विदुः ॥ १५ ॥
यथा [28]काष्ठमयो हस्ती यथा [28]चर्म्ममयो मृगः ।
यश्च विप्रोऽ[29]नधीयानस् त्रयस् ते नाम [30]बिभ्रति ॥ १६ ॥
[31]सेवेतेमांस् तु [32]नियमान् ब्रह्मचारी [33]गुरौ वसन् ।
[34]सन्नियम्येन्द्रिय.ग्रामं तपो.[35]वृद्ध्यर्थम् आत्मनः ॥ १७ ॥
चोदितो गुरुणा नित्यम् अप्रचोदित एव वा ।
[36]कुर्य्याद् [37]अध्ययने यत्नम् आचार्य्यस्य हितेषु च ॥ १८ ॥
आचार्य्यश्च पिता चैव माता भ्राता च [38]पूर्व्व.जः ।
[39]नार्त्तेनाप्य् अवमन्तव्या ब्राह्मणेन विशेषतः ॥ १९ ॥
यं [40]माता.पितरौ क्लेशं [41]सहेते सम्भवे [42]नृणां ।
न तस्य [43]निष्कृतिः [44]शक्या कर्त्तुं [45]वर्ष.शतैर् अपि ॥ २० ॥

15) r. 6. 16) p. 151. *a.* 17) ब्रह्म, "the Vedas"; वादिन्, "an expounder," p. 149. *a.* 18) p. 52. note. 19) इरिण, n. "barren soil." 20) ब्राह्म, adj. "relating to Brahmā," "divine," p. 23. viii. 21) r. 66. 22) *swa* is here used generally ("own") and not reflexively. 23) nom. case, sing. masc. of शासितृ, p. 115. p. 149. 2. 24) p. 152. *a.* 25) पलित, adj. "gray" (as the hair). 26) nom. case, sing. of the pres. part. ātm. of अधी, "to read," p. 113. and r. 124. 27) p. 95. note. 28) p. 23. xii. 29) r. 135. 30) p. 117. 31) for सेवेत इमान्, r. 5. r. 20.: *seveta* is the 3d sing. pot. ātm. of *sev*, "to serve," "practise." 32) See verse 62. 33) *i.e.* गुरुसमीपे, com. "at his Guru's." 34) indec. part. of *yam*, "to restrain," with prep. *sam* and *ni.* 35) p. 177. *c.* 36) p. 102. 37) p. 195. *b.* 38) "born first," "elder." 39) p. 140. *l.* 40) r. 152. *b.* 41) 3d dual pres. ātm. of *sah*, "to bear." 42) p. 37. †. 43) "acquittance," "discharge of a debt." 44) p. 198. *a.* 45) r. 180.

तयोर् नित्यं प्रियं कुर्य्याद् आचार्य्यस्य च सर्व्वदा ।
तेष्व् एव त्रिषु तुष्टेषु तपः सर्व्वं समाप्यते ॥ २१ ॥
तेषां त्रयाणां शुश्रूषा परमं तप उच्यते[46] ।
न तैर् अभ्यननुज्ञातो[47] धर्म्मम् अन्यं समाचरेत् ॥ २२ ॥
अभिवादन[48]शीलस्य नित्यं वृद्धोपसेविनः[49] ।
चत्वारि[50] सम्प्रवर्द्धन्ते[1] आयुर् विद्या यशो बलं ॥ २३ ॥
यथा खनन् खनित्रेण नरो वार्य्य्[2] अधिगच्छति ।
तथा गुरुगतां विद्यां शुश्रूषुर्[3] अधिगच्छति ॥ २४ ॥
विषाद् अप्य् अमृतं ग्राह्यं बालाद् अपि सुभाषितं ।
श्रद्दधानः[4] शुभां विद्याम् आददीता[5]वराद् अपि ॥ २५ ॥
अथ तेन परो धर्म्मो विद्या शौचं[6] सुभाषितं ।
विविधानि च शिल्पानि[7] समादेयानि[8] सर्व्वतः ॥ २६ ॥
इन्द्रियाणां विचरतां[9] विषयेष्व्[10] अपहारिषु[11] ।
संयमे यत्नम् आतिष्ठेद्[12] विद्वान् यन्तेव[13] वाजिनां ॥ २७ ॥

46) p. 90. *f.* r. 190. 47) "unpermitted." This insertion of the negative prefix *an* (r. 135.) between the two prepositions is remarkable, and the more so, as the metre would equally admit of अनभ्यनुज्ञातो. 48) अभिवादन, "salutation." 49) उपसेविन्, "one who serves or honours," p. 149. *a.* 50) p. 48.
1) 3d plur. pres. ātm. of the root वृध्, 1st conj. with prep. *sam* and *pra.* 2) r. 7.
3) lit. "desirous to hear," r. 40. 4) श्रद्दधान, "possessing श्रत्, belief," r. 124. *a.* 5) 3d sing. pot. ātm. of *dā* with prep. *ā*, p. 174. 6) "purity," from शुचि, "pure," by p. 23. viii. 7) nom. plur. n. of शिल्प, "an art." 8) "to be collected," fut. part. of *dā* (p. 147. *c.*) with prep. *sam* and *ā.* 9) gen. plur. of pres. part. of चर् (r. 123.) with prep. *vi*, p. 175. 10) loc. plur. r. 7. 11) अपहारिन्, "a seizer," from हृ (p. 149. *a.*) with prep. *apa.* 12) root *sthā* with prep. *ā*, "to follow up," "apply"; यत्नम् आस्था is a common phrase in Manu for "to make effort." 13) यन्ता, nom. sing. masc. "a driver," from यम्, "to restrain" (r. 131. 2.).

न जातु[14] कामः कामानाम् उपभोगेन शाम्यति[15] ।
हविषा कृष्णवर्त्मेव[16] भूय[17] एवाभिवर्द्धते[18] ॥ २८ ॥
इन्द्रियाणां प्रसङ्गेन दोषम् ऋच्छत्य्[19] असंशयं[20] ।
सन्नियम्य तु तान्य् एव ततः सिद्धिं नियच्छति[21] ॥ २९ ॥
वेदास् त्यागश्च यज्ञाश्च नियमाश्च तपांसि च ।
न विप्रदुष्टभावस्य[22] सिद्धिं गच्छन्ति कर्हिचित्[23] ॥ ३० ॥
वशे कृत्वेन्द्रियग्रामं संयम्य[24] च मनस् तथा ।
सर्व्वान् संसाधयेद् अर्थान् अक्षिण्वन्[25] योगतस्[26] तनुं[27] ॥ ३१ ॥
इन्द्रियाणां तु सर्व्वेषां यद्य्[28] एकं क्षरतीन्द्रियं[29] ।
तेनास्य क्षरति प्रज्ञा दृतेः[30] पादाद्[31] इवोदकं ॥ ३२ ॥
यस्य वाङ्मनसे[32] शुद्धे सम्यग्गुप्ते च सर्व्वदा ।
स वै सर्व्वम् अवाप्नोति वेदान्त[33]ोपगतं[34] फलं ॥ ३३ ॥
सम्मानाद्[35] ब्राह्मणो नित्यम् उद्विजेत[36] विषाद् इव ।
अमृतस्येव चाकाङ्क्षेद्[37] अवमानस्य[38] सर्व्वदा ॥ ३४ ॥

14) p. 153. *f.* 15) p. 109. 16) कृष्णवर्त्मन्, masc. "fire" (nom. case -र्त्मा). 17) p. 153. *d.* 18) root वृध् with prep. अभि. 19) 3d sing. pres. of root ऋ, "to go to," "incur," r. 191. *b.* 20) r. 171. *b.* 21) root यम् with नि, "to obtain"; com. लभते. 22) "depraved," pass. part. of दुष् (p. 139. *i.*) with prep. *vi* and *pra.* 23) r. 133. 24) यम् with prep. सम्. 25) nom. case sing. of the pres. part. of क्षि, "to harass," 5th conj. r. 123. r. 135. 26) योग, "religious meditation," p. 152. *a.* 27) तनु, fem. "the body." 28) r. 136. *b.* r. 7. 29) 3d sing. pres. of क्षर्, 1st conj. "to ooze out," "to disappear gradually." 30) दृति, "a leather skin." 31) r. 195. 32) r. 152. *a.* मनस्, when compounded with वाक्, becomes मनस. Pāṇini, 5. 4. 77. 33) see p. २. 7. 34) उपगत, "obtained," lit. "undergone." 35) r. 195. *a.* 36) root विज्, 6th conj. with उत्, "to fear." 37) root कांक्ष् with आ, "to be desirous of." 38) gen. case of अवमान, n. "dishonour."

सुखं ह्य् अवमतः शेते[39] सुखं च प्रतिबुध्यते ।
सुखं चरति लोकेऽस्मिन्[40] अवमन्ता[41] विनश्यति[42] ॥ ३५ ॥
एवं चरति यो विप्रो ब्रह्मचर्य्यम् अविप्लुतः[43] ।
स गच्छत्य् उत्तमं स्थानं न चेहाजायते[44] पुनः ॥ ३६ ॥

Duties of the Brahman in the second Order, or Quarter of his Life, as a Grihastha, or Householder.

चतुर्थम्[1] आयुषो भागम्[2] उषित्वा[3]द्यं गुरौ[4] द्विजः ।
द्वितीयम् आयुषो भागं कृत.दारो[5] गृहे वसेत् ॥ ३७ ॥
अद्रोहेणैव[6] भूतानाम् अल्प.द्रोहेण[7] वा पुनः ।
अक्लेशेन शरीरस्य कुर्वीत धन.सञ्चयं ॥ ३८ ॥
धर्म्मार्थाव्[8] उच्यते[9] श्रेयः कामार्थौ धर्म्म एव च ।
अर्थ एवेह वा श्रेयस् त्रिवर्ग इति तु स्थितिः ॥ ३९ ॥
सन्तोषं परम् आस्थाय सुखार्थी संयतो[10] भवेत् ।
सन्तोष.मूलं[11] हि सुखं दुःख.मूलं विपर्य्ययः ॥ ४० ॥

39) p. 113. 40) r. 9. r. 19. 41) r. 131. 2. 42) p. 175. 43) अ, "not," and विप्लुत, "deviating." 44) 3d sing. pres. of root, जन्, 4th conj. (r. 89. *a.*), "to be born," with prep. आ. If from this may be derived a noun आजाति, the phrase शतम् आजातीः (p. 155. *a.*) might be explained, without making आ govern the accusative. 1) p. 44. †. 2) acc. case (r. 180. *a.*) of भाग, "part." 3) p. 143. *a.* 4) *i.e.* गुरुकुले, com. 5) दार, "a wife," p. 169. *a.* p. 32. †. 6) अ, "not"; द्रोह, m. "injury." 7) p. 103. 8) r. 152. *a.* r. 190. 9) p. 90. *f.* 10) "restrained." 11) These two compounds well illustrate the difference between a relative and absolute dependent compound; the first is used relatively, and as an epithet of सुखं, it must therefore be translated "has its root," or "is founded in contentment"; the second is not used relatively to विपर्य्ययः, or it would be written दुःखमूलः; it must, therefore, be translated as an absolute dependent, "the root of misery," see p. 167. *a.*

वेदोदितं [12]स्वकं कर्म्म नित्यं कुर्य्याद् अतन्द्रितः ।
[13]तद्धि [14]कुर्व्वन् यथा.शक्ति [15]प्राप्नोति परमां गतिं ॥ ४१ ॥
इन्द्रियार्थेषु सर्व्वेषु न [16]प्रसज्येत कामतः ।
सर्व्वान् [17]परित्यजेद् अर्थान् [18]स्वाध्यायस्य [19]विरोधिनः ॥ ४२ ॥
वयसः कर्म्मणोऽर्थस्य श्रुतस्या[20]भिजनस्य च ।
[21]वेष.वाग्.बुद्धि.[22]सारूप्यम् [23]आचरन् विचरेद् इह ॥ ४३ ॥
न [24]सीदन् अपि धर्म्मे[25]ण मनोऽधर्म्मे निवेशयेत् ।
अधार्म्मिकाणां पापानाम् [26]आशु पश्यन् विपर्य्ययं ॥ ४४ ॥
नाधर्म्मश् [27]चरितो लोके [28]सद्यः फलति [29]गौर् इव ।
[30]शनैर् [31]आवर्त्तमानस् तु [32]कर्त्तुर् मूलानि [33]कृन्तति ॥ ४५ ॥
यदि नात्मनि पुत्रेषु न चेत् पुत्रेषु [34]नप्तृषु ।
न त्व् एव तु कृतोऽधर्म्मः कर्त्तुर् भवति [35]निष्फलः ॥ ४६ ॥
व्यसनस्य च मृत्योश् च व्यसनं [36]कष्टम् उच्यते ।
[37]व्यसन्य् [38]अधोऽधो व्रजति [39]स्वर् [40]यात्य् अव्यसनी मृतः ॥ ४७ ॥

12) स्वक, "own," p. 23. xii. 13) for तद् हि, r. 18. 14) r. 123. 15) p. 120. 16) 3d sing. pot. pass. of सञ्ज्, "to adhere to," p. 90. *d.* 17) p. 174. 18) स्वाध्याय, "inaudible reading to one's self of scripture." 19) acc. case plur. of विरोधिन्, "adverse to," "inconsistent," from रुध्, by p. 149. *a.* 20) gen. case sing. of अभिजन, "family rank." 21) also written वेश, "dress." 22) "sameness of form," from सरूप, by p. 23. vii. Cf. also p. ९०. note 51. 23) r. 123. and p. 174. 24) root *sad*, p. 107. and r. 123. r. 19. 25) p. 182. *b.* 26) p. 153. *e.* 27) "committed," p. 139. *h.* 28) p. 153. *f.* 29) nom. case (r. 27. *a.*) of *go*, "the earth," meaning also "a cow," p. 39. †. 30) p. 151. *b.* 31) lit. "rolling on," root वृत् with आ, r. 124. 32) p. 37. 33) p. 65. *b.* 34) loc. plur. of नप्तृ, "a grandson, p. 37. 35) "without फल, "fruit," p. 154. *e.* and p. 15. note. 36) कष्ट, "the most grievous," used as a superlative. 37) for व्यसनी (r. 7.) p. 27. iv. 38) p. 156. *e.* 39) स्वर्, indecl. "heaven." 40) p. 112.

नास्तिक्यं[41] वेद.निन्दां च देवतानां च कुत्सनं[42] ।
द्वेषं दम्भं च मानं च क्रोधं तैक्ष्ण्यं[43] च वर्ज्जयेत् ॥ ४८ ॥
नारुन्तुदः[44] स्याद् आर्त्तोऽपि न पर.द्रोह.कर्म्म.धीः[45] ।
ययास्योद्विजते वाचा परो न ताम् उदीरयेत्[46] ॥ ४९ ॥
सत्यं ब्रूयात् प्रियं ब्रूयान्[47] न ब्रूयात् सत्यम् अप्रियं ।
प्रियं च नानृतं ब्रूयाद् एष धर्म्मः सनातनः[48] ॥ ५० ॥
यद् यत्[49] पर.वशं कर्म्म तत् तद् यत्नेन[50] वर्ज्जयेत् ।
यद् यद् आत्म.वशं तु स्यात् तत् तत् सेवेत यत्नतः[51] ॥ ५१ ॥
सर्व्वं पर.वशं दुःखं सर्व्वम् आत्म.वशं सुखं ।
एतद् विद्यात् समासेन लक्षणं सुख.दुःखयोः[52] ॥ ५२ ॥
पूजयेद् अशनं[53] नित्यम् अद्याच्[54] चैतद् अकुत्सयन्[55] ।
दृष्ट्वा हृष्येत् प्रसीदेच्[56] च प्रतिनन्देच्[57] च सर्व्वशः ॥ ५३ ॥
अनारोग्यम्[58] अनायुष्यम्[59] अस्वर्ग्यं[60] चातिभोजनं[1] ।
अपुण्यं लोक.विद्विष्टं तस्मात् तत् परिवर्ज्जयेत् ॥ ५४ ॥

41) "atheism," from नास्ति, "there is not (a God)." 42) "contempt." 43) from तीक्ष्ण, "sharp," "cruel," by p. 23. vii. 44) अरुन्तुद, "acrimonious," "galling." 45) This is a very anomalous compound. 46) 3d sing. pot. of root ईर् with prep. *ut*, "to utter." 47) r. 15. 48) "perpetual." 49) r. 86. 50) P. 182. *d.* 51) p. 152. *a.* 52) r. 152. *a.* 53) "food," from अश्, by p. 22. iii. 54) 3d sing. pot. of root अद्, "to eat," 2d conj. r. 16. 55) nom. case sing. of pres. part. (r. 123.) of root कुत्स्, 10th conj. "to contemn," r. 135. 56) 3d sing. pot. of root *sad* (p. 107.) with *pra*, "to be calm," "contented." 57) 3d sing. pot. of नन्द् with प्रति, "to receive with pleasure and thankfulness." प्रणम्य प्राञ्जलिः कथयेत् । अस्माकं नित्यम् अस्त्वेतद् इति, com. 58) अन् not आरोग्य, adj. "belonging to health," formed from अरोग, by p. 23. vii. 59) अन् not आयुष्य, "belonging to life," p. 23. vii. 60) अ not स्वर्ग्य, "belonging to heaven," p. 23. vii. 1) r. 135. *a.*

सम्प्राप्ताय त्व् अतिथये[2] प्रदद्याद्[3] आसनोदके[4] ।
अन्नं चैव यथा.शक्ति सत्कृत्य विधि.पूर्व्वकं[5] ॥ ५५ ॥
न वै स्वयं तद् अश्नीयाद्[6] अतिथिं यन् न भोजयेत् ।
धन्यं[7] यशस्यम्[7] आयुष्यं[7] स्वर्ग्यं[7] चातिथि.पूजनं[8] ॥ ५६ ॥
यत्किंचिद् अपि दातव्यं याचितेनानसूयया ।
परितुष्टेन भावेन पात्रम्[10] आसाद्य[11] शक्तितः ॥ ५७ ॥
येन येन तु भावेन यद् यद् दानं प्रयच्छति[12] ।
तत् तत् तेनैव भावेन प्राप्नोति प्रतिपूजितः[13] ॥ ५८ ॥
न विस्मयेत[14] तपसा[15] न दत्त्वा परिकीर्त्तयेत्[16] ।
विस्मयात् क्षरति तपो दानं च परिकीर्त्तनात् ॥ ५९ ॥
न धर्म्मस्यापदेशेन[17] पापं कृत्वा व्रतं चरेत् ।
व्रतेन पापं प्रच्छाद्य[18] कुर्व्वन् स्त्री.शूद्र.दम्भनं[19] ॥ ६० ॥
यो ऽन्यथा सन्तम्[20] आत्मानम् अन्यथा सत्सु[21] भाषते ।
स पाप.कृत्तमो[22] लोके स्तेन आत्मापहारकः[23] ॥ ६१ ॥

2) dat. case, p. 33. and r. 194. 3) 3d sing. pot. of दा (p. 118.) with प्र. 4) r. 152. *a*. 5) lit. "preceded by rule"; पूर्व्वक is very commonly added to a word in modern Sanscrit and Bengāli, to express the manner in which, or the state of mind with which, any thing is done. 6) p. 124. 7) p. 23. vii. 8) r. 147. पूजन, "the act of honouring." 9) r. 187. 10) "a fit object," properly "a vessel." 11) root *sad* with *ā*, "to meet with." 12) *yam* (r. 88. *c*.) with *pra*, "to bestow." 13) "honoured in return," p. 175. 14) 3d sing. pot. ātm. of *smi*, 1st conj. with *vi*, "to admire," "feel pride in." 15) r. 175. *b*. 16) root कृत्, 10th conj. irreg. with परि, "to proclaim." 17) अपदेश, "disguise." 18) indec. part. of the root छद्, 10th conj. "to cover," with prep. प्र, p. 145. *i*. 19) दम्भन, "deceit." 20) r. 123. 21) r. 197. 22) r. 42. r. 71. 23) root हृ, "to seize" (p. 150. *b*.), with prep. *apa*.

यमान्[24] सेवेत् सततं न नित्यं नियमान्[24] बुधः ।
यमान् पतत्य् अकुर्वाणो[25] नियमान् केवलान् भजन्[26] ॥ ६२ ॥
धर्म्मं शनैः सञ्चिनुयाद्[27] वल्मीकम् इव पुत्तिकाः[28] ।
पर.लोक.सहायार्थं[29] सर्व्व.भूतान्य् अपीडयन्[30] ॥ ६३ ॥
नामुत्र[31] हि सहायार्थं पिता माता च तिष्ठतः ।
न पुत्र.दारं[32] न ज्ञातिर् धर्म्मस् तिष्ठति केवलः ॥ ६४ ॥
एकः प्रजायते जन्तुर् एक एव प्रलीयते[33] ।
एको ऽनुभुङ्क्ते[34] सु.कृतम् एक एव च दुष्कृतं ॥ ६५ ॥
मृतं शरीरम् उत्सृज्य[35] काष्ठ.लोष्ट.समं क्षितौ ।
विमुखा बान्धवा यान्ति[36] धर्म्मस् तम् अनुगच्छति ॥ ६६ ॥
तस्माद् धर्म्मं सहायार्थं नित्यं सञ्चिनुयाच्[37] छनैः ।
धर्म्मेण हि सहायेन तमस्[38] तरति दुस्तरं ॥ ६७ ॥
धर्म्म.प्रधानं पुरुषं तपसा हत.किल्बिषं[39] ।
पर.लोकं नयत्य् आशु भास्वन्तं[40] ख.शरीरिणं[41] ॥ ६८ ॥

24) The *yamāh*, or "moral duties," according to the scholiast, are purity of thought, chastity, compassion, patience, truth, religious meditation, honesty, freedom from malice, mildness, and self-restraint: the *niyamāh*, or "ceremonial duties," are ablution, fasting, sacrificing, reading of scripture, and religious silence. 25) r. 124. *a.* 26) root भज, "to serve," "perform," r. 123. 27) 3d sing. pot. of root *chi* (p. 95.) with prep. *sam.* 28) nom. plur. of पुत्तिका, "a kind of ant"; पिपीलिकाप्रभेदाः, Com. According to Wilkins, these ant-hills are seen in Bengal eight or ten feet high. 29) r. 171. *c.* 30) nom. case sing. of the pres. part. of root पीड्, 10th conj. "to pain," r. 135. 31) p. 152. *b.* 32) r. 153. *a.* 33) 3d sing. pres. ātm. of ली, 4th conj. "to perish." 34) 3d sing. pres. ātm. of भुज्, 7th conj. "to eat," r. 96. and see युज्, p. 122. 35) p. 110., p. 145. *f.* 36) p. 112. 37) r. 17. 38) r. 60. 39) हत from हन्, "to destroy," p. 140. *o.* किल्बिष, n. "sin," p. 169. *a.* 40) acc. case of भास्वत्, "luminous," formed from भास्, "light," by r. 42. i. 41) acc. case of खशरीरिन्, "having a celestial body," from ख, "heaven," and शरीर, "body," p. 27. iv.

Duties of the Grihastha's Wife.

पाणिग्राहस्य[1] साध्वी[2] स्त्री जीवतो वा मृतस्य वा ।
पति.लोकम् अभीप्सन्ती[3] नाचरेत् किञ्चिद् अप्रियं ॥ ६९ ॥
उपचर्य्यः[4] स्त्रिया साध्व्या[5] सततं देव.वत्[6] पतिः ।
पतिं शुश्रूषते येन तेन स्वर्गे महीयते[7] ॥ ७० ॥
सदा प्रहृष्टया[8] भार्य्यं गृह.कार्य्येषु दक्षया[9] ।
सु.संस्कृतोपस्करया[10] व्यये चामुक्त.हस्तया[11] ॥ ७१ ॥
पतिं या नाभिचरति[12] मनो.वाग्.देह.संयता ।
इहाग्र्यां[13] कीर्त्तिम् आप्नोति पति.लोकं परत्र[14] च ॥ ७२ ॥
न च नामापि गृह्णीयात् पत्यौ[15] प्रेते[16] परस्य तु ।
आसीत[17] आमरणात्[18] क्षान्ता[19] नियता ब्रह्मचारिणी ॥ ७३ ॥

1) gen. case of पाणिग्राह, "one who takes by the hand," "a husband." 2) nom. fem. of साधु, "virtuous," p. 46. 3) nom. fem. of pres. part. (p. 136. *b.*) of desid. form of *āp* (p. 130. *c.*) with prep. *abhi.* 4) "to be served," root *char* with prep. *upa*, p. 147. *g.* 5) inst. case, r. 49. 6) p. 152. *f.* 7) 3d sing. pres. of an irregular nominal verb महीय्, "to be exalted," "honoured," formed from महत्, "great," com. पूज्यते. 8) तया, "by her (understood) भार्य्यं, it is to be (p. 147. *d.*) प्रहृष्टया, cheerful," see p. 203. *c.* 9) inst. fem. of दक्ष, "skilful." 10) p. 169. *a.* उपस्कर, "an article of household furniture." Com. कुण्डकटाहादि, "pots," "pans," "crockery," &c. 11) inst. fem. of अमुक्तहस्त, lit. "whose hand is not free," p. 169. *a.* 12) चर् with अभि, "to transgress," "to deal treacherously with." 13) acc. fem. of अग्र्य, "chief." 14) p. 152. *b.* 15) p. 35. †. 16) loc. case of प्रेत, "deceased," root इ, "to go," with प्र, p. 138. *b.* 17) 3d sing. pot. ātm. of root आस्, 2d conj. "to remain." 18) आ, "until"; मरणात्, abl. case "death," p. 155. *a.* 19) "patient," p. 141.

Duties of the Brahman in the third Order, or Quarter of his Life, as a Vānaprastha, or Hermit.

गृहस्थस् तु यदा पश्येद् वली[20].पलितम् आत्मनः ।
पुत्रेषु[21] भार्यां निक्षिप्य[22] तदारण्यं समाश्रयेत्[23] ॥ ७४ ॥
यद् भक्ष्यं स्यात् ततो दद्याद् बलिं भिक्षां च शक्तितः[24] ।
अम्मूल[25].फल.भिक्षाभिर्[26] अर्चयेद् आश्रमागतान्[27] ॥ ७५ ॥
स्वाध्याये नित्य.युक्तः[28] स्याद् दान्तो[29] मैत्रः[30] समाहितः[31] ।
दाता[32] नित्यम् अनादाता[33] सर्व.भूतानुकम्पकः[34] ॥ ७६ ॥
अप्रयत्नः सुखार्थेषु यथावद् विजितेन्द्रियः ।
धरा.शयो[35]ऽममश्चैव[36] वृक्ष.मूल.निकेतनः[37] ॥ ७७ ॥
तपश् चरन् उग्रतरं[38] शोषयेद्[39] देहम् आत्मनः ।
वीत[40].शोक.भयो विप्रो ब्रह्म.लोके महीयते ॥ ७८ ॥

Duties of the Brahman in the fourth Order, or Quarter of his Life, as a Bhikshu, or religious Mendicant.

वनेषु तु विहृत्यैवं[1] तृतीयं भागम् आयुषः ।
चतुर्थम् आयुषो भागं त्यक्त्वा सङ्गान् परिव्रजेत्[2] ॥ ७९ ॥

20) वली, "a wrinkle." 21) r. 197. 22) p. 145. *f.* 23) root श्रि, 1st conj. with *sam* and *ā*, "to have recourse to." 24) p. 152. *a.* 25) अप्, "water," p. 46. †; प is changed to म् by the same rule that a final क् is changed to ङ before a nasal, r. 15. 26) r. 151. *a.* 27) r. 143. 28) युक्त, "intent on." 29) p. 141. 30) "amicable," from मित्र, "a friend," by p. 23. viii. 31) "composed," from *dhā* with prep. *sam* and *ā*, p. 130. *c.* 32) p. 37. 33) अन् not आदाता, "a receiver," p. 174. 34) from root कम्प् with prep. अनु (p. 150. *b.*), lit. "trembling after," "easily moved with commiseration." 35) धरा, "the ground"; शय, "who sleeps," from शी, "to sleep," p. 140. 1. 36) "free from selfishness"; अ, "not," and मम, "of me." 37) निकेतन, n. "a habitation," p. 32. †. 38) उग्र, "severe," r. 71. 39) root शुष्, 10th conj. (p. 87. *e.*), "to dry up." 40) वीत, "freed from," lit. "gone," root इ with prep. वि, p. 138. *b.* 1) root हृ with वि, p. 175., p. 144. *a.* 2) root व्रज् with परि, "to wander about," especially as a mendicant.

क्लृप्त.केश.नख.श्मश्रुः पात्री दण्डी[4] कुसुम्भवान्[5] ।
विचरेन् नियतो नित्यं सर्व.भूतान्य् अपीडयन् ॥ ८० ॥
नाभिनन्देत मरणं नाभिनन्देत जीवितं ।
कालम् एव प्रतीक्षेत[6] निर्देशं[7] भृतको[8] यथा ॥ ८१ ॥
इन्द्रियाणां निरोधेन[9] राग.द्वेष.क्षयेण च ।
अहिंसया च भूतानाम् अमृतत्वाय[10] कल्पते[11] ॥ ८२ ॥
अतिवादांस्[12] तितिक्षेत[13] नावमन्येत कञ्चन ।
क्रुध्यन्तं न प्रतिक्रुध्येद्[14] आक्रुष्टः[15] कुशलं[16] वदेत् ॥ ८३ ॥
अल्पान्नाभ्यवहारेण[17] रहः[18] स्थानासनेन[19] च ।
ह्रियमाणानि[20] विषयैर् इन्द्रियाणि निवर्त्तयेत्[21] ॥ ८४ ॥
जरा.शोक.समाविष्टं[22] रोगायतनम् आतुरं ।
रजस्वलम्[23] अनित्यं च भूतावासम्[24] इमं त्यजेत् ॥ ८५ ॥

3) "having a पात्र or dish," p. 27. iv. 4) "having a दण्ड or staff," p. 27. iv. 5) "having a कुसुम्भ or water-pot," r. 42. i. 6) 3d sing. pot. âtm. of root ईक्ष्, 1st conj. with प्रति, "to expect." 7) "wages," भृति, com. 8) "a hired labourer." 9) inst. case of निरोध, "restraint." 10) dat. case of अमृतत्व, "immortality," p. 22. vi. r. 194. 11) 3d sing. pres. âtm. of क्लृप्, 1st conj. (p. 64. *a.*), "to be fit for." 12) acc. case plur. (r. 20.) of अतिवाद, "opprobrious language." 13) p. 129. r. 119. 14) p. 175. 15) root क्रुश् with आ, "to curse," p. 130. *i.* 16) lit. "welfare." 17) अभ्यवहार, "eating." 18) रहस्, adv. "in private." 19) r. 153. 20) nom. plur. neut. of the pres. part. of the passive of हृ, r. 124. 21) caus. of root वृत् with नि, "to cause to cease." 22) root विश् with सम् and आ, "to enter," "occupy," p. 139. *i.* 23) "possessed of रजस्, or the quality of passion," p. 23. xii. 24) भूत, "element"; आवास, "habitation," *i.e.* देहं पृथिव्यादिभूतनिर्म्मितं, "a body formed of the five elements, earth, fire, water, air, and æther."

अनेन विधिना[25] सर्व्वांस्[26] त्यक्त्वा सङ्गान् शनैः शनैः ।
सन्न्यासेना[27]पहत्यै[28]नः[29] प्राप्नोति परमां गतिं ॥ ८६ ॥
चतुर्भिर् अपि चैवै[30]तैर् नित्यम् आश्रमिभिर्[31] द्विजैः ।
दश.[32]लक्षणको धर्म्मः सेवितव्यः प्रयत्नतः ॥ ८७ ॥
धृतिः[33] क्षमा दमो ऽस्तेयं[34] शौचम् इन्द्रिय.निग्रहः ।
धीर्[35] विद्या[36] सत्यम् अक्रोधो दशकं धर्म्म.लक्षणं ॥ ८८ ॥

THE SECOND OR MILITARY CLASS (OR KSHATRIYAS).

The King.

ब्राह्मं प्राप्तेन संस्कारं क्षत्रियेण यथा.[37]विधि ।
सर्व्वस्यास्य यथा.[37]न्यायं कर्त्तव्यं परिरक्षणं ॥ ८९ ॥
नाब्रह्म[38] क्षत्रम्[39] ऋध्नोति[40] नाक्षत्रं ब्रह्म वर्द्धते ।
ब्रह्म क्षत्रं च सम्पृक्तम्[41] इह चामुत्र वर्द्धते ॥ ९० ॥
अराजके[42] हि लोके ऽस्मिन् सर्व्वतो विद्रुते भयात् ।
रक्षा[43]र्थम् अस्य सर्व्वस्य राजानम् असृजत्[44] प्रभुः ॥ ९१ ॥

25) p. 182. *d.* 26) r. 20. 27) root अस् with सम् and नि, "to give up all worldly affections." 28) root हन् with अप, "to expel," p. 145. *g.* 29) acc. neut. of एनस्, "sin," r. 69. r. 6. 30) for च एव एतैः, r. 6. r. 27. *a.* 31) inst. plur. of आश्रमिन्, "belonging to an order," p. 27. iv. 32) लक्षण, "a sign," "characteristic," p. 23. xii. 33) com. सन्तोष. 34) अ, "not," and स्तेय, "theft." 35) com. शास्त्रादितत्त्वज्ञानं, "knowledge of the principles of the shāstras. 36) com. आत्मज्ञानं, "knowledge of self." 37) r. 171. *b.* 38) nom. case neut. of अब्रह्मन्, "having no Brahman," "without the Brahmanical class." 39) nom. case neut. "the military body." 40) ऋध्, 5th conj. "to prosper," r. 94. 41) root पृच् with सम्, "to unite," p. 130. *i.* 42) अराजक, "having no king." 43) p. 177. *c.* 44) p. 110.

बालोऽपि नावमन्तव्यो मनुष्य[43] इति भूमिपः ।
महती देवता ह्य् एषा नर[44]रूपेण तिष्ठति ॥ ९२ ॥
परमं यत्नम् आतिष्ठेत् स्तेनानां निग्रहे[45] नृपः ।
स्तेनानां निग्रहाद्[46] अस्य यशो राष्ट्रं च वर्द्धते ॥ ९३ ॥
रक्षणाद् आर्य्य.वृत्तानां कण्टकानां च शोधनात् ।
नरेन्द्रास्[47] त्रिदिवं[48] यान्ति प्रजा.पालन.तत्पराः ॥ ९४ ॥
यथोद्धरति[49] निर्द्दाता[50] कक्षं[1] धान्यं च रक्षति ।
तथा रक्षेन् नृपो राष्ट्रं हन्याच्[2] च परिपन्थिनः[3] ॥ ९५ ॥
अशासंस्[4] तस्करान् यस् तु बलिं गृह्णाति पार्थिवः ।
तस्य प्रक्षुभ्यते[5] राष्ट्रं स्वर्गाच् च परिहीयते ॥ ९६ ॥
निर्भयं[6] तु भवेद्[7] यस्य राष्ट्रं बाहु.बलाश्रितं[8] ।
तस्य तद् वर्द्धते नित्यं सिच्यमान[9] इव द्रुमः ॥ ९७ ॥
अधार्म्मिकं त्रिभिर् न्यायैर्[10] निगृह्णीयात्[11] प्रयत्नतः ।
निरोधनेन[12] बन्धेन विविधेन बधेन च ॥ ९८ ॥

43) p. 206. *b.* 44) p. 182. *d.* 45) p. 195. *b.* 46) r. 177. *a.* 47) nom. plur. of नरेन्द्र, "a king," lit. "the chief of men." 48) "paradise," the place where the three great gods sport. 49) root हृ with उत्, p. 174. 50) nom. case masc. of निर्द्दातृ, "a reaper," root दो, "to cut," with निर्, see p. 110. *c.* p. 149. 2. 1) कक्ष, m. "grass," "weeds." 2) p. 115. 3) acc. case plur. of परिपन्थिन्, lit. "one who attacks on the पथिन् or road." 4) अ, "not," and शासन्, "punishing" (r. 20.) nom. case of pres. part. of शास् (p. 115.). Properly this should be अशासत्, see p. 136. *c.*, but such violations of Grammar are not uncommon in metrical composition. 5) root क्षुभ्, 4th conj. ātm. "to be shaken," with प्र. 6) p. 154. *e.* 7) r. 203. *a.* 8) आश्रित, "depending on," "resting on," root श्रि, p. 138. *b.* 9) pres. part. of the pass. of सिच्, "to irrigate," r. 124. 10) inst. plur. of न्याय, "an act of policy." 11) p. 124. 12) निरोधन, "prevention."

यदि न प्रणयेद्[13] राजा दण्डं दण्ड्येष्व्[14] अतन्द्रितः ।
शूले[15] मत्स्यान् इवापक्ष्यन्[16] दुर्ब्बलान् बलवत्तराः ॥ ९९ ॥
अद्यात्[17] काकः पुरोडाशं[18] श्वा च लिह्याद्[19] हविस्[20] तथा ।
स्वाम्यं च न स्यात्[21] कस्मिंश्चिद् भिद्येरन्[22] सर्व्व.सेतवः ॥ १०० ॥
सर्व्वो दण्ड.जितो लोको दुर्लभो हि शुचिर् नरः ।
दण्डस्य हि भयात् सर्व्वं जगद् भोगाय[23] कल्पते ॥ १०१ ॥
यावान्[24] अवध्यस्य वधे तावान् वध्यस्य मोक्षणे[25] ।
अधर्म्मो नृपतेर् दृष्टो धर्म्मस् तु विनियच्छतः[26] ॥ १०२ ॥
इन्द्रियाणां जये योगं समातिष्ठेद् दिवा[27].निशं ।
जितेन्द्रियो हि शक्नोति वशे स्थापयितुं[28] प्रजाः ॥ १०३ ॥

Administration of Justice.

नोत्पादयेत्[29] स्वयं कार्य्यं राजा नाप्य् अस्य पूरुषः ।
न च प्रापितम् अन्येन ग्रसेद्[30] अर्थं कथञ्चन ॥ १०४ ॥
यथा नयत्य्[31] असृक्.पातैर्[32] मृगस्य मृगयुः[33] पदं ।
नयेत् तथानुमानेन धर्म्मस्य नृपतिः पदं ॥ १०५ ॥

13) 3d sing. pot. of root नी with प्र, "to inflict," p. 175. 14) दण्ड्य, "deserving punishment," root दण्ड्, "to punish," p. 147. *g.* 15) शूल, n. "an iron pin or spit." 16) r. 210. 17) 3d sing. pot. of अद्, 2d conj. "to eat." 18) acc. case masc. of पुरोडाश, "an oblation of clarified butter mixed with cakes of barley meal." 19) root लिह्, 2d conj. "to lick." 20) हविस्, n. "clarified butter," r. 18. 21) r. 203. *b.* 22) 3d plur. pot. of the pass. of भिद्, "to break," p. 99. 23) r. 194. 24) p. 181. *c.* 25) loc. of मोक्षण, "liberation." 26) root यम् with वि and नि, p. 64. *c.* p. 136. Com. यथाशास्त्रं दण्डं कुर्व्वतः, "inflicting punishment in a legal manner." 27) r. 153. 28) p. 87. *d.* 29) root पद् in caus. with उत्, "to excite." 30) root ग्रस्, "to devour," "seize upon"; but the scholiast explains it by उपेक्षेत, "should neglect." 31) root नी (p. 64. *a.*) here, "to track." 32) पात, "a falling," "dropping." 33) "a hunter."

धर्म्मो विद्धस्[34] त्व् अधर्म्मेण सभां यत्रोपतिष्ठते[35] ।
शल्यं[36] चास्य न कृन्तन्ति[37] विद्वांस् तत्र सभासदः[38] ॥ १०६ ॥
सभां वा न प्रवेष्टव्यं[39] वक्तव्यं वा समञ्जसं[40] ।
अब्रुवन् विब्रुवन् वापि नरो भवति किल्बिषी[41] ॥ १०७ ॥
सत्येन पूयते[42] साक्षी धर्म्मः सत्येन वर्द्धते ।
तस्मात् सत्यं हि वक्तव्यं सर्व्व.वर्णेषु साक्षिभिः ॥ १०८ ॥
अन्धो मत्स्यान् इवाश्नाति[43] स नरः कण्टकैः सह ।
यो भाषते ऽर्थ.वैकल्यम्[44] अप्रत्यक्षं सभां गतः ॥ १०९ ॥
जन्म.प्रभृति[45] यत्किञ्चित् पुण्यं भद्र त्वया कृतं ।
तत् ते सर्व्वं शुनो[46] गच्छेद् यदि ब्रूयास् त्वम् अन्यथा ॥ ११० ॥
अवाक्.शिरास्[47] तमस्य् अन्धे[48] किल्बिषी नरकं व्रजेत् ।
यः प्रश्नं[49] वितथं[50] ब्रूयात् पृष्टः सन् धर्म्म.निश्चये ॥ १११ ॥
मन्यन्ते वै पाप.कृतो[1] न कश्चित् पश्यतीति नः ।
तांस्[2] तु देवाः प्रपश्यन्ति स्वस्यैवान्तरपूरुषः[3] ॥ ११२ ॥
एको ऽहम् अस्मीत्य्[4] आत्मानं यत् त्वं कल्याण मन्यसे ।
नित्यं स्थितस्[5] ते हृद्य्[6] एष पुण्य.पापेक्षिता[7] मुनिः[8] ॥ ११३ ॥

[34]) root व्यध्, "to pierce," p. 140. *n*. [35]) 3d sing. pres. ātm. of स्था with उप (p. 107.), "to approach." [36]) शल्य, m. n. "a dart." [37]) root कृत्, r. 90. *b*., for उत्कृत्, "to extract," Com. उद्धरन्ति. [38]) सभासद्, "one of an assembly"; सभा, "an assembly"; सद्, "to sit," p. 25. r. 42. [39]) p. 203. *b*. [40]) समञ्जस, neuter, "truth." [41]) nom. case masc. of किल्बिषिन्, "possessing किल्बिष, sin," p. 27. iv. [42]) p. 99. [43]) p. 124. [44]) "the state of being विकल, mutilated, defective," p. 23. vii. [45]) p. 178. *f*. [46]) acc. plur. of श्वन्, p. 42. †. [47]) nom. case masc. "having the head downwards." [48]) loc. case of अन्ध, "blind," here "total." [49]) r. 199. *a*. [50]) वि, "not," and तथ, "true," p. 154. *e*.

[1]) p. 39. [2]) r. 20. [3]) अन्तरपूरुष, lit. "the inner man," "the internal spirit." [4]) p. 205. *a*. [5]) p. 139. *c*. [6]) loc. case of हृद्, r. 60. [7]) nom. case masc. of ईक्षितृ, "an inspector," p. 149. 2. [8]) मुनि, "a holy sage," here it refers to "the soul," "the intelligent spirit."

आत्मैव ह्य् आत्मनः साक्षी गतिर् आत्मा तथात्मनः ।
मा[10]वमंस्थाः स्वम् आत्मानं नृणां साक्षिणम् उत्तमं ॥११४॥
द्यौर् भूमिर् आपो हृदयं चन्द्रार्काग्नि[11].यमानिलाः ।
रात्रिः सन्ध्ये[12] च धर्मश्च वृत्त.ज्ञाः सर्व.देहिनां ॥११५॥

THE THIRD OR COMMERCIAL CLASS (OR VAISHYAS).

वैश्यस् तु कृत.संस्कारः कृत्वा दार[13].परिग्रहं ।
वार्त्ता[14]यां नित्य.युक्तः स्यात् पशूनां चैव रक्षणे ॥११६॥
प्रजा[15]पतिर् हि वैश्याय सृष्ट्वा[16] परिददे[17] पशून् ।
ब्राह्मणाय च राज्ञे च सर्वाः परिददे प्रजाः ॥११७॥
वीजानाम् उप्ति[18]विच्च स्यात् क्षेत्र.दोष.गुणस्य च ।
सारा[19]सारं च भाण्डानां देशानां च गुणागुणान्[19] ॥११८॥
मणि.मुक्ता.प्रवाला[20]नां लोहानां तान्तवस्य[21] च ।
गन्धानां च रसानां च विद्याद् अर्घ[22].बलाबलं ॥११९॥
भृत्यानां च भृतिं विद्याद् भाषाश्च विविधा नृणां ।
द्रव्याणां स्थान.योगां[23]श्च क्रय.विक्रयम् एव च ॥१२०॥
धर्मेण च द्रव्य.वृद्धाव्[24] आतिष्ठेद् यत्नम् उत्तमं ।
दद्याच्च सर्व[25].भूतानाम् अन्नम् एव प्रयत्नतः ॥१२१॥

9) गति, "that to which one goes for refuge." 10) 2d sing. of 3d pret. of मन् with अव, "to contemn," p. 82. *e.*, the augment being dropped by r. 208. 11) r. 151. 12) nom. dual of सन्ध्या, "twilight." 13) दार, "wife," परिग्रह, "taking." 14) loc. c. of वार्त्ता, "agriculture and trade." 15) a name of Brahmā, "the lord of all beings." 16) root सृज्, p. 143. *a.* 17) 2d pret. ātm. of दा (p. 118.) with परि. 18) उप्ति, "sowing," विद्, "to know," r. 42. r. 16. 19) r. 153. *b.* 20) प्रवाल, "coral," r. 151. *a.* 21) तान्तव, n. "woven cloth." 22) lit. "the price strong and weak" (r. 153. *b.*), *i.e.* "dear and cheap." 23) योग is sometimes joined to another word, without much obvious meaning. 24) loc. c. r. 8. 25) r. 196.

THE FOURTH OR SERVILE CLASS (OR SHŪDRAS).

विप्राणां वेद.विदुषां गृहस्थानां यशस्विनां[26] ।
शुश्रूषैव तु शूद्रस्य धर्म्मो नैःश्रेयसः[27] परः ॥ १२२ ॥
शुचिर् उत्कृष्ट.शुश्रूषुर् मृदु.वाग्[28] अनहङ्कृतः[29] ।
ब्राह्मणाद्याश्रयो नित्यम् उत्कृष्टां जातिम् अश्नुते ॥ १२३ ॥
अहिंसा सत्यम् अस्तेयं शौचम् इन्द्रिय.निग्रहं ।
एतं सामासिकं धर्म्मं चातुर्वर्ण्ये[30]ऽब्रवीन् मनुः ॥ १२४ ॥

[26]) "possessed of यशस् fame," p. 27. v. [27]) formed from निःश्रेयस्, "final beatitude, by p. 23. viii. [28]) r. 45. [29]) अन्, "not," and अहङ्कृत, "proud"; lit. "making much of self." [30]) loc. c. "the four classes" collectively, from चतुर्वर्ण, by p. 23. vii.

TRANSLATION OF THE FOREGOING SELECTIONS FROM THE INSTITUTES OF MANU.

Introductory Remarks.

THE precise time at which the Institutes of Manu were compiled is uncertain. Sir William Jones places the date about twelve hundred years before Christ, and Mr. Elphinstone about nine hundred, or about the age of Homer. It will be observed, by a reference to the translation (verses 69—73.), that the burning of the Satī, or Indian widow, is not even hinted at, which, of itself, fixes the time of the compilation of the laws far anterior to the era of Alexander the Great, the Macedonians having found this cruel and revolting custom prevalent at the period of their invasion. But whatever may be the date of this code, the matter it contains cannot fail to strike the most superficial observer as full of interest and importance. No one, it is presumed, will read the subjoined translation without admiring the lofty and almost Christian tone of morality that pervades it: and when it is remembered that we are entirely without historical account of the Hindus at these early ages, every one must admit the importance of a work, which, presenting us with a complete picture of their laws, religion, and social habits, may serve as a guide to many points in their political history.

Let not, however, the reader suppose that the translation we have here given of the most striking passages in these Institutes is intended to serve as a sample of the whole, or he will derive from its perusal a very exalted and a very false notion of the state of Hindu morality at this early epoch. The original work is polluted by numerous rules and prohibitions, having reference to practices which could only have prevailed in a corrupt and degraded state of moral feeling. It should, moreover, be borne in mind, that the compiler of this code, who was probably some learned Brahman of the day, collected from the literature of his country, and the opinions of his own time, what *ought to be* the laws which should regulate the community, rather than what those laws actually were; and that he doubtless mixed up with the existing state of things many of his own ideas upon questions of religion, morality, and law. Nevertheless, however much the minuter parts of the picture presented to us in this book are to be attributed to the imagination of the legislator, and however much it may be necessary to soften down the particular features of the landscape, still, taken as a whole, it furnishes us with a very valuable representation of the early condition of the Hindu people. And its importance will be enhanced, when it is remembered that the natives of India at the present day regard it not only as the oldest, but as the most sacred text after the Vedas, and that it still furnishes the basis of Hindu jurisprudence.

The original work is entirely wanting in arrangement, and the preceding extracts have been selected from various parts so as to give the cream of the whole with as much continuity and connexion as the subject would admit. The reader must understand that the most remarkable feature in Hindu society, as depicted in the Institutes, is the division of the people into four classes or castes: 1st, The Sacerdotal; 2d, The Military; 3d, The Commercial; 4th, The Servile. The first three classes, though by no means equal, were admitted into one common pale, and called by the common name of "twice-born." With reference to them alone were these Institutes composed, the 4th class being in that state of degradation which would seem to indicate that they were the aborigines of the soil, subject to a conquering race. As to the 1st, or Sacerdotal Class, the Brahmans who formed it were held to be the chief of all human beings; they were even superior to the king, and their lives and property were protected by the most stringent laws. They were to divide their lives into four quarters (or orders), living for the first quarter as students with their preceptors; for the second, as householders with their families; for the third, as anchorites in the woods; for the fourth, as religious mendicants, wandering from house to house, and emaciating their bodies by mortification and austerity. As to the 2d, or Military Class, although much inferior in rank to the Sacerdotal, they enjoyed great privileges, and, inasmuch as the king and his ministers were taken from their body, must have been practically the most powerful. As to the 3d, or Commercial, they were not held in much esteem, their duties being to keep cattle, till the ground, and engage in trade. The 4th, or Servile Class, were excluded from all political and religious privileges; and although it does not appear that they were the slaves of the state like those of Europe, their only duties were made to consist in serving the other three classes.

Mr. Elphinstone notices two great peculiarities in the society thus constituted: 1st, the little importance attached to the direction of public worship and religious ceremonies by the Brahmans; 2dly, the strictness with which all the actions of the Brahmans are regulated, as if living in a convent, and not scattered over a vast tract of country, without head or council or ecclesiastical government.

The annexed translation is partly founded upon that of Sir William Jones; but although, in some passages, the words of that distinguished oriental scholar have been followed, it has been thought desirable to introduce many alterations in the present version.

TRANSLATION.

ORIGIN OF THE FOUR CLASSES, AND GENERAL VIEW OF THEIR DUTIES.

1. For the sake of the preservation of all this creation, the Supreme in glory assigned separate duties to those who sprang respectively from his mouth, his arm, his thigh, and his foot.

2. To *Brahmans* he assigned the duties of teaching, of reading, of sacrificing, of assisting at sacrifices, of giving, and (if indigent) of receiving.

3. The (duties) of a *Kshatriya* are, in brief, the defence of the people, giving, sacrificing, reading, freedom from attachment to sensual pleasures.

4. To the *Vaishya* (he assigned the duties of) keeping cattle, giving, sacrificing, reading, trading, lending money at interest, and agriculture.

5. To the *Shūdra*, the Supreme Ruler appointed one single duty, the service of these (other) classes ungrudgingly.

6. Of created things, the most excellent are those which are animated; of the animated, those endued with intellectual life;

of the intelligent, mankind; and of men, Brahmans (or the sacerdotal class).

7. Of Brahmans, those who are learned (in the ritual); of the learned, those whose minds are acquainted with their duty; of those who are acquainted with their duty, such as perform it; of such as perform it, those who have acquaintance with the Supreme Spirit.

8. The seniority of Brahmans (or priests) is from sacred learning; of Kshatriyas (or soldiers) from valour; of Vaishyas (or merchants and husbandmen) from (abundance of) grain and money; of Shūdras (or slaves) from priority of birth alone.

9. The Brahman, the Kshatriya, and the Vaishya are the three twice-born classes (their sacred birth taking place at their investiture with the sacred thread); but the fourth class, or Shūdra, is once-born (as being excluded from investiture with the thread); there is no fifth class (except those which are mixed and impure).

THE FIRST, OR SACERDOTAL CLASS (OR BRAHMANS).

Duties of the Brahman in the first Order (Āshrama) or Quarter of his Life, as a Brahmachārī, or Student of Religion, subject to his Guru or Preceptor.

10. Learning, having approached a Brahman, said to him, "I am thy divine treasure, preserve me, deliver me not to a scorner; so (preserved) I shall become supremely strong.

11. But communicate me to that student who will be a careful guardian of the treasure, and whom thou shalt know to be pure, self-governed, and a Brahmachārī."

12. Where virtue and worldly means (sufficient to secure it) are not found, or diligent attention proportioned (to the holiness of the subject), in that soil divine knowledge must not be sown, like good seed on barren land.

13. A teacher of the Veda should be willing to die with his learning rather than sow it in sterile soil, even though he be in grievous distress.

14. A Brahman who is the causer of spiritual birth, the teacher of proper duties, even though a child, becomes by right the father of an old man.

15. A man is not therefore aged because his head is gray; him surely the gods consider as aged, who, though young, is well read in Scripture.

16. As an elephant made of wood, as an antelope made of leather, so is an unread Brahman; these three (merely) bear the name.

17. These (following) rules must a Brahmachārī observe, whilst dwelling with his preceptor, keeping all his passions under controul, for the sake of increasing his habitual devotion.

18. When commanded by his preceptor, and even when he has received no command, let him always be diligent in reading and in friendly offices toward his teacher.

19. A teacher, a father, a mother, and an elder brother, are not to be treated with disrespect, especially by a Brahman, even though he be much irritated.

20. That trouble which a mother and father undergo in rearing their children is a debt which cannot be repaid even in hundreds of years.

21. Let a man constantly do what may please these (his parents), and on all occasions what may please his preceptor; when these three are satisfied, his whole course of devotion is accomplished.

22. Obedience to these three is called the highest devotion, and without their approbation he must perform no other duty.

23. Of (the youth) who habitually greets and constantly reveres the aged, four things obtain increase—life, knowledge, fame, strength.

24. As a man who digs deep with a spade comes to a spring of water, so he who is diligent in serving (his preceptor) attains the knowledge which lies in his teacher's mind.

25. Even from poison nectar may be taken, even from a child gentleness of speech: a believer in Scripture may receive a good lesson even from a man of the lowest class.

26. Therefore the highest virtue, learning, purity, gentleness of speech, and various liberal arts should be collected by him from all quarters.

27. In the restraint of the organs which run wild among

ravishing objects of sense, a wise man should apply diligent care, like a charioteer in managing (restive) steeds.

28. Desire is never satisfied with the enjoyment of desired objects, as the fire (is not appeased) by clarified butter, it only blazes more vehemently.

29. By addiction to his sensual organs a man undoubtedly incurs guilt; but having kept them in subjection, he thence attains heavenly bliss.

30. Neither the Vedas, nor almsgiving, nor sacrifices, nor strict observances, nor pious austerities, ever lead that man to heavenly felicity who is inwardly depraved.

31. Having kept all his organs of sense under controul, and obtained command over his heart also, he will accomplish every object, even though he reduce not his body by religious austerities.

32. But when one among all his organs gives way, by that single defect his knowledge of divine truth passes away, as water leaks through (a single crack in) a leathern vessel.

33. He whose discourse and heart are pure and ever perfectly guarded, attains all the fruit acquired by a complete course of studying the Veda.

34. Let a Brahman constantly shrink from worldly honour as he would poison, and rather always earnestly desire disrespect as he would nectar.

35. For though scorned he may sleep with pleasure; with pleasure may he awake; with pleasure may he pass through this life; but the scorner utterly perishes.

36. The Brahman who thus without deviation passes the time of his studentship, ascends (after death) to the most exalted regions, and is not again subject to birth in this lower world.

Duties of the Brahman in the second order or quarter of his life, as a Grihastha, or Householder.

37. Let a Brahman, having dwelt with a preceptor for the first quarter of his life, pass the second quarter of life in his own house, as a married man.

38. With no injury to animated beings, or with as little injury

as possible, and without toil to his own body, let him accumulate riches.

39. The chief temporal good is by some declared to be virtue and wealth; (by some) pleasure and wealth; and (by some) virtue alone; (by others) wealth alone; but the chief good here below is an assemblage of all three: this is a sure decision.*

40. If he seek happiness, let him be moderate (in the acquisition of riches), pursuing perfect contentment: for happiness has its root in content, and discontent is the root of misery.

41. Let him daily, without sloth, perform his peculiar duty prescribed by the Veda; for performing that duty to the best of his ability he obtains supreme bliss.

42. Let him not from carnal desire be too strongly attached to all objects of sense: let him wholly abandon all pursuits that are incompatible with the study of Scripture.

43. Let him pass through this world, bringing his apparel, his discourse, and his intellectual acquirements into conformity with his age, his occupations, his means, his divine knowledge, and his station in life.

44. Though sinking (into penury) in consequence of his righteous dealings, let him never apply his mind to unrighteousness, observing the speedy overthrow of iniquitous and sinful men.

45. Iniquity practised in this world, like the earth, does not bear fruit at the moment: but advancing little by little it eradicates the author of it.

46. Yes; iniquity, once committed, fails not of producing fruit to him who wrought it; if not in his person, yet in his sons; or if not in his sons, yet in his grandsons.

47. Of death and of vice, vice is pronounced the more dreadful; since after death a vicious man sinks to the lowest depths of hell, while a man, free from vice, reaches heaven.

48. Let him, therefore, shun atheism, disbelief of Scripture, contempt of the deities, malice, hypocrisy, pride, anger, and cruelty.

---

* This passage will call to the mind of the classical scholar the 5th and 6th chapters of the 1st book of Aristotle's Ethics.

49. Let him not wound the feelings of others, even though irritated; let him not injure another in thought or deed; let him not even utter a word by which his fellow-creature may suffer uneasiness.

50. Let him say what is true, let him say what is pleasing; let him speak no disagreeable truth, nor let him speak agreeable falsehood: this is a perpetual law.

51. Whatever act depends (for its accomplishment) on another, that act let him carefully shun; but whatever depends on himself, to that let him diligently attend.

52. Every thing which depends (for its attainment) on the favour of another causes unhappiness, but every thing which depends on one's own individual exertions causes happiness: let him know this to be in a few words the definition of pleasure and pain.

53. Let him always honour his food, and eat it without contempt; when he sees it, let him rejoice, and be content, and ever return thanks for it (praying that he may always obtain it).

54. Excessive eating is prejudicial to health, to life, and to the prospect of attaining heaven; it is destructive to merit, and odious amongst men; therefore, he should by all means avoid it.

55. To a guest who has arrived at his house let him offer a seat and water and food, such as may be in his power, treating him with hospitality, according to prescribed rule.

56. Let him never eat any thing himself which he has not first set before his guest: reverence of a guest is conducive to wealth, to fame, to life, and to a heavenly reward.

57. When asked, he should give something, though it be a mere trifle, ungrudgingly, with a cheerful heart, and to the best of his means, having met with a worthy object of charity.

58. With whatever spirit a man bestows any gift, with the very same spirit, being honoured in return, he shall receive a similar recompense.

59. Let not a man pride himself on his religious observances; having made a donation let him never proclaim it: by pride, the merit of devotion is lost, and the merit of almsgiving by ostentatiously proclaiming it.

60. Let him not having committed sin perform a penance

under the pretext of religion, disguising his crime under mere bodily austerity, and deceiving (only) women and the lowest class of men.

61. He who being of one character describes himself to the good as of another is the most sinful wretch in the world, the worst of thieves, a stealer of men's minds.

62. A wise man should constantly discharge all the moral duties,* though he perform not constantly the ceremonies of religion; since he falls low, if, performing ceremonial acts only, he discharges not his moral duties.

63. Giving pain to no creature, let him, for the sake of obtaining a companion to the next world, accumulate virtue by degrees, as the white ants (collect the soil into) a hillock.

64. For neither father, nor mother, nor wife, nor son, nor kinsman, will remain as his companion in his passage to the next world; his virtue alone will adhere to him.

65. Single is every living being born, single he passes away, single he eats the fruit of his good deeds, and single the fruit of his evil deeds.

66. When he leaves his dead body, like a log or a lump of clay, on the ground, his kindred retire with averted faces, but his virtue accompanies his soul.

67. Continually, therefore, and by degrees, let him accumulate virtue, for the sake of securing an inseparable associate; since with virtue as his companion he will traverse a gloom, hard indeed to be traversed.

68. The man who is eminent in piety, and whose offences have been expiated by devotion, such a man does his virtue instantly convey after death to another world with a radiant form and a body of celestial substance.

Duties of the Grihastha's Wife.

69. A faithful wife, wishing to attain in heaven the mansion of her husband, must do nothing unkind to that husband, be he living or dead.

70. A husband must constantly be served as a god by a vir-

* See p. २५. note 24.

tuous wife. As far only as she is obedient to her lord, so far is she exalted in heaven.

71. She must always be cheerful, skilful in her management of the affairs of the house, careful in cleaning the household furniture, and not too lavish in her expenditure.

72. She who commits no offence against her lord, but is devoted to him in mind, speech, and body, acquires high renown in this world, and in the next the same abode with her husband.

73. And when her husband is dead, let her not even pronounce the name of another man, but let her continue till her own death, forgiving all injuries, performing austerities, and avoiding every sensual pleasure.

Duties of the Brahman in the third order or quarter of his life, as a Vānaprastha, or Hermit.

74. When the householder perceives wrinkles on his body, and his hair gray, consigning his wife to the care of his sons, let him then have recourse to the forest.

75. From such food as himself may eat, let him to the best of his ability make offerings and give alms, and with water, roots, fruit, and other presents let him honour all who visit his hermitage.

76. Let him be constantly engaged in the study of Scripture, patient of extremities, benevolent, composed in mind, a constant giver but no receiver of gifts, tenderly affectionate towards all animated bodies.

77. Not solicitous for the means of gratification, his organs properly kept in subjection, sleeping on the bare ground, without one selfish affection, dwelling at the roots of trees.

78. Let him emaciate his bodily frame, enduring harsher and harsher mortifications. A Brahman who has banished sorrow and fear becomes exalted in the divine world.

Duties of the Brahman in the fourth order or quarter of his life, as a Bhikshu, or Religious Mendicant.

79. Having thus passed his time in the forests during the third portion of his life, let him for the fourth portion of it become a Parivrājaka (or religious mendicant), abandoning all sensual connexions.

80. His hair, nails, and beard being clipped, bearing with him a dish, a staff, and a water-pot, intent on religious meditation, let him wander about continually without causing pain to any creature.

81. Let him not long for death, let him not long for life, let him expect his appointed time as a hired servant his wages.

82. By the restraint of his sensual organs, by the gradual extinction of affection and hatred, and by abstinence from injury to sentient beings, he becomes fit for immortality.

83. Let him bear opprobrious speech with patience, let him not treat any one with contempt, with an angry man let him not in his turn be angry, when cursed let him utter a blessing.

84. By eating little food, and by standing and sitting in solitary places, let him suppress those organs that are hurried away by sensual objects.

85. A mansion infested by decrepitude and sorrow, the seat of malady, harassed by pains, haunted with the darkness of passion, transient and formed of earth, such a mansion let him cheerfully quit.

86. In this manner having by little and little abandoned all earthly attachments, and having by devotion of himself to God effaced sin, he then attains the supreme path of glory.

87. By Brahmans, placed in these four orders, a (system of) duty having ten characteristics must be sedulously practised.

88. Contentment, returning good for evil, self-command, honesty, purification, coercion of the organs, knowledge of science, wisdom, veracity, and freedom from anger, form their tenfold system of duty.

THE SECOND, OR MILITARY CLASS (OR KSHATRIYAS).

The King.

89. By a Kshatriya (or man of the military class), who has received in due form the investiture prescribed by the Vedas, the protection of all these (his dominions) is to be made according to rule.

90. The military class does not flourish without the sacerdotal, nor does the sacerdotal prosper without the military; the sacerdotal and military classes, when associated together, obtain increase in this world and the next.

91. For if the world were without a king it would be agitated by fear, therefore the Supreme Ruler created a king for the sake of the protection of all this (universe).

92. A king, even though a child, must not be treated with contempt from an idea that he is a mere mortal; for he is a mighty divinity that appears in human shape.

93. A king should apply all his efforts to the suppression of robbers; for by the suppression of such wicked men his fame and territory obtain increase.

94. By the protection of the virtuous and the extirpation of evil doers, monarchs who devote themselves to the care of their subjects attain paradise.

95. As a husbandman plucks up weeds and preserves his corn, thus let a king destroy the iniquitous and protect his country.

96. But that monarch who takes a revenue without restraining the wicked, of such an one the dominions become troubled, and he himself is excluded from heaven.

97. But of him whose realm is supported by the strength of his arm and free from terror, the dominions continually flourish like a tree duly watered.

98. Let him diligently suppress the unrighteous by three methods—by coercion, by confinement, and by various kinds of capital punishment.

99. If the king were not with the greatest activity to inflict punishment on the guilty, the stronger would roast the weak like fish on a spit.

100. The crow would peck the consecrated offering, and the dog would lick the clarified butter; ownership would remain with nobody, all barriers would be broken down.

101. The whole human race is kept under controul by punishment, for an innocent man is difficult to be found: through fear of punishment the whole universe is fitted for the enjoyment of its blessings.

102. Injustice is considered to attach to a king as much in releasing the man who deserves punishment, as in punishing the man who deserves it not; but justice to one who inflicts it with proper discrimination.

103. Day and night must he exert every effort to gain the victory over his passions, since that king alone whose passions are subdued can keep his subjects also in subjection.

Administration of Justice.

104. Neither the king himself nor the king's officer ought ever to promote litigation, or to neglect a law-suit when brought before him by another.

105. As a hunter tracks the lurking-place of the (wounded) deer by the drops of blood, so must a king investigate the direction in which justice lies by deliberate arguments.

106. Where justice, being wounded by iniquity, approaches the court, and the judges extract not the dart, there those judges also shall be wounded by it.

107. Either the court must not be entered, or truth must be declared: that man is criminal who either remains silent or says what is false.

108. By truth is a witness purified from sin; by truth is justice advanced: truth must, therefore, be spoken by witnesses of every class.

109. The man who, being arrived in a court of justice, gives an imperfect account of a transaction, the truth of which he has not clearly ascertained, shall resemble a blind man who eats fish along with the bones.

110. The merit of every virtuous act which thou hast done, O good man, since thy birth, shall depart from thee to the dogs, if thou speak falsely.

111. Headlong in utter darkness shall the guilty wretch tumble into hell, who, being asked a question in judicial inquiry, answers falsely.

112. The sinful say in their hearts, "None sees us." Yes; the gods distinctly see them, and so does the spirit within their breasts.

113. Though thou thinkest to thyself, O good friend, "I am alone," there resides in thy bosom an Omniscient being, the inspector of thy goodness or of thy wickedness.

114. The soul itself is its own witness; the soul itself is its own refuge: offend not thy own soul, the supreme internal witness of men.

115. The firmament, the earth, the waters, the human heart, the moon, the sun, the fire, the Judge of departed souls, the wind, the night, the two twilights, and justice, are acquainted with the conduct of all corporeal beings.

THE THIRD OR COMMERCIAL CLASS (OR VAISHYAS).

116. Let the Vaishya, having received investiture with the sacrificial thread, and having married a wife, be always attentive to his business of agriculture and trade, and the tending of cattle.

117. Since the Lord of the world, having created cattle, intrusted them to the care of the Vaishya, while he intrusted the whole human species to the Brahman and Kshatriya.

118. Let him be acquainted with the proper seasons for sowing seeds, and with the bad or good qualities of land, the excellence or defects of commodities, the advantages and disadvantages of different regions.

119. Of gems, pearls, and coral; of metals, woven cloths, perfumes, and condiments, let him know the prices both high and low.

120. Let him know the just wages of servants, and the various dialects of men, the best mode of keeping goods, and every thing connected with purchase and sale.

121. Let him exert his utmost efforts to augment his property by all righteous means; and let him, to the best of his power, contribute toward the support and nourishment of all creatures.

THE FOURTH OR SERVILE CLASS (OR SHŪDRAS).

122. Attendance on illustrious Brahmans, who are householders and learned in the Vedas, is of itself the highest duty of a Shūdra, and conducive to his heavenly reward.

123. Pure (in body and mind), serving the three higher classes, mild in speech, never arrogant, ever firm in his dependence on the sacerdotal class, he may obtain the highest class in another transmigration.

124. Avoidance of injury to animated beings, veracity, honesty, cleanliness, and command over the organs of sense, form the compendious system of duties which Manu has ordained for all the four classes.

SCHEME OF THE SHLOKA, OR ANUṢHṬUBH METRE.

The Institutes of Manu are written in the *shloka*, or *anuṣhṭubh metre*. This is the commonest of all the infinite variety of Sanscrit metres, and is that which chiefly prevails in the great epic poems of the East. It consists of two lines of sixteen syllables each, but the rules which regulate one line apply equally to the other. The scheme is as follows:—

1	2	3	4	|	5	6	7	8	||	9	10	11	12	|	13	14	15	16
·	·	·	·	|	⏑	⏓	⏓	·	||	·	·	·	·	|	⏑	—	⏑	·

The 1st, 2d, 3d, 4th, 9th, 10th, 11th, and 12th syllables may be either long or short. The 16th, as ending the line, is also common. But the line may be considered as divided into two parts at the 8th syllable, since it is an almost universal rule that this syllable must end a word, *whether simple or compound.* Hence it follows that the usual privilege of a final syllable is conceded to the 8th also.

The 5th syllable ought always to be short. The 6th may be either long or short, but if long then the 7th ought to be long also, and if short then the 7th ought to be short also. But occasional variations from these last rules occur.

The last four syllables form two iambics, the 13th being always short, the 14th always long, and the 15th always short.

Every shloka, or couplet of two lines, must form a complete sentence in itself, and contain both subject and predicate. Not unfrequently, however, in the Rāmāyaṇa and Mahābhārata, three lines are united to form a triplet.